Bloom's Classic Critical Views

JOHN MILTON

Bloom's Classic Critical Views

Bloom's Classic Critical Views

JOHN MILTON

Edited and with an Introduction by
Harold Bloom
Sterling Professor of the Humanities
Yale University

BLOOM'S
LITERARY CRITICISM
An imprint of Infobase Publishing

Bloom's Classic Critical Views: John Milton
Copyright © 2011 Infobase Publishing
Introduction © 2011 by Harold Bloom

Bloom's Literary Criticism
An imprint of Infobase Publishing
132 West 31st Street
New York NY 10001

Library of Congress Cataloging-in-Publication Data
John Milton / edited and with an introduction by Harold Bloom.
     p. cm.—(Bloom's classic critical views)
     A selection of important older literary criticism on John Milton.
     Includes bibliographical references and index.
     ISBN 978-1-60413-702-6 (hardcover : alk. paper)   1. Milton, John, 1608–1674—
Criticism and interpretation.   I. Bloom, Harold.
     PR3588.J6535 2010
     821'.4—dc22
                                        2010030615

You can find Bloom's Literary Criticism on the World Wide Web at
http://www.chelseahouse.com

Volume editor: Carol Blessing
Cover design by Takeshi Takahashi
Composition by IBT Global, Troy NY
Cover printed by IBT Global, Troy NY
Book printed and bound by IBT Global, Troy NY
Date printed: December 2010
Printed in the United States of America
10 9 8 7 6 5 4 3 2 1

Contents

Contents

Series Introduction

Bloom's Classic Critical Views is a new series presenting a selection of the most important older literary criticism on the greatest authors commonly read in high school and college classes today. Unlike the Bloom's Modern Critical Views series, which for more than 20 years has provided the best contemporary criticism on great authors, Bloom's Classic Critical Views attempts to present the authors in the context of their time and to provide criticism that has proved over the years to be the most valuable to readers and writers. Selections range from contemporary reviews in popular magazines, which demonstrate how a work was received in its own era, to profound essays by some of the strongest critics in the British and American tradition, including Henry James, G.K. Chesterton, Matthew Arnold, and many more.

Some of the critical essays and extracts presented here have appeared previously in other titles edited by Harold Bloom, such as the New Moulton's Library of Literary Criticism. Other selections appear here for the first time in any book by this publisher. All were selected under Harold Bloom's guidance.

In addition, each volume in this series contains a series of essays by a contemporary expert, who comments on the most important critical selections, putting them in context and suggesting how they might be used by a student writer to influence his or her own writing. This series is intended above all for students, to help them think more deeply and write more powerfully about great writers and their works.

Volume Introduction by Harold Bloom

Milton's *Paradise Lost* is as difficult as it is magnificent; Milton's "minor poems" would be major for everyone else. "Lycidas" and *Samson Agonistes* are both astonishing works; to appreciate and to understand them is an activity wholly appropriate to the compassionate mind and the understanding heart. Both "Lycidas" and *Samson Agonistes* are unique poetic splendors; nothing else in the language authentically resembles them. They are, in many ways, the alpha and omega of poetic experience in the English language.

Milton was a great iconoclast in religion and politics, but in literature he was a baroque elaborist of tradition: of Homer and Virgil, Athenian tragedy, the Bible, Tasso and Spenser, and, most significantly, of Shakespeare. "Lycidas," the most influential elegy in English, deliberately stations its allusions to Theocritus and Virgil, Petrarch and Spenser so as to overgo the entire history of pastoral lament. The poem's echoes of *A Midsummer Night's Dream* seem to me involuntary, as though Shakespeare, most dangerous of influences, enters without Milton's consent. Though "Lycidas" ostensibly is Milton's dirge for a college acquaintance, it is as much an elegy for the self as are Shelley's *Adonais* and Whitman's "When Lilacs Last in the Dooryard Bloom'd." Milton, fearless in all else, expresses the implicit anxiety of being cut short before he can write the immortal epic that became *Paradise Lost*. It would be difficult to find another poem in the language of middle length (200 lines or less) that rivals "Lycidas" in imaginative intensity and splendor.

Samson Agonistes is an extraordinary poem, which demands energy of mind and grand resources of emotional strength. Taking his form from Euripides and his story from the book of Judges, Milton ruggedly associates his own heroic obduracy and tragic blindness with the Hebrew hero's. Though the poem concludes in "calm of mind all passion spent," we remember it for its shapely turbulence, as when the enchained Samson frightens away the Philistine bully Harapha with the superb line "My heels are fettered, but my fist is free." The fighting spirit of crucial psalms of David revives in John Milton, who molds Euripidean tragedy into a vast psalm of 1,758 lines, totally imbued with Yahwistic fervor. Milton stood at last for Yahweh alone, which pragmatically meant an absolutely solitary stance, a sect of one. His own tragic hero, the formidable Milton remains the most severe and admonishing emblem that our waning culture affords us.

Milton and His Precursors

No poet compares to Milton in his intensity of self-consciousness as an artist and in his ability to overcome all negative consequences of such concern. Milton's highly deliberate and knowingly ambitious program necessarily involved him in direct competition with Homer, Virgil, Lucretius, Ovid, Dante, and Tasso, among other major precursors. More anxiously, it brought him very close to Spenser, whose actual influence on *Paradise Lost* is deeper, subtler, and more extensive than scholarship so far has recognized. Most anxiously, the ultimate ambitions of *Paradise Lost* gave Milton the problem of expanding Scripture without distorting the Word of God.

A reader, thinking of Milton's style, is very likely to recognize that style's most distinctive characteristic as being the density of its allusiveness. Perhaps only Gray compares to Milton in this regard, and Gray is only a footnote, though an important and valuable one, to the Miltonic splendor. Milton's allusiveness has a distinct design, which is to enhance both the quality and the extent of his inventiveness. His handling of allusion is his highly individual and original defense against poetic tradition, his revisionary stance in writing what is in effect a tertiary epic, following after Homer in primary epic and Virgil, Ovid, and Dante in secondary epic. Most vitally, Miltonic allusion is the crucial revisionary ratio by which *Paradise Lost* distances itself from its most dangerous precursor, *The Faerie Queene*, for Spenser had achieved a national romance of epic greatness in the vernacular and in the service of moral and theological beliefs not far from Milton's own.

The map of misprision moves between the poles of *illusio*—irony as a figure of speech, or the reaction formation I have termed *clinamen*—and allusion, particularly as the scheme of transumption or metaleptic reversal that I have named *apophrades* and analogized to the defenses of introjection and projection. As the common root of their names indicates, *illusio* and allusion are curiously related, both being a kind of mockery, rather in the sense intended by the title of Geoffrey Hill's poem on Campanella that "Men are a mockery of Angels." The history of *allusion* as an English word goes from an initial meaning of "illusion" on to an early Renaissance use as meaning a pun or word play in general. But by the time of Bacon it meant any symbolic likening, whether in allegory, parable, or metaphor, as when in *The Advancement of Learning* poetry is divided into "Narrative, representative, and allusive." A fourth meaning, which is still the correct modern one, follows rapidly by the very early seventeenth century and involves any implied, indirect, or hidden reference. The fifth meaning, still incorrect but bound to establish itself, now equates allusion with direct, overt reference. Since the root meaning is "to play with, mock, jest at," allusion is uneasily allied to words like *ludicrous* and *elusion*, as we will remember later.

Thomas McFarland, formidably defending Coleridge against endlessly repetitive charges of plagiarism, has suggested that plagiarism ought to be added as a seventh revisionary ratio. Allusion is a comprehensive enough ratio to contain plagiarism also under the heading of *apophrades*, which the Lurianic Kabbalists called *gilgul*. Allusion as covert reference became in Milton's control the most powerful and successful figuration that any strong poet has ever employed against his strong precursors.

Milton, who would not sunder spirit from matter, would not let himself be a receiver, object to a subject's influencings. His stance against dualism and influence alike is related to his exaltation of unfallen pleasure, his appeal not so much to his reader's senses as to his reader's yearning for the expanded senses of Eden. Precisely here is the center of Milton's own influence on the romantics, and here also is why he surpassed them in greatness, since what he could do for himself was the cause of their becoming unable to do the same for themselves. His achievement became at once their starting point, their inspiration, yet also their goad, their torment.

Yet he too had his starting point: Spenser. Spenser was "the soothest shepherd that e'er piped on plains," "sage and serious." "Milton has acknowledged to me, that Spenser was his original," Dryden testified, but the paternity required no acknowledgment. A darker acknowledgment can be read in Milton's astonishing mistake about Spenser in *Areopagitica*, written more than 20 years before *Paradise Lost* was completed:

> . . . It was from out the rind of one apple tasted, that the knowledge of good and evil, as two twins cleaving together, leaped forth into the world. And perhaps this is that doom which Adam fell into of knowing good and evil, that is to say of knowing good by evil. As therefore the state of man is, what wisdom can there be to choose, what continence to forbear, without the knowledge of evil? He that

can apprehend and consider vice with all her baits and seeming pleasures, and yet abstain, and yet distinguish, and yet prefer that which is truly better, he is the true warfaring Christian. I cannot praise a fugitive and cloistered virtue, unexercised and unbreathed, that never sallies out and sees her adversary, but slinks out of the race, where that immortal garland is to be run for, not without dust and heat. Assuredly we bring not innocence into the world, we bring impurity much rather; that which purifies us is trial, and trial is by what is contrary. That virtue therefore which is but a youngling in the contemplation of evil, and knows not the utmost that vice promises to her followers, and rejects it, is but a blank virtue, not a pure; her whiteness is but an excremental whiteness; which was the reason why our sage and serious poet Spenser, whom I dare be known to think a better teacher than Scotus or Aquinas, describing true temperance under the person of Guyon, brings him in with his palmer through the cave of Mammon, and the bower of earthly bliss, that he might see and know, and yet abstain.

Spenser's cave of Mammon is Milton's Hell; far more than the descents to the underworld of Homer and Virgil, more even than Dante's vision, the prefiguration of books 1 and 2 of *Paradise Lost* reverberates in book 2 of *The Faerie Queene*. Against Acrasia's bower, Guyon enjoys the moral guidance of his unfaltering Palmer but necessarily in Mammon's cave Guyon has to be wholly on his own, even as Adam and Eve must withstand temptation in the absence of the affable Raphael. Guyon stands, though at some cost; Adam and Eve fall, but both the endurance and the failure are independent. Milton's is no ordinary error, no mere lapse in memory but is itself a powerful misinterpretation of Spenser and a strong defense against him. For Guyon is not so much Adam's precursor as he is Milton's own, the giant model imitated by the Abdiel of *Paradise Lost*. Milton rewrites Spenser so as to *increase the distance* between his poetic father and himself. St. Augustine identified memory with the father, and we may surmise that a lapse in a memory as preternatural as Milton's is a movement against the father.

Milton's full relation to Spenser is too complex and hidden for any rapid description or analysis to suffice, even for my limited purposes in this essay. Here I will venture that Milton's transumptive stance in regard to all his precursors, including Spenser, is founded on Spenser's resourceful and bewildering (even Joycean) way of subsuming his precursors, particularly Virgil, through his labyrinthine syncretism. Spenserian allusiveness has been described by Angus Fletcher as collage: "Collage is parody drawing attention to the *materials* of art and life." Fletcher follows Harry Berger's description of the technique of conspicuous allusion in Spenser: "the depiction of stock literary motifs, characters, and genres in a manner which emphasizes their conventionality, displaying at once their debt to and their existence in a conventional climate—Classical, medieval, romance, etc.—which is archaic when seen from Spenser's retrospective viewpoint." This allusive collage or conspicuousness is readily assimilated to Spenser's peculiarly metamorphic elegiacism, which becomes the particular legacy of Spenser to all his poetic descendants, from Drayton and Milton down to Yeats and Stevens. For Spenser began that internalization of quest romance that is or became what we call romanticism. It is the Colin Clout of Spenser's book 6 who is the father of Milton's "Il Penseroso," and from Milton's visionary stems the later Spenserian transformations of Wordsworth's Solitary and all of the Solitary's children in the wanderers of Keats, Shelley, Browning, Tennyson, and Yeats until the parodistic climax in Stevens's comedian Crispin. Fletcher, in his study of Spenser, *The Prophetic Moment*, charts this genealogy of introspection, stressing the intervention of Shakespeare between Spenser and Milton, since from Shakespeare Milton learned to contain the Spenserian elegiacism or "prophetic strain" within what Fletcher calls "transcendental forms." In his study of *Comus* as such a form, *The Transcendental Masque*, Fletcher emphasizes the "enclosed vastness" in which Milton, like Shakespeare, allows reverberations of the Spenserian resonance, a poetic diction richly dependent on allusive echoings of precursors. *Comus* abounds in *apophrades*, the return of many poets dead and gone, with Spenser and Shakespeare especially prominent among them. Following Berger and Fletcher, I would call the allusiveness of *Comus* still "conspicuous" and so still Spenserian, still part of the principle of echo. But, with *Paradise Lost*, Miltonic allusion is transformed into a mode of transumption, and poetic tradition is radically altered in consequence.

Fletcher, the most daemonic and inventive of modern allegorists, is again the right guide into the mysteries of transumptive allusion, through one of the brilliant footnotes in his early book *Allegory: The Theory of a Symbolic Mode* (p. 241, n. 33). Studying what he calls "difficult ornament" and the transition to modern allegory, Fletcher meditates on Johnson's ambivalence toward Milton's style. In his *Life of Milton*, Johnson observes that "the heat of Milton's mind might be said to sublimate his learning." Hazlitt, a less ambivalent admirer of Milton, asserted that Milton's learning had the effect of intuition. Johnson, though so much more grudging, actually renders the greater homage, for Johnson's own immense hunger of imagination was overmatched by Milton's, as he recognized:

Whatever be his subject, he never fails to fill the imagination. But his images and descriptions of the scenes or operations of Nature do not seem to be always copied from original form, nor to have the freshness, raciness, and energy of immediate observation. He saw Nature, as Dryden expresses it, *through the spectacles of books*; and on most occasions calls learning to his assistance. . . .

. . . But he does not confine himself within the limits of rigorous comparison: his great excellence is amplitude, and he expands the adventitious image beyond the dimensions which the occasion required. Thus, comparing the shield of Satan to the orb of the Moon, he crowds the imagination with the discovery of the telescope, and all the wonders which the telescope discovers.

This Johnsonian emphasis on allusion in Milton inspires Fletcher to compare Miltonic allusion to the trope of transumption or metalepsis, Puttenham's "far-fetcher":

Johnson stresses allusion in Milton: "the spectacles of books" are a means of sublimity, since at every point the reader is led from one scene to an allusive second scene, to a third, and so on. Johnson's Milton has, we might say, a "transumptive" style. . . .

Here is the passage that moved Johnson's observation, *Paradise Lost*, book 1, 283–313. Beelzebub has urged Satan to address his fallen legions, who still lie "astounded and amazed" on the lake of fire:

He scarce had ceas't when the superior Fiend
Was moving toward the shore; his ponderous 0shield
Ethereal temper, massy, large and round,
Behind him cast; the broad circumference
Hung on his shoulders like the Moon, whose Orb
Through Optic Glass the *Tuscan* Artist views
At Ev'ning from the top of *Fesole*,
Or in *Valdarno*, to descry new Lands,
Rivers or Mountains in her spotty Globe.
His Spear, to equal which the tallest Pine
Hewn on *Norwegian* hills, to be the Mast
Of some great Ammiral, were but a wand,
He walkt with to support uneasy steps

Over the burning Marl, not like those steps
On Heaven's Azure, and the torrid Clime
Smote on him sore besides, vaulted with Fire;
Nathless he so endur'd, till on the Beach
Of that inflamed Sea, he stood and call'd
His Legions, Angel Forms, who lay intrans't
Thick as Autumnal Leaves that strow the Brooks
In *Vallembrosa*, where th' *Etrurian* shades
High overarch't imbow'r; or scatter'd sedge
Afloat, when with fierce Winds *Orion* arm'd
Hath vext the Red-Sea Coast, whose waves o'erthrew
Busiris and his *Memphian* Chivalry,
While with perfidious hatred they pursu'd
The Sojourners of *Goshen*, who beheld
From the safe shore thir floating Carcasses
And broken Chariot Wheels, so thick bestrown
Abject and lost lay these, covering the Flood,
Under amazement of thir hideous change.

The transumption of the precursors here is managed by the juxtaposition between the far-fetching of Homer, Virgil, Ovid, Dante, Tasso, Spenser, the Bible, and the single near-contemporary reference to Galileo, "the Tuscan artist," and his telescope. Milton's aim is to make his own belatedness into an earliness, and his tradition's priority over him into a lateness. The critical question to be asked of this passage is: Why is Johnson's "adventitious image," Galileo and the telescope, present at all? Johnson, despite his judgment that the image is extrinsic, implies the right answer: because the expansion of this apparently extrinsic image crowds the reader's imagination, by giving Milton the true priority of interpretation, the powerful reading that insists on its own uniqueness and its own accuracy. Troping on his forerunners' tropes, Milton compels us to read as he reads and to accept his stance and vision as our origin, his time as true time. His allusiveness introjects the past and projects the future but at the paradoxical cost of the present, which is not voided but is yielded up to an experiential darkness, as we will see, to a mingling of wonder (discovery) and woe (the fallen Church's imprisonment of the discoverer). As Frank Kermode remarks, *Paradise Lost* is a wholly contemporary poem, yet surely its sense of the present is necessarily more of loss than of delight.

Milton's giant simile comparing Satan's shield to the moon alludes to the shield of Achilles in the *Iliad*, XIX, 373–80:

. . . and caught up the great shield, huge and heavy next, and from
it the light glimmered far, as from the moon.
 And as when from across water a light shines to mariners from
a blazing fire, when the fire is burning high in the mountains in a
desolate standing, as the mariners are carried unwilling by storm
winds over the fish-swarming sea, far away from their loved ones;
so the light from the fair elaborate shield of Achilleus shot into the
high air.

(Lattimore version)

Milton is glancing also at the shield of Radigund in *The Faerie Queene,*
(V.v.3):

And on her shoulder hung her shield, bedeckt
Upon the bosse with stones, that shined wide,
As the faire Moone in her most full aspect,
That to the Moone it mote be like in each respect.

Radigund, princess of the Amazons, is dominated by pride and anger,
like Achilles. Satan, excelling both in his bad eminence, is seen accurately
through the optic glass of the British artist's transumptive vision, even as
Galileo sees what no one before him has seen on the moon's surface. Galileo,
when visited by Milton (as he tells us in *Areopagitica*), was working while
under house arrest by the Inquisition, a condition not wholly unlike Milton's
own in the early days of the Restoration. Homer and Spenser emphasize the
moonlike brightness and shining of the shields of Achilles and Radigund;
Milton emphasizes size, shape, weight as the common feature of Satan's shield
and the moon, for Milton's post-Galilean moon is more of a world and less of
a light. Milton and Galileo are *late*, yet they see more, and more significantly,
than Homer and Spenser, who were *early*. Milton gives his readers the light
yet also the true dimensions and features of reality, even though Milton, like
the Tuscan artist, must work on while compassed around by experiential
darkness, in a world of woe.
 Milton will not stop with his true vision of Satan's shield but transumes
his precursors also in regard to Satan's spear, and to the fallen-leaves aspect
of the satanic host. Satan's spear evokes passages of Homer, Virgil, Ovid,
Tasso, and Spenser, allusions transumed by the contemporary reference
to a flagship ("ammiral") with its mast made of Norwegian fir. The central
allusion is probably to Ovid's vision of the Golden Age (Golding's version,
I, 109–16):

The loftie Pyntree was not hewen from mountaines where it stood,
In seeking straunge and forren landes to rove upon the flood.
Men knew none other countries yet, than where themselves did keepe:
There was no towne enclosed yet, with walles and ditches deepe.
No horne nor trumpet was in use, no sword nor helmet worne.
The worlde was suche, that souldiers helpe might easly be forborne.
The fertile earth as yet was free, untoucht of spade or plough,
And yet it yeelded of it selfe of every things inough.

Ovid's emblem of the passage from Golden Age to Iron Age is reduced to "but a wand," for Satan will more truly cause the fall from golden to iron. As earlier Satan subsumed Achilles and Radigund, now he contains and metaleptically reverses the Polyphemus of Homer and of Virgil, the Tancredi and Argantes of Tasso, and the proud giant Orgoglio of Spenser:

a club, or staff, lay there along the fold—
an olive tree, felled green and left to season
for Kyklops' hand. And it was like a mast
a lugger of twenty oars, broad in the beam—
a deep-sea-going craft—might carry:
so long, so big around, it seemed.

(*Odyssey*, IX, 322–27, Fitzgerald version)

. . . we saw
upon a peak the shepherd Polyphemus;
he lugged his mammoth hulk among the flocks,
searching along familiar shores—an awful
misshapen monster, huge, his eyelight lost.
His steps are steadied by the lopped-off pine
he grips. . . .

(*Aeneid,* III, 660–66;
Mandelbaum version, 849–55)

These sons of Mavors bore, instead of spears,
  Two knotty masts, which none but they could lift;
Each foaming steed so fast his master bears,
  That never beast, bird, shaft, flew half so swift:
Such was their fury, as when Boreas tears
  The shatter'd crags from Taurus' northern clift:
Upon their helms their lances long they brake,

And up to heav'n flew splinters, sparks, and smoke.

> (*Jerusalem Delivered*, VI, 40, Fairfax version)

So growen great through arrogant delight
  Of th'high descent, whereof he was yborne,
  And through presumption of his matchlesse might,
  All other powres and knighthood he did scorne.
  Such now he marcheth to this man forlorne,
  And left to losse: his stalking steps are stayde
  Upon a snaggy Oke, which he had torne
  Out of his mothers bowelles, and it made
  His mortall mace, wherewith his foemen he dismayde.

> (*Faerie Queene*, I, vii, x)

The Wild Men, Polyphemus the Cyclops, and the crudely proud Orgoglio, as well as the Catholic and Circassian champions, Tancredi and Argantes, all become late and lesser versions of Milton's earlier and greater Satan. The tree and the mast become interchangeable with the club, and all three become emblematic of the brutality of Satan as the Antichrist, the fallen son of God who walks in the darkness of his vainglory and perverts nature to the ends of war by sea and war by land, Job's Leviathan and Behemoth. Milton's present age is again an experiential darkness—of naval warfare—but his backward glance to satanic origins reveals the full truth of which Homer, Virgil, Tasso give only incomplete reflections. Whether the transumption truly overcomes Spenser's Orgoglio is more dubious, for he remains nearly as satanic as Milton's Satan, except that Satan is more complex and poignant, being a son of heaven and not, like the gross Orgoglio, a child of earth.

The third transumption of the passage, the fiction of the leaves, is surely the subtlest and the one most worthy of Milton's greatness. He tropes here on the tropes of Isaiah, Homer, Virgil, and Dante and with the Orion allusion on Job and Virgil. The series is capped by the references to Exodus and Ovid, with the equation of Busiris and Satan. This movement from fallen leaves to starry influence over storms to the overwhelming of a tyrannous host is itself a kind of transumption, as Milton moves from metonymy to metonymy before accomplishing a final reduction.

Satan's fallen hosts, poignantly still called "angel forms," most directly allude to a prophetic outcry of Isaiah 34:4:

> And all the host of heaven shall be dissolved, and the heavens
> shall be rolled together as a scroll; and all their host shall fall

down, as the leaf falleth off from the vine, and as a falling fig from
the fig tree.

Milton is too wary to mark this for transumption; his trope works on a
series of Homer, Virgil, Dante:

. . . why ask of my generation?
As is the generation of leaves, so is that of humanity.
The wind scatters the leaves on the ground, but the fine timber
burgeons with leaves again in the season of spring returning.
So one generation of men will grow while another dies. . . .

(Iliad, VI, 145–50, Lattimore version)

thick as the leaves that with the early frost
of autumn drop and fall within the forest,
or as the birds that flock along the beaches,
in flight from frenzied seas when the chill season
drives them across the waves to lands of sun.
They stand; each pleads to be the first to cross
the stream; their hands reach out in longing for
the farther shore. But Charon, sullen boatman,
now takes these souls, now those; the rest he leaves;
thrusting them back, he keeps them from the beach.

(Aeneid, VI, 310–19;
Mandelbaum version, 407–16)

. . . But those forlorn and naked souls changed color, their teeth
chattering, as soon as they heard the cruel words. They cursed God,
their parents, the human race, the place, the time, the seed of their
begetting and of their birth. Then, weeping loudly, all drew to the
evil shore that awaits every man who fears not God. The demon
Charon, his eyes like glowing coals, beckons to them and collects
them all, beating with his oar whoever lingers.

As the leaves fall away in autumn, one after another, till the
bough sees all its spoils upon the ground, so there the evil seed of
Adam: one by one they cast themselves from that shore at signals,
like a bird at its call. Thus they go over the dark water, and before
they have landed on the other shore, on this side a new throng
gathers.

(Inferno, III, 100–120, Singleton version)

Homer accepts grim process; Virgil accepts yet plangently laments, with his unforgettable vision of those who stretch forth their hands out of love for the farther shore. Dante, lovingly close to Virgil, is more terrible, since his leaves fall even as the evil seed of Adam falls. Milton remembers standing, younger and then able to see, in the woods at Vallombrosa, watching the autumn leaves strew the brooks. His characteristic metonymy of shades for woods allusively puns on Virgil's and Dante's images of the shades gathering for Charon and by a metalepsis carries across Dante and Virgil to their tragic Homeric origin. Once again, the precursors are projected into belatedness, as Milton introjects the prophetic source of Isaiah. Leaves fall from trees, generations of men die, because once one-third of the heavenly host came falling down. Milton's present time again is experiential loss; he watches no more autumns, but the optic glass of his art sees fully what his precursors saw only darkly, or in the vegetable glass of nature

By a transition to the "scattered sedge" of the Red Sea, Milton calls up Virgil again, compounding two passages on Orion:

Our prows were pointed there when suddenly,
rising upon the surge, stormy Orion
drove us against blind shoals. . . .
(*Aeneid*, I, 534–36; Mandelbaum version, 753–55)

. . . he marks Arcturus,
the twin Bears and the rainy Hyades,
Orion armed with gold; and seeing all
together in the tranquil heavens, loudly
he signals. . . .

(*Aeneid*, III, 517–21;
Mandelbaum version, 674–78)

Alastair Fowler notes the contrast to the parallel biblical allusions:

He is wise in heart, and mighty in strength: who hath hardened himself against him, and hath prospered?
. . . Which alone spreadeth out the heavens, and treadeth upon the waves of the sea.
Which maketh Arcturus, Orion, and Pleiades, and the chambers of the south.

(Job 9:4,8–9)

Seek him that maketh the seven stars and Orion, and turneth the
shadow of death into the morning, and maketh the day dark with
night: that calleth for the waters of the sea, and poureth them out
upon the face of the earth: The LORD is his name. . . .

(Amos 5:8)

In Virgil, Orion rising marks the seasonal onset of storms. In the Bible,
Orion and all the stars are put into place as a mere sign system, demoted
from their pagan status as powers. Milton says "hath vexed" to indicate that
the sign system continues in his own day, but he says "o'erthrew" to show
that the satanic stars and the hosts of Busiris the Pharaoh fell once for all,
pharaoh being a type of Satan. Virgil, still caught in a vision that held Orion
as a potency, is himself again transumed into a sign of error.

I have worked through this passage's allusions in some detail so as to
provide one full instance of a transumptive scheme in *Paradise Lost*. Johnson's insight is validated, for the "adventitious image" of the optic glass is
shown to be not extrinsic at all but rather to be the device that "crowds the
imagination," compressing or hastening much transumption into a little
space. By arranging his precursors in series, Milton figuratively reverses his
obligation to them, for his stationing crowds them between the visionary
truth of his poem (carefully aligned with biblical truth) and his darkened
present (which he shares with Galileo). Transumption murders time, for by
troping on a trope, you enforce a state of rhetoricity or word consciousness,
and you negate fallen history. Milton does what Bacon hoped to do; Milton
and Galileo become ancients, and Homer, Virgil, Ovid, Dante, Tasso, and
Spenser become belated moderns. The cost is a loss in the immediacy of the
living moment. Milton's meaning is remarkably freed of the burden of ante-
riority, but only because Milton himself is already one with the future, which
he introjects.

It would occupy too many pages to demonstrate another of Milton's transumptive schemes in its largest and therefore most powerful dimensions, but
I will outline one, summarizing rather than quoting the text and citing rather
than giving the allusions. My motive is not only to show that the "optic glass"
passage is hardly unique in its arrangement, but to analyze more thoroughly
Milton's self-awareness of both his war against influence and his use of rhetoricity as a defense. Of many possibilities, book 1, lines 670–798 seems to me
the best, for this concluding movement of the epic's initial book has as its
hidden subject both the anxiety of influence and an anxiety of morality about
the secondariness of any poetic creation, even Milton's own. The passage

describes the sudden building, out of the deep, of Pandaemonium, the palace of Satan, and ends with the infernal peers sitting there in council.

This sequence works to transume the crucial precursors again—Homer, Virgil, Ovid, and Spenser—but there are triumphant allusions here to Lucretius and Shakespeare also (as Fowler notes). In some sense, the extraordinary and reverberating power of the Pandaemonium masque (as John Hollander terms it, likening it to transformation scenes in court masques) depends on its being a continuous and unified allusion to the very idea of poetic tradition, and to the moral problematic of that idea. Metalepsis or transumption can be described as an extended trope with a missing or weakened middle, and for Milton literary tradition is such a trope. The illusionistic sets and complex machinery of the masque transformation scene are emblematic, in the Pandaemonium sequence, of the self-deceptions and morally misleading machinery of epic and tragic convention.

Cunningly, Milton starts the sequence with a transumption to the fallen near-present, evoking the royal army in the civil war as precise analogue to the satanic army. Mammon leads on the advance party, in an opening allusion to Spenser's Cave of Mammon canto, since both Mammons direct gold-mining operations. With the next major allusion, to the same passage in Ovid's *Metamorphoses* I that was evoked in the Galileo sequence, Milton probes the morality of art:

> Let none admire
> That riches grow in Hell; that soil may best
> Deserve the precious bane. And here let those
> Who boast in mortal things, and wond'ring tell
> Of *Babel*, and the works of *Memphian* Kings,
> Learn how their greatest Monuments of Fame,
> And Strength and Art are easily outdone
> By Spirits reprobate, and in an hour
> What in an age they with incessant toil
> And hands innumerable scarce perform.

Milton presumably would not have termed the *Iliad* or the *Aeneid* "precious bane," yet the force of his condemnation extends to them, and his anxiety necessarily touches his own poem as well. Pandaemonium rises in baroque splendor, with a backward allusion to Ovid's Palace of the Sun, also designed by Mulciber (*Metamorphoses* II, 1–4), and with a near-contemporary allusion to St. Peter's in Rome and, according to Fowler, to Bernini's colonnade in the piazza of St. Peter's. Mulciber, archetype not only of Bernini but more darkly of all artists, including epic poets, becomes the center of the sequence:

> Men call'd him *Mulciber,* and how he fell
> From Heav'n, they fabl'd, thrown by angry *Jove*
> Sheer o'er the Crystal Battlements: from Morn
> To Noon he fell, from Noon to dewy Eve,
> A Summer's day; and with the setting Sun
> Dropt from the Zenith like a falling Star,
> On *Lemnos* th' Ægœan Isle: thus they relate,
> Erring; for he with this rebellious rout
> Fell long before; nor aught avail'd him now
> To have built in Heav'n high Towrs; nor did he scape
> By all his Engines, but was headlong sent
> With is industrious crew to build in hell.

The devastating "Erring" of line 747 is a smack at Homer by way of the *errat* of Lucretius (*De rerum natura*, I, 393, as Fowler notes). The contrast with Homer's passage illuminates the transumptive function of Milton's allusiveness, for Homer's Hephaistos (whose Latin name was Vulcan or Mulciber) gently fables his own downfall:

> . . . It is too hard to fight against the Olympian.
> There was a time once before now I was minded to help you, and he caught
> me by the foot and threw me from the magic threshold,
> and all day long I dropped helpless, and about sunset
> I landed in Lemnos. . . .
>
> (*Iliad,* I, 589–93, Lattimore version)

Milton first mocks Homer by overaccentuating the idyllic nature of this fall and then reverses Homer completely. In the dark present, Mulciber's work is still done when the bad eminence of baroque glory is turned to the purposes of a fallen Church. So, at line 756, Pandaemonium is called "the high capital" of Satan, alluding to two lines of Virgil (*Aeneid*, VI, 836 and VIII, 348), but the allusion is qualified by the complex simile of the bees that continues throughout lines 768–75 and which relies on further allusions to *Iliad*, II, 87–90 and *Aeneid*, 430–36, where Achaian and Carthaginian heroes respectively are compared to bees. One of the most remarkable of Milton's transumptive returns to present time is then accomplished by an allusion to

Shakespeare's *A Midsummer Night's Dream*, II, i, 28ff. A "belated peasant" beholds the "Faery Elves" even as we, Milton's readers, see the giant demons shrink in size. Yet our belatedness is again redressed by metaleptic reversal, with an allusion to *Aeneid*, VI, 451–54, where Aeneas recognizes Dido's "dim shape among the shadows (just as one who either sees or thinks he sees ... the moon rising)." So the belated peasant "sees, or dreams he sees" the elves, but like Milton we know we see the fallen angels metamorphosed from giants into pygmies. The Pandaemonium sequence ends with the great conclave of "a thousand demi-gods on golden seats," in clear parody of ecclesiastical assemblies reconvened after the Restoration. As with the opening reference to the advance party of the royal army, the present is seen as fallen on evil days, but it provides vantage for Milton's enduring vision.

So prevalent throughout the poem is this scheme of allusion that any possibility of inadvertence can be ruled out. Milton's design is wholly definite, and its effect is to reverse literary tradition, at the expense of the presentness of the present. The precursors return in Milton, but only at his will, and they return to be corrected. Perhaps only Shakespeare can be judged Milton's rival in allusive triumph over tradition, yet Shakespeare had no Spenser to subsume but only a Marlowe, and Shakespeare is less clearly in overt competition with Aeschylus, Sophocles, and Euripides than Milton is with Homer, Virgil, Ovid, Dante, and Tasso.

Hobbes, in his *Answer to Davenant's Preface* (1650), had subordinated wit to judgment and so implied also that rhetoric was subordinate to dialectic:

> From knowing much, proceedeth the admirable variety and novelty of metaphors and similitudes, which are not possibly to be lighted on in the compass of a narrow knowledge. And the want whereof compelleth a writer to expressions that are either defaced by time or sullied with vulgar or long use. For the phrases of poesy, as the airs of music, with often hearing become insipid; the reader having no more sense of their force, than our flesh is sensible of the bones that sustain it. As the sense we have of bodies, consisteth in change and variety of impression, so also does the sense of language in the variety and changeable use of words. I mean not in the affectation of words newly brought home from travel, but in new (and withal, significant) translation to our purposes, of those that be already received, and in far fetched (but withal, apt, instructive, and comely) similitudes. . . .

Had Milton deliberately accepted this as challenge, he could have done no more both to fulfill and to refute Hobbes than *Paradise Lost* already does.

What Davenant and Cowley could not manage was a complete translation to their own purposes of received rhetoric; but Milton raised such translation to sublimity. In doing so, he also raised rhetoric over dialectic, *contra* Hobbes, for his farfetchedness (Puttenham's term for transumption) gave similitudes the status and function of complex arguments. Milton's wit, his control of rhetoric, was again the exercise of the mind through all her powers and not a lower faculty subordinate to judgment. Had Hobbes written his *Answer* twenty years later, and after reading *Paradise Lost*, he might have been less confident of the authority of philosophy over poetry.

BIOGRAPHY

JOHN MILTON
1608–1674

John Milton was born in Cheapside, London, on December 9, 1608, the son of a scrivener and moneylender who had been disinherited for converting to Protestantism. Milton probably entered St. Paul's School in 1620, although he may have begun as early as 1615. In addition, he had a private tutor. His earliest known poems were rhymed paraphrases of Psalms 114 and 136, probably written when he was 15.

In 1625, Milton entered Christ's College, Cambridge University, receiving a B.A. in 1629 and an M.A. in 1632. Because of his delicate appearance and abstemious behavior, Milton was called "the Lady" at college. There, however, Milton wrote six Italian sonnets and his Christmas ode, "On the Morning of Christ's Nativity" (1629). It is believed that Milton wrote the companion poems "L'Allegro" and "Il Penseroso" during a long vacation in 1631. He also wrote many Latin poems while at college.

After leaving Cambridge in 1632, Milton settled into a five-year-long retirement in his father's household, first at Hammersmith and then at Horton, Buckinghamshire. He continued his studies and his writing. Probably in 1632 he wrote a short masque, *Arcades*, at the request of a friend, the composer Henry Lawes. This was followed by a longer masque, also written at Lawes's request, *A Maske Presented at Ludlow Castle 1634: on Michaelmasse Night*. Now known as *Comus*, this pastoral was first performed on September 29, 1634, before John Egerton, earl of Bridgwater. In 1637, Milton contributed the elegy "Lycidas" to a volume of elegies centering on the drowning of a college friend, Edward King.

Milton spent the next few years abroad, chiefly in Italy. He wrote a number of Latin poems, including "Mansus," an epistle. Soon after his return to England in 1639, he wrote the Latin pastoral elegy "Epitaphium Damonis," in honor of Charles Diodati, who had been his friend since childhood.

Having returned to England because of the increasing political tensions there, Milton settled in London. He initially took in pupils but became more and more dedicated to the causes of civil and religious liberty, convictions that were to dominate his life and writings from 1641 to 1660. During these years he wrote numerous tracts and pamphlets on a wide range of topics. A collection of his early poems was published in 1645.

His early pamphlets concerned freedom of religion and included such works as *Of Reformation Touching Church-Discipline in England* (1641) and *Reason of Church-Government* (1642). He also wrote four tracts between 1643 and 1645 advocating the right to divorce. In 1642, Milton had married Mary Powell, who left him after one month; she returned three years later. Mary Milton bore four children, of whom three, all daughters, survived. She died in childbirth in 1652. Milton married twice again, first to Catherine Woodcocke, who with her infant daughter died in childbirth, and then to Elizabeth Minshull, who survived her husband.

Milton's tract writing continued through the years of the civil war and the Commonwealth. *Of Education* was published in 1644 as was the celebrated *Areopagitica*, which advocated freedom of the press. The political tract *The Tenure of Kings and Magistrates* (1649), Milton's first, appeared two weeks after the execution of Charles I. Soon afterward, Milton was asked to be Latin, or foreign, secretary to Cromwell. Milton also edited the Commonwealth newspaper *Mercurius Politicus* and continued writing numerous tracts, including *Eikonoklastes* (1649); the two *Defences of the English People* (1649, 1654), against the Royalist claims of Salmasius and Alexander More; *A Treatise of Civil Power in Ecclesiastical Causes* (1659); and his last political pamphlet, *The Readie and Easie Way to Establish a Free Commonwealth* (1660).

Milton went blind in the winter of 1651–52, while still Latin secretary. He wrote a sonnet on his blindness; this, along with some 17 other sonnets and versifications of various psalms, represents the poetry he wrote while otherwise engaged in 20 years of public service. In the months following the Restoration, Milton was in serious danger of being hanged for treason. He was initially hidden and protected by friends. Although arrested and briefly imprisoned in 1660, he was released and pardoned, perhaps with the help of his friends Andrew Marvell and William Davenant.

It is believed that *Paradise Lost* was begun while Milton was still Latin secretary, perhaps between 1655 and 1658. His work was dictated—to assistants, relatives, his younger daughters, and friends—in a daily routine that Milton likened to being "milked." The first edition, consisting of ten books, was finished in 1665 and published in 1667. The second and final edition was published in 1674, and it contained, along with minor revisions, 12 books, as books 7 and 10 were each divided in half. The sequel, *Paradise Regained*, concerns Christ in the wilderness overcoming Satan's temptations and was published in 1671. In that same year, Milton published *Samson Agonistes*, which chronicles the triumph of the blind Samson and is modeled on the principles of Greek drama.

For most of the remainder of his life, Milton lived at Cripplegate, enjoying a peaceful life in the company of his third wife, whom he married in 1663. During the plague in 1665, Milton moved to the rural village of Chalfont St. Giles, 25 miles from London, with his wife and possibly Deborah, his daughter and scribe. It is believed he finished *Paradise Lost* while residing in his small cottage there and returned to London in 1666. Milton died on November 8, 1674, "of the gout struck in" and is buried along with his father in St. Giles-in-the-Fields.

PERSONAL

The following selections provide insight into John Milton's life and reputation, ranging in their bases from personal knowledge to hearsay and speculation. The authors' judgments of Milton hinge on their personal political, religious, and artistic views, with the resulting legacy a mixture of praise and declamation. Several repeated points emerge from the accounts, however; Milton was a handsome and somewhat feminine-looking youth; he was a serious student, always committed and perhaps overly committed to his studies; his personal habits were austere; his devotion to religion and politics won him both praise and censure; he loved music and was skilled in playing the organ; and his later blindness provoked pathos as well as admiration for his continued work.

Milton's own account focuses on both the high standing of his parents and his singleminded focus on reading, including its debilitating effect on his eyesight. Several accounts are from friends or relations of Milton. Edward Phillips (1630-96?), Milton's nephew, lived for a time with Milton and was both Milton's student and scribe. Thomas Ellwood, an English Quaker whom Milton hired to read to him in Latin, credits himself for Milton's writing of *Paradise Regained*, as Ellwood had asked the poet "what hast thou to say of Paradise found?" after reading *Paradise Lost*.

Later accounts are interposed by editors of Milton's works. The famed painter, critic, and art theorist Jonathan Richardson provides a secondhand and quite visual account of Milton's last years. Thomas Newton, bishop and literary scholar, produced an edition of *Paradise Lost* that included much of the commentary on the work produced up to his time; he focuses on Milton's strictly regulated practices in this period of the poet's life. British historian and Anglican priest Thomas Birch presents a regimented but complimentary and idealized portrait of Milton.

Eighteenth-century biographies are often critical of Milton's politics, especially his support of regicide and his puritanical religion. Politically, the two English parties, the Tories (those who stand with the monarchy) and Whigs (those supporting populist politics) not surprisingly divide their opinions of Milton along party lines. With the advent of the French Revolution and romanticism, Milton became, in his commentators' eyes, a heroic advocate of political, religious, and personal liberty. His voice influenced many British romantic poets, who appropriated his nonconformity in their own time. In particular, Milton's developed character of Satan in *Paradise Lost* inspired a new strain of antihero, captured by George Gordon, Lord Byron; Percy Bysshe Shelley; and William Blake in their works. In the process of elevating Milton's Satan, his religious views were often misinterpreted or undermined. Later, nineteenth-century Victorian biographers focused on Milton's classicism, universal appeal, and the "incandescence" of his thought and poetry, rather than his theological and political views and personal life. Early twentieth-century commentators concentrated more on his Renaissance humanism and less on his religion. Each age, therefore, re-created Milton in its own image, according to prevailing attitudes about politics, religion, and literary tastes.

JOHN MILTON (1654)

I was born in London, of an honorable family. My father was a man of supreme integrity, my mother a woman of purest reputation, celebrated throughout the neighborhood for her acts of charity. My father destined me in early childhood for the study of literature, for which I had so keen an appetite that from my twelfth year scarcely ever did I leave my studies for my bed before the hour of midnight. This was the first cause of injury to my eyes, whose natural weakness was augmented by frequent headaches. Since none of these defects slackened my assault upon knowledge, my father took care that I should be instructed daily both in school and under other masters at home. When I had thus become proficient in various languages and had tasted by no means superficially the sweetness of philosophy, he sent me to Cambridge, one of our two universities. There, untouched by any reproach, in the good graces of all upright men, for seven years I devoted myself to the traditional disciplines and liberal arts, until I had attained the degree of Master, as it is called, *cum laude*. Then, far from fleeing to Italy, as that filthy rascal alleges, of my own free will I returned home, to the regret of most of the fellows of the college, who bestowed on me no little honor. At my father's country place, whither he had retired to spend his declining years, I devoted myself entirely to the study of Greek and Latin writers, completely at leisure, not, however, without sometimes exchanging the country for the city, either to purchase books or to become acquainted with some new discovery in mathematics or music, in which I then took the keenest pleasure.

—John Milton, A *Second Defence of the English People*, 1654, tr. North

JOHN MILTON (1667)

On evil days though fallen, and evil tongues; In darkness, and with dangers compassed round, And solitude; yet not alone.

—John Milton, *Paradise Lost*, 1667, book 7

GERARD LANGBAINE (1691)

An Author that liv'd in the Reign of King *Charles* the Martyr. Had his Principles been as good as his Parts, he had been an Excellent Person; but his demerits towards his Sovereign, has very much sullied his Reputation.

—Gerard Langbaine, *An Account of the English Dramatick Poets*, 1691, p. 375

ANTHONY À WOOD (1691)

Having obtained a B.A. and M.A. from Oxford University, historian Anthony à Wood (1632–95) documented in several volumes a history of Oxford's graduates and those who, like Milton, a Cambridge graduate, had even marginal connections with the university. He used Aubrey's research as well as other secondhand sources that he abridged and supplemented, with a resulting work that sometimes lacks accuracy. Wood casts a negative light on Milton's political radicalism but praises his education and wit.

This year (1635) was incorporated Master of Arts *John Milton*, not that it appears so in the Register, for the reason I have told you in the Incorporations 1629, but from his own mouth to my friend, who was well acquainted with, and had from him, and from his Relations after his death, most of this account of his life and writings following. (1) That he was born in *Breadstreet* within the City of London, between 6 and 7 a clock in the morning of the ninth of *Decemb.* an. 1608. (2) That his father *Joh. Milton* who was a Scrivner living at the *Spread Eagle*[1] in the said street, was a Native of *Halton* in *Oxfordshire*, and his mother named *Sarah* was of the antient family of the *Bradshaws*. (3) That his Grandfather *Milton* whose Christian name was *John*, as he thinks, was an

Under-Ranger or Keeper of the Forest of *Shotover* near to the said town of
Halton, but descended from those of his name who had lived beyond all record
at *Milton* near *Halton* and *Thame* in *Oxfordshire*. Which Grandfather being a
zealous Papist, did put away, or, as some say, disinherit, his Son, because he
was a Protestant, which made him retire to *London*, to seek, in a manner, his
fortune. (4) That he the said *John Milton* the Author, was educated mostly in
Pauls school under *Alex. Gill* senior, and thence at 15 years of age was sent to
Christs Coll. in *Cambridge*, where he was put under the tuition of *Will. Chap-
pell*, afterwards Bishop of *Ross* in *Ireland*, and there, as at School for 3 years
before, 'twas usual with him to sit up till midnight at his book, which was the
first thing that brought his eyes into the danger of blindness. By this his indefatigable study he profited exceedingly, wrot then several Poems, paraphras'd
some of *David's Psalms*, performed the collegiate and academical exercise to
the admiration of all, and was esteemed to be a vertuous and sober person, yet
not to be ignorant of his own parts. (5) That after he had taken the degrees in
Arts, he left the University of his own accord, and was not expelled for misde-
meanors, as his Adversaries have said. Whereupon retiring to his Fathers house
in the Country, he spent some time in turning over Latin and Greek Authors,
and now and then made[2] excursions into the great City to buy books, to the
end that he might be instructed in Mathematicks and Musick, in which last he
became excellent, and by the help of his Mathematicks could compose a Song
or Lesson. (6) That after five years being thus spent, and his Mother (who was
very charitable to the poor) dead, he did design to travel, so that obtaining the
rudiments of the Ital. Tongue, and Instructions how to demean himself from Sir
Hen. Wotton, who delighted in his company, and gave him Letters of commendation to certain persons living at *Venice*, he travelled into *Italy*, an. 1638. (7)
That in his way thither, he touched at *Paris*, where *Joh. Scudamoure*, Vicount
Slego, Embassador from K. *Ch.* I. to the French king, received him kindly, and
by his means became known to *Hugo Grotius*, then and there Embassador from
the Qu. of *Sweden*; but the manners and genius of that place being not agreeable to his mind, he soon left it. (8) That thence by *Geneva* and other places of
note, he went into *Italy*, and thro *Legorne, Pisa*, &c. he went to *Florence*, where
continuing two months, he became acquainted with several learned men, and
familiar with the choicest Wits of that great City, who introduced and admitted
him into their private Academies, whereby he saw and learn'd their fashions
of literature. (9) That from thence he went to *Sena* and *Rome*, in both which
places he spent his time among the most learned there, *Lucas Holsteinius* being
one; and from thence he journied to *Naples*, where he was introduced into the
acquaintance *otjoh. Bapt. Mansus* an Italian Marquess (to whom *Torquatus
Tassus* an Italian poet wrot his book *De Amicitia*) who shewed great civilities

to him, accompanied him to see the rarieties of that place, visited him at his Lodgings, and sent to, the testimony of his great esteem for, him, in this Distich,

Ut mens, forma, decor, mos, si pietas sic,
Non Anglus, verum hercule Angelus ipse fores.

And excus'd himself at parting for not having been able to do him more honour, by reason of his resolute owning his (Protestant) religion: which resoluteness he using at *Rome,* many there were that dared not to express their civilities towards him, which otherwise they would have done: And I have heard it confidently related, that for his said Resolutions, which out of policy, and for his own safety, might have been then spared, the English Priests at *Rome* were highly disgusted, and it was question'd whether the Jesuits his Countrymen there, did not design to do him mischief. Before he left *Naples* he return'd the Marquess an acknowledgment of his great favours in an elegant copy of verses entit. Mansus, which is among the Latin poems. (10) That from thence *(Naples)* he thought to have gone into *Sicily* and *Greece,* but upon second thoughts he continued in *Italy,* and went to *Luca, Bononia, Ferrara,* and at length to *Venice;* where continuing a month, he went and visited *Verona* and *Millan.* (11) That after he had ship'd the books and other goods which he had bought in his travels, he returned thro *Lombardy,* and over the *Alpes* to *Geneva,* where spending some time, he became familiar with the famous *Joh. Deodate* D. D. Thence, going thro *France,* he returned home, well fraught with Knowledge and Manners, after he had been absent one year and three months. (12) That soon after he setled in an house in S. *Bride's* Churchyard, near *Fleetstreet,* in *London,* where he instructed in the Lat. Tongue two Youths named *John* and *Edw. Philips,* the Sons of his Sister Anne by her Husband *Edward Philips:* both which were afterwards Writers, and the eldest principl'd as his Uncle. But the times soon after changing, and the Rebellion thereupon breaking forth, *Milton* sided with the Faction, and being a man of parts, was therefore more capable than another of doing mischief, especially by his pen, as by those books which I shall anon mention, will appear. (13) That at first we find him a Presbyterian and a most sharp and violent opposer of Prelacy, the established ecclesiastical Discipline and the orthodox Clergy. (14) That shortly after he did set on foot and maintained very odd and novel Positions concerning Divorce, and then taking part with the Independents, he became a great Anti-monarchist, a bitter Enemy to K. *Ch.* I. and at length arrived to that monstrous and unparallel'd height of profligate impudence, as in print to justify the most execrable Murder of him the best of Kings, as I shall anon tell you. Afterwards being made Latin Secretary to the Parliament, we find him a Commonwealths man, a hater of all things that looked towards a single person, a great reproacher of the Universities, scholas-tical degrees, decency and uniformity in the Church. (15) That when *Oliver* ascended the Throne, he became the Latin Secretary, and proved to him very serviceable when employed in business of weight and moment, and did great matters to obtain a name and wealth. To conclude, he was a person of wonderful parts, of a very sharp, biting and satyrical wit. He was a good Philosopher and Historian, an excellent Poet, Latinist, Grecian and Hebritian, a good Mathematician and Musitian, and so rarely endowed by nature, that had he been but honestly principled, he might have been highly useful to that party, against which he all along appeared with much malice and bitterness.

Notes

1. The arms that *Joh. Milton* did use and seal his letters with, were,
   Argent a spread eagle with two heads gules, legg'd and beak'd sable.
   See in Joh. Milton's book intit. *Defensio secunda:* edit. *Hag.* Com. 1654, p. 61, &c.

—Anthony à Wood, from *Fasti Oxonienses*, 1691

EDWARD PHILLIPS "THE LIFE OF MR. JOHN MILTON" (1694)

Edward Phillips (1630–96?) was John Milton's nephew, the son of Milton's eldest sister, who had lived with and was tutored by Milton. Later, Phillips served as one of Milton's scribes. Despite his familial connection and residence with the poet, Phillips's account of Milton famously misreports his birth year as 1606, instead of 1608, and his death year as 1673, instead of 1674. Phillips is, however, the only early biographer to record all 11 of Milton's London residences and to provide some unusually candid details of his family life. Phillips is the first to make note of Milton's habit of having his daughters read to him in languages with which they were unfamiliar. The passage that follows gives an amusing account of Milton's unsuccessful attempt to educate his daughters in Greek, Latin, and modern European languages.

He had three Daughters who surviv'd him many years (and a Son) all by his first Wife : *Anne* his Eldest as abovesaid, and *Mary* his Second, who were both born at his House in *Barbican*; and *Debora* the youngest, who is yet living, born at his House in *Petty-France,* between whom and his Second Daughter, the Son, named *John*, was born as above-mention'd, at his Apartment in *Scotland Yard*. By his Second Wife, *Catharine* the Daughter of Captain *Woodcock* of *Hackney*, he had only one Daughter, of which the Mother the first year after her Marriage died in Child bed, and the Child also within a Month after. By his Third Wife *Elizabeth* the daughter of one Mr. *Minshal* of *Cheshire* (and Kinswoman to Dr. *Paget*), who surviv'd him, and is said to be yet living, he never had any Child; and those he had by the First he made serviceable to him in that very particular in which he most wanted their Service, and supplied his want of Eye-sight by their Eyes and Tongue; for though he had daily about him one or other to Read to him, some persons of Man's Estate, who of their own accord greedily catch'd at the opportunity of being his Readers, that they might as well reap the benefit of what they Read to him, as oblige him by the benefit of their reading; others of younger years sent by their Parents to the same end; yet excusing only the Eldest Daughter by reason of her bodily Infirmity, and difficult utterance of Speech, (which to say truth I doubt was the Principal cause of excusing her), the other two were Condemn'd to the performance of Reading, and exactly pronouncing of all the Languages of whatever Book he should at one time or other think fit to peruse; Viz. The *Hebrew* (and I think the *Syriac*), the *Greek*, the *Latin*, the *Italian*, *Spanish* and *French*. All which sorts of Books to be confined to Read, without understanding one word, must needs be a Tryal of Patience, almost beyond endurance; yet it was endured by both for a long time; yet the irksomeness of this imployment could not always be concealed, but broke out more and more into expressions of uneasiness; so that at length they were all (even the Eldest also) sent out to learn some Curious and Ingenious sorts of Manufacture, that are proper for Women to learn, particularly Imbroideries in Gold or Silver. It had been happy indeed if the Daughters of such a Person had been made in some measure Inheritrixes of their Father's Learning; but since Fate otherwise decreed, the greatest Honour that can be ascribed to this now living (and so would have been to the others, had they lived) is to be Daughter to a man of his extraordinary Character.

—Edward Philips, "The Life of Mr. John Milton,"
Letters of State, English edition, 1694

JOHN AUBREY "JOHN MILTON" (1669–96)

John Aubrey (1626–97), seventeenth-century antiquarian and biographer, was commissioned by Anthony à Wood to gather information on Milton for his historical publications. Milton's relations—including nephew Edward Phillips, widow Elizabeth, and brother Christopher, as well as others connected to Milton—were primary sources for Aubrey. With his encyclopedic materials, Aubrey created a relatively unedited and extremely detailed account of Milton, with many firsthand anecdotes, albeit little literary analysis. The following selection shows Aubrey's lack of organization but contains interesting insights into the everyday aspects of Milton's life. Rather than shaping his autobiography into a portrayal of a saintlike subject, Aubrey journalistically reports without commentary all the information he has garnered.

Mr. John Milton was of an Oxfordshire familie. His Grandfather was a Roman Catholic of Holton, in Oxfordshire, near Shotover.

His father was brought-up in the University of Oxon, at Christ Church, and his grandfather disinherited him because he kept not to the Catholique Religion (he found a Bible in English, in his Chamber). So therupon he came to London, and became a Scrivener (brought up by a friend of his; was not an Apprentice) and gott a plentiful estate by it, and left it off many yeares before he dyed. He was an ingeniose man; delighted in musique; composed many Songs now in print, especially that of *Oriana*. I have been told that the Father composed a Song of fourscore parts for the Lantgrave of Hess, for which his Highnesse sent a meddall of gold, or a noble present. He dyed about 1647; buried in Cripple-gate-church, from his house in the Barbican.

His son John was borne the 9th of December, 1608, *die Veneris,* half an hour after 6 in the morning, in Bread Street, in London, at the Spread Eagle, which was his house (he had also in that street another howse, the Rose; and other houses in other places). Anno Domini 1619, he was ten yeares old; and was then a Poet. His school-master then was a Puritan, in Essex, who cutt his haire short.

He went to Schoole to old Mr. Gill, at Paule's Schoole. Went at his owne Chardge only, to Christ's College in Cambridge at fifteen, where he stayed eight yeares at least. Then he travelled into France and Italie (had Sir H. Wotton's commendatory letters). At Geneva he contracted a great friendship with the learned Dr. Deodati of Geneva. He was acquainted with Sir Henry Wotton, Ambassador at Venice, who delighted in his company. He was severall yeares beyond Sea, and returned to England just upon the breaking-out of the Civill Warres.

From his brother, Christopher Milton:—when he went to Schoole, when he was very young, he studied very hard, and sate-up very late, commonly till twelve or one a clock at night, and his father ordered the mayde to sitt-up for him, and in those yeares (10) composed many Copies of Verses which might well become a riper age. And was a very hard student in the University, and performed all his exercises there with very good Applause. His first Tutor there was Mr. Chapell; from whom receiving some unkindnesse (whipt him) he was afterwards (though it seemed contrary to the Rules of the College) transferred to the Tuition of one Mr. Tovell, who dyed Parson of Lutterworth. He went to travell about the year 1638 and was abroad about a year's space, chiefly in Italy.

Immediately after his return he took a lodging at Mr. Russell's, a Taylour, in St. Bride's Churchyard, and took into his tuition his sister's two sons, Edward and John Philips, the first 10, the other 9 years of age; and in a yeare's time made them capable of interpreting a Latin authour at sight. And within three years they went through the best of Latin and Greek Poetts—Lucretius and Manilius, of the Latins (and with him the use of the Globes, and some rudiments of Arithmetic and Geometry.) Hesiod, Aratus, Dionysius Afer, Oppian, Apollonii *Argonautica,* and Quintus Calaber. Cato, Varro and Colu-mella *De re rustica* were the very first Authors they learn't. As he was severe on the one hand, so he was most familiar and free in his conversation to those to whome most sowre in his way of education. N.B. he mad his Nephews Songsters, and sing, from the time they were with him.

His first wife (Mrs. Powell, a Royalist) was brought up and lived where there was a great deale of company and merriment, dancing, etc. And when she came to live with her husband, at Mr. Russell's, in St. Bride's Church-yard, she found it very solitary; no company came to her; oftimes heard his Nephews beaten and cry. This life was irkesome to her, and so she went to her Parents at Fost-hill. He sent for her, after some time; and I thinke his servant was evilly entreated: but as for matter of wronging his bed, I never heard the least suspicions; nor had he, of that, any Jealousie.

Two opinions doe not well on the same Boulster; she was a Royalist, and went to her mother to the King's quarters, neer Oxford. I have perhaps so much charity to her that she might not wrong his bed: but what man, espe-cially contemplative, would like to have a young wife environ'd and storm'd by the Sons of Mars, and those of the enemi partie? He parted from her, and wrote the Triplechord about divorce.

He had a middle wife, whose name was Katharin Woodcock. No child living by her.

He maried his third wife, Elizabeth Minshull, the year before the Sick-nesse: a gent. person, a peacefull and agreable humour.

Hath two daughters living: Deborah was his amanuensis (he taught her Latin, and to reade Greeke to him when he had lost his eie-sight).

His sight began to faile him at first upon his writing against Salmasius, and before 'twas full compleated one eie absolutely faild. Upon the writing of other bookes, after that, his other eie decayed. His eie-sight was decaying about 20 yeares before his death. His father read without spectacles at 84. His mother had very weake eies, and used spectacles presently after she was thirty yeares old.

His harmonicall and ingeniose Soul did lodge in a beautifull and well proportioned body. He was a spare man. He was scarce so tall as I am (*quaere*, *quot feet I am high*: *resp.,* of middle stature).

He had abroun hayre. His complexion exceeding faire—he was so faire that they called him *the Lady of Christ's College.* Ovall face. His eie a darke gray.

He was very healthy and free from all diseases: seldome tooke any physique (only sometimes he tooke manna): only towards his latter end he was visited with the Gowte, Spring and Fall.

He had a delicate tuneable Voice, and had good skill. His father instructed him. He had an Organ in his howse; he played on that most. Of a very cheerfull humour. He would be chearfull even in his Gowte-fitts, and sing.

He had a very good Memorie; but I believe that his excellent Method of thinking and disposing did much to helpe his Memorie.

His widowe haz his picture, drawne very well and like, when a Cambridge-schollar, which ought to be engraven; for the Pictures before his bookes are not at all like him.

His exercise was chiefly walking. He was an early riser (*scil.* at 4 a clock *mane)* yea, after he lost his sight. He had a man to read to him. The first thing he read was the Hebrew bible, and that was at 4 h. *mane, Vi* h. plus. Then he contemplated.

At 7 his man came to him again, and then read to him again, and wrote till dinner; the writing was as much as the reading. His daughter, Deborah, could read to him in Latin, Italian and French, and Greeke. Maried in Dublin to one Mr. Clarke (sells silke, etc.) very like her father. The other sister is Mary, more like her mother.

After dinner he used to walke 3 or four houres at a time (he always had a Garden where he lived) went to bed about 9.

Temperate man, rarely dranke between meales. Extreme pleasant in his conversation, and at dinner, supper, etc.; but Satyricall. (He pronounced the letter R (*littera canina*) very hard—a certaine signe of a Satyricall Witt—*from John Dreyden.)*

All the time of writing his *Paradise Lost,* his veine began at the Autumnall Aequinoctiall, and ceased at the Vernall or thereabouts (I believe about May) and this was 4 or 5 yeares of his doeing it. He began about 2 yeares before the King came-in, and finished about three yeares after the King's restauracion.

In the 4th booke of *Paradise Lost* there are about six verses of Satan's Exclamation to the Sun, which Mr. E. Philips remembers about 15 or 16 yeares before ever his Poem was thought of, which verses were intended for the Beginning of a Tragoedie which he had designed, but was diverted from it by other businesse.

He was visited much by the learned; more then he did desire. He was mightily importuned to goe into France and Italic Foraigners came much to see him, and much admired him, and offer'd to him great preferments to come over to them; and the only inducement of severall foreigners that came over into England, was chiefly to see Oliver Protector, and Mr. John Milton; and would see the hous and chamber wher he was borne. He was much more admired abrode then at home.

His familiar learned Acquaintance were Mr. Andrew Marveil, Mr. Skinner, Dr. Pagett, M.D.

John Dreyden, Esq., Poet Laureate, who very much admires him, went to him to have leave to putt his *Paradise Lost* into a Drame in rythme. Mr. Milton recieved him civilly, and told him *he would give him leave to tagge his Verses.*

His widowe assures me that Mr. T. Hobbs was not one of his acquaintance, that her husband did not like him at all, but he would acknowledge him to be a man of great parts, and a learned man. Their Interests and Tenets did run counter to each other.

Whatever he wrote against Monarchic was out of no animosity to the King's person, or owt of any faction or interest, but out of a pure Zeale to the Liberty of Mankind, which he thought would be greater under a fre state than under a Mon-archiall government. His being so conversant in Livy and the Roman authors, and the greatness he saw donne by the Roman common-wealth, and the vertue of their great Commanders induc't him to.

Mr. John Milton made two admirable Panegyricks, as to Sublimitie of Witt, one on Oliver Cromwel, and the other on Thomas, Lord Fairfax, both which his nephew Mr. Philip hath. But he hath hung back these two yeares, as to imparting copies to me for the Collection of mine. Were they made in commendation of the Devill, 'twere all one to me: 'tis the *hypsos* that I looke after. I have been told that 'tis beyond Waller's or anything in that kind.

—John Aubrey, "John Milton,"
Brief Lives, 1669–96

Thomas Ellwood (1714)

Quaker Thomas Ellwood (1639–1713) made an arrangement with Milton in 1662 to read to the poet in exchange for Latin instruction, initiating a

friendship that continued until Milton's death. Ellwood was also responsible for locating a residence in Chalfont St. Giles for Milton to inhabit,
in 1665–66, during the plague of London. Ellwood is best known for his
remark, upon reading *Paradise Lost*, "Thou hast said much here of *Paradise
Lost*, but what hast thou to say of *Paradise Found*?" This is reported to have
inspired Milton's writing of the second epic, which he showed to Ellwood
in 1666, although scholars dispute the date of composition for *Paradise
Regained* and whether it indeed was written after the encounter with
Ellwood.

(Isaac Penington) had an intimate acquaintance with Dr. Paget, a physician
of note in London, and he with John Milton, a gentleman of great note for
learning throughout the learned world, for the accurate pieces he had written
on various subjects and occasions.

This person, having filled a public station in the former times, lived now
a private and retired life in London, and having wholly lost his sight, kept
always a man to read to him, which usually was the son of some gentleman of
his acquaintance, whom in kindness he took to improve in his learning.

Thus, by the mediation of my friend Isaac Penington with Dr. Paget, and
of Dr. Paget with John Milton, was I admitted to come to him, not as a servant
to him (which at that time he needed not), nor to be in the house with him,
but only to have the liberty of coming to his house at certain hours when I
would, and to read to him what books he should appoint me, which was all
the favour I desired.

But this being a matter which would require some time to bring about, I
in the meanwhile returned to my father's house in Oxfordshire.

I committed the care of the house to a tenant of my father's who lived
in the town, and taking my leave of Crowell, went up to my sure friend
Isaac Penington again; where understanding that the mediation used for my
admittance to John Milton had succeeded so well that I might come when I
would, I hastened to London, and in the first place went to wait upon him.

He received me courteously, as well for the sake of Dr. Paget, who introduced me, as of Isaac Penington, who recommended me; to both whom he
bore a good respect. And having inquired divers things of me with respect to
my former progression in learning, he dismissed me, to provide myself with
such accommodation as might be most suitable to my future studies.

I went therefore and took myself a lodging as near to his house (which
was then in Jewyn Street) as conveniently as I could, and from thenceforward went every day in the afternoon, except on the first days of the week,

and sitting by him in his dining-room read to him in such books in the Latin tongue as he pleased to hear me read.

At my first sitting to read to him, observing that I used the English pronunciation, he told me, if I would have the benefit of the Latin tongue, not only to read and understand Latin authors, but to converse with foreigners, either abroad or at home, I must learn the foreign pronunciation. To this I consenting, he instructed me how to sound the vowels; so different from the common pronunciation used by the English, who speak Anglice their Latin, that—with some few other variations in sounding some consonants in particular cases, as c before e or i like *ch, sc* before i like *sh*, etc.—the Latin thus spoken seemed as different from that which was delivered, as the English generally speak it, as if it were another language.

I had before, during my retired life at my father's, by unwearied diligence and industry, so far recovered the rules of grammar, in which I had once been very ready, that I could both read a Latin author and after a sort hammer out his meaning. But this change of pronunciation proved a new difficulty to me. It was now harder to me to read than it was before to understand when read. But

> *Labor omnia vincit*
> *Improbus.*
> Incessant pains,
> The end obtains.

And so did I. Which made my reading the more acceptable to my master. He, on the other hand, perceiving with what earnest desire I pursued learning, gave me not only all the encouragement but all the help he could; for, having a curious ear, he understood by my tone when I understood what I read and when I did not; and accordingly would stop me, examine me, and open the most difficult passages to me.

Thus went I on for about six weeks' time, reading to him in the afternoons; and exercising myself with my own books in my chamber in the forenoons, I was sensible of an improvement.

—Thomas Ellwood, *The History of the Life of*
Thomas Ellwood, 1714, edited by Crump, pp. 88–90

JONATHAN RICHARDSON (1734)

Artist and author Jonathan Richardson (1665–1745) expressed his admiration for Milton in both verbal and visual matter. In addition to documenting Milton's biography from the accounts of Milton's acquaintances and others, his *Explanatory Notes and Remarks on Milton's Paradise Lost* discusses the influence Milton's works had in his own life, as well as imagery and story analysis of the major epic. Richardson painted a portrait of Milton based on a pastel portrait by William Faithorne and also produced a rendering of Milton's head influenced by a work of Samuel Cooper; Richardson's drawing in turn influenced an engraving by George Vertue. This excerpt focuses primarily on the latter years of Milton's life.

One that had Often seen him, told me he us'd to come to a House where He Liv'd, and he has also Met him in the Street, Led by *Millington*, the same who was so Famous an Auctioneer of Books about the time of the Revolution, and Since. This Man was then a Seller of Old Books in *Little Britain*, and *Milton* lodg'd at his house. This was 3 or 4 Years before he Dy'd. he then wore no Sword that My Informer remembers, though Probably he did, at least 'twas his Custom not long before to wear one with a Small Silver-Hilt, and in Cold Weather a Grey Camblet Coat, his Band was Usually not of the Sort as That in the Print I have given, That is, as my Original is, but like What are in the Common Prints of him, the Band usually wore at That time; to have a more Exact Idea of his Figure, let it be remembered that the Fashion of the Coat Then was not Much Unlike what the Quakers Wear Now.

I have heard many Years Since that he Us'd to Sit in a Grey Coarse Cloath Coat at the Door of his House, near *Bun-hill* Fields Without *Moor-gate*, in Warm Sunny Weather to Enjoy the Fresh Air, and So, as well as in his Room, received the Visits of People of Distinguish'd Parts, as well as Quality, and very Lately I had the Good Fortune to have Another Picture of him from an Ancient Clergy-man in *Dorsetshire*, Dr. *Wright*; He found him in a Small House, he thinks but One Room on a Floor; in That, up One pair of Stairs, which was hung with a Rusty Green, he found *John Milton*, Sitting in an Elbow Chair, Black Cloaths, and Neat enough, Pale, but not Cadaverous, his Hands and Fingers Gouty, and with Chalk Stones, among Other Discourse He exprest Himself to This Purpose; that was he Free from the Pain This gave him, his Blindness would be Tolerable.

Sufficient Care had not been taken of This Body, he had a Partiality for his Mind; but All that Temperance, Chastity, and every Wholesom Vertue could do, was done; Nor did he forbear Sometimes to Walk and Use Exercise, as himself says, *Eleg* I. 50. VII. 51. and in a Passage in his *Apol.* for *Smectym-mtus* which will be Quoted Anon on Another Occasion, but This was not Enough to Support him Under that Intense Study and Application which he took to be his Portion *in This* Life. He lov'd the Country, but was little There, nor do we hear any thing of his Riding, Hunting, Dancing, &c. When he was Young he learnt to Fence, probably as a Gentlemanly Accomplishment, and that he might be Able to do Himself Right in Case of an Affront, which he wanted not Courage nor Will for, as Himself intimates, though it does not appear he ever made This Use of his Skill, after he was Blind he us'd a Swing for Exercise.

Musick he Lov'd Extreamly, and Understood Well, 'tis said he Compos'd, though nothing of That has been brought down to Us. he diverted Himself with Performing, which they say he did Well on the Organ and Bas-Viol. and This was a great Relief to him after he had lost his Sight.

in relation to his Love of Musick, and the Effect it had upon his Mind, I remember a Story I had from a Friend I was Happy in for many Years, and who lov'd to talk of *Milton,* as he Often Did. *Milton* hearing a Lady Sing Finely, *now will I Swear"* (says he) *This Lady is Handsom."* his Ears Now were Eyes to Him.

—Jonathan Richardson, *Explanatory Notes and*
Remarks on Milton's Paradise Lost, 1734

Thomas Newton "Life of Milton" (1749–59)

Anglican cleric Thomas Newton (1704–82) became bishop of Bristol and eventually dean of St. Paul's Cathedral in 1768. He was an editor and biographer of Milton, documenting his edition of *Paradise Lost* with his own annotations coupled with extensive notes gleaned from printed and unprinted sources. His first edition was a three-volume set that appeared in 1749; it was followed, in 1752, with a single volume edition containing a new biography of Milton and a postscript on the plagiarism charges leveled by William Lauder. Notably, Newton's life of Milton included an interview with Milton's granddaughter Elizabeth Foster.

In his way of living he was an example of sobriety and temperance. He was very sparing in the use of wine or strong liquors of any kind. He was likewise very abstemious in his diet, not fastidiously nice or delicate in his choice of dishes, but content with anything that was most in season, or easiest to be procured; eating and drinking (according to the distinction of the philosopher) that he might live, and not living that he might eat or drink. So that probably his gout descended by inheritance from one or other of his parents; or, if it was of his own acquiring, it must have been owing to his studious and sedentary life.

—Thomas Newton, "Life of Milton," *Milton's*
Poetical Works, 1749–59, edited by Newton

Thomas Birch (1753)

In his youth he is said to have been extremely handsome, and while he was a student at Cambridge, he was called "the Lady of Christ's-College," and he took notice of this himself in one of his Public Prolusions before that university; "A *quibusdam audivi nuper domina.*" The colour of his hair was a light brown; the symmetry of his features exact; enlivened with an agreeable air, and a beautiful mixture of fair and ruddy. Mr. Wood observes, that "his eyes were none of the quickest." His stature, as we find it measured by himself, did not exceed the middle-size; he was neither too lean, nor too corpulent; his limbs well proportioned, nervous, and active, serviceable in all respects to his exercising the sword, in which he much delighted, and wanted neither skill, nor courage, to resent an affront from men of the most athletic constitutions. In his diet he was abstemious; not delicate in the choice of his dishes; and strong liquors of all kinds were his aversion. Being too sadly convinced how much his health had suffered by night-studies in his younger years, he used to go early (seldom later than nine) to rest; and rose commonly in the summer at four, and in the winter at five in the morning; but when he was not disposed to rise at his usual hours, he always had one to read to him by his bed-side. At his first rising he had usually a chapter read to him out of the Hebrew bible; and he commonly studied all the morning till twelve, then used some exercise for an hour, afterwards dined, and after dinner played on the organ, and either sung himself, or made his wife sing, who, he said, had a good voice, but no ear, and then he went up to study again till six, when his friends came to visit him, and sat with him till eight. Then he went down to supper, which was usually olives and some light thing; and after supper he smoked his pipe, and drank a glass of water, and went to bed. When his blindness restrained him from other exercises, he had a machine to swing in for the preservation of his health; and diverted himself in his chamber with playing on an organ. He had a delicate ear and excellent voice, and great skill in vocal and instrumental music. His deportment was erect, open and affable; and his conversation easy, cheerful, and instructive.

—Thomas Birch, An *Historical and Critical Account of the Life and Writings of Mr. John Milton,* 1753

Samuel Johnson "John Milton" (1779)

Dr. Samuel Johnson (1709–84), an author and biographer, was also the leading Enlightenment literary critic, whose opinion shaped much of the reading public's sensibilities. He compiled the first English dictionary and wrote satires, essays, and poetry, including the renowned *Rasselas*, a work of prose fiction. As a staunch royalist and Anglican, Johnson castigates Milton's antimonarchical political focus and anti-Church religious views, but as a neoclassicist, he categorically praises Milton's use of Greek and Roman sources.

Because Johnson was primarily a literary conservative, seeing literature as ultimately reinforcing the best values of society and the order of authority, his judgments of Milton's republicanism and religious nonconformity colored his assessments of the author's literary accomplishments and were influential to other eighteenth-century thinkers. Johnson's evaluations of Milton's personality and much of his works mix strong negatives in with fewer positives, as seen in the Works section of this volume.

His literature was unquestionably great. He read all the languages which are considered either as learned or polite: Hebrew, with its two dialects, Greek, Latin, Italian, French, and Spanish. In Latin his skill was such as places him in the first rank of writers and critics; and he appears to have cultivated Italian with uncommon diligence. The books in which his daughter, who used to read to him, represented him as most delighting, after Homer, which he could almost repeat, were Ovid's *Metamorphoses* and Euripides. His Euripides is, by Mr. Cradock's kindness, now in my hands: the margin is sometimes noted; but I have found nothing remarkable.

Of the English poets he set most value upon Spenser, Shakespeare, and Cowley. Spenser was apparently his favourite: Shakespeare he may easily be supposed to like, with every skilful reader; but I should not have expected that Cowley, whose ideas of excellence were different from his own, would have had much of his approbation. His character of Dryden, who sometimes visited him, was, that he was a good rhymist, but no poet.

His theological opinions are said to have been first Cal-vinistical; and afterwards, perhaps when he began to hate the Presbyterians, to have tended towards Arminianism. In the mixed questions of theology and government he never thinks that he can recede far enough from popery or prelacy; but what Baudius says of Erasmus seems applicable to him—*magis habuit quod fugeret, quam quod sequeretur*. He had determined rather what to condemn, than what to approve. He has not associated himself with any denomination of Protestants: we know rather what he was not than what he was. He was not of the Church of Rome; he was not of the Church of England.

To be of no Church is dangerous. Religion, of which the rewards are distant, and which is animated only by faith and hope, will glide by degrees out of the mind, unless it be invigorated and reimpressed by external ordinances, by stated calls to worship, and the salutary influence of example. Milton, who appears to have had a full conviction of the truth of Christianity, and to have regarded the Holy Scriptures with the pro-foundest veneration, to have been untainted by any heretical peculiarity of opinion, and to have lived in a confirmed belief of the immediate and occasional agency of Providence, yet grew old without any visible worship. In the distribution of his hours there was no hour of prayer, either solitary or with his household; omitting public prayers, he omitted all.

Of this omission the reason has been sought upon a supposition, which ought never to be made, that men live with their own approbation, and justify their conduct to themselves. Prayer certainly was not thought superfluous by him who represents our first parents as praying acceptably in the state of innocence, and efficaciously after their fall. That he lived without prayer can hardly be affirmed; his studies and meditations were an habitual prayer. The neglect of it in his family was probably a fault for which he condemned himself, and which he intended to correct, but that death, as too often happens, intercepted his reformation.

His political notions were those of an acrimonious and surly republican, for which it is not known that he gave any better reason than that *a popular government was the most frugal; for the trappings of a monarchy would set up an ordinary commonwealth.* It is surely very shallow policy that supposes money to be the chief good; and even this, without considering that the support and expense of a Court is, for the most part, only a particular kind of traffic, for which money is circulated without any national impoverishment.

Milton's republicanism was, I am afraid, founded in an envious hatred of greatness, and a sullen desire of independence; in petulance impatient of control, and pride disdainful of superiority. He hated monarchs in the State, and prelates in the Church; for he hated all whom he was required to obey. It is to be suspected that his predominant desire was to destroy rather than establish, and that he felt not so much the love of liberty as repugnance to authority.

It has been observed that they who most loudly clamour for liberty do not most liberally grant it. What we know of Milton's character in domestic relations is that he was severe and arbitrary. His family consisted of women; and there appears in his books something like a Turkish contempt of females, as subordinate and inferior beings. That his own daughters might not break the ranks, he suffered them to be depressed by a mean and penurious education. He thought woman made only for obedience, and man only for rebellion.

—Samuel Johnson, "John Milton,"
Lives of the Poets, 1779

WILLIAM WORDSWORTH (1805)

Famed English romantic poet William Wordsworth (1770–1850) wrote commentaries on Milton's life and works, crediting Milton as one of his own important literary influences. As a child, Wordsworth's father had him memorize passages of Milton's works. Wordsworth shared Milton's belief that religion was a personal experience, not to be mediated by the state, and that the poet's highest calling was to function as prophet.

Wordsworth's important lengthy autobiographical poem, *The Prelude,* cited in this selection, owed much to *Paradise Lost,* as Wordsworth lamented his childhood self's loss of a paradisiacal connection to nature, portraying himself as a type of Adam. Both poets integrated politics into their art, as they both castigated tyrannical authority. This excerpt portrays Milton as a prophet speaking difficult truths; like most of the romantics, Wordsworth views Milton as a freethinker, a true individual, and a poetic genius.

Yea, our blind Poet, who in his later day,
Stood almost single; uttering odious truths—
Darkness before, and danger's voice behind,
Soul awful—if the earth has ever lodged
An awful soul—I seemed to see him here
Familiarly, and in his scholar's dress
Bounding before me, yet a stripling youth—
A boy, no better, with his rosy cheeks
Angelical, keen eye, courageous look,
And conscious step of purity and pride.

—William Wordsworth,
The Prelude, 1799–1805, book 2

FRANÇOIS RENÉ (1837)

François René, vicomte de Chateaubriand (1768–1848), was a French nobleman and writer of romantic sensibilities who admired Milton's works and translated *Paradise Lost* into French prose. He studied religion, became a knight of the Order of Malta, and wrote books on Catholicism and the role of religion in literature. In his *Genie du Christianism*, Chateaubriand discusses Milton's portrayals of Satan, Hell, Adam, Eve, and the angels. His *Essai sur la littérature anglaise* also includes an extensive analysis of *Paradise Lost*. Here, he praises Milton's support of Oliver Cromwell and unwavering republicanism, recording an incident in which Milton showed his fortitude to Charles II.

Milton alone remained faithful to the memory of Cromwell. While minor authors, vile, perjured, bought by restored power, insulted the ashes of a great man at whose feet they had grovelled, Milton gave him an asylum in his genius, as in an inviolable temple. Milton might have been reinstated in office. His third wife (for he espoused two after the death of Mary Powell) beseeching him to accept his former place as Secretary, he replied, "You are a woman, and would like to keep your carriage; but I will die an honest man." Remaining a Republican, he wrapped himself in his principles, with his Muse and his poverty. He said to those who reproached him with having served a tyrant, "He delivered us from kings." Milton affirmed that he had only fought for the cause of God and of his country. One day, walking in St. James's Park, he suddenly heard repeated near him, "The king! the king!" "Let us withdraw," he said to his guide, "I never loved kings." Charles II. accosted the blind man. "Thus, Sir, has Heaven punished you for having conspired against my father." "Sire," he replied, "if the ills that afflict us in this world be the chastisements for our faults, your father must have been very guilty."

—François René, vicomte de Chateaubriand,
Sketches of English Literature, 1837, volume 2, p. 80

WILLIAM H. PRESCOTT "CHATEAUBRIAND'S ENGLISH LITERATURE" (1839)

Indignant at every effort to crush the spirit, and to cheat it, in his own words, "of that liberty which rarefies and enlightens it like the influence of heaven," he proclaimed the rights of man as a rational immortal being, undismayed by menace and obloquy, amid a generation of servile and unprincipled sycophants. The blindness which excluded him from the things of earth opened to him more glorious and spiritualized conceptions of heaven, and aided him in exhibiting the full influence of those sublime truths which the privilege of free inquiry in religious matters had poured upon the mind.

—William H. Prescott, "Chateaubriand's English
Literature," 1839, *Biographical and Critical
Miscellanies,* 1845

WILLIAM HOWITT (1847)

English writer William Howitt (1792–1879) wrote works of poetry, fiction, history, and travel writing both in conjunction with his wife, Mary, and as sole author. The two were Quakers, who combined their moral didacticism with romantic sensibilities, particularly focusing on a love of nature and the need for societal reform for the working class. He is best known for *The Rural Life of England* (1838).

The following passage from *Homes and Haunts of the Most Eminent British Poets* (1847) characterizes Howitt as one who possessed a natural curiosity and loved to walk; his selections on literary figures were quite popular, including this passage describing Milton's grave, the monument honoring one of England's greatest literary figures.

Perhaps no man ever inhabited more houses than our great epic poet, yet scarcely one of these now remains. We come now to Milton's last house, the narrow house appointed for all living, in which he laid his bones beside those of his father. This was in the church of St. Giles, Cripplegate. He died on Sunday, the 8th of November, 1674, and was buried on the 12th. His funeral is stated to have been very splendidly and numerously attended. By the parish registry we find that he was buried in the chancel: "John Milton, gentleman. Consumption. Chancell. 12. Nov., 1674." Dr. Johnson supposed that he had no inscription, but Aubrey distinctly states that "when the two steppes to the communion-table were raysed in 1690, his stone was removed." Milton's grave remained a whole century without a mark to point out where the great poet lay, till in 1793 Mr. Whitbread erected a bust and an inscription to his memory. What is more, there is every reason to believe that his remains were, on this occasion of raising the chancel and removing the stone, disturbed. The coffin was disinterred and opened, and numbers of relic-hunters were eager to seize and convey off fragments of his bones. The matter at the time occasioned a sharp controversy, and the public were at length persuaded to believe that they were not the remains of Milton, but of a female, that by mistake had been thus treated. But when the workmen had the inscribed stone before them, and dug down directly below it, what doubt can there be that the remains were those of the poet? By an alteration in the church when it was repaired in 1682, that which was the old chancel ceased to be the present one, and the remains of Milton thus came to lie in the great central aisle. The monument erected by Whitbread marks, as near as possible, the place. The bust is by Bacon. It is attached to a pillar, and beneath it is this inscription:

John Milton,
Author of Paradise Lost,
Born Dec.ʳ- 1608
Died Nov.ʳ- 1674.
His father, John Milton, died March, 1646.
They were both interred in this church.
Samuel Whitbread posuit, 1793.
—William Howitt, *Homes and Haunts of the Most*
Eminent British Poets, 1847, volume 1, pp. 75–115

ALPHONSE DE LAMARTINE "MILTON" (1854)

The best portraits of Milton represent him seated at the foot of an oak at sunset, his face turned towards the beams of the departing luminary, and dictating his verses to his well-beloved Deborah, listening attentively to the voice of her father; while his wife Elizabeth looks on him as Eve regarded her husband after her fault and punishment. His two younger daughters meanwhile gather flowers from the meadows, that he may inhale some of the odors of Eden which perfumed his dreams. Our thoughts turn involuntarily to the lot of that wife and daughters, after the death of the illustrious old man on whom they were attending; and the poet, thus brought back to our eyes again, becomes more interesting than the poem. Happy are they whose glory is watered with tears! Such reputation penetrates to the heart, and in the heart alone the poet's name becomes immortal.

—Alphonse de Lamartine, "Milton,"
Memoirs of Celebrated Characters, 1854

THOMAS KEIGHTLEY (1855)

With respect to the worldly circumstances of this great man, little is known with certainty. It is evident that during his travels, and after his return, the allowance made him by his father was liberal. It was adequate, we may see, to the support of himself and his two nephews, for it is not likely that his sister paid him anything for them. He must also have considered himself able to support a family, without keeping school, when he married Miss Powell. He of course inherited the bulk of his father's property, but of the amount of it we are ignorant; all we know is that it included the interest in his house in Bread-street. His losses were not inconsiderable. A sum of £2000, which he had invested in the Excise Office, was lost at the

Restoration, as the Government refused to recognize the obligations of the Commonwealth; according to the account of his granddaughter, he lost another sum of £2000, by placing it in the hands of a money-scrivener; and he also lost at the Restoration a property of £60 a year out of the lands of the Dean and Chapter of Westminster, which he very probably had purchased. His house in Bread-street was destroyed by the Great Fire. The whole property which he left behind him, exclusive of his claim on the Powell family for his wife's fortune, and of his household goods, did not exceed £1500, including the produce of his library, a great part of which he is said to have disposed of before his death.

—Thomas Keightley, *An Account of the Life,*
Opinions, and Writings of John Milton, 1855, p. 75

PETER BAYNE (1878)

He attends no church, belongs to no communion, and has no form of worship in his family; notable circumstances, which we may refer, in part at least, to his blindness, but significant of more than that. His religion was of the spirit, and did not take kindly to any form. Though the most Puritan of the Puritans, he had never stopped long in the ranks of any Puritan party, or given satisfaction to Puritan ecclesiastics and theologians. In his youth he had loved the night; in his old age he loves the pure sunlight of early morning as it glimmers on his sightless eyes. The music which had been his delight since childhood has still its charm, and he either sings or plays on the organ or bass violin every day. In his grey coat, at the door of his house in Bunhill Fields, he sits on clear afternoons; a proud, ruggedly genial old man, with sharp satiric touches in his talk, the untunable fibre in him to the last. Eminent foreigners come to see him; friends approach reverently, drawn by the splendour of his discourse. It would range, one can well imagine, in glittering freedom, like "arabesques of lightning," over all ages and all literatures. He was the prince of scholars; a memory of superlative power waiting as handmaid on the queenliest imagination. The whole spectacle of ancient civilisation, its cities, its camps, its landscapes, was before him. There he sat in his grey coat, like a statue cut in granite. He recanted nothing, repented of nothing. England had made a sordid failure, but he had not failed. His soul's fellowship was with the great Republicans of Greece and Rome, and with the Psalmist and Isaiah and Oliver Cromwell.

—Peter Bayne, *The Chief Actors in the Puritan*
Revolution, 1878, p. 345

MARK PATTISON (1879)

I do not find that Milton, though he wrote against paid ministers as hirelings, ever expressly formulated an opinion against ministers as such. But as has already been hinted, there grew up in him, in the last period of his life, a secret sympathy with the mode of thinking which came to characterise the Quaker sect. Not that Milton adopted any of their peculiar fancies. He affirms categorically the permissibility of oaths, of military service, and requires that women should keep silence in the congregation. But in negativing all means of arriving at truth except the letter of Scripture interpreted by the inner light, he stood upon the same platform as the followers of George Fox.

—Mark Pattison, *Milton*, 1879, p. 148

MATTHEW ARNOLD "A FRENCH CRITIC ON MILTON" (1879)

Matthew Arnold (1822–88) was the premier Victorian critic, as well as a widely read essayist and poet. After serving as private secretary to Lord Lansdowne, he became an inspector of schools, which enabled him to visit schools in continental Europe for comparison. Often critical of the English middle class, Arnold used examples of European culture and literature in his critiques of his native land. Poetry formed much of the bulk of his earlier writing; dissatisfaction with his own work caused him to shift almost exclusively to essays, including literary criticism, social criticism, and writings on religion and education. His works particularly acknowledged the role of the burgeoning middle class in England's future, which he viewed as narrowminded and anti-intellectual. Arnold placed great faith in "culture" as a way to raise society; great literature and art were major components of that culture.

The brief selection here showcases Arnold's belief that literature should serve as a moral touchstone. He prizes Milton's "grand style," that is, his use of rhythm and diction, in his 1888 *Essays in Criticism* and defends Milton's works from negative readings of other critics, especially Samuel Johnson. Although Arnold disliked Milton's puritanical thinking, which he viewed as the stumbling block of Victorian Britain's middle class, he praised Milton's art as a timeless part of the high culture Arnold espoused.

As a man, too, not less than as a poet, Milton has a side of unsurpassable grandeur. A master's touch is the gift of nature. Moral qualities, it is commonly thought, are in our own power. Perhaps the germs of such qualities are in their greater or less strength as much a part of our natural constitution as the sense for style. The range open to our own will and power, however, in developing and establishing them, is evidently much larger. Certain high moral dispositions Milton had from nature, and he sedulously trained and developed them until they became habits of great power.

—Matthew Arnold, "A French Critic on Milton,"
Mixed Essays, 1879, p. 269

C. M. INGLEBY (1883)

On the 4th of August, 1790, according to a small volume written by Philip Neve, Esq. (of which two editions were published in the same year), Milton's coffin was removed and his remains exhibited to the public on the 4th and 5th of that month. Mr. George Stevens, the great editor of Shakspere, who justly denounced the indignity intended, not offered, to the great Puritan poet's remains by Royalist Land-sharks, satisfied himself that the corpse was that of a woman of fewer years than Milton. . . . Mr. Stevens's assurance gives us good reason for believing that Mr. Philip Neve's indignant protest is only good in general, and that Milton's hallowed reliques still rest undisturbed within their peaceful shrine.

—C. M. Ingleby, *Shakespeare's Bones,* 1883

GEORGE SAINTSBURY (1887)

George Edward Bateman Saintsbury (1845–1933) was a prolific and influential British literary critic of the late Victorian and Edwardian periods. He attended Oxford University, where he was influenced by the Oxford Movement, a High Church religious movement led by John Henry Newman that focused on combating the perceived secularization of the Anglican Church by reviving some Catholic liturgical and ceremonial practices. After serving as a grammar school teacher and newspaper writer in Manchester, Saintsbury became classical master at St. Elizabeth's School on the island of Guernsey, then the headmaster of Elgin Educational Institute in Morayshire, Scotland. Saintsbury began writing literary criticism for the *Fortnightly Review* and was commissioned by the *Encyclopaedia Britannica* editors to write 30 essays on French literature. He published numerous book-length studies of French and English literature, raising his reputation especially with his 1887 *History of Elizabethan Literature,* from which the following selection is drawn. Despite his journalistic beginnings, Saintsbury was respected enough to earn an appointment to the Regius Professorship of English at the

University of Edinburgh in September 1895. He continued to write books of note, including the multivolume sets *A History of Criticism and Literary Taste in Europe from the Earliest Texts to the Present Day* and *A History of English Prosody from the Twelfth Century to the Present Day.*

Saintsbury visualized the ideal critic as one who had read widely and could appreciate and articulate the pleasures that the best texts produce in the reader. In the following excerpt, Milton's biography shapes Saintsbury's perception of his work; negative character traits of the author, such as Milton's "tyrannical" personality, cause the audience to have a less pleasurable experience when reading the author's works.

On the whole, Milton's character was not an amiable one, nor even wholly estimable. It is probable that he never in the course of his whole life did anything that he considered wrong; but unfortunately, examples are not far to seek of the facility with which desire can be made to confound itself with deliberate approval. That he was an exacting, if not a tyrannical husband and father, that he held in the most peremptory and exaggerated fashion the doctrine of the superiority of man to woman, that his egotism in a man who had actually accomplished less would be held ludicrous and half disgusting, that his faculty of appreciation beyond his own immediate tastes and interests was small, that his intolerance surpassed that of an inquisitor, and that his controversial habits and manners outdid the license even of that period of controversial abuse,—these are propositions which I cannot conceive to be disputed by any competent critic aware of the facts. If they have ever been denied, it is merely from the amiable but uncritical point of view which blinks all a man's personal defects in consideration of his literary genius. That we cannot afford to do here, especially as Milton's personal defects had no small influence on his literary character.

—George Saintsbury, *A History of
Elizabethan Literature*, 1887, p. 317

Augustine Birrell "John Milton" (1887)

There is something very fascinating in the records we have of Milton's one visit to the Continent. A more impressive Englishman never left our shores. Sir Philip Sidney perhaps approaches him nearest. Beautiful beyond praise, and just sufficiently conscious of it to be careful never to appear at a disadvantage, dignified in manners, versed in foreign tongues, yet full of the ancient learning,—a gentleman, a scholar, a poet, a musician, and a

Christian,—he moved about in a leisurely manner from city to city, writing Latin verses for his hosts and Italian sonnets in their ladies' albums, buying books and music, and creating, one cannot doubt, an all too flattering impression of an English Protestant.

—Augustine Birrell, "John Milton," *Obiter Dicta, Second Series*, 1887, p. 14

LESLIE STEPHEN (1894)

Leslie Stephen (1832–1904) typified the Victorian propensity for cataloging knowledge in his role as the first editor of the *Dictionary of National Biography*, a reference guide to famous British personages. Although he had been ordained as an Anglican priest, he later denounced his faith to embrace agnosticism. Besides biographies, Stephen wrote and edited other compendia, including *Essays on Free Thinking and Plain Speaking*, and served as editor of the *Cornhill Magazine*, which featured work from leading writers of his time. He is famously the father of author Virginia Woolf, her sister Vanessa Bell, and half-sister Laura Makepeace Stephen. This passage recounts Milton's days at Cambridge University.

Milton was nicknamed the "lady" at college, from his delicate complexion and slight make. He was, however, a good fencer, and thought himself a "match for any one." Although respected by the authorities, his proud and austere character probably kept him aloof from much of the coarser society of the place. He shared the growing aversion to the scholasticism against which one of his exercises is directed. Like Henry More, who entered Christ's in Milton's last year, he was strongly attracted by Plato, although he was never so much a philosopher as a poet. He already considered himself as dedicated to the utterance of great thoughts, and to the strictest chastity and self-respect, on the ground that he who would "write well hereafter in laudable things ought himself to be a true poem."

—Leslie Stephen, *Dictionary of National Biography*, 1894, volume 38, p. 25

EDWARD DOWDEN "THE TEACHING OF ENGLISH LITERATURE" (1895)

Irish scholar, poet, and critic Edward Dowden (1843–1913) was friends with John Butler Yeats (father of William Butler Yeats) at Trinity College, Dublin, where Dowden received his undergraduate and graduate degrees and later served as professor of English literature. His first full-length work, *Shakspere: A Critical Study of His Mind and Art* (1875), established him as a respected critic. Dowden's work on Shakespeare and his plays has continued to be his most enduring contribution. He also wrote books on Robert Southey, Edmund Spenser, Percy Bysshe Shelley, Robert Browning, and Michel de Montaigne, in addition to collected essays on other eras and writers. The following excerpt reveals Dowden's transcendentalist tendency to focus on the beauty of Milton's work, rather than its puritanical and polemical attributes.

In Milton's life, as in Milton's prose writings, occur passages which are not admirable, which are indeed the reverse of admirable. The student of literature, we may presume, is a lover of beauty, and the temptation with him to shirk the ugly passages of a life is a temptation easily understood. Here he may say, as Mr. Matthew Arnold has said of Shelley, here, in *Comus* and *Samson,* here in the Council Chamber sheltering Davenant from dangers incurred through his Royalist ardours, here, in company with Lawrence, listening to the lute well touched, is the Milton we desire to know, the Milton who delights. Let us, at least as long as we are able, avert our eyes from the Milton who disgusts, from the unamiable Milton, the Milton who calls his opponent "an idiot by breeding and a solicitor by presumption," the Milton who helped to embitter his daughters' lives, and remembered them as "unkind children" in his will. What is gained by forcing this disgusting Milton on our attention? We choose, if we can, to retain a charming picture of the great poet. The delightful Milton is the true Milton after all. Ah, give us back the delightful Milton!

—Edward Dowden, "The Teaching of English Literature," *New Studies in Literature,* 1895, p. 442

William Vaughn Moody
"Life of Milton" (1899)

It was fortunate for the harmonious development of Milton's genius that during the critical years between youth and manhood, years which in most men's lives are fullest of turmoil and dubiety, he was enabled to live a life of quiet contemplation. His nature was fiercely polemical, and without this period of calm set between his college life and his life as a public disputant, the sweeter saps of his mind would never have come to flower and fruitage.

It was particularly fortunate, too, that this interim should be passed in the country, where the lyric influences were softest, where all that was pastoral and genial in his imagination was provoked. The special danger of men of his stamp, in whom will and doctrine are constantly president over impulse, is the loss of plasticity, the stiffening of imagination in its bonds.

—William Vaughn Moody, "Life of Milton," *Poetical*
Works of Milton, 1899, Cambridge edition, p. xiii

WILLIAM P. TRENT (1899)

But he is more than idealist or artist—he was a superlatively noble, brave, truly conscientious man, who could never have intentionally done a mean thing; who was pure and clean in thought, speech, and action; who was patriotic to the point of sublime self-sacrifice; who loved his neighbor to the point of risking his life for republican principles of liberty; who, finally, spent his every moment as in the sight of the God he both worshiped and loved. Possessed of sublime powers, his thought was to make the best use of them to the glory of God and the good of his fellow-man. We may not think that he always succeeded; but who among the men of our race save Washington is such an exemplar of high and holy and effective purpose? Beside his white and splendid flame nearly all the other great spirits of earth burn yellow, if not low. Truly, as Wordsworth said, his soul was like a star; and, if it dwelt apart, should we therefore love it the less? It is more difficult to love the sublime than to love the approximately human, but the necessity for such love is the essence of the first and greatest commandment.

—William P. Trent, *John Milton: A Short Study of*
His Life and Works, 1899, p. 55

GENERAL

As one of the major (if not the ultimate) poets in all of English literature, John Milton has attracted critical attention from the time of his earliest publications to today. For English commentators, he is a national commodity, ranking with Chaucer and Shakespeare as a principal player in the field of letters, a source of pride, although not universally applauded for all aspects of his work. Critics could raise their reputation by producing critical analysis of Milton's poetry, and we see that a host have, both in the following selections and those in the Works section. Milton's writings have been judged through the ages based on the critics' views of his theology, politics, and aesthetics.

John Milton's reputation during his lifetime and until the end of the seventeenth century centered on his religious and political radicalism. Indeed, he solicited controversy by authoring a series of polemical tracts; his "Doctrine and Discipline of Divorce" allowed for divorce in instances in which the couple is not compatible, alienating religious conservatives within both Anglican and Puritan groups. Milton's political prose helped stir public opinion against Charles I and monarchy in general, and his tracts have been blamed for stirring insurrection against King Charles I, which clumintated in his public beheading. Those political ideas filtered into Milton's poetry as well and, as a result, made his life and works impossible to separate. *Paradise Lost* most famously has been viewed as linking Satan with courtly corruption, for example. Milton's puritanical beliefs that provoked his vitriolic condemnation of the Church of England for its corruption and connection with the monarchy manifest themselves not only in such prose work as *Reason of Church Government* but less centrally in Milton's imaginative works as well.

Commentators tended to focus on the aspects of Milton's thought with which they agreed or disagreed, basing their critical judgments on the points most odious or applaudable to them. To British conservatives who were writing under sovereign rule and were members of the Church of England, Milton's views were often heretical and unpatriotic. Others, primarily the romantic thinkers, who sought personal liberties in worship, social practices, and intellect, were quick to see in Milton a kindred spirit. Therefore, a vast ideological and evaluative gulf lies between some of the excerpts contained in this section.

Despite some negative eighteenth-century views, Milton's works were often awarded the accolade of being sublime, the chief evaluative notion of the era, a concept that also extended into the nineteenth century. Taken from the classical critic Longinus, the term was used by Joseph Addison and developed in the works of Edmund Burke, who separated the concepts of beauty and the sublime. Burke saw the sublime as evident in grand parts of nature, as opposed to beauty, which can be noted in the smaller units; he further saw strong emotions linked to self-preservation, such as terror, as evocative of the sublime. Above all, the sublime could be measured in its effects on the perceiver, rather than the object itself. *Paradise Lost* is especially labeled as sublime in some of the following criticism, for its massive scope and its effect on the emotions of the readers in, for example, presenting Satan and Hell.

In addition to the religious and political evaluations of Milton, the critiques grounded in the aesthetic range widely. In his epics, Milton chose to use blank verse, unrhymed iambic pentameter as his preferred form. He even introduced *Paradise Lost* with an apologia for this style, citing classical writers and holding unrhymed poetry as more suitable to serious subjects. As this aesthetic was counter to prevailing English tastes, he received criticism for not rhyming his epics. John Dryden, a contemporary poet, in fact rewrote *Paradise Lost* into rhymed verse for his opera based on the work, while Milton's friend and secretary, Andrew Marvell, defended Milton for his style. The staunch eighteenth-century neoclassicists, notably Samuel Johnson, often chastised Milton for violating Aristotelian criteria for genres and for mixing together "pagan" and Christian materials.

Milton's diction or word choice was a subject of critical discourse as well. For some British critics especially, his use of Latinate, rather than Anglo-Saxon, words was deemed pretentious or overly pedantic. Milton also coined new words, particularly in *Paradise Lost*, a poetic trait not universally acclaimed.

As a reminder to the contemporary reader who may be versed in literary criticism that incorporates a theoretical perspective in order to analyze the works, the earlier criticism included in this section focuses more on value judgments in determining the strengths and weaknesses of the author's works, the fitness of the author to speak for others, and the overall achievement of the author in creating works of lasting quality.

Humphrey Moseley "The Stationer to the Reader" (1645)

One of the earliest publishers of Milton's works, Humphrey Mosley produced an edition of the 1645 poems from his shop, the Prince's Arms at St. Paul's Churchyard, London. Moseley published works by poets and writers of good repute, including Launcelot Andrews, Francis Bacon, Abraham Cowley, William Crashaw, Henry Lawes, and John Donne. At the time this edition was compiled, Milton had published only a few poetic works, including "Lycidas" and an anonymous version of *Comus*, in addition to some prose. Here, Mosley writes an introduction to attract the type of reader who has purchased Mosley's other distinguished authors.

It is not any private respect of gain, Gentle Reader (for the slightest Pamphlet is nowadays more vendible than the works of learnedest men), but it is the love I have to our own Language that hath made me diligent to collect and set forth such Pieces, both in Prose and Verse, as may renew the wonted honour and esteem of our English tongue; and it's the worth of these both English and Latin Poems, not the flourish of any prefixed encomions, that can invite thee to buy them—though these are not without the highest commendations and applause of the learnedest Academicks, both domestic and foreign, and, amongst those of our own country, the unparalleled attestation of that renowned Provost of Eton, Sir Henry Wotton. The author's more peculiar excellency in those studies was too well known to conceal his papers, or to keep me from attempting to solicit them from him. Let the event guide itself which way it will, I shall deserve of the age by bringing into the light as true a birth as the Muses have brought forth since our famous Spenser wrote; whose Poems in these English ones are as rarely imitated as sweetly excelled. Reader, if thou art eagle-eyed to censure their worth, I am not fearful to expose them to thy exactest perusal.

—Humphrey Moseley, "The Stationer to the Reader," Milton's Poems, 1645

William Winstanley (1687)

John Milton was one, whose natural parts might deservedly give him a place amongst the principal of our English Poets, having written two Heroick

Poems and a Tragedy; namely, *Paradice Lost, Paradice Regain'd,* and *Sampson Agonista*. But his Fame is gone out like a Candle in a Snuff, and his Memory will always stink, which might have ever lived in honourable Repute, had not he been a notorious Traytor, and most impiously and villainously bely'd that blessed Martyr King *Charles* the First.

—William Winstanley, *The Lives of the Most Famous English Poets,* 1687

JOHN DRYDEN "LINES ON MILTON" (1688)

John Dryden (1631–1700) was a major playwright, poet, satirist, and critic of the later seventeenth century. Although he grew up in a Puritan home, he became a loyal royalist. After graduating from Trinity College, Cambridge, Dryden began his writing career with political verse on the death of Oliver Cromwell and the coronation of King Charles II and then turned to writing for the Restoration stage. He achieved more success, however, through his witty verse; some of his best-known works include *Absalom and Achitophel,* a short satirical epic referencing rebellions related to the successor of Charles II, and *MacFlecknoe,* a hilariously scathing sendup of his poetic rival, Thomas Shadwell. Dryden's theological interests culminated in his "Religio Laici," or "Layman's Faith," defending the Anglican Church against deism and Catholicism.

Dryden's admiration of Milton's works inspired him to base an opera on *Paradise Lost,* although Dryden's dislike for Milton's blank verse was revealed in his rhymed operatic adaptation titled *The State of Innocence,* which was never performed because of the prohibitive cost. Dryden composed an epigrammatic poem titled "Lines on Milton" for the 1688 edition of *Paradise Lost,* placed below an engraving of Milton's bust on the title page. In keeping with the classical visual representation of Milton, Dryden praises the poet above Homer and Virgil. Dryden's assessment of Milton follows the belief that modern writers could exceed the ancients, by dint of having learned from the older works and improved on them.

Three *Poets,* in three distant *Ages* born,
Greece, Italy, and *England* did adorn.
The *First* in loftiness of thought Surpass'd;
The *Next* in Majesty; in both the *Last.*
The force of *Nature* cou'd no farther goe:
To make a *Third* she joynd the former two.

—John Dryden, "Lines on Milton," 1688

Joseph Addison "An Account of the Greatest English Poets" (1694)

Joseph Addison (1672–1719) was a poet, critic, and essayist acquainted with Milton's daughter Deborah. An Oxford graduate and scholar of Latin poetry, he wrote a series of articles on *Paradise Lost* in both *The Tatler*, a newspaper founded by Sir Richard Steele, and *The Spectator*, the newspaper Addison co-founded with Steele in 1711–12. Despite his political stance as a Whig, Addison largely disagreed with Milton's advocacy of the execution of Charles I. While praising Milton for his genius, imagination, universal subject matter, and verse form in *Paradise Lost*, Addison criticizes him for violating the eighteenth century critical stance on the Aristotelian unities. Milton's epic, according to Addison, contains too many digressions and improbabilities, the language is too labored or obscure at times, and the heroic element was not properly realized. Nonetheless, he feels that Milton was able to demonstrate his mastery of the sublime in passages of *Paradise Lost*. Addison's *Spectator* essays on Milton were collected and published as a single volume, which was highly influential in Milton criticism throughout the eighteenth century.

But Milton, next, with high and haughty stalks,
Unfetter'd in majestick numbers walks;
No vulgar hero can his muse ingage;
Nor earth's wide scene confine his hallow'd rage.
See! see, he upward springs, and tow'ring high
Spurns the dull province of mortality,
Shakes heaven's eternal throne with dire alarms,
And sets the Almighty thunderer in arms.
What-e'er his pen describes I more than see,
Whilst ev'ry verse arrayed in majesty,
Bold, and sublime, my whole attention draws,
And seems above the critick's nicer laws.
How are you struck with terror and delight,
When angel with arch-angel copes in fight!
When great Messiah's out- spread banner shines,
How does the chariot rattle in his lines!
What sounds of brazen wheels, what thunder, scare,
And stun the reader with the din of war!
With fear my spirits and my blood retire,

To see the seraphs sunk in clouds of fire;
But when, with eager steps, from hence I rise,
And view the first gay scenes of Paradise;
What tongue, what words of rapture can express
A vision so profuse of pleasantness.
Oh had the poet ne'er profan'd his pen,
To varnish o'er the guilt of faithless men;
His other works might have deserv'd applause!
 But now the language can't support the cause;
While the clean current, tho' serene and bright,
Betrays a bottom odious to the sight.

—Joseph Addison, "An Account of the
Greatest English Poets," 1694

Laurence Echard (1718)

Had his education, and first display'd his Parts in *Christ-Colledge* in *Cambridge,* which he improv'd by his Travels and his indefatigable industry to that Degree, that he became the Wonder of the Age, tho' always affecting uncommon and heterodoxical Opinions. He was made *Latine* Secretary to the long Parliament, and afterwards to *Cromwell* Himself; in which Stations he shew'd himself a most inveterate and unexampled Enemy to the Memory of the Murder'd and Martyr'd King; insomuch that at the Restoration some of his Books were order'd to be burnt, and he himself was in great Danger. He was certainly a Man of prodigious Parts, and wrot many Books; but what did most, and most justly distinguish him was his Poetry, particularly his *Paradise lost,* in which he manifested such a wonderful sublime Genius, as perhaps was never exceeded in any Age or Nation in the World.

—Laurence Echard, *The History of England,*
1718, volume 3, p. 369

James Thomson "Summer" (1727)

Is not each great, each amiable Muse
Of classic ages in thy Milton met?
A genius universal as his theme,
Astonishing as Chaos, as the bloom
Of blowing Eden fair, as Heaven sublime!

—James Thomson, "Summer," *The Seasons,* 1727

ALEXANDER POPE (1737–39)

A leading eighteenth-century poet, satirist, and essayist, Alexander Pope (1688–1744) wrote the 1711 *Essay on Criticism*, which encapsulated the literary tastes of the English Enlightenment, including neoclassical adulation for ancient writers and a strong belief in universal values. Pope was influenced greatly by Milton in his works, despite the following critical excerpt, which reflects his age's preference for the rhymed heroic couplet. While Pope as a Catholic was theologically oppositional to Milton, the fact that both were in disfavor with the royalist authorities over religious issues might have contributed to Pope's admiration for Milton. There are more than 200 passages from Milton's works in Pope's opus, including his well-known mock-epic poems *The Rape of the Lock* and *The Dunciad*. His *Essay on Man* purports to "vindicate the ways of God to man," echoing Milton's *Paradise Lost*'s intention to "justify God's ways to men." Pope, however, extends Milton's Christian theology to a universal humanistic focus.

I have nothing to say for rhyme, but that I doubt whether a poem can support itself without it, in our language; unless it be stiffened with such strange words, as are likely to destroy our language itself. The high style, that is affected so much in blank verse, would not have been borne, even in Milton, had not his subject turned so much on such strange out-of-the-world things as it does.

—Alexander Pope, *Spence's Anecdotes*, 1737–39

THOMAS GRAY "OBSERVATIONS ON ENGLISH METRE" (CA. 1761)

Poet and Oxford professor Thomas Gray (1716–71) applauds Milton's musicality in this passage. Gray was particularly indebted to Milton's "L'Allegro" and "Il Penseroso" in his own work "Ode to Music."

The best example of an exquisite ear that I can produce. The more we attend to the composition of Milton's harmony, the more we shall be sensible how he loved to vary his pauses, his measures, and his feet, which gives that enchanting air of freedom and wildness to his versification, unconfined by any rules but those which his own feeling and the nature of his subject demanded. Thus he mixes the line of eight syllables with that of seven, the

Trochee and the Spondee with the Iambic foot, and the single rhyme with
the double.

—Thomas Gray, "Observations on English Metre,"
ca. 1761, *Works*, volume 1, pp. 332–33

DAVID HUME (1762)

Scottish philosopher and historian David Hume (1711–76) began his studies
at Edinburgh University when he was 11, focusing primarily on literature, history, and philosophy. After graduation, he continued to study for three more
years, with the goal of becoming a philosopher and scholar, and wrote his *A
Treatise on Human Nature* by the time he was 26. The work evidenced Hume's
rejection of metaphysics in favor of empiricism, which was to distinguish him
as the major British philosopher of all time. His point of view, however, was
unpopular, earning him charges of being a skeptic and an atheist.

Hume published *Essays, Moral and Political* in 1741 and 1742 but was
soon after rejected from two academic chairman positions, from the Universities of Edinburgh and Glasgow. While in Europe on a diplomatic mis-
sion, he published *Philosophical Essays Concerning Human Understanding*.
Hume eventually became librarian to the Edinburgh Faculty of Advo-
cates, which allowed him research materials to write a six-volume *History
of England*, published from 1754 to 1762. Though his post was in jeopardy
when he purchased books for the library that were seen as unsuitable,
he managed to finish the series, resigning upon its completion. Hume
later accepted a position as secretary to the ambassador to France, Lord
Hertford, enabling him to spend three years in Paris and meet philosopher Jean-Jacques Rousseau, whom he brought back with him to England; their friendship ended soon after, as Rousseau erroneously believed
Hume was conspiring against him.

Hume continued to write and publish compilations of his essays, arranging for the controversial *Dialogues Concerning Natural Religion* to be
published in 1779, three years after his death. In the selection that follows, Hume castigates Milton's theology and religious polemics, blaming
the author's historical period for deficiencies in his art.

It is, however, remarkable, that the greatest genius by far that shone out in
England during this period was deeply engaged with these fanatics, and
even prostituted his pen in theological controversy in factious disputes, and
in justifying the most violent measures of the party. This was John Milton,

whose poems are admirable, though liable to some objections; his prose writings disagreeable, though not altogether defective in genius. Nor are all his poems equal; his *Paradise Lost,* his *Comus,* and a few others, shine out amidst some flat and insipid compositions; even in the *Paradise Lost,* his capital performance, there are very long passages, amounting to near a third of the work, almost wholly destitute of harmony and elegance, nay of all vigour of imagination. This natural inequality in Milton's genius was much increased by the inequalities in his subject; of which some parts are of themselves the most lofty that can enter into human conception, others would have required the most laboured elegance of composition to support them. It is certain, that this author, when in a happy mood, and employed on a noble subject, is the most wonderfully sublime of any poet in any language, Homer and Lucretius and Tasso not excepted. More concise than Homer, more simple than Tasso, more nervous than Lucretius; had he lived in a later age, and learned to polish some rudeness in his verses; had he enjoyed better fortune, and possessed leisure to watch the returns of genius in himself, he had attained the pinnacle of perfection, and borne away the palm of epic poetry.

—David Hume, *History of England,* 1762

SAMUEL JOHNSON "JOHN MILTON" (1779)

Samuel Johnson (1709–84) was the leading eighteenth-century critical voice, as well as a renowned essayist of works published in *The Rambler,* a writer of fiction (most notably *Rasselas*), and a poet in his own right. His was the first published dictionary of English in 1755. Although he attended Oxford University, he never completed his degree because of his father's bleak financial circumstances; he initially turned to writing as a way of supporting himself and helping his family. He continues to be one of the most famous critics of Milton, always outspoken in regard to what he viewed as Milton's flaws.

The following excerpt contains portions of Johnson's extensive evaluative overview of Milton's works, following his biography of Milton. Throughout, Johnson mixes scant praise with more censure. Johnson's readings typify eighteenth-century biases against Milton: The poet is admonished for inconsistencies and improbabilities that violate neoclassical unities of character and action. The linkage of "pagan" and Christian elements particularly perplexes Johnson, as well as the pairing of high moral subjects with lesser details. At times, he also finds Milton's poetic style irregular.

Johnson's judgment of the greatness of a literary work included the pleasure experienced by the reader, a mode of thought that extended

Aristotelian criteria and anticipated contemporary reader-response criticism. He categorically dismisses "Lycidas" as a poem few would read or enjoy if they did not know its author and castigates much of *Comus* for its dramatic deficiencies; he praises "L'Allegro" and "Il Penseroso," though, for their overall unified effect. While Johnson esteems *Paradise Lost* for its moral lessons, he also essentially deems it overly lengthy and tedious. Most famously, Johnson makes the following claim echoed through the ages by overworked students, "*Paradise Lost* is one of the books which the reader admires and lays down, and forgets to take up again. None ever wished it longer than it is." As the arch-classicist, Johnson sees the work is lesser than Homer's epics, "only because it is not the first," but nonetheless feels it demonstrates Milton's independent thought.

———

In the examination of Milton's poetical works I shall pay so much regard to time as to begin with his juvenile productions. For his early pieces he seems to have had a degree of fondness not very laudable; what he has once written he resolves to preserve, and gives to the public an unfinished poem, which he broke off because he was *nothing satisfied with what he had done,* supposing his readers less nice than himself. These preludes to his future labours are in Italian, Latin, and English. Of the Italian I cannot pretend to speak as a critic; but I have heard them commended by a man well qualified to decide their merit. The Latin pieces are lusciously elegant; but the delight which they afford is rather by the exquisite imitation of the ancient writers, by the purity of the diction, and the harmony of the numbers, than by any power of invention, or vigour of sentiment. They are not all of equal value; the elegies excel the odes; and some of the exercises on *Gunpowder Treason* might have been spared.

The English poems, though they make no promises of *Paradise Lost,* have this evidence of genius, that they have a cast original and unborrowed. But their peculiarity is not excellence: if they differ from verses of others, they differ for the worse; for they are too often distinguished by repulsive harshness; the combinations of words are new, but they are not pleasing; the rhymes and epithets seem to be laboriously sought, and violently applied.

That in the early parts of his life he wrote with much care appears from his manuscripts, happily preserved at Cambridge, in which many of his smaller works are found as they were first written, with the subsequent corrections. Such relics show how excellence is acquired; what we hope ever to do with ease we must learn first to do with diligence.

Those who admire the beauties of this great poet sometimes force their own judgment into false approbation of his little pieces, and prevail upon themselves to think that admirable which is only singular. All that short compositions can commonly attain is neatness and elegance. Milton never learned the art of doing little things with grace; he overlooked the milder excellence of suavity and softness; he was a *lion* that had no skill *in dandling the kid.*

One of the poems on which much praise has been bestowed is "Lycidas," of which the diction is harsh, the rhymes uncertain, and the numbers unpleasing. What beauty there is we must therefore seek in the sentiments and images. It is not to be considered as the effusion of real passion; for passion runs not after remote allusions and obscure opinions. Passion plucks no berries from the myrtle and ivy, nor calls upon Arethuse and Mincius, nor tells of rough *satyrs* and *fauns with cloven heel.* Where there is leisure for fiction there is little grief.

In this poem there is no nature, for there is nothing new. Its form is that of a pastoral, easy, vulgar, and therefore disgusting; whatever images it can supply are long ago exhausted, and its inherent improbability always forces dissatisfaction on the mind. When Cowley tells of Hervey, that they studied together, it is easy to suppose how much he must miss the companion of his labours, and the partner of his discoveries; but what image of tenderness can be excited by these lines?—

We drove a field, and both together heard
What time the grey fly winds her sultry horn,
Battening our flocks with the fresh dews of night.

We know that they never drove a field, and that they had no flocks to batten; and though it be allowed that the representation may be allegorical, the true meaning is so uncertain and remote that it is never sought because it cannot be known when it is found.

Among the flocks, and copses, and flowers, appear the heathen deities— Jove and Phoebus, Neptune and Æolus, with a long train of mythological imagery, such as a college easily supplies. Nothing can less display knowledge, or less exercise invention, than to tell how a shepherd has lost his companion, and must now feed his flocks alone, without any judge of his skill in piping; and how one god asks another god what is become of Lycidas, and how neither god can tell. He who thus grieves will excite no sympathy; he who thus praises will confer no honour.

This poem has yet a grosser fault. With these trifling fictions are mingled the most awful and sacred truths, such as ought never to be polluted with such irreverend combinations. The shepherd likewise is now a feeder of sheep, and afterwards an ecclesiastical pastor, a superintendent of a Christian flock. Such equivocations are always unskilful; but here they are indecent, and at least approach to impiety, of which, however, I believe the writer not to have been conscious.

Such is the power of reputation justly acquired, that its blaze drives away the eye from nice examination. Surely no man could have fancied that he read "Lycidas" with pleasure had he not known its author.

Of the two pieces, "L'Allegro" and "Il Penseroso," I believe opinion is uniform; every man that reads them reads them with pleasure. The author's design is not, what Theobald has remarked, merely to show how objects derive their colours from the mind, by representing the operation of the same things upon the gay and the melancholy temper, or upon the same man as he is differently disposed; but rather how, among the successive variety of appearances, every disposition of mind takes hold on those by which it may be gratified.

The *cheerful* man hears the lark in the morning; the *pensive* man hears the nightingale in the evening. The *cheerful* man sees the cock strut, and hears the horn and hounds echo in the wood; then walks, *not unseen,* to observe the glory of the rising sun, or listen to the singing milkmaid, and view the labours of the ploughman and the mower; then casts his eyes about him over scenes of smiling plenty, and looks up to the distant tower, the residence of some fair inhabitant; thus he pursues rural gaiety through a day of labour or of play, and delights himself at night with the fanciful narratives of superstitious ignorance.

The *pensive* man, at one time, walks *unseen* to muse at midnight; and at another hears the sullen curfew. If the weather drives him home, he sits in a room lighted only by *glowing embers,* or by a lonely lamp outwatches the north star, to discover the habitation of separate souls, and varies the shades of meditation by contemplating the magnificent or pathetic scenes of tragic and epic poetry. When the morning comes, a morning gloomy with rain and wind, he walks into the dark trackless woods, falls asleep by some murmuring water, and with melancholy enthusiasm expects some dream of prognostication, or some music played by aerial performers.

Both Mirth and Melancholy are solitary, silent inhabitants of the breast, that neither receive nor transmit communication; no mention is therefore made of a philosophical friend, or a pleasant companion. The seriousness does not arise from any participation of calamity, nor the gaiety from the pleasures of the bottle.

The man of *cheerfulness,* having exhausted the country, tries what *towered cities* will afford, and mingles with scenes of splendour gay assemblies and nuptial festivities; but he mingles a mere spectator, as, when the learned comedies of Jonson or the wild dramas of Shakespeare are exhibited, he attends the theatre.

The *pensive* man never loses himself in crowds, but walks the cloister, or frequents the cathedral. Milton probably had not yet forsaken the Church.

Both his characters delight in music; but he seems to think that cheerful notes would have obtained from Pluto a complete dismission of Eurydice, of whom solemn sounds only procured a conditional release.

For the old age of Cheerfulness he makes no provision; but Melancholy he conducts with great dignity to the close of life. His cheerfulness is without levity, and his pensiveness without asperity.

Through these two poems the images are properly selected, and nicely distinguished; but the colours of the diction seem not sufficiently discriminated. I know not whether the characters are kept sufficiently apart. No mirth can indeed be found in his melancholy; but I am afraid that I always meet some melancholy in his mirth. They are two noble efforts of imagination.

The greatest of his juvenile performances is the *Masque of Comus*, in which may very plainly be discovered the dawn or twilight of *Paradise Lost*. Milton appears to have formed very early that system of diction, and mode of verse, which his maturer judgment approved, and from which he never endeavoured nor desired to deviate.

Nor does *Comus* afford only a specimen of his language; it exhibits likewise his power of description and his vigour of sentiment employed in the praise and defence of virtue. A work more truly poetical is rarely found; allusions, images, and descriptive epithets, embellish almost every period with lavish decoration. As a series of lines, therefore, it may be considered as worthy of all the admiration with which the votaries have received it.

As a drama it is deficient. The action is not probable. A masque, in those parts where supernatural intervention is admitted, must indeed be given up to all the freaks of imagination; but, so far as the action is merely human, it ought to be reasonable, which can hardly be said of the conduct of the two brothers, who, when their sister sinks with fatigue in a pathless wilderness, wander both away together in search of berries too far to find their way back, and leave a helpless Lady to all the sadness and danger of solitude. This, however, is a defect overbalanced by its convenience.

What deserves more reprehension is, that the prologue spoken in the wild wood by the attendant Spirit is addressed to the audience; a mode of communication so contrary to the nature of dramatic representation, that no precedents can support it.

The discourse of the Spirit is too long—an objection that may be made to almost all the following speeches; they have not the sprightliness of a dialogue animated by reciprocal contention, but seem rather declamations deliberately composed, and formally repeated, on a moral question. The auditor therefore listens as to a lecture, without passion, without anxiety.

The song of Comus has airiness and jollity; but, what may recommend Milton's morals as well as his poetry, the invitations to pleasure are so general, that they excite no distinct images of corrupt enjoyment, and take no dangerous hold on the fancy.

The following soliloquies of Comus and the Lady are elegant, but tedious. The song must owe much to the voice, if it ever can delight. At last the Brothers enter, with too much tranquillity; and when they have feared lest their sister should be in danger, and hoped that she is not in danger, the Elder makes a speech in praise of chastity, and the Younger finds how fine it is to be a philosopher.

Then descends the Spirit in form of a shepherd, and the Brother, instead of being in haste to ask his help, praises his singing, and inquires his business in that place. It is remarkable, that at this interview the Brother is taken with a short fit of rhyming. The Spirit relates that the Lady is in the power of Comus; the Brother moralises again; and the Spirit makes a long narration, of no use because it is false, and therefore unsuitable to a good being.

In all these parts the language is poetical, and the sentiments are generous; but there is something wanting to allure attention.

The dispute between the Lady and Comus is the most animated and affecting scene of the drama, and wants nothing but a brisker reciprocation of objections and replies to invite attention and detain it.

The songs are vigorous, and full of imagery; but they are harsh in their diction, and not very musical in their numbers.

Throughout the whole the figures are too bold, and the language too luxuriant for dialogue. It is a drama in the epic style, inelegantly splendid, and tediously instructive.

The Sonnets were written in different parts of Milton's life, upon different occasions. They deserve not any particular criticism; for of the best it can only be said, that they are not bad; and perhaps only the eighth and twenty-first are truly entitled to this slender commendation. The fabric of a sonnet, however adapted to the Italian language, has never succeeded in ours, which, having greater variety of termination, requires the rhymes to be often changed.

Those little pieces may be despatched without much anxiety; a greater work calls for greater care. I am now to examine *Paradise Lost*; a poem which, considered with respect to design, may claim the first place, and with respect to performance, the second, among the production of the human mind.

By the general consent of critics the first praise of genius is due to the writer of an epic poem, as it requires an assemblage of all the powers which are singly sufficient for other compositions. Poetry is the art of uniting pleasure with truth, by calling imagination to the help of reason. Epic poetry undertakes to teach the most important truths by the most pleasing precepts, and therefore relates some great event in the most affecting manner. History must supply the writer with the rudiments of narration, which he must improve and exalt by a nobler art, must animate by dramatic energy, and diversify by retrospection and anticipation; morality must teach him the exact bounds, and different shades, of vice and virtue; from policy, and the practice of life, he has to learn the discriminations of character, and the tendency of the passions, either single or combined; and physiology must supply him with illustrations and images. To put these materials to poetical use, is required an imagination capable of painting nature and realising fiction. Nor is he yet a poet till he has attained the whole extension of his language, distinguished all the delicacies of phrase, and all the colours of words, and learned to adjust their different sounds to all the varieties of metrical modulation.

Bossu is of opinion that the poet's first work is to find a *moral,* which his fable is afterwards to illustrate and establish. This seems to have been the process only of Milton; the moral of other poems is incidental and consequent; in Milton's only it is essential and intrinsic. His purpose was the most useful and the most arduous; to *vindicate the ways of God to man;* to show the reasonableness of religion, and the necessity of obedience to the Divine Law.

To convey this moral, there must be a *fable,* a narration artfully constructed, so as to excite curiosity, and surprise expectation. In this part of his work Milton must be confessed to have equalled every other poet. He has involved in his account of the Fall of Man the events which preceded, and those that were to follow it: he has interwoven the whole system of theology with such propriety, that every part appears to be necessary; and scarcely any recital is wished shorter for the sake of quickening the progress of the main action.

The subject of an epic poem is naturally an event of great importance. That of Milton is not the destruction of a city, the conduct of a colony, or the foundation of an empire. His subject is the fate of worlds, the revolutions of heaven and of earth; rebellion against the Supreme King, raised by the highest order of created beings; the overthrow of their host, and the punishment of their crime; the creation of a new race of reasonable creatures; their original happiness and innocence, their forfeiture of immortality, and their restoration to hope and peace.

Great events can be hastened or retarded only by persons of elevated dignity. Before the greatness displayed in Milton's poem, all other greatness shrinks away. The weakest of his agents are the highest and noblest of human beings, the original parents of mankind; with whose actions the elements consented; on whose rectitude, or deviation of will, depended the state of terrestrial nature, and the condition of all the future inhabitants of the globe.

Of the other agents in the poem, the chief are such as it is irreverence to name on slight occasions. The rest were lower powers;

—of which the least could wield
Those elements, and arm him with the force
Of all their regions;

powers which only the control of Omnipotence restrains from laying creation waste, and filling the vast expanse of space with ruin and confusion. To display the motives and actions of beings thus superior, so far as human reason can examine them, or human imagination represent them, is the task which this mighty poet has undertaken and performed.

In the examination of epic poems much speculation is commonly employed upon the *characters*. The characters in the *Paradise Lost*, which admit of examination, are those of angels and of man; of angels good and evil; of man in his innocent and sinful state.

Among the angels, the virtue of Raphael is mild and placid, of easy condescension and free communication; that of Michael is regal and lofty, and, as may seem, attentive to the dignity of his own nature. Abdiel and Gabriel appear occasionally, and act as every incident requires; the solitary fidelity of Abdiel is very amiably painted.

Of the evil angels the characters are more diversified. To Satan, as Addison observes, such sentiments are given as suit *the most exalted and most depraved being*. Milton has been censured by Clarke for the impiety which sometimes breaks from Satan's mouth. For there are thoughts, as he justly remarks, which no observation of character can justify, because no good man would willingly permit them to pass, however transiently, through his own mind. To make Satan speak as a rebel, without any such expressions as might taint the reader's imagination, was indeed one of the greatest difficulties in Milton's undertaking, and I cannot but think that he has extricated himself with great happiness. There is in Satan's speeches little that can give pain to a pious ear. The language of rebellion cannot be the same with that of obedience. The malignity of Satan foams in haughtiness and obstinacy; but his expressions are commonly general, and no otherwise offensive than as they are wicked.

The other chiefs of the celestial rebellion are very judiciously discriminated in the first and second books; and the ferocious character of Moloch appears, both in the battle and the council, with exact consistency.

To Adam and to Eve are given, during their innocence, such sentiments as innocence can generate and utter. Their love is pure benevolence and mutual veneration; their repasts are without luxury, and their diligence without toil. Their addresses to their Maker have little more than the voice of admiration and gratitude. Fruition left them nothing to ask; and Innocence left them nothing to fear.

But with guilt enter distrust and discord, mutual accusation and stubborn self-defence; they regard each other with alienated minds, and dread their Creator as the avenger of their transgression. At last they seek shelter in his mercy, soften to repentance, and melt in supplication. Both before and after the Fall the superiority of Adam is diligently sustained.

Of the *probable* and the *marvellous,* two parts of a vulgar epic poem which immerge the critic in deep consideration, the *Paradise Lost* requires little to be said. It contains the history of a miracle, of Creation and Redemption; it displays the power and the mercy of the Supreme Being; the probable therefore is marvellous, and the marvellous is probable. The substance of the narrative is truth; and as truth allows no choice, it is, like necessity, superior to rule. To the accidental or adventitious parts, as to everything human, some slight exceptions may be made. But the main fabric is immoveably supported.

It is justly remarked by Addison, that this poem has, by the nature of its subject, the advantage above all others, that it is universally and perpetually interesting. All mankind will, through all ages, bear the same relation to Adam and to Eve, and must partake of that good and evil which extend to themselves.

Of the *machinery,* so called from *Theos apo mechanes* by which is meant the occasional interposition of supernatural power, another fertile topic of critical remarks, here is no room to speak, because everything is done under the immediate and visible direction of Heaven; but the rule is so far observed, that no part of the action could have been accomplished by any other means.

Of *episodes,* I think there are only two, contained in Raphael's relation of the war in heaven, and Michael's prophetic account of the changes to happen in this world. Both are closely connected with the great action; one was necessary to Adam as a warning, the other as a consolation.

To the completeness or *integrity* of the design nothing can be objected; it has distinctly and clearly what Aristotle requires, a beginning, a middle, and an end. There is perhaps no poem, of the same length, from which so little can be taken without apparent mutilation. Here are no funeral games, nor is there any long description of a shield. The short digressions at the beginning of the third, seventh, and ninth books might doubtless be spared; but superfluities so beautiful, who would take away? or who does not wish that the author of the *Iliad* had gratified succeeding ages with a little knowledge of himself? Perhaps no passages are more frequently or more attentively read than those extrinsic paragraphs; and, since the end of poetry is pleasure, that cannot be unpoetical with which all are pleased.

The questions, whether the action of the poem be strictly *one,* whether the poem can be properly termed *heroic,* and who is the hero, are raised by such readers as draw their principles of judgment rather from books than from reason. Milton, though he entitled *Paradise Lost* only a *poem,* yet calls it himself *heroic song.* Dryden, petulantly and indecently, denies the heroism of Adam, because he was overcome; but there is no reason why the hero should not be unfortunate, except established practice, since success and virtue do not go necessarily together. Cato is the hero of Lucan; but Lucan's authority will not be suffered by Quintilian to decide. However, if success be necessary, Adam's deceiver was at last crushed; Adam was restored to his Maker's favour, and therefore may securely resume his human rank.

After the scheme and fabric of the poem, must be considered its component parts, the sentiments and the diction.

The *sentiments,* as expressive of manners, or appropriated to characters, are for the greater part unexceptionally just.

Splendid passages, containing lessons of morality, or precepts of prudence, occur seldom. Such is the original formation of this poem, that as it admits no human manners till the Fall, it can give little assistance to human conduct. Its end is to raise the thoughts above sublunary cares or pleasures. Yet the praise of that fortitude with which Abdiel maintained his singularity of virtue against the scorn of multitudes, may be accommodated to all times; and Raphael's reproof of Adam's curiosity after the planetary motions, with the answer returned by Adam, may be confidently opposed to any rule of life which any poet has delivered.

The thoughts which are occasionally called forth in the progress are such as could only be produced by an imagination in the highest degree fervid and active, to which materials were supplied by incessant study and unlimited curiosity. The heat of Milton's mind might be said to sublimate his learning, to throw off into his work the spirit of science, unmingled with its grosser parts.

He had considered creation in its whole extent, and his descriptions are therefore learned. He had accustomed his imagination to unrestrained indulgence, and his conceptions therefore were extensive. The characteristic quality of his poem is sublimity. He sometimes descends to the elegant, but his element is the great. He can occasionally invest himself with grace; but his natural port is gigantic loftiness. He can please when pleasure is required; but it is his peculiar power to astonish.

He seems to have been well acquainted with his own genius, and to know what it was that nature had bestowed upon him more bountifully than upon others; the power of displaying the vast, illuminating the splendid, enforcing the awful, darkening the gloomy, and aggravating the dreadful; he therefore chose a subject on which too much could not be said, on which he might tire his fancy without the censure of extravagance.

The appearances of nature, and the occurrences of life, did not satiate his appetite of greatness. To paint things as they are requires a minute attention, and employs the memory rather than the fancy. Milton's delight was to sport in the wide regions of possibility; reality was a scene too narrow for his mind. He sent his faculties out upon discovery, into worlds where only imagination can travel, and delighted to form new modes of existence, and furnish sentiment and action to superior beings, to trace the counsels of hell, or accompany the choirs of heaven. But he could not be always in other worlds; he must sometimes revisit earth, and tell of things visible and known. When he cannot raise wonder by the sublimity of his mind, he gives delight by its fertility.

Whatever be his subject, he never fails to fill the imagination. But his images and descriptions of the scenes or operations of nature do not seem to be always copied from original form, nor to have the freshness, raciness, and energy of immediate observation. He saw nature, as Dryden expresses it, *through the spectacles of books;* and on most occasions calls learning to his assistance. The garden of Eden brings to his mind the vale of Enna, where Proserpine was gathering flowers. Satan makes his way through fighting elements, like Argo between the Cyanean rocks, or Ulysses between the two Sicilian whirlpools, when he shunned Charybdis on the *larboard.* The mythological allusions have been justly censured, as not being always used with notice of their vanity; but they contribute variety to the narration, and produce an alternate exercise of the memory and the fancy.

His similes are less numerous and more various than those of his predecessors. But he does not confine himself within the limits of rigorous comparison: his great excellence is amplitude, and he expands the adventitious image beyond the dimensions which the occasion required. Thus, comparing the shield of Satan to the orb of the moon, he crowds the imagination with the discovery of the telescope, and all the wonders which the telescope discovers.

Of his moral sentiments it is hardly praise to affirm that they excel those of all other poets; for this superiority he was indebted to his acquaintance with the sacred writings. The ancient epic poets, wanting the light of revelation, were very unskilful teachers of virtue: their principal characters may be great, but they are not amiable. The reader may rise from their works with a greater degree of active or passive fortitude, and sometimes of prudence; but he will be able to carry away few precepts of justice, and none of mercy.

From the Italian writers it appears that the advantages of even Christian knowledge may be possessed in vain. Ariosto's pravity is generally known; and though the *Deliverance of Jerusalem* may be considered as a sacred subject, the poet has been very sparing of moral instruction.

In Milton every line breathes sanctity of thought and purity of manners, except when the train of the narration requires the introduction of the rebellious spirits; and even they are compelled to acknowledge their subjection to God, in such a manner as excites reverence and confirms piety.

Of human beings there are but two; but those two are the parents of mankind, venerable before their fall for dignity and innocence, and amiable after it for repentance and submission. In their first state their affection is tender without weakness, and their piety sublime without presumption. When they have sinned, they show how discord begins in mutual frailty, and how it ought to cease in mutual forbearance, how confidence of the Divine favour is forfeited by sin, and how hope of pardon may be obtained by penitence and prayer. A state of innocence we can only conceive, if indeed in our present misery it be possible to conceive it; but the sentiments and worship proper to a fallen and offending being we have all to learn, as we have all to practise.

The poet, whatever be done, is always great. Our progenitors in their first state conversed with angels; even when folly and sin had degraded them, they had not in their humiliation *the port of mean suitors;* and they rise again to reverential regard when we find that their prayers were heard.

As human passions did not enter the world before the Fall, there is in the *Paradise Lost* little opportunity for the pathetic; but what little there is has not been lost. That passion which is peculiar to rational nature, the anguish arising from the consciousness of transgression, and the horrors attending the sense of the Divine displeasure, are very justly described and forcibly impressed. But the passions are moved only on one occasion; sublimity is the general and prevailing quality of this poem; sublimity variously modified, sometimes descriptive, sometimes argumentative.

The defects and faults of *Paradise Lost*—for faults and defects every work of man must have—it is the business of impartial criticism to discover. As, in displaying the excellence of Milton, I have not made long quotations, because of selecting beauties there had been no end, I shall in the same general manner mention that which seems to deserve censure; for what Englishman can take delight in transcribing passages which, if they lessen the reputation of Milton, diminish in some degree the honour of our country?

The generality of my scheme does not admit the frequent notice of verbal inaccuracies; which Bentley, perhaps better skilled in grammar than poetry, has often found, though he sometimes made them, and which he imputed to the obtrusions of a reviser, whom the author's blindness obliged him to employ; a supposition rash and groundless if he thought it true, and vile and pernicious if, as is said, he in private allowed it to be false.

The plan of *Paradise Lost* has this inconvenience, that it comprises neither human actions nor human manners. The man and woman who act and suffer are in a state which no other man or woman can ever know. The reader finds no transaction in which he can by any effort of imagination place himself; he has therefore little natural curiosity or sympathy.

We all, indeed, feel the effects of Adam's disobedience; we all sin like Adam, and like him must all bewail our offences: we have restless and insidious enemies in the fallen angels, and in the blessed spirits we have guardians and friends; in the redemption of mankind we hope to be included; in the description of heaven and hell we are surely interested, as we are all to reside hereafter either in the regions of horror or bliss.

But these truths are too important to be new; they have been taught to our infancy; they have mingled with our solitary thoughts and familiar conversation, and are habitually interwoven with the whole texture of life. Being therefore not new, they raise no unaccustomed emotion in the mind; what we knew before, we cannot learn; what is not unexpected, cannot surprise.

Of the idea suggested by these awful scenes, from some we recede with reverence, except when stated hours require their association; and from others we shrink with horror, or admit them only as salutary inflictions, as counterpoises to our interests and passions. Such images rather obstruct the career of fancy than incite it.

Pleasure and terror are indeed the genuine sources of poetry; but poetical pleasure must be such as human imagination can at least conceive, and poetical terrors such as human strength and fortitude may combat. The good and evil of eternity are too ponderous for the wings of wit; the mind sinks under them in passive helplessness, content with calm belief and humble adoration.

Known truths, however, may take a different appearance, and be conveyed to the mind by a new train of intermediate images. This Milton has undertaken, and performed with pregnancy and vigour of mind peculiar to himself. Whoever considers the few radical positions which the Scriptures afforded him, will wonder by what energetic operation he expanded them to such extent, and ramified them to so much variety, restrained as he was by religious reverence from licentiousness of fiction.

Here is a full display of the united force of study and genius; of a great accumulation of materials, with judgment to digest, and fancy to combine them: Milton was able to select from nature, or from story, from an ancient fable, or from modern science, whatever could illustrate or adorn his thoughts. An accumulation of knowledge impregnated his mind, fermented by study, and exalted by imagination.

It has been therefore said, without an indecent hyperbole, by one of his encomiasts, that in reading *Paradise Lost* we read a book of universal knowledge.

But original deficience cannot be supplied. The want of human interest is always felt. *Paradise Lost* is one of the books which the reader admires and lays down, and forgets to take up again. None ever wished it longer than it is. Its perusal is a duty rather than a pleasure. We read Milton for instruction, retire harassed and overburdened, and look elsewhere for recreation; we desert our master and seek for companions.

Another inconvenience of Milton's design is, that it requires the description of what cannot be described, the agency of spirits. He saw that immateriality supplied no images, and that he could not show angels acting but by instruments of action; he therefore invested them with form and matter. This, being necessary, was therefore defensible; and he should have secured the consistency of his system, by keeping immateriality out of sight, and enticing his reader to drop it from his thoughts. But he has unhappily perplexed his poetry with his philosophy. His infernal and celestial powers are sometimes pure spirit, and sometimes animated body. When Satan walks with his lance upon the *burning marie,* he has a body; when, in his passage between hell and the new world, he is in danger of sinking in the vacuity, and is supported by a gust of rising vapours, he has a body; when he animates the toad, he seems to be mere spirit, that can penetrate matter at pleasure; when he *starts up in his own shape,* he has at least a determined form; and when he is brought before Gabriel, he has *a spear and a shield,* which he had the power of hiding in the toad, though the arms of the contending angels are evidently material.

The vulgar inhabitants of Pandaemonium, being *incorporeal spirits,* are *at large, though without number,* in a limited space: yet in the battle, when they were overwhelmed by mountains, their armour hurt them, *crushed in upon their substance, now grown gross by sinning.* This likewise happened to the uncorrupted angels, who were overthrown the *sooner for their arms, for unarmed they might easily as spirits have evaded by contraction or remove.* Even as spirits they are hardly spiritual; for *contraction* and *remove* are images of matter; but if they could have escaped without their armour, they might have escaped from it, and left only the empty cover to be bartered. Uriel, when he rides on a sunbeam, is material; Satan is material when he is afraid of the prowess of Adam.

The confusion of spirit and matter which pervades the whole narration of the war of heaven fills it with incongruity; and the book in which it is related is, I believe, the favourite of children, and gradually neglected as knowledge is increased.

After the operation of immaterial agents, which cannot be explained, may be considered that of allegorical persons, which have no real existence. To exalt causes into agents, to invest abstract ideas with form, and animate them with activity, has always been the right of poetry. But such airy beings are, for the most part, suffered only to do their natural office, and retire. Thus Fame tells a tale, and Victory hovers over a general, or perches on a standard; but Fame and Victory can do more. To give them any real employment, or ascribe to them any material agency, is to make them allegorical no longer, but to shock the mind by ascribing effects to non-entity. In the *Prometheus* of Æschylus we see Violence and Strength, and in the *Alcestis* of Euripides we see Death brought upon the stage, all as active persons of the drama; but no precedents can justify absurdity.

Milton's allegory of Sin and Death is undoubtedly faulty. Sin is indeed the mother of Death, and may be allowed to be the portress of hell; but when they stop the journey of Satan, a journey described as real, and when Death offers him battle, the allegory is broken. That Sin and Death should have shown the way to hell, might have been allowed; but they cannot facilitate the passage by building a bridge, because the difficulty of Satan's passage is described as real and sensible, and the bridge ought to be only figurative. The hell assigned to the rebellious spirits is described as not less local than the residence of man. It is placed in some distant part of space, separated from the regions of harmony and order by a chaotic waste and an unoccupied vacuity; but Sin and Death worked up a *mole* of *aggravated soil,* cemented with *asphaltus;* a work too bulky for ideal architects.

This unskilful allegory appears to me one of the greatest faults of the poem; and to this there was no temptation but the author's opinion of its beauty.

To the conduct of the narrative some objection may be made. Satan is with great expectation brought before Gabriel in Paradise, and is suffered to go away unmolested. The creation of man is represented as the consequence of the vacuity left in heaven by the expulsion of the rebels; yet Satan mentions it as a report *rife in heaven* before his departure.

To find sentiments for the state of innocence was very difficult; and something of anticipation perhaps is now and then discovered. Adam's discourse of dreams seems not to be the speculation of a new-created being. I know not whether his answer to the angel's reproof for curiosity does not want something of propriety; it is the speech of a man acquainted with many other men. Some philosophical notions, especially when the philosophy is false, might have been better omitted. The angel, in a comparison, speaks of *timorous deer* before deer were yet timorous, and before Adam could understand the comparison.

Dryden remarks, that Milton has some flats among his elevations. This is only to say that all the parts are not equal. In every work one part must be for the sake of others; a palace must have passages; a poem must have transitions. It is no more to be required that wit should always be blazing than that the sun should always stand at noon. In a great work there is a vicissitude of luminous and opaque parts, as there is in the world a succession of day and night. Milton, when he has expatiated in the sky, may be allowed sometimes to revisit earth; for what other author ever soared so high, or sustained his flight so long?

Milton, being well versed in the Italian poets, appears to have borrowed often from them; and as every man catches something from his companions, his desire of imitating Ariosto's levity has disgraced his work with the "Paradise of Fools"—a fiction not in itself ill-imagined, but too ludicrous for its place.

His play on words, in which he delights too often; his equivocations, which Bentley endeavours to defend by the example of the ancients; his unnecessary and ungraceful use of terms of art, it is not necessary to mention, because they are easily remarked, and generally censured, and at last bear so little proportion to the whole that they scarcely deserve the attention of a critic. Such are the faults of that wonderful performance *Paradise Lost,* which he who can put in balance with its beauties must be considered not as nice but as dull, as less to be censured for want of candour, than pitied for want of sensibility.

Of *Paradise Regained,* the general judgment seems now to be right, that it is in many parts elegant, and everywhere instructive. It was not to be supposed that the writer of *Paradise Lost* could ever write without great effusions of fancy, and exalted precepts of wisdom. The basis of *Paradise Regained* is narrow: a dialogue without action can never please like an union of the narrative and dramatic powers. Had this poem been written not by Milton, but by some imitator, it would have claimed and received universal praise.

If *Paradise Regained* has been too much depreciated, *Samson Agonistes* has in requital been too much admired. It could only be by long prejudice, and the bigotry of learning, that Milton could prefer the ancient tragedies, with their encumbrance of a chorus, to the exhibitions of the French and English stages; and it is only by a blind confidence in the reputation of Milton that a drama can be praised in which the intermediate parts have neither cause nor consequence, neither hasten nor retard the catastrophe.

In this tragedy are however many particular beauties, many just sentiments and striking lines; but it wants that power of attracting the attention which a well-connected plan produces.

Milton would not have excelled in dramatic writing; he knew human nature only in the gross, and had never studied the shades of character, nor the combinations of concurring, or the perplexity of contending, passions. He had read much, and knew what books could teach, but had mingled little in the world, and was deficient in the knowledge which experience must confer.

Through all his greater works there prevails an uniform peculiarity of *diction,* a mode and cast of expression which bears little resemblance to that of any former writer, and which is so far removed from common use that an unlearned reader, when he first opens his book, finds himself surprised by a new language.

This novelty has been, by those who can find nothing wrong in Milton, imputed to his laborious endeavours after words suitable to the grandeur of his ideas. *Our language,* says Addison, *sunk under him.* But the truth is that, both in prose and verse, he had formed his style by a perverse and pedantic principle. He was desirous to use English words with a foreign idiom. This in all his prose is discovered and condemned; for there judgment operates freely, neither softened by the beauty nor awed by the dignity of his thoughts; but such is the power of his poetry, that his call is obeyed without resistance, the reader feels himself in captivity to a higher and nobler mind, and criticism sinks in admiration.

Milton's style was not modified by his subject; what is shown with greater extent in *Paradise Lost* may be found in *Comus.* One source of his peculiarity was his familiarity with the Tuscan poets; the disposition of his words is, I think, frequently Italian, perhaps sometimes combined with other tongues.

Of him, at last may be said what Jonson says of Spenser, that *he wrote no language,* but has formed what Butler calls a *Babylonish dialect,* in itself harsh and barbarous, but made, by exalted genius and extensive learning, the vehicle of so much instruction and so much pleasure that, like other lovers, we find grace in its deformity.

Whatever be the faults of his diction, he cannot want the praise of copiousness and variety: he was master of his language in its full extent; and has selected the melodious words with such diligence, that from his book alone the Art of English Poetry might be learned.

After his diction, something must be said of his *versification.* The *measure,* he says, *is the English heroic verse without rhyme.* Of this mode he had many examples among the Italians, and some in his own country. The Earl of Surrey is said to have translated one of Virgil's books without rhyme; and, besides our tragedies, a few short poems had appeared in blank verse, particularly one tending to reconcile the nation to Raleigh's wild attempt upon Guiana, and probably written by Raleigh himself. These petty performances cannot be supposed to have much influenced Milton, who more probably took his hint from Trissino's *Italia Liberata;* and, finding blank verse easier than rhyme, was desirous of persuading himself that it is better.

Rhyme, he says, and says truly, *is no necessary adjunct of true poetry.* But, perhaps, of poetry as a mental operation, metre or music is no necessary adjunct: it is, however, by the music of metre that poetry has been discriminated in all languages; and, in languages melodiously constructed with a due proportion of long and short syllables, metre is sufficient. But one language cannot communicate its rules to another: where metre is scanty and imperfect, some help is necessary. The music of the English heroic line strikes the ear so faintly, that it is easily lost, unless all the syllables of every line co-operate together; this co-operation can be only obtained by the preservation of every verse unmingled with another as a distinct system of sounds; and this distinctness is obtained and preserved by the artifice of rhyme. The variety of pauses, so much boasted by the lovers of blank verse, changes the measures of an English poet to the periods of a declaimer; and there are only a few happy readers of Milton who enable their audience to perceive where the lines end or begin. *Blank verse,* said an ingenious critic, *seems to be verse only to the eye.*

Poetry may subsist without rhyme, but English poetry will not often please; nor can rhyme ever be safely spared but where the subject is able to support itself. Blank verse makes some approach to that which is called the *lapidary style;* has neither the easiness of prose, nor the melody of numbers, and therefore tires by long continuance. Of the Italian writers without rhyme, whom Milton alleges as precedents, not one is popular; what reason could urge in its defence has been confuted by the ear.

But, whatever be the advantage of rhyme, I cannot prevail on myself to wish that Milton had been a rhymer; for I cannot wish his work to be other than it is; yet, like other heroes, he is to be admired rather than imitated. He that thinks himself capable of astonishing may write blank verse; but those that hope only to please must condescend to rhyme.

The highest praise of genius is original invention. Milton cannot be said to have contrived the structure of an epic poem, and therefore owes reverence to that vigour and amplitude of mind to which all generations must be indebted for the art of poetical narration, for the texture of the fable, the variation of incidents, the interposition of dialogue, and all the strategems that surprise and enchain attention. But, of all the borrowers from Homer, Milton is perhaps the least indebted. He was naturally a thinker for himself, confident of his own abilities, and disdainful of help or hindrance: he did not refuse admission to the thoughts or images of his predecessors, but he did not seek them. From his contemporaries he neither courted nor received support; there is in his writings nothing by which the pride of other authors might be gratified, or favour gained: no exchange of praise, nor solicitation of support. His great works were performed under discountenance, and in blindness, but difficulties vanished at his touch; he was born for whatever is arduous; and his work is not the greatest of heroic poems, only because it is not the first.

—Samuel Johnson, from "John Milton,"
Lives of the English Poets, 1779

HORACE WALPOLE (1785)

Author of the first gothic novel, *The Castle of Otranto*, Horace Walpole (1717–97) was a member of Parliament, eventually the fourth earl of Oxford, and a friend of Thomas Gray, whose collection of poetry he printed using his own press. Walpole had reconstructed an estate into a gothic castle named Strawberry Hill, part of the inspiration for his novel. This excerpt shows his interest in Italian style, garnered from his tour of the European continent after withdrawing from Cambridge.

Milton had such superior merit, that I will only say, that if his angels, his Satan, and his Adam, have as much dignity as the Apollo Belvedere, his Eve has all the delicacy and graces of the Venus of Medici, as his description of Eden has the colouring of Albano. Milton's tenderness imprints ideas as graceful as Guido's Madonnas: and the *Allegro, Penseroso,* and *Comus* might be denominated from the Three Graces, as the Italians gave singular titles to two or three of Petrarch's best sonnets.

—Horace Walpole, letter to John Pinkerton,
June 26, 1785, *Correspondence*, volume 16,
edited by Lewis, p. 270

ROBERT BURNS "POEM ON PASTORAL POETRY" (CA. 1796)

In Homer's craft Jock Milton thrives.

—Robert Burns, "Poem on Pastoral Poetry," ca. 1796

SAMUEL TAYLOR COLERIDGE "NOTES ON MILTON" (1796)

Samuel Taylor Coleridge (1772–1834) was a poet and leader of the romantic movement whose deep admiration for Milton wove its way through his own poetry in a variety of allusions and stylistic borrowings. The son of an Anglican vicar, Coleridge intended to pursue a clerical career when he entered Jesus College in Cambridge but, through his relationship with the Unitarian William Frend, began to grow disenchanted with the state religion. En route to Wales, Coleridge met Robert Southey, and the two began a philosophical kinship that culminated in their idea of a pantisocracy, a utopian ideal influenced by Plato's *Republic* in which all would be equal and share in governing. After Southey decided to pursue a law career and abandon the idea of founding a pantisocracy on the banks of the Susquehanna River in Pennsylvania, Coleridge turned to a writing career, never completing his Cambridge degree.

While a young radical, Coleridge wrote political sonnets predicated on Milton's, supported Milton's antiroyalism, and admired Milton's religious independence. Coleridge worked to emulate Milton by increasing his own knowledge, as Milton had, studying Milton's works and learning from Milton's style and subject matter. Coleridge's more direct poetic borrowings include the use of a line from *Samson Agonistes* in "Dejection: An Ode" and appropriating portions of *Paradise Lost* in "Religious Musings" and in his prose literary critical work *Biographia Literaria*. He unsuccessfully tried his hand at composing an epic in imitation of Milton. The brief passage that follows expresses Coleridge's belief that Milton is the best of thinkers, one who challenges the readers in his works.

The reader of Milton must be always on his duty: he is surrounded with sense; it rises in every line; every word is to the purpose. There are no lazy intervals; all has been considered, and demands and merits observation. If this be called obscurity, let it be remembered that it is such an obscurity as is a compliment to the reader; not that vicious obscurity, which proceeds from a muddled head.

—Samuel Taylor Coleridge, "Notes on Milton"
(1796), *Literary Remains,* volume 1, edited by
Coleridge, p. 184

WILLIAM GODWIN
"MILTON AND CLARENDON" (1797)

Philosopher and author William Godwin (1756–1836) wrote on politics, education, and history after leaving his position as a Presbyterian minister. He became a deist and anarchist, publishing *Enquiry into Political Justice* in 1787. In 1797, he married Mary Wollstonecraft; she died later that year giving birth to their child Mary. Godwin wrote *Memoirs of the Author of a Vindication of the Rights of Women* in his late wife's honor.

Godwin discussed Milton and his works in at least two essays with *The Enquirer,* terming *Paradise Lost* "a sublime poem." He also borrowed the plot of Milton's *Comus* for his own work *Imogen: A Pastoral Romance,* comically claiming that the two works shared a common manuscript.

The fact seems to be, that Milton was dissatisfied with the shapeless chaos in which our language appeared in former writers and set himself, with that ardour which always distinguished him, to reform it. His success indeed is not entitled to unlimited encomium. The gigantic structure of his genius perhaps somewhat misled him. He endeavoured to form a language of too lofty and uniform a port. The exuberance of his mind led him to pour out his thoughts with an impetuosity, that often swept away with it the laws of simplicity and even the rules of grammatical propriety. His attempt however to give system to the lawless dialect of our ancestors, was the mark of a generous spirit, and entitles him to our applause. If we compare the style of Milton to that of later writers, and particularly to that of our own days, undoubtedly nothing but a very corrupt taste can commend it. But the case is altered, if we compare it with the writings of his predecessors. An impartial critic would perhaps find no language in any writer that went before Milton, of so much merit as that of Milton himself.

—William Godwin, "Milton and Clarendon,"
The Enquirer, 1797, p. 405

William Wordsworth "London, 1802" (1802)

Wordsworth was influenced by Milton's 23 sonnets in composing his own 150 sonnets; the following work "London" encapsulates Wordsworth's adulation of Milton's genius. The occasion of the poem was Wordsworth's return from France, as he compared what he considered the decadence of English life during a time of war to Milton's austere puritanism and political sacrifice in working for the English Revolution.

Milton! thou shouldst be living at this hour:
England hath need of thee: she is a fen
Of stagnant waters: altar, sword, and pen,
Fireside, the heroic wealth of hall and bower,
Have forfeited their ancient English dower
Of inward happiness. We are selfish men;
Oh! raise us up, return to us again;
And give us manners, virtue, freedom, power.
Thy soul was like a Star, and dwelt apart:
Thou hadst a voice whose sound was like the sea:
Pure as the naked heavens, majestic, free,
So didst thou travel on life's common way,
In cheerful godliness; and yet thy heart
The lowliest duties on herself did lay.
                    —William Wordsworth, "London, 1802," 1802

William Blake "Excerpt from *Milton, Book the First*" (1804)

Poet and artist William Blake (1757–1827) was a major force in the early British romantic movement and the poet most indebted to Milton, finding in the predecessor the best English model of the divinely inspired poet-prophet. Blake himself claimed to have mystical visions as a child and continued to write about his spiritual insights throughout in life. Sent to drawing school while young and apprenticed to an engraver at age 14, he would later self-illustrate much of his poetry. Many of the engravings produced throughout his life were in response to Milton's *Paradise Lost*, Blake producing several sets of illustrations for the epic.

In 1789, Blake produced *Songs of Innocence*, expanding it in 1794 to *Songs of Innocence and Experience* to encompass the dual nature of human life, the carefree time of childhood and the darker realities of adulthood.

He followed that work with several poems on sustained topics, *The Marriage of Heaven and Hell*—which is certainly a response to *Paradise Lost*—*The French Revolution, America, A Prophecy,* and *Europe.* In 1800, Blake and his wife, Catherine, moved from London to the village of Felpham on the seacoast; there, he wrote his epic poem *Milton,* illustrating it with his own engravings after returning to London in 1803, when he also wrote and illustrated a second epic poem, *Jerusalem: The Emanation of the Giant Albion.* In 1825, he was commissioned to create engravings for an edition of Dante's *Divine Comedy;* Blake died two years later before finishing the project.

The following passage is taken from Blake's *Milton,* his epic that expresses both admiration and criticism for his poetic forefather. Milton's Satan represents all that holds him back intellectually and stylistically from being the true prophet who can redeem society. One of the stumbling blocks for Milton, from Blake's point of view, is his adherence to classical literary models; another is external religion, rather than inner inspiration. Blake contrasts the Daughters of Memory, representing traditions that are fettering Milton, with the Daughters of Inspiration, the divinely breathed sources of truth that Milton is meant to portray. Because he has allowed error to weaken his prophetic message, Milton is here identified with Satan, who must be cast into Hell.

Then Milton rose up from the heavens of Albion ardorous!
The whole Assembly wept prophetic, seeing in Milton's face
And in his lineaments divine the shades of Death & Ulro
He took off the robe of the promise, & ungirded himself from

   the oath of God.

And Milton said, I go to Eternal Death! The Nations still
Follow after the detestable Gods of Priam; in pomp
Of warlike selfhood, contradicting and blaspheming.
When will the Resurrection come; to deliver the sleeping body
From corruptibility; O when Lord Jesus wilt thou come?
Tarry no longer; for my soul lies at the gates of death.
I will arise and look forth for the morning of the grave.
I will go down to the sepulchre to see if morning breaks!
I will go down to self annihilation and eternal death,

Lest the Last Judgment come & find me unannihilate
And I be seiz'd & giv'n into the hands of my own Selfhood
The Lamb of God is seen thro' mists & shadows, hov'ring
Over the sepulchres in clouds of Jehovah & winds of Elohim,
A disk of blood, distant; & heav'ns & earth's roll dark between.
What do I here before the Judgment? without my Emanation?
With the daughters of memory, & not with the daughters of inspiration
I in my Selfhood am that Satan: I am that Evil one!
He is my Spectre! In my obedience to loose him from my Hells
To claim the Hells, my Furnaces, I go to Eternal Death.

And Milton said, I go to Eternal Death! Eternity shudder'd
For he took the outside course, among the graves of the dead
A mournful shade. Eternity shudderd at the image of eternal death

Then on the verge of Beulah he beheld his own Shadow:
A mournful form double; hermaphroditic: male & female
In one wonderful body, and he enterd into it
In direful pain for the dread shadow, twenty-seven-fold
Reachd to the depths of direst Hell, & thence to Albion's land:
Which is this earth of vegetation on which now I write.

The Seven Angels of the Presence wept over Milton's shadow!

—William Blake, excerpt from
Milton, Book the First, 1804

George Gordon, Lord Byron
"Dedication to *Don Juan*" (1818)

English romantic poet George Gordon, Lord Byron (1788–1824) wrote *Childe Harold's Pilgrimage* and the 17-canto epic *Don Juan*, rewriting the famed Lothario into an easily seduced man accosted by forward females, rather than a male aggressor. Like most romantic writers, Byron prized Milton's genius and individualism and admired how his predecessor dared to live his life in opposition to corrupt political and religious norms. Here, Byron commends Milton for standing fast against both kings Charles I and II.

If, fallen in evil days on evil tongues,
Milton appeal'd to the Avenger, Time,

If Time, the Avenger, execrates his wrongs,
And makes the word "Miltonic" mean *"sublime,"*
He deign'd not to belie his soul in songs,
Nor turn his very talent to a crime;
He did not loathe the Sire to laud the Son,
But closed the tyrant-hater he begun.

—George Gordon, Lord Byron, "Dedication"
to *Don Juan,* 1818, stanza 10

JOHN KEATS "ON A LOCK OF MILTON'S HAIR" (1818)

English poet John Keats (1795–1821) lost both parents by the time he was 15, was taken in as a surgeon's apprentice, and then left behind his medical ambitions to pursue literature. He befriended other romantic authors and thinkers, such as Percy Shelley, William Wordsworth, and Leigh Hunt. After taking care of his brother Tom, who had a fatal case of consumption, Keats developed consumption himself, leaving him in weakened health. On the advice of his doctor, Keats moved to Italy in 1820, where he died in Rome in 1821. Despite his short life, he produced poetry that is still powerful and popular.

The amount of influence John Milton's works had on Keats is a point of great critical contention among literary critics who focus on the romantics. While some may have overly exaggerated the connection, it is clear that Keats both admired and wrestled with the works of Milton, which Keats's friends had compelled him to study. The long poem *Hyperion* was so indebted to *Paradise Lost* that Keats rewrote it into *The Fall of Hyperion* in order to make it less so; the rewrite still shows significant stylistic influences nonetheless.

In "On Seeing a Lock of Milton's Hair," Keats voices praise for what he perceives as Milton's timeless genius, the embodiment of the Platonic values conflating beauty and truth that Keats celebrates as well in "Ode on a Grecian Urn."

Chief of organic numbers!
Old Scholar of the Spheres!
Thy spirit never slumbers,
But rolls about our ears
For ever and for ever!
O what a mad endeavour
Worketh He,
Who to thy sacred and ennobled hearse

Would offer a burnt sacrifice of verse
And melody.
How heavenward thou soundest!
Live Temple of sweet noise,
And Discord unconfoundest,
Giving Delight new joys,
And Pleasure nobler pinions
O where are thy dominions?
    Lend thine ear
To a young Delian oath—ay, by thy soul,
By all that from thy mortal lips did roll,
And by the kernel of thy earthly love,
Beauty in things on earth and things above.
I swear!
When every childish fashion
Has vanished from my rhyme,
Will I, grey gone in passion,
Leave to an after-time
Hymning and Harmony
Of thee and of thy works, and of thy life;
But vain is now the burning and the strife;
Pangs are in vain, until I grow high-rife
With old Philosophy,
And mad with glimpses of futurity.
For many years my offerings must be hush'd;
When I do speak, I'll think upon this hour,
Because I feel my forehead hot and flushed,
Even at the simplest vassal of thy power.
A lock of thy bright hair,—
Sudden it came,
And I was startled when I caught thy name
Coupled so unaware;
Yet at the moment temperate was my blood—
thought I had beheld it from the flood!

          —John Keats, "On a Lock of Milton's Hair," 1818

Thomas Campbell (1819)

Scottish poet Thomas Campbell (1777–1844) attended Glasgow University, leaving for Edinburgh to become a tutor, where he began his career as a writer. Many of his better-known poems center on issues of justice and freedom, as he was influenced by the American and French revolutions. His early lengthy poem "The Pleasures of Hope," written in 1799, looks to a better world freed from exploitation and corruption. He then wrote a series of martial poems, "Ye Mariners of England," "The Battle of the Baltic," and "Hohenlinden," celebrating British naval power, Horatio Nelson's victory, and a French-Austrian land battle, successively. He also wrote historical, biographical, and literary critical essays for periodical and book publication to help supplement his income. The following selection on Milton's greatness is excerpted from the introduction to *Specimens of the British Poets* (1819).

He stood alone and aloof above his times, the bard of immortal subjects, and, as far as there is perpetuity in language, of immortal fame. The very choice of those subjects bespoke a contempt for any species of excellence that was attainable by other men. There is something that overawes the mind in conceiving his long deliberated selection of that theme—his attempting it when his eyes were shut upon the face of nature—his dependence, we might almost say, on supernatural inspiration, and in the calm air of strength with which he opens *Paradise Lost,* beginning a mighty performance without the appearance of an effort. Taking the subject all in all, his powers could nowhere else have enjoyed the same scope. It was only from the height of this great argument that he could look back upon eternity past, and forward upon eternity to come; that he could survey the abyss of infernal darkness, open visions of Paradise, or ascend to heaven and breathe empyreal air.

—Thomas Campbell,
An Essay on English Poetry, 1819

Percy Bysshe Shelley
"Excerpt from *Adonais*" (1821)

Written upon the death of friend and fellow poet John Keats, Percy Bysshe Shelley's lament *Adonais* was influenced in part by Milton's elegy "Lycidas."

Most musical of mourners, weep again!
Lament anew, Urania!—He died,
Who was the Sire of an immortal strain,
Blind, old, and lonely, when his country's pride,
The priest, the slave, and the liberticide,

Trampled and mocked with many a loathèd rite
Of lust and blood; he went, unterrified,
Into the gulf of death; but his clear Sprite
Yet reigns o'er earth; the third among the sons of light.
> —Percy Bysshe Shelley, *Adonais*, 1821, stanza 4

ROBERT SOUTHEY (1821)

The brother-in-law of Samuel Taylor Coleridge, Robert Southey (1774–1843) was a prolific writer of both poetry and prose. He began studies at Oxford University to prepare for the ministry, but his deist and revolutionary leanings precipitated his withdrawal after two terms. While there, he wrote his first successful work, *Joan of Arc, An Epic Poem*, which showcased his revolutionary spirit. He married a working-class woman, Edith Fricker, and met Coleridge in 1794, which was to become the most important relationship of his writing career. The two worked on plans for creating a pantisocracy (equal rule by all) in the Susquehanna Valley of Pennsylvania, which never came to fruition because of economic shortfalls and ideological differences between the friends. Coleridge had meanwhile married Edith Fricker's sister Sarah. Southey went on to study law and travel to Spain and Portugal, where he wrote poetry and was inspired to produce his 1807 *Letters from England: By Don Manuel Alvarez Espriella*, a collection of works by a fictitious Spanish traveler who was, of course, Southey. Returning to England, Southey practiced law in London and resumed his friendship with Coleridge, visiting his home Greta Hall in Keswick in 1803 after a series of deaths in Southey's family. Coleridge left his wife and home, placing Southey in charge of Greta Hall, where he primarily remained until his death.

Southey continued writing poetry, including the epics *Thabala the Destroyer* (1801), *Madoc* (1805), *The Curse of Kehama* (1810), and *Roderick, the Last of the Goths* (1814). He then turned to biographies, developing a controlled prose style that has been highly praised, in contrast to his poetry that was often met with mixed reviews. However, it was his poetry that won him a position with the Tory court as poet laureate in 1813; many of his libertarian friends saw Southey as a political traitor. He wrote biographies of Methodism founder John Wesley; poet William Cowper; and patriotic figures Lord Nelson and the Duke of Wellington, among others. The older, more conservative Southey still held out hopes for a better society, focusing on instilling moral virtue through education, including reading the works of authors who could instill proper values in their readers, thus anticipating the work of Matthew Arnold.

With other emotion
Milton's severer shade I saw and, in reverence humbled
Gazed on that soul sublime: of passion now as of blindness
Heal'd, and no longer here to Kings and to Hierarchs hostile,
He was assoil'd from taint of the fatal fruit; and in Eden
Not again to be lost, consorted an equal with Angels.

—Robert Southey, *A Vision of Judgment*, 1821, section 9

WILLIAM ELLERY CHANNING (1826)

New England Unitarian preacher and theologian William Ellery Channing (1780–1842) was born in Newport, Rhode Island, and graduated from Harvard University. His theology countered the idea of New England Calvinism and influenced Ralph Waldo Emerson and the transcendental movement, as Channing believed. The minister was influenced by the writings of Frances Hutcheson, that humans are not basically evil by nature but are capable of unselfish generosity. His focus on self-culture, that is, developing inner spirituality, was the basis of Unitarian thought. Here, we see Channing's focus on Milton's self, rather than his religion.

This character of power runs through all Milton's works. His descriptions of nature show a free and bold hand. He has no need of the minute, graphic skill which we prize in Cowper or Crabbe. With a few strong or delicate touches, he impresses, as it were, his own mind on the scenes which he would describe, and kindles the imagination of the gifted reader to clothe them with the same radiant hues under which they appeared to his own. This attribute of power is universally felt to characterize Milton. His sublimity is in every man's mouth. Is it felt that his poetry breathes a sensibility and tenderness hardly surpassed by its sublimity? We apprehend that the grandeur of Milton's mind has thrown some shade over his milder beauties; and this it has done, not only by being more striking and imposing, but by the tendency of vast mental energy to give a certain calmness to the expression of tenderness and deep feeling.

—William Ellery Channing, *Remarks on the Character and Writings of John Milton*, 1826

John Sterling "Shades of the Dead" (1829)

Milton was abundantly skilled in the dialectic art; he had a divine intuition into the logic of poetry; but he was not particularly remarkable, among men of genius, for penetrating and comprehensive intellect. This is very clear from his political and theological writings. His scheme of Government is that of a purely ideal commonwealth, and has the fault common to the greater number of such conceptions, that it never could be practised, except among beings for whom no government at all would be necessary. His opinions as to a Church Establishment are of an exactly similar description; and no imagination less powerful than his could have realized such visions to any mind. Nor could these phantom plans have obtained, in the thoughts of a nation, the living force necessary to their action, unless every man had been able to breathe into them from himself a breath of existence as powerful as that with which they were imbued by their creator.

—John Sterling, "Shades of the Dead," 1829, Essays
and Tales, 1848, volume 1, edited by Hare, p. 76

James Montgomery (1833)

Milton frequently innovates upon the high harmonies of his *accented* verse with the substitution of *quantities;* sometimes difficult at first sight to master, but generally admirable in effect, and heightening,—even when harshest, the majesty of his strains like a momentary crash of discord, thrown by the skilful organist, into the full tide of instrumental music, which gives intenser sweetness to what follows.

—James Montgomery, *Lectures on General
Literature,* 1833, p. 92

Thomas De Quincey (1835)

Essayist Thomas De Quincey (1785–1859) was a native of Manchester, England, and admirer of William Wordsworth, whom he tried to visit in Grasmere in 1802. De Quincey's shyness overtook him, so he visited Wales instead and then attended Oxford University from 1803 to 1808 without completing his examinations. Finally, in 1807, he met William and Dorothy Wordsworth and their circle of friends, a group of thinkers who were highly influential on De Quincey's life and works. He later worked on editing and publishing one of Wordsworth's pamphlets and came to live with the Wordsworths before moving to nearby Dove Cottage, their former home.

Dividing his time studying law in London and staying in other parts of England, including Grasmere, De Quincey continued using the opium with which he had first experimented in Oxford. His marriage to farmer's daughter Margaret Simpson in 1817, following the birth of their child, alienated him from the Wordsworths. He became editor of the *Westmoreland Gazette* in 1818, to which he brought a sensationalistic and polemical stance, angering the owners of the paper and hastening his resignation in 1819. De Quincey's turning point came in 1821 with the two-part publication by *London Magazine* of his *Confessions of an English Opium Eater*, a major work that translated the psychological probing of romantic poetry into prose. Following a positive reception from the magazine's readers, De Quincey published the work in book version. This important autobiography launched his career as journalist-essayist, in which he wrote biographies, coverage of historical events, and literary criticism.

In the following passage on Milton, from De Quincey's entry written for *Encylopedia Brittanica*, the author comments on Milton's diction, noting primarily his introduction of word choice that is other than Anglo-Saxon.

Milton was not an extensive or discursive thinker, as Shakspeare was; for the motions of his mind were slow, solemn, sequacious, like those of the planets; not agile and assimilative; not attracting all things within its own sphere; not multiform: repulsion was the law of his intellect—he moved in solitary grandeur. Yet, merely from this quality of grandeur, unapproachable grandeur, his intellect demanded a larger infusion of Latinity into his diction. For the same reason (and without such aids he would have had no proper element in which to move his wings) he enriched his diction with Hellenisms and with Hebraisms; but never, as could be easy to show, without a full justification in the result. Two things may be asserted of all his exotic idioms—1st, That they express what could not have been expressed by any native idiom; 2nd, That they harmonize with the English language, and give a colouring of the antique, but not any sense of strangeness, to the diction.

—Thomas De Quincey, Autobiography, 1835

EDWIN GUEST (1838)

It will not be easy to acquit Milton, altogether, of injustice towards his countryman; but if he disdained to mention Surrey, he also disdained to copy from him—both the merits and the faults of Milton's versification are *his own!* . . . Perhaps no man ever paid the same attention to the quality of his rhythm as Milton. What other poets affect, as it were, by chance, Milton achieved by the aid of science and of art; he *studied* the aptness of his numbers, and diligently tutored an ear, which nature had gifted with the most delicate sensibility. In the flow of his rhythm, in the quality of his letter-sounds, in the disposition of his pauses, his verse almost ever *fits* the subject; and so insensibly does poetry blend with this—the last beauty of exquisite versification, that the reader may sometimes doubt whether it be the thought itself, or merely the happiness of its expression, which is the source of a gratification so deeply felt.

—Edwin Guest, *A History of English Rhythms*, 1838, volume 2, pp. 240–42

Thomas Carlyle (1838)

The British essayist Thomas Carlyle (1795–1881) was an outspoken and sometimes controversial lecturer and biographer who was immensely influential in shaping Victorian political, spiritual, and aesthetic concepts. Born in Scotland, he attended Edinburgh University, which he left without taking a degree, with the initial aim of entering the clergy; but his readings in philosophers Edmund Gibbon and David Hume made him question his faith. Carlyle later became friends with philosopher John Stuart Mill, who also influenced his thought. Carlyle developed a sense of spirituality that ran counter to Scottish Calvinism and other modes of established Christianity but also to skepticism; he called his mode of belief "natural supernaturalism," a secular religion based on late romantic notions of wonder and imagination.

Commissioned by *London Magazine* in 1823 to write an essay on German romantic writer Friedrich Schiller, Carlyle began his career in crafting biographies of those whom he deemed important. The article was expanded to book length, the first of many literary biographies Carlyle would produce. He saw writing the lives of great personages as an important means for society to understand the genesis of great ideas; he wanted readers to see and feel the subjects' lives deeply. In addition to his work on Schiller, Carlyle wrote on other German writers, helping to shape the public's taste for their works. He wrote biographies of Walter Scott, an essay on Boswell's *Life of Johnson* (re-evaluating the writer and critic Samuel Johnson), Michel de Montaigne, John Sterling, and Friederich II, as well a volume on the French Revolution. In *On Heroes, Hero-Worship & the Heroic in History*, an 1840 compilation of a series of lectures on literature and history, Carlyle reasserts his belief in the artist as priest of the divine workings of the universe; art flourishes when the established religions begin to crumble, as in the age of Shakespeare, transitioning from Catholic to Anglican belief.

The following excerpt, from a lecture on Milton, reflects Carlyle's preference for Shakespeare, whom he views as universal in his appeal, over Milton, precisely because of the latter's adherence to too narrow a religious vision.

He must not be ranked with Shakespeare. He stands relative to Shakespeare as Tasso or Ariosto does to Dante, as Virgil to Homer. He is conscious of writing an epic, and of being the great man he is. No great man ever felt so great a consciousness as Milton. That consciousness was the measure of his greatness; he was not one of those who reach into actual contact with the deep fountain of greatness. His *Paradise Lost* is not an epic in its composition as Shakespeare's utterances are epic. It does not come out of the heart of things; he hadn't it lying there to pour it out in one gush; it seems rather to have been welded together afterward. His sympathies with things are much narrower than Shakespeare's—too sectarian. In universality of mind there is no hatred; it doubtless rejects what is displeasing, but not in hatred for it. Everything has a right to exist. Shakespeare was not polemical: Milton was polemical altogether.

—Thomas Carlyle, *Lectures on the History of Literature*, 1838, p. 165

RALPH WALDO EMERSON "MILTON" (1838)

Associated with the American transcendentalist movement, Ralph Waldo Emerson (1803–82) was born in Boston, Massachusetts, to a Unitarian minister and a Puritan mother. Emerson attended Harvard as an undergraduate and proceeded on to Harvard Divinity School; vision problems precluded earning his master's degree there, but he was ordained and served at Second Church in Boston. After his first wife's death and grappling with issues of faith, he resigned his ministerial post. Later, he married Lydia Jackson and moved to Concord, Massachusetts, where he entertained friends Margaret Fuller and Henry Thoreau, among others, and began a lecturing and writing career, primarily focusing on letters, poetry, and essays. In 1840, Emerson began the magazine *The Dial* in conjunction with Bronson Alcott (brother of Louisa May Alcott), George Ripley, and Margaret Fuller. His small volume *Nature* was instrumental in precipitating the transcendentalist movement, which borrowed in turn from European romanticism, particularly metaphysical ideas about the importance of learning through the natural world, to which the human spirit is tied. He began the Transcendental Club with other adherents of the movement. Emerson's best-known essay, *Self-Reliance*, epitomizes his nonconformist philosophy.

Emerson's letters and journals record his reading and unwavering admiration of many of Milton's works, though he criticizes him for more polemical pieces. Above all, Emerson sees in Milton an independent thinker in a difficult age, a like-minded man who loves and celebrates the greatness of nature and the human spirit.

The discovery of the lost work of Milton, the treatise *Of the Christian Doctrine,* in 1823, drew a sudden attention to his name. For a short time the literary journals were filled with disquisitions on his genius; new editions of his works, and new compilations of his life, were published. But the newfound book having in itself less attraction than any other work of Milton, the curiosity of the public as quickly subsided, and left the poet to the enjoyment of his permanent fame, or to such increase or abatement of it only as is incidental to a sublime genius, quite independent of the momentary challenge of universal attention to his claims.

But if the new and temporary renown of the poet is silent again, it is nevertheless true that he has gained, in this age, some increase of permanent praise. The fame of a great man is not rigid and stony like his bust. It changes with time. It needs time to give it due perspective. It was very easy to remark an altered tone in the criticism when Milton reappeared as an author, fifteen years ago, from any that had been bestowed on the same subject before. It implied merit indisputable and illustrious; yet so near to the modern mind as to be still alive and life-giving. The aspect of Milton, to this generation, will be part of the history of the nineteenth century. There is no name in English literature between his age and ours that rises into any approach to his own. And as a man's fame, of course, characterizes those who give it, as much as him who receives it, the new criticism indicated a change in the public taste, and a change which the poet himself might claim to have wrought.

The reputation of Milton had already undergone one or two revolutions long anterior to its recent aspects. In his lifetime, he was little or not at all known as a poet, but obtained great respect from his contemporaries as an accomplished scholar and a formidable pamphleteer. His poems fell unregarded among his countrymen. His prose writings, especially the *Defence of the English People,* seem to have been read with avidity. These tracts are remarkable compositions. They are earnest, spiritual, rich with allusion, sparkling with innumerable ornaments; but as writings designed to gain a practical point, they fail. They are not effective, like similar productions of Swift and Burke; or, like what became also controversial tracts, several masterly speeches in the history of the American Congress. Milton seldom deigns a glance at the obstacles that are to be overcome before that which he proposes can be done. There is no attempt to conciliate,—no mediate, no preparatory course suggested,—but, peremptory and impassioned, he demands, on the instant, an ideal justice. Therein they are discriminated from modern writings, in which a regard to the actual is all but universal.

Their rhetorical excellence must also suffer some deduction. They have no perfectness. These writings are wonderful for the truth, the learning, the subtility and pomp of the language; but the whole is sacrificed to the particular. Eager to do fit justice to each thought, he does not subordinate it so as to project the main argument. He writes whilst he is heated; the piece shows all the rambles and resources of indignation, but he has never *integrated* the parts of the argument in his mind. The reader is fatigued with admiration, but is not yet master of the subject.

Two of his pieces may be excepted from this description, one for its faults, the other for its excellence. The *Defence of the People of England,* on which his contemporary fame was founded, is, when divested of its pure Latinity, the worst of his works. Only its general aim, and a few elevated passages, can save it. We could be well content if the flames to which it was condemned at Paris, at Toulouse, and at London, had utterly consumed it. The lover of his genius will always regret that he should not have taken counsel of his own lofty heart at this, as at other times, and have written from the deep convictions of love and right, which are the foundations of civil liberty. There is little poetry or prophecy in this mean and ribald scolding. To insult Salmasius, not to acquit England, is the main design. What under heaven had Madame de Saumaise, or the manner of living of Saumaise, or Salmasius, or his blunders of grammar, or his niceties of diction, to do with the solemn question whether Charles Stuart had been rightly slain? Though it evinces learning and critical skill, yet, as an historical argument, it cannot be valued with similar disquisitions of Robertson and Hallam, and even less celebrated scholars. But when he comes to speak of the reason of the thing, then he always recovers himself. The voice of the mob is silent, and Milton speaks. And the peroration, in which he implores his countrymen to refute this adversary by their great deeds, is in a just spirit. The other piece is his *Areopagitica,* the discourse, addressed to the Parliament, in favor of removing the censorship of the press; the most splendid of his prose works. It is, as

Luther said of one of Melancthon's writings, "alive, hath hands and feet,—and not like Erasmus's sentences, which were made, not grown." The weight of the thought is equalled by the vivacity of the expression, and it cheers as well as teaches. This tract is far the best known and the most read of all, and is still a magazine of reasons for the freedom of the press. It is valuable in history as an argument addressed to a government to produce a practical end, and plainly presupposes a very peculiar state of society.

But deeply as that peculiar state of society, in which and for which Milton wrote, has engraved itself in the remembrance of the world, it shares the destiny which overtakes everything local and personal in Nature; and the accidental facts on which a battle of principles was fought have already passed, or are fast passing, into oblivion. We have lost all interest in Milton as the redoubted disputant of a sect; but by his own innate worth this man has steadily risen in the world's reverence, and occupies a more imposing place in the mind of men at this hour than ever before.

It is the aspect which he presents to this generation, that alone concerns us. Milton the polemic has lost his popularity long ago; and if we skip the pages of *Paradise Lost* where "God the Father argues like a school divine," so did the next age to his own. But, we are persuaded, he kindles a love and emulation in us which he did not in foregoing generations. We think we have seen and heard criticism upon the poems, which the bard himself would have more valued than the recorded praise of Dryden, Addison and Johnson, because it came nearer to the mark; was finer and closer appreciation; the praise of intimate knowledge and delight; and, of course, more welcome to the poet than the general and vague acknowledgment of his genius by those able but unsympathizing critics. We think we have heard the recitation of his verses by genius which found in them that which itself would say; recitation which told, in the diamond sharpness of every articulation,that now first was such perception and enjoyment possible; the perception and enjoyment of all his varied rhythm, and his perfect fusion of the classic and the English styles. This is a poet's right; for every masterpiece of art goes on for some ages reconciling the world unto itself, and despotically fashioning the public ear. The opposition to it, always greatest at first, continually decreases and at last ends; and a new race grows up in the taste and spirit of the work, with the utmost advantage for seeing intimately its power and beauty.

But it would be great injustice to Milton to consider him as enjoying merely a critical reputation. It is the prerogative of this great man to stand at this hour foremost of all men in literary history, and so (shall we not say?) of all men, in the power *to inspire*. Virtue goes out of him into others. Leaving out of view the pretensions of our contemporaries (always an incalculable influence), we think no man can be named whose mind still acts on the cultivated intellect of England and America with an energy comparable to that of Milton. As a poet, Shakspeare undoubtedly transcends, and far surpasses him in his popularity with foreign nations; but Shakspeare is a voice merely; who and what he was that sang, that sings, we know not. Milton stands erect, commanding, still visible as a man among men, and reads the laws of the moral sentiment to the new-born race. There is something pleasing in the affection with which we can regard a man who died a hundred and sixty years ago in the other hemisphere, who, in respect to personal relations, is to us as the wind, yet by an influence purely spiritual makes us jealous for his fame as for that of a near friend. He is identified in the mind with all select and holy images, with the supreme interests of the human race. If hereby we attain any more precision, we proceed to say that we think no man in these later ages, and few men ever, possessed so great a conception of the manly character. Better than any other he has discharged the office of every great man, namely, to raise the idea of Man in the minds of his contemporaries and of posterity,—to draw after Nature a life of man, exhibiting such a composition of grace, of strength and of virtue, as poet had not described nor hero lived. Human nature in these ages is indebted to him for its best portrait. Many philosophers in England, France and Germany have formally dedicated their study to this problem; and we think it impossible to recall one in those countries who communicates the same vibration of hope, of self-reverence, of piety, of delight in beauty, which the name of Milton awakens. Lord Bacon, who has written much and with prodigious ability on this science, shrinks and falters before the absolute and uncourtly Puritan. Bacon's Essays are the portrait of an ambitious and profound calculator,—a great man of the vulgar sort. Of the upper world of man's being they speak few and faint words. The man of Locke is virtuous without enthusiasm, and intelligent without poetry. Addison, Pope, Hume and Johnson, students, with very unlike temper and success, of the same subject, cannot, taken together, make any pretension to the amount or the quality of Milton's inspirations. The man of Lord Chesterfield is unworthy to touch his garment's hem. Franklin's man is a frugal, inoffensive, thrifty citizen, but savors of nothing heroic. The genius of France has not, even in her best days, yet culminated in any one head—not in Rousseau, not in Pascal, not in Fenelon—into such perception of all the attributes of humanity as to entitle it to any rivalry in these lists. In Germany, the greatest writers are still too recent to institute a comparison; and yet we are tempted to say that art and not life seems to be the end of their effort. But the idea of a purer existence than any he saw around him, to be realized in the life and conversation of men, inspired every act and every writing of John Milton. He defined the object of education to be, "to fit a man to perform justly, skilfully and magnanimously all the offices, both private and public, of peace and war." He declared that "he who would aspire to write well hereafter in laudable things, ought himself to be a true poem; that is, a composition and pattern of the best and honorablest things, not presuming to sing high praises of heroic men or famous cities, unless he have in himself the experience and the practice of all that which is praiseworthy." Nor is there in literature a more noble outline of a wise external education than that which he drew up, at the age of thirty-six, in his Letter to Samuel Hartlib. The muscles, the nerves and the flesh with which this skeleton is to be filled up and covered exist in his works and must be sought there.

For the delineation of this heroic image of man, Milton enjoyed singular advantages. Perfections of body and of mind are attributed to him by his biographers, that, if the anecdotes had come down from a greater distance of time, or had not been in part furnished or corroborated by political enemies, would lead us to suspect the portraits were ideal, like the Cyrus of Xenophon, the Telemachus of Fenelon, or the popular traditions of Alfred the Great.

Handsome to a proverb, he was called the lady of his college. Aubrey says, "This harmonical and ingenuous soul dwelt in a beautiful, well-proportioned body." His manners and his carriage did him no injustice. Wood, his political opponent, relates that "his deportment was affable, his gait erect and manly, bespeaking courage and undauntedness." Aubrey adds a sharp trait, that "he pronounced the letter R very hard, a certain sign of satirical genius." He had the senses of a Greek. His eye was quick, and he was accounted an excellent master of his rapier. His ear for music was so acute that he was not only enthusiastic in his love, but a skilful performer himself; and his voice, we are told, was delicately sweet and harmonious. He insists that music shall make a part of a generous education.

With these keen perceptions, he naturally received a love of Nature and a rare susceptibility to impressions from external beauty. In the midst of London, he seems, like the creatures of the field and the forest, to have been tuned in concord with the order of the world; for, he believed, his poetic vein only flowed from the autumnal to the vernal equinox; and in his essay on Education, he doubts whether, in the fine days of spring, any study can be accomplished by young men. "In those vernal seasons of the year, when the air is calm and pleasant, it were an injury and sullenness against Nature not to go out and see her riches and partake in her rejoicing with heaven and earth." His sensibility to impressions from beauty needs no proof from his history; it shines through every page. The form and the voice of Leonora Baroni seemed to have captivated him in Rome, and to her he addressed his Italian sonnets and Latin epigrams.

To these endowments it must be added that his address and his conversation were worthy of his fame. His house was resorted to by men of wit, and foreigners came to England, we are told, "to see the Lord Protector and Mr. Milton." In a letter to one of his foreign correspondents, Emeric Bigot, and in reply apparently to some compliment on his powers of conversation, he writes: "Many have been celebrated for their compositions, whose common conversation and intercourse have betrayed no marks of sublimity or genius. But as far as possible, I aim to show myself equal in thought and speech to what I have written, if I have written anything well."

These endowments received the benefit of a careful and happy discipline. His father's care, seconded by his own endeavor, introduced him to a profound skill in all the treasures of Latin, Greek, Hebrew and Italian tongues; and, to enlarge and enliven his elegant learning, he was sent into Italy, where he beheld the remains of ancient art, and the rival works of Raphael, Michael Angelo and Correggio; where, also, he received social and academical honors from the learned and the great. In Paris, he became acquainted with Grotius; in Florence or Rome, with Galileo; and probably no traveller ever entered that country of history with better right to its hospitality, none upon whom its influences could have fallen more congenially.

Among the advantages of his foreign travel, Milton certainly did not count it the least that it contributed to forge and polish that great weapon of which he acquired such extraordinary mastery,—his power of language. His lore of foreign tongues added daily to his consummate skill in the use of his own. He was a benefactor of the English tongue by showing its capabilities. Very early in life he became conscious that he had more to say to his fellow men than they had fit words to embody. At nineteen years, in a college exercise, he addresses his native language, saying to it that it would be his choice to leave trifles for a grave argument,—

Such as may make thee search thy coffers round,
Before thou clothe my fancy in fit sound;
Such where the deep transported mind may soar
Above the wheeling poles, and at Heaven's door
Look in, and see each blissful deity,
How he before the thunderous throne doth lie.

Michael Angelo calls "him alone an artist, whose hands can execute what his mind has conceived." The world, no doubt, contains many of that class of men whom Wordsworth denominates *silent poets,* whose minds teem with images which they want words to clothe. But Milton's mind seems to have no thought or emotion which refused to be recorded. His mastery of his native tongue was more than to use it as well as any other; he cast it into new forms. He uttered in it things unheard before. Not imitating but rivalling Shakspeare, he scattered, in tones of prolonged and delicate melody, his pastoral and romantic fancies; then, soaring into unattempted strains, he made it capable of an unknown majesty, and bent it to express every trait of beauty, every shade of thought; and searched the kennel and jakes as well as the palaces of sound for the harsh discords of his polemic wrath. We may even apply to his performance on the instrument of language, his own description of music:—

Notes, with many a winding bout
Of linked sweetness long drawn out,
With wanton heed and giddy cunning,
The melting voice through mazes running,
Untwisting all the chains that tie
The hidden soul of harmony.

But whilst Milton was conscious of possessing this intellectual voice, penetrating through ages and propelling its melodious undulations forward through the coming world, he knew that this mastery of language was a secondary power, and he respected the mysterious source whence it had its spring; namely, clear conceptions and a devoted heart. "For me," he said, in his *Apology for Smectymnuus,* "although I cannot say that I am utterly untrained in those rules which best rhetoricians have given, or unacquainted with those examples which the prime authors of eloquence have written in any learned tongue, yet true eloquence I find to be none but the serious and hearty love of truth; and that whose mind soever is fully possessed with a fervent desire to know good things, and with the dearest charity to infuse the knowledge of them into others, when such a man would speak, his words, by what I can express, like so many nimble and airy servitors, trip about him at command, and in well-ordered files, as he would wish, fall aptly into their own places."

But as basis or fountain of his rare physical and intellectual accomplishments, the man Milton was just and devout. He is rightly dear to mankind, because in him, among so many perverse and partial men of genius,—in him humanity rights itself; the old eternal goodness finds a home in his breast, and for once shows itself beautiful. His gifts are subordinated to his moral sentiments; and his virtues are so graceful that they seem rather talents than labors. Among so many contrivances as the world has seen to make holiness ugly, in Milton at least it was so pure a flame that the foremost impression his character makes is that of elegance. The victories of the conscience in him are gained by the commanding charm which all the severe and restrictive virtues have for him. His virtues remind us of what Plutarch said of Timoleon's victories, that they resembled Homer's verses, they ran so easy and natural. His habits of living were austere. He was abstemious in diet, chaste, an early riser, and industrious. He tell us, in a Latin poem, that the lyrist may indulge in wine and in a freer life; but that he who would write an epic to the nations must eat beans and drink water. Yet in his severity is no grimace or effort. He serves from love, not from fear. He is innocent and exact, because his taste was so pure and delicate. He acknowledges to his friend Diodati, at the age of twenty-one, that he is enamoured, if ever any was, of moral perfection: "For whatever the Deity may have bestowed upon me in other respects, he has certainly inspired me, if any ever were inspired, with a passion for the good and fair. Nor did Ceres, according to the fable, ever seek her daughter Proserpine with such unceasing solicitude as I have sought this *tou kalou idean,* this perfect model of the beautiful in all forms and appearances of things."

When he was charged with loose habits of living, he declares that "a certain niceness of nature, an honest haughtiness and self-esteem either of what I was or what I might be, and a modesty, kept me still above those low descents of mind beneath which he must deject and plunge himself that can agree" to such degradation. "His mind gave him," he said, "that every free and gentle spirit, without that oath of chastity, ought to be born a knight; nor needed to expect the gilt spur, or the laying of a sword upon his shoulder, to stir him up, by his counsel and his arm, to secure and protect" attempted innocence.

He states these things, he says, "to show that though Christianity had been but slightly taught him, yet a certain reservedness of natural disposition and moral discipline, learned out of the noblest philosophy, was enough to keep him in disdain of far less incontinences than these" that had been charged on him. In like spirit, he replies to the suspicious calumny respecting his morning haunts. "Those morning haunts are where they should be, at home; not sleeping, or concocting the surfeits of an irregular feast, but up and stirring, in winter, often ere the sound of any bell awake men to labor or devotion; in summer, as oft with the bird that first rouses, or not much tardier, to read good authors, or cause them to be read, till the attention be weary, or memory have its perfect fraught; then with useful and generous labors preserving the body's health and hardiness, to render lightsome, clear and not lumpish obedience to the mind, to the cause of religion and our country's liberty, when it shall require firm hearts in sound bodies to stand and cover their stations. These are the morning practices." This native honor never forsook him. It is the spirit of *Comus,* the loftiest song in the praise of chastity that is in any language. It always sparkles in his eyes. It breathed itself over his decent form. It refined his amusements, which consisted in gardening, in exercise with the sword and in playing on the organ. It engaged his interest in chivalry, in courtesy, in whatsoever savored of generosity and nobleness. This magnanimity shines in all his life. He accepts a high impulse at every risk, and deliberately undertakes the defence of the English people, when advised by his physicians that he does it at the cost of sight. There is a forbearance even in his polemics. He opens the war and strikes the first blow. When he had cut down his opponents, he left the details of death and plunder to meaner partisans. He said, "he had learned the prudence of the Roman soldier, not to stand breaking of legs, when the breath was quite out of the body."

To this antique heroism, Milton added the genius of the Christian sanctity. Few men could be cited who have so well understood what is peculiar in the Christian ethics, and the precise aid it has brought to men, in being an emphatic affirmation of the omnipotence of spiritual laws, and, by way of marking the contrast to vulgar opinions, laying its chief stress on humility. The indifference of a wise mind to what is called high and low, and the fact that true greatness is a perfect humility, are revelations of Christianity which Milton well understood. They give an inexhaustible truth to all his compositions. His firm grasp of this truth is his weapon against the prelates. He celebrates in the martyrs "the unresistible might of weakness. " He told the bishops that "instead of showing the reason of their lowly condition from divine example and command, they seek to prove their high preeminence from human consent and authority." He advises that in country places, rather than to trudge many miles to a church, public worship be maintained nearer home, as in a house or barn. "For notwithstanding the gaudy superstition of some still devoted ignorantly to temples, we may be well assured that he who disdained not to be born in a manger disdains not to be preached in a barn." And the following passage, in the *Reason of Church Government,* indicates his own perception of the doctrine of humility. "Albeit I must confess to be half in doubt whether I should bring it forth or no, it being so contrary to the eye of the world, that I shall endanger either not to be regarded, or not to be understood. For who is there, almost, that measures wisdom by simplicity, strength by suffering, dignity by lowliness?" Obeying this sentiment, Milton deserved the apostrophe of Wordsworth:—

Pure as the naked heavens, majestic, free,
So didst thou travel on life's common way
In cheerful godliness; and yet thy heart
The lowliest duties on itself did lay.

He laid on himself the lowliest duties. Johnson petulantly taunts Milton with "great promise and small performance," in returning from Italy because his country was in danger, and then opening a private school. Milton, wiser, felt no absurdity in this conduct. He returned into his revolutionized country, and assumed an honest and useful task, by which he might serve the state daily, whilst he launched from time to time his formidable bolts against the enemies of liberty. He felt the heats of that "love" which "esteems no office mean." He compiled a logic for boys; he wrote a grammar; and devoted much of his time to the preparing of a Latin dictionary. But the religious sentiment warmed his writings and conduct with the highest affection of faith. The memorable covenant, which in his youth, in the second book of the *Reason of Church Government,* he makes with God and his reader, expressed the faith of his old age. For the first time since many ages, the invocations of the Eternal Spirit in the commencement of his books are not poetic forms, but are thoughts, and so are still read with delight. His views of choice of profession, and choice in marriage, equally expect a divine leading.

Thus chosen, by the felicity of his nature and his breeding, for the clear perception of all that is graceful and all that is great in man, Milton was not less happy in his times. His birth fell upon the agitated years when the discontents of the English Puritans were fast drawing to a head against the tyranny of the Stuarts. No period has surpassed that in the general activity of mind. It is said that no opinion, no civil, religious, moral dogma can be produced that was not broached in the fertile brain of that age. Questions that involve all social and personal rights were hasting to be decided by the sword, and were searched by eyes to which the love of freedom, civil and religious, lent new illumination. Milton, gentle, learned, delicately bred in all the elegancy of art and learning, was set down in England in the stern, almost fanatic society of the Puritans. The part he took, the zeal of his fellowship, make us acquainted with the greatness of his spirit as in tranquil times we could not have known it. Susceptible as Burke to the attractions of historical prescription, of royalty, of chivalry, of an ancient church illustrated by old martyrdoms and installed in cathedrals,—he threw himself, the flower of elegancy, on the side of the reeking conventicle; the side of humanity, but unlearned and unadorned. His muse was brave and humane, as well as sweet. He felt the dear love of native

land and native language. The humanity which warms his pages begins, as
it should, at home. He preferred his own English, so manlike he was, to the
Latin, which contained all the treasures of his memory. "My mother bore me,"
he said, "a speaker of what God made mine own, and not a translator." He
told the Parliament that "the imprimaturs of Lambeth House had been writ
in Latin; for that our English, the language of men ever famous and foremost
in the achievements of liberty, will not easily find servile letters enow to spell
such a dictatory presumption." At one time he meditated writing a poem on
the settlement of Britain, and a history of England was one of the three main
tasks which he proposed to himself. He proceeded in it no further than to the
Conquest. He studied with care the character of his countrymen, and once
in the *History,* and once again in the *Reason of Church Government,* he has
recorded his judgment of the English genius.

Thus drawn into the great controversies of the times, in them he is
never lost in a party. His private opinions and private conscience always
distinguish him. That which drew him to the party was his love of liberty,
ideal liberty; this therefore he could not sacrifice to any party. Toland
tells us, "As he looked upon true and absolute freedom to be the greatest
happiness of this life, whether to societies or single persons, so he thought
constraint of any sort to be the utmost misery; for which reason he used to
tell those about him the entire satisfaction of his mind that he had constantly
employed his strength and faculties in the defence of liberty, and in direct
opposition to slavery." Truly he was an apostle of freedom; of freedom in
the house, in the state, in the church; freedom of speech, freedom of the
press; yet in his own mind discriminated from savage license, because that
which he desired was the liberty of the wise man, containing itself in the
limits of virtue. He pushed, as far as any in that democratic age, his ideas of
civil liberty. He proposed to establish a republic, of which the federal power
was weak and loosely defined, and the substantial power should remain
with primary assemblies. He maintained that a nation may try, judge and
slay their king, if he be a tyrant. He pushed as far his views of *ecclesiastical*
liberty. He taught the doctrine of unlimited toleration. One of his tracts is
writ to prove that no power on earth can compel in matters of religion. He
maintained the doctrine of *literary* liberty, denouncing the censorship of the
press, and insisting that a book shall come into the world as freely as a man,
so only it bear the name of author or printer, and be responsible for itself
like a man. He maintained the doctrine of *domestic* liberty, or the liberty of
divorce, on the ground that unfit disposition of mind was a better reason
for the act of divorce than infirmity of body, which was good ground in

law. The tracts he wrote on these topics are, for the most part, as fresh and pertinent to-day as they were then. The events which produced them, the practical issues to which they tend, are mere occasions for this philanthropist to blow his trumpet for human rights. They are all varied applications of one principle, the liberty of the wise man. He sought absolute truth, not accommodating truth. His opinions on all subjects are formed for man as he ought to be, for a nation of Miltons. He would be divorced when he finds in his consort unfit disposition; knowing that he should not abuse that liberty, because with his whole heart he abhors licentiousness and loves chastity. He defends the slaying of the king, because a king is a king no longer than he governs by the laws; "it would be right to kill Philip of Spain making an inroad into England, and what right the king of Spain hath to govern us at all, the same hath the king Charles to govern tyrannically." He would remove hirelings out of the church, and support preachers by voluntary contributions; requiring that such only should preach as have faith enough to accept so self-denying and precarious a mode of life, scorning to take thought for the aspects of prudence and expediency. The most devout man of his time, he frequented no church; probably from a disgust at the fierce spirit of the pulpits. And so, throughout all his actions and opinions, is he a consistent spiritualist, or believer in the omnipotence of spiritual laws. He wished that his writings should be communicated only to those who desired to see them. He thought nothing honest was low. He thought he could be famous only in proportion as he enjoyed the approbation of the good. He admonished his friend "not to admire military prowess, or things in which force is of most avail. For it would not be matter of rational wonder, if the wethers of our country should be born with horns that could batter down cities and towns. Learn to estimate great characters, not by the amount of animal strength, but by the habitual justice and temperance of their conduct."

Was there not a fitness in the undertaking of such a person to write a poem on the subject of Adam, the first man? By his sympathy with all Nature; by the proportion of his powers; by great knowledge, and by religion, he would reascend to the height from which our nature is supposed to have descended. From a just knowledge of what man should be, he described what he was. He beholds him as he walked in Eden:—

His fair large front and eye sublime declared
Absolute rule; and hyacinthine locks
Round from his parted forelock manly hung
Clustering, but not beneath his shoulders broad.

And the soul of this divine creature is excellent as his form. The tone of his thought and passion is as healthful, as even and as vigorous as befits the new and perfect model of a race of gods.

The perception we have attributed to Milton, of a purer ideal of humanity, modifies his poetic genius. The man is paramount to the poet. His fancy is never transcendent, extravagant; but as Bacon's imagination was said to be "the noblest that ever contented itself to minister to the understanding," so Milton's ministers to the character. Milton's sublimest song, bursting into heaven with its peals of melodious thunder, is the voice of Milton still. Indeed, throughout his poems, one may see, under a thin veil, the opinions, the feelings, even the incidents of the poet's life, still reappearing. The sonnets are all occasional poems. "L'Allegro" and "Il Penseroso" are but a finer autobiography of his youthful fancies at Harefield; the *Comus* a transcript, in charming numbers, of that philosophy of chastity, which, in the *Apology for Smectymnuus,* and in the *Reason of Church Government,* he declares to be his defence and religion. The *Samson Agonistes* is too broad an expression of his private griefs to be mistaken, and is a version of the *Doctrine and Discipline of Divorce.* The most affecting passages in *Paradise Lost* are personal allusions; and when we are fairly in Eden, Adam and Milton are often difficult to be separated. Again, in *Paradise Regained,* we have the most distinct marks of the progress of the poet's mind, in the revision and enlargement of his religious opinions. This may be thought to abridge his praise as a poet. It is true of Homer and Shakspeare that they do not appear in their poems; that those prodigious geniuses did cast themselves so totally into their song that their individuality vanishes, and the poet towers to the sky, whilst the man quite disappears. The fact is memorable. Shall we say that in our admiration and joy in these wonderful poems we have even a feeling of regret that the men knew not what they did; that they were too passive in their great service; were channels through which streams of thought flowed from a higher source, which they did not appropriate, did not blend with their own being? Like prophets, they seem but imperfectly aware of the import of their own utterances. We hesitate to say such things, and say them only to the unpleasing dualism, when the man and the poet show like a double consciousness. Perhaps we speak to no fact, but to mere fables, of an idle mendicant Homer, and of a Shakspeare content with a mean and jocular way of life. Be it how it may, the genius and office of Milton were different, namely, to ascend by the aids of his learning and his religion—by an equal perception, that is, of the past and the future—to a higher insight and more lively delineation of the heroic life of man. This was his poem; wherof all his indignant pamphlets and all his soaring verses are only single cantos or detached stanzas. It was plainly needful that his poetry should be a version of his own life, in order to give weight and solemnity to his thoughts; by which they might penetrate and possess the imagination and the will of mankind. The creations of Shakspeare are cast into the world of thought to no further end than to delight. Their intrinsic beauty is their excuse for being. Milton, fired "with dearest charity to infuse the knowledge of good things into others," tasked his giant imagination and exhausted the stores of his intellect for an end beyond, namely, to teach. His own conviction it is which gives such authority to his strain. Its reality is its force. If out of the heart it came, to the heart it must go. What schools and epochs of common rhymers would it need to make a counterbalance to the severe oracles of his muse:—

In them is plainest taught and easiest learnt,
What makes a nation happy, and keeps it so.

The lover of Milton reads one sense in his prose and in his metrical compositions; and sometimes the muse soars highest in the former, because the thought is more sincere. Of his prose in general, not the style alone but the argument also is poetic; according to Lord Bacon's definition of poetry, following that of Aristotle, "Poetry, not finding the actual world exactly conformed to its idea of good and fair, seeks to accommodate the shows of things to the desires of the mind, and to create an ideal world better than the world of experience." Such certainly is the explanation of Milton's tracts. Such is the apology to be entered for the plea for freedom of divorce; an essay, which, from the first, until now, has brought a degree of obloquy on his name. It was a sally of the extravagant spirit of the time, overjoyed, as in the French Revolution, with the sudden victories it had gained, and eager to carry on the standard of truth to new heights. It is to be regarded as a poem on one of the griefs of man's condition, namely, unfit marriage. And as many poems have been written upon unfit society, commending solitude, yet have not been proceeded against, though their end was hostile to the state; so should this receive that charity which an angelic soul, suffering more keenly than others from the unavoidable evils of human life, is entitled to.

We have offered no apology for expanding to such length our commentary on the character of John Milton; who, in old age, in solitude, in neglect, and blind, wrote the *Paradise Lost;* a man whom labor or danger never deterred from whatever efforts a love of the supreme interests of man prompted. For are we not the better; are not all men fortified by the remembrance of the bravery, the purity, the temperance, the toil, the independence and the angelic devotion of this man, who, in a revolutionary age, taking counsel only of himself, endeavored, in his writings and in his life, to carry out the life of man to new heights of spiritual grace and dignity, without any abatement of its strength?

—Ralph Waldo Emerson, "Milton," 1838,
Complete Works, volume 12, 1904, pp. 247–49

WILLIAM SMYTH (1840)

The invectives of this great poet against prelates and Presbyterians will perfectly astonish those, who as yet are conversant only with his immortal work, his descriptions of the Garden of Eden, and the piety and innocence of our first parents.

—William Smyth, *Lectures on Modern History*, 1840

LEIGH HUNT "MILTON" (1844)

Poet and literary critic James Henry Leigh Hunt (1784–1859) was born to American parents who had returned to England during the American Revolution. He received an education in the classics at Christ's Hospital School, published a collection of poems when he was 17, was apprenticed as a legal clerk to his brother, and soon left that post to pursue literary journalism. Beginning by writing theater reviews, Hunt moved on to become editor in 1808 of the *Examiner*, a newspaper begun by his brother John. Leigh Hunt served in that position until 1821, writing articles on politics and literature, and also edited the *Reflector* from 1811 to 1812. Convicted of slandering the Prince Regent in a *Reflector* essay, Hunt served two years in prison from 1813 to 1815, all the while being allowed to continue editing the *Examiner*, have his family with him, and see important visitors Charles Lamb, William Hazlitt, and George Gordon, Lord Byron. He later edited several other magazines, including the *Literary Pocket-Book*, the *Indicator*, and the *Liberal* (a magazine he worked with Shelley and Byron to establish), as well as several short-lived periodicals. He wrote also for the *New Monthly Magazine* and began publishing book-length works, including *Lord Byron and Some of His Contemporaries*, *Christianism: or Belief and Unbelief Reconciled*, which later was expanded and reissued as *The Religion of the Heart: a Manual of Faith and Duty*, collections of his poetry, a novel, *Sir Ralph Ester*, set in the Restoration, and a two-volume autobiography.

Hunt published several volumes of his collected literary essays; the following selection on Milton is one of his many critical articles. Praising Milton for demonstrating the romantic qualities of imagination and for being a "changer," that is, demonstrating politically forward thinking,

Hunt nonetheless finds *Paradise Lost* lacking in true piety and prefers Milton's "L'Allegro" and "Il Penseroso."

Milton was a very great poet, second only (if second) to the very greatest, such as Dante and Shakspeare; and, like all great poets, equal to them in particular instances. He had no pretensions to Shakspeare's universality; his wit is dreary; and (in general) he had not the faith in things that Homer and Dante had, apart from the intervention of words. He could not let them speak for themselves without helping them with his learning. In all he did, after a certain period of youth (not to speak it irreverently), something of the schoolmaster is visible; and a gloomy religious creed removes him still farther from the universal gratitude and delight of mankind. He is understood, however, to have given this up before he died. He had then run the circle of his knowledge, and probably come round to the wiser, more cheerful, and more poetical beliefs of his childhood.

In this respect, "Allegro'" and "Penseroso" are the happiest of his productions; and in none is the poetical habit of mind more abundantly visible. They ought to precede the "Lycidas" (not unhurt with theology) in the modern editions of his works, as they did in the collection of minor poems made by himself. *Paradise Lost* is a study for imagination and elaborate musical structure. Take almost any passage, and a lecture might be read from it on contrasts and pauses, and other parts of metrical harmony; while almost every word has its higher poetical meaning and intensity; but all is accompanied with a certain oppressiveness of ambitious and conscious power. In the "Allegro" and "Penseroso," &c., he is in better spirits with all about him; his eyes had not grown dim, nor his soul been forced inwards by disappointment into a proud self-esteem, which he narrowly escaped erecting into self-worship. He loves nature, not for the power he can get out of it, but for the pleasure it affords him; he is at peace with town as well as country, with courts and cathedral-windows; goes to the play and laughs; to the village-green and dances; and his study is placed, not in the Old Jewry, but in an airy tower, from whence he good-naturedly hopes that his candle—I beg pardon, his "lamp" (for he was a scholar from the first, though not a Puritan)—may be "seen" by others. His mirth, it is true, is not excessively merry. It is, as Warton says, the "dignity of mirth;" but it is happy, and that is all that is to be desired. The mode is not to be dictated by the mode of others; nor would it be so interesting if it were. The more a man is himself the better, provided he add a variation to the stock of comfort, and not of sullenness. Milton was born in a time of great changes; he was bred to be one of the changers; and in the order of events, and the working of good out of ill, we are bound to be grateful to what was of a mixed nature in himself, without arrogating for him that exemption from the mixture which belongs to no man. But upon the same principle on which nature herself loves joy better than grief, health than disease, and a general amount of welfare than the reverse (urging men towards it where it does not prevail, and making many a form of discontent itself but a mode of pleasure and self-esteem), so Milton's great poem never has been, and never can be popular (sectarianism apart) compared with his minor ones; nor does it, in the very highest sense of popularity, deserve to be. It does not work out the very piety it proposes; and the piety which it does propose wants the highest piety of an intelligible charity and reliance. Hence a secret preference for his minor poems among many of the truest and selectest admirers of *Paradise Lost,*—perhaps with all who do not admire power in any shape above truth in the best; hence Warton's found edition of them, delightful for its luxurious heap of notes and parallel passages.

—Leigh Hunt, "Milton," *Imagination and Fancy,*
1844

THOMAS B. SHAW (1847)

No species of literature, no language, no book, no art or science seems to have escaped his curiosity, or resisted the combined ardour and patience of his industry. His works may be considered as a vast arsenal of ideas drawn from every region of human speculation, and either themselves the condensed quintessence of knowledge and wisdom, or dressing and adoring the fairest and most majestic conceptions.

—Thomas B. Shaw, *Outlines of English Literature,*
1847, p. 162

EDWIN R. WHIPPLE "AUTHORS IN THEIR RELATIONS TO LIFE" (1850)

No one can fitly reverence Milton who has not studied the character of the age of Charles II., in which his later fortunes were cast. He was Dryden's contemporary in time, but not his master or disciple in slavishness. He was under the anathema of power; a republican, in days of abject servility; a Christian, among men whom it would be charity to call infidels; a man of pure life and high principle, among sensualists and renegades. On nothing external could he lean for support. In his own domain of imagination perhaps the greatest poet that ever lived, he was still doomed to see such pitiful and stupid poetasters as Shadwell and Settle bear away the shining rewards of letters. Well might he declare that he had fallen on evil times! The genius of Milton is indeed worthy of all the admiration we award marvellous intellectual endowment; but how much more do we venerate the whole man, when we find it riveted to that high and hardy moral courage which makes his name thunder rebuke to all power that betrays freedom, to all genius that is false to virtue!

—Edwin R. Whipple, "Authors in Their Relations to Life," *Lectures on Subjects Connected with Literature and Life*, 1850, pp. 24–25

George Meredith
"The Poetry of Milton" (1851)

While known primarily as a Victorian novelist, George Meredith (1828–1909) wrote poetry in the beginning of his writing career. Born in Portsmouth, he was sent to boarding schools in England and Germany after his mother's death and began writing poetry in his early twenties, influenced by the works of John Keats and Alfred, Lord Tennyson. Soon after, he founded with Edward Gryffydh Peacock the *Monthly Observer*, a literary magazine to which he contributed poems and essays. Meredith also wrote for a number of established periodicals, distinguishing himself as a journalist and critic, and was acclaimed for his lecture *An Essay on Comedy and the Uses of the Comic Spirit* printed in 1877 in the *New Quarterly Magazine*. He shifted to fiction with his 1856 novel, *The Shaving of Shagpat: An Arabian Entertainment*, which showed his propensity for social satire. This culminated in his mature and popular 1879 novel, *The Egoist*. He then turned his subject matter to more psychological and moral topics in works such as *Diana of the Crossways* in 1885 and *The Amazing Marriage* in 1895. All told, Meredith wrote 15 novels, numerous shorter fictive works, and published six volumes of poetry.

The selection that follows, from Meredith's first volume of poetry, was part of a grouping of short verse celebrating those whom he considered the greatest British poets: Chaucer, Spenser, Shakespeare, Milton, Southey, Coleridge, Shelley, Wordsworth, and Keats.

Like to some deep-chested organ whose grand
    inspiration,
Serenely majestic in utterance, lofty and calm,

Interprets to mortals with melody great as its burthens,
The mystical harmonies chiming for ever throughout the bright spheres.
　　　　　　　—George Meredith, "The Poetry of Milton," 1851,
　　　　　　　　　　　　　　　　　　　　　　　　　Works, volume 31, p. 139

FREDERICK DENISON MAURICE
"THE FRIENDSHIP OF BOOKS" (1856)

He was the most learned of all our poets, the one who from his childhood upwards was a devourer of Greek and Latin books, of the romances of the Middle Ages, of French and Italian poetry, above all of the Hebrew Scriptures. All these became his friends; for all of them connected themselves with the thoughts that occupied men in his own time, with the deep religious and political controversies which were about to bring on a civil war. Many persons think that the side which he took in that war must hinder us from making his books our friends; that we may esteem him as a great poet, but that we cannot meet him cordially as a man. No one is more likely to entertain that opinion than an English clergyman, for Milton dealt his blow unsparingly enough, and we come in for at least our full share of them. I know all that, and yet I must confess that I have found him a friend, and a very valuable friend, even when I have differed from him most and he has made me smart most.

　　　　　　　—Frederick Denison Maurice, "The Friendship of
　　　　　　　　　Books," 1856, The Friendship of Books and Other
　　　　　　　　　　　　　　　　Lectures, 1874, edited by Hughes, p. 14

GEORGE WILLIAM CURTIS "THE DUTY
OF THE AMERICAN SCHOLAR" (1856)

Graced with every intellectual gift, he was personally so comely that the romantic woods of Vallambrosa are lovelier from their association with his youthful figure sleeping in their shade. He had all the technical excellences of the scholar. At eighteen he wrote better Latin verses than have been written in England. He replied to the Italian poets who complimented him in Italian pure as their own. He was profoundly skilled in theology, in science, and in the literature of all languages. These were his accomplishments, but his genius was vast and vigorous. While yet a youth he wrote those minor poems which have the simple perfection of productions of nature; and in the ripeness of his wisdom and power he turned his blind eyes to heaven, and sang the lofty song which has given him a twin glory with Shakespeare in English renown.

It is much for one man to have exhausted the literature of other nations and to have enriched his own. But other men have done this in various degrees. Milton went beyond it to complete the circle of his character as the scholar. You know the culmination of his life. The first scholar in England and in the world at that time fulfilled his office. His vocation making him especially the representative of liberty, he accepted the part to which he was naturally called, and turning away from all the blandishments of ease and fame, he gave himself to liberty and immortality.

—George William Curtis, "The Duty of the American Scholar" (1856), *Orations and Addresses*, 1893, volume 1, p. 12

Charles Kingsley "Plays and Puritans" (1859)

Anglican clergyman, social and political reformer, literary critic, and author, the Reverend Charles Kingsley (1819–75) was born in Devonshire and went to Cambridge University as an undergraduate. After ordination, he realized that religion must improve the physical condition of the disenfranchised, as well as their spiritual condition, and he combined social reform with his office of curate of Eversley, becoming involved in the Christian socialist movement. A prolific writer, Kingsley wrote a drama, *The Saint's Tragedy: or, The True Story of Elizabeth of Hungary*, in 1848, *Yeast; a Problem*, a series of essays on living conditions of farmers printed in *Fraser's Magazine* in 1848 and published in book form in 1851, and *Alton Locke*, an 1850 novel of a poet struggling to survive in deplorable London squalor. In addition to many more novels on historical themes as well as the first science book for children, Kingsley produced his most famous creation, *The Water-Babies; A Fairy Tale for a Land-Baby* in 1863, a children's story that melded social criticism of unsanitary conditions with moral teaching and that was ultimately responsible for the 1864 Chimney Sweepers Act. He also had an academic career, serving one year as professor of English literature at Queen's College in 1848, and from 1860–69 as Regius Professor of Modern History at Cambridge.

   The following selection is taken from one of Kingsley's literary criticism volumes, *Plays and Puritans*, in which he deems seventeenth-century dramatic works as generally growing less artistic and more immoral after Shakespeare. Restoration drama was, in particular, bawdy rather than uplifting, according to the author. Kingsley portrays Milton as the exceptional writer of the Caroline period, who as a Puritan is "one who, instead of trusting himself and his hopes of the universe to second-hand hearsays, systems, and traditions, had looked God's Word and his own soul in the face, and determined to act on that which he had found."

Take any,—the most hackneyed passage of *Comus*, the "L'Allegro," the "Penseroso," the *Paradise Lost*, and see the freshness, the sweetness, and the simplicity, which is strangely combined with the pomp, the self-restraint, the earnestness of every word; take him even, as an *experimentum crucis*, when he trenches upon ground heathen and questionable, and tries the court poets at their own weapons,—

Or whether (as some sages sing),
The frolic wind that breathes the spring,
Zephyr with Aurora playing,
As he met her once a-maying,
There on beds of violets blue,
And fresh-blown roses washed in dew.

but why quote what all the world knows?—Where shall we find such real mirth, ease, sweetness, dance and song of words in any thing written for five-and-twenty years before him? True, he was no great dramatist. He never tried to be one: but there was no one in his generation who could have written either *Comus* or *Samson Agonistes*. And if, as is commonly believed, and as his countenance seems to indicate, he was deficient in humour, so were his contemporaries, with the sole exception of Cartwright. Witty he would be, and bitter: but he did not live in a really humorous age; and if he has none of the rollicking fun of the fox-hound puppy, at least he has none of the obscene gibber of the ape.

—Charles Kingsley, "Plays and Puritans" (1859),
Plays and Puritans and Other Historical Essays, 1873

SAMUEL LEIGH SOTHEBY (1861)

British book collector and auctioneer Samuel Leigh Sotheby was the last of the Sotheby family to oversee the eponymously named auctionhouse. He produced a large quantity of book collection catalogs as well as edited books on physical qualities of the antiquarian works, such as *Ramblings in the Elucidation of the Autograph of Milton*, 1861, the source of the following selection.

Milton does not appear to have derived any pecuniary advantage from his labours as a Poet. His juvenile productions, and a few other minor pieces, were published for the first time in 1645. His Poems were evidently at that period not more esteemed than many of the contemporaneous poetical volumes of similar character. If we may judge from the fact of those poems being issued without any of those commendatory verses,—the tribute of praise so generally accorded by way of introduction to the effusions of a brother poet,—we may fairly come to the conclusion that Milton was, at that period, comparatively little known in the poetical world. Unlike also the works of other poets of the day, those of Milton are not inscribed to any patron, but are merely introduced to the public by an address from Humphrey Moseley the publisher. The volume bears no indication that it had been even published under the superintendence of the author. The Poems are arranged without much attention to their chronological order; and some of the Sonnets are without the headings that occur in the originals in the Trinity College Manuscript. Besides this, several of the Sonnets written before 1645, are omitted, as also other of his early poetical productions.

—Samuel Leigh Sotheby, *Ramblings in the Elucidation of the Autograph of Milton*, 1861, p. 12

Alfred, Lord Tennyson "Milton" (1863)

Alfred, Lord Tennyson (1809–92), famed Victorian poet, began writing at an early age to escape difficulties in his home life. He was born into a family of 12 children, his father, an Anglican rector, was sometimes unstable and abusive, and several of Tennyson's brothers had either inherited epilepsy or abused drugs or alcohol. By the time he was 18, Alfred Tennyson had published *Poems by Two Brothers*, which was primarily a collection of his poetry with a few selections by his older brothers Frederick and Charles.

Entering Trinity College, Cambridge, he met Arthur Hallam, who was to be the tragic subject of Tennyson's most enduring work, *In Memoriam A.H.H.* While at Cambridge, Tennyson published a blank-verse poem, *Timbuctoo*, and *Poems: Chiefly Lyrical* in 1830. After leaving Cambridge because of his father's death, Tennyson published another volume in 1832, *Poems*, which contained works written while travelling with Hallam through the Pyrenees, including "Mariana in the South" and "The Lotos-Eaters," as well as "The Lady of Shalott." Though many of the poems are now praised, negative reviews prevailed at the time. In 1833, Hallam died of a brain hemorrhage while on a Vienna trip with Tennyson, devastating both Tennyson and his sister Emily, who had been engaged to Hallam. Tennyson increased his poetic output, finally publishing in 1842 a two-volume set that included new poems plus rewrites of formerly published ones.

After a mental breakdown caused by financial losses, emotional up-heavals, and lack of care for his health, Tennyson spent several periods of time in a hydropathic hospital for treatment, where he finally learned that the trances he thought were epileptic seizures were actually brought on by gout. He published a long narrative poem in blank verse, *The Princess*, in 1847, and the 3,000-line work that had consumed years of his time, *In Memoriam A.H.H.*, in 1850. The latter made him the most renowned poet in England, and he became poet laureate and later a beloved friend of Queen Victoria. Later publications showed an interest in English legend and his-tory, including *Idylls of the King* (1859), *The Holy Grail and Other Poems* (1869), *Queen Mary: A Drama* (1875), [King] *Harold: A Drama* (1876), *The Foresters, Robin Hood and Maid Marian* (1892), and *Becket* (1894). Altogether, Tenny-son produced more than 20 volumes of poetry and plays and was awarded a peerage in 1833, creating his title of Baron Tennyson of Aldworth and Freshwater. He also received honorary doctorates from Edinburgh and Ox-ford, turning down the thrice-made offer from Cambridge.

Tennyson's writings were indebted to Milton's blank verse, which he adapted in many works, and to "Lycidas," an influence on *In Memoriam A.H.H.* Like Milton, Tennyson viewed the role of a poet as a divinely in-spired prophet and portrayed the tension between reason and passion in his works, notably *Idylls of the King*. The following sonnet is Tennyson's homage to the poet he regarded as the most sublime.

O mighty-mouth'd inventor of harmonies,
O skill'd to sing of Time or Eternity,
God-gifted organ-voice of England,
Milton, a name to resound for ages;
Whose Titan angels, Gabriel, Abdiel,
Starr'd from Jehovah's gorgeous armouries,
Tower, as the deep-domed empyrean
Rings to the roar of an angel onset—
Me rather all that bowery loneliness,
The brooks of Eden mazily murmuring,
And bloom profuse and cedar arches
Charm, as a wanderer out in ocean,
Where some refulgent sunset of India
Streams o'er a rich ambrosial ocean isle,

And crimson-hued the stately palm-woods
Whisper in odorous heights of even.

—Alfred, Lord Tennyson, "Milton," 1863

HENRY MORLEY (1868)

Milton put off his singing robes to labour for the State, and between the springtime of his genius and the glorious harvest of its autumn, gave the summer of his life to direct service of the country. He was then the pen of the Commonwealth, the voice of England to the outer world. And in his earlier and later verse, not less than in the middle period of his prose writing, Milton's genius was rich with the life of his own time, although he thought apart from the crowd, and spoke for himself, royally, with independent power. No poet is for all time who is not also for his age, reflecting little or much of its outward manner, but a part of its best mind.

—Henry Morley, introduction to
The King and the Commons, 1868, p. xx

GEORGE MACDONALD (1868)

British Victorian poet and novelist George Macdonald (1824–1905) made a lasting name for himself primarily through his fantasy works. Born in a Scottish village, he became enamored with German romanticism at King's College, Aberdeen. After further theological training, he became pastor of Trinity Congregational Church, Arundel, but his unorthodox and mystical religious views—including divine goodness as opposed to damnation and salvation for non-Christians and animals—alienated his congregation, so he resigned his post and worked as a travelling lecturer.

Macdonald's publications *Within and Without* (1855) and *Phantastes* (1858) began to bring him recognition, and soon he devoted himself to writing, producing nearly 30 novels by the end of his life. He had relocated to a home in London, The Retreat, in 1859, where he welcomed fellow Victorian writers Matthew Arnold and Alfred Tennyson and theologian Frederick Denison Maurice. The latter helped Macdonald become professor of English literature at Bedford College and served as the subject of his novel *David Elginbrod* (1863). Macdonald's works contained his romantic spiritual social views, including famed fairy stories such as *The Princess and the Goblin* (1872), which castigated the materialism of corrupt society. In his own life, he lived close to poverty, rejecting the pastorate of a wealthy New York congregation after his American lecture tour.

Interspersed with his creative works are book-length studies of literature, including a work on *Hamlet* and a rewriting of Sir Philip Sidney's
works, in addition to *England's Antiphon*, on English religious poetry, and
excerpted here, praising Milton's art of poetry.

If George Herbert's utterance is like the sword-play of one skilful with the
rapier, that of Milton is like the sword-play of an old knight, flashing his huge
but keen-cutting blade in lightnings about his head. Compared with Herbert,
Milton was a man in health. He never *shows*, at least, any diseased regard of
himself. His eye is fixed on the truth, and he knows of no ill-faring. While a
man looks thitherward, all the movements of his spirit reveal themselves only
in peace. The unity of his being is the strength of Milton. He is harmony, sweet
and bold, throughout. Not Philip Sidney, not George Herbert loved words and
their melodies more than he; while in their use he is more serious than either,
and harder to please, uttering a music they have rarely approached.

—George Macdonald,
England's Antiphon, 1868, pp. 194–95

John Robert Seeley
"Milton's Political Opinions" (1868)

Milton was a pamphleteer, only a pamphleteer of original genius. Had he
less originality, with the same power of language, he would probably have
figured more in the history of the time, because he would have become
more distinctly the mouthpiece of a party. But because the weight of his
mind always carries him below the surface of the subject, because in these
pamphlets he appeals constantly to first principles, opens the largest questions, propounds the most general maxims, we are not therefore unfairly to
compare them with complete treatises on politics, or to forget that they are
essentially pamphlets still.

—John Robert Seeley, "Milton's Political
Opinions," *Macmillan's Magazine*, 1868, p. 302

Hippolyte Taine (1871)

Hippolyte Taine (1828–93) was a French historian and literary critic famous
for his desire to apply the scientific method to the humanities. As a leading
member of the Positivist movement, he was pivotal in focusing on historical
studies of literature, seeing writers as a product of their race, environment,

and era. His *L'Histoire de la littérature anglaise* (1871) was a major achievement but not without its detractors, who viewed Taine's approach at times
too narrow, inconsistent, or shallowly applied. Here, Taine focuses on
Milton's biography, using generalizations to characterize him and his work.

John Milton was not one of those fevered souls, void of self-command,
whose rapture takes them by fits, whom a sickly sensibility drives for ever
to the extreme of sorrow or joy, whose pliability prepares them to produce
a variety of characters, whose inquietude condemns them to paint the
insanity and contradictions of passion. Vast knowledge, close logic, and
grand passion: these were his marks. His mind was lucid, his imagination limited. He was incapable of disturbed emotion or of transformation.
He conceived the loftiest of ideal beauties, but he conceived only one. He
was not born for the drama, but for the ode. He does not create souls, but
constructs arguments and experiences emotions. Emotions and arguments,
all the forces and actions of his soul, assemble and are arranged beneath a
unique sentiment, that of the sublime; and the broad river of lyric poetry
streams from him, impetuous, with even flow, splendid as a cloth of gold.
. . . He was speculative and chimerical. Locked up in his own ideas, he sees
but them, is attracted but by them. . . . He lived complete and untainted to
the end, without loss of heart or weakness; experience could not instruct
nor misfortune depress him; he endured all, and repented of nothing. . . .
When Milton wishes to joke, he looks like one of Cromwell's pikemen, who,
entering a room to dance, should fall upon the floor, and that with the extra
momentum of his armour.

> —Hippolyte Taine, *History of English Literature,*
> 1871, volume 1, translated by Van Laun,
> book 2, chapter 6

HENRY WADSWORTH LONGFELLOW
"MILTON" (1873)

American poet Henry Wadsworth Longfellow (1807–82) was well loved in
his own day, though his poetry has now declined in readership. Born in
Portland, Maine, which was at the time part of Massachusetts, he attended Bowdoin College, where he became professor after graduating and
studying languages in Europe. His time in Germany was spent reading
the German romantics. Subsequent travels to England and continental
Europe increased his acquaintance with esteemed authors, including

Thomas Carlyle and Charles Dickens. In 1834, Longfellow was appointed chairman of French and Spanish at Harvard University. He produced many longer narrative poems, including *Evangeline, A Tale of Acadie,* 1847; *The Song of Hiawatha,* 1855; *The Courtship of Miles Standish,* 1858; and immensely popular shorter poems, such as "The Children's Hour," 1859, and "Paul Revere's Ride" in *Tales of a Wayside Inn,* 1863. Longfellow is the sole American poet to receive recognition in Poets' Corner of Westminster Abbey, where a bust of him was installed in 1884.

In addition to composing his own verse, Longfellow also translated European works into English, including Dante's *Divine Comedy* in 1867, demonstrating his interest in serious literary study. He produced a series of sonnets on other poets as well, including Chaucer and Shakespeare. This selection reproduces his sonnet to Milton, which showcases Longfellow's romantic and transcendentalist emotional sensibilities and love of nature in comparing Milton's poetic prowess to a mighty wave pounding the shore.

I pace the sounding sea-beach and behold,
How the voluminous billows roll and run,
Upheaving and subsiding, while the sun
Shines through their sheeted emerald far unrolled,
And the ninth wave, slow gathering fold by fold
All its loose-folding garments into one,
Plunges upon the shore, and floods the dun
Pale reach of sands, and changes them to gold.
So in majestic cadence rise and fall
The mighty undulations of thy song,
O sightless bard, England's Maeonides!
And ever and anon, high over all
Uplifted, a ninth wave superb and strong,
Floods all the soul with its melodious seas.

> —Henry Wadsworth Longfellow,
> "Milton," *A Book of Sonnets,* 1873

JOHN CAMPBELL SHAIRP (1877)

With Milton, Nature was not his first love, but held only a secondary place in his affections. He was in the first place a scholar, a man of letters, with the theologian and polemic latent in him. A lover of all artistic beauty he was, no doubt, and of Nature mainly as it lends itself to this perception. And as is his mode of apprehending Nature, such is the language in which he describes her.

—John Campbell Shairp,
On Poetic Interpretation of Nature, 1877, p. 186

WILLIAM MICHAEL ROSSETTI (1878)

Less famous than his siblings, the poets Dante Gabriel and Christina Rossetti, William Michael Rossetti (1829–1919) was a British art and literary critic and editor. He served as art critic for *The Spectator*, editor of the Pre-Raphaelite journal *The Germ*, wrote a biography of his brother Dante Gabriel, compiled volumes of letters and papers of Pre-Raphaelite artists, and produced editions of Walt Whitman and William Blake and studies of Dante and other earlier poets. In the following passage, Rossetti reflects on the common reactions to Milton; overwhelmed by his difficult style, readers often are somewhat critical of his faults but are sympathetic to him because of his blindness.

An ordinary mind contemplating Milton can realize to itself the feeling of the Athenian who resented hearing Aristides for ever styled "the Just." Such a mind feels a little and excusably provoked at the serene and severe loftiness of a Milton, and casts about to find him blame-worthy in his very superiority—an exacting husband and father, an over-learned writer, cumbrous or stilted in prose and scholastically accoutred in verse, a political and religious extremist. There may be something in these objections, or the smaller kind of souls will please themselves by supposing there is something in them. Honour is the predominant emotion naturally felt towards Milton—hardly enthusiasm—certainly not sympathy. Perhaps a decided feeling of unsympathy would affect many of us, were it not for the one great misfortune of the poet. Nature has forbidden him to be infirm in himself, but gave him a crown of accidental or physical infirmity, and bowed him somewhat—a little lower than the angels—towards sympathy.

—William Michael Rossetti,
Lives of Famous Poets, 1878, p. 76

JAMES ANTHONY FROUDE (1880)

Admire as we may *Paradise Lost*; try as we may to admire *Paradise Regained*; acknowledge as we must the splendour of the imagery and the stately march of the verse—there comes upon us irresistibly a sense of the unfitness of the subject for Milton's treatment of it. If the story which he tells us is true, it is too momentous to be played with in poetry. We prefer to hear it in plain prose, with a minimum of ornament and the utmost possible precision of statement. Milton himself had not arrived at thinking it to be a legend, a picture, like a Greek Mythology. His poem falls between two modes of treatment and two conceptions of truth; we wonder, we recite, we applaud, but something comes in between our minds and a full enjoyment, and it will not satisfy us better as time goes on.

—James Anthony Froude, *Bunyan*, 1880, p. 116

John Dennis (1883)

Milton is the most sublime of our poets, and next to Wordsworth, he is perhaps the most intense. I mean that every line he utters, every scene he describes, is felt and seen by the writer; that his poetry is the expression of his innermost life, and that his individuality pervades it. Unlike Spenser and Shakespeare, Milton can seldom escape from himself, but his egotism is of the noblest order. We see this egotism in the earliest poems, in the sonnets written in middle age, and again in his latest work, the *Samson Agonistes*, in which, as in a mirror, may be witnessed the struggles of his soul and the sorrows of his life.

—John Dennis, *Heroes of Literature*, 1883, p. 127

Richard Henry Stoddard (1883)

The greatness of the man was conspicuous in his blindness, for though he was fallen on evil days and evil tongues, he was unchanged, and though he was in solitude he was not alone. Urania visited his slumbers nightly, and governed his song, and found an audience—fit audience though few. The Spirit of Heavenly Song attained its greatest height with *Paradise Lost* in 1667, and, slowly wheeling through the firmament of English Verse, began to descend in 1671 with *Paradise Regained* and *Samson Agonistes*. It reached the lowest deep in the next half century in the Psalms and Hymns of Watts.

—Richard Henry Stoddard, introduction to
English Verse: Chaucer to Burns, 1883, p. xxxviii

Hutcheson Macaulay Posnett (1886)

The essence of the Greek pastoral elegy is the contrast of man's individual life with Nature's apparent eternity—a melancholy sentiment becoming the lisp of a modern materialist, but in the author of "Lycidas," the poetical champion of a faith before which the material universe is but dust and ashes compared with the soul of the veriest wretch who wears the form of man, almost grotesquely out of place. Why should Nature lament the escape of a divinity greater than herself from its clay prison? The Greek chorus in the social life of the Hebrews speaking the Puritanism of England in *Samson Agonistes* is not a stranger union of incongruities than the poet of individual immortality repeating the materialism of the Greek in lamentations for Edward King. Plainly the individualism of the sixteenth and seventeenth centuries did not know whether it was of earth or the infinite; and this confused judgment made it willing to look on Nature partially as a beautiful machine, its exquisite mechanism worthy of such word-pictures as "L'Allegro" and "Il Penseroso" contain, partially as a pagan god to be duly invoked only in good old pagan fashion, and partially as a perishable nullity destined to be "rolled together as a scroll"—in any case connected by no profoundly real links with man's social and individual life.

—Hutcheson Macaulay Posnett,
Comparative Literature, 1886, p. 384

Harry Lyman Koopman "Milton" (1888)

O Milton, thou hast only half thy praise
In having lowered the heavens within man's ken;
Thine other, equal labor was to raise
The human spirit up to heaven again;
So, underneath thy forehead's aureole blaze,
Thine awful eyes are mild with love to men.

—Harry Lyman Koopman, "Milton," Orestes and
Other Poems, 1888, p. 148

Matthew Arnold "Milton" (1888)

Matthew Arnold's essay is framed by an event that crosses continents, the gifting of a window in England in honor of Milton's second widow, Catherine Woodcock, by a Philadelphia benefactor. The essay was originally written as Arnold's address at the dedication of the Milton Memorial Window in St. Margaret's Church, Westminister. The occasion provokes Arnold's discussion of Milton's transcendence, most especially as an English writer, extending the superior Anglo-Saxon legacy into the United States and beyond. Arnold elevates Milton as the greatest of all writers because of his "grand style" that

is superior even to Shakespeare's and thus most effective in its universal
ambassadorial role of promoting English culture.

The most eloquent voice of our century uttered, shortly before leaving the
world, a warning cry against 'the Anglo-Saxon contagion.' The tendencies
and aims, the view of life and the social economy of the ever-multiplying and
spreading Anglo-Saxon race, would be found congenial, this prophet feared,
by all the prose, all the vulgarity amongst mankind, and would invade and
overpower all nations. The true ideal would be lost, a general sterility of mind
and heart would set in.

  The prophet had in view, no doubt, in the warning thus given, us and
our colonies, but the United States still more. There the Anglo-Saxon race is
already most numerous, there it increases fastest; there material interests are
most absorbing and pursued with most energy; there the ideal, the saving
ideal, of a high and rare excellence, seems perhaps to suffer most danger of
being obscured and lost. Whatever one may think of the general danger to
the world from the Anglo-Saxon contagion, it appears to me difficult to deny
that the growing greatness and influence of the United States does bring
with it some danger to the ideal of a high and rare excellence. The *average
man* is too much a religion there; his performance is unduly magnified, his
shortcomings are not duly seen and admitted. A lady in the State of Ohio sent
to me only the other day a volume on American authors; the praise given
throughout was of such high pitch that in thanking her I could not forbear
saying that for only one or two of the authors named was such a strain of
praise admissible, and that we lost all real standard of excellence by praising
so uniformly and immoderately. She answered me with charming good
temper, that very likely I was quite right, but it was pleasant to her to think
that excellence was common and abundant. But excellence is not common
and abundant; on the contrary, as the Greek poet long ago said, excellence
dwells among rocks hardly accessible, and a man must almost wear his heart
out before he can reach her. Whoever talks of excellence as common and
abundant, is on the way to lose all right standard of excellence. And when the
right standard of excellence is lost, it is not likely that much which is excellent
will be produced.

  To habituate ourselves, therefore, to approve, as the Bible says, things
that are really excellent, is of the highest importance. And some apprehen-
sion may justly be caused by a tendency in Americans to take, or, at any rate,
attempt to take, profess to take, the average man and his performances too
seriously, to overrate and overpraise what is not really superior.

But we have met here to-day to witness the unveiling of a gift in Milton's honour, and a gift bestowed by an American, Mr. Childs of Philadelphia; whose cordial hospitality so many Englishmen, I myself among the number, have experienced in America. It was only last autumn that Stratford-upon-Avon celebrated the reception of a gift from the same generous donor in honour of Shakspeare. Shakspeare and Milton—he who wishes to keep his standard of excellence high, cannot choose two better objects of regard and honour. And it is an American who has chosen them, and whose beautiful gift in honour of one of them, Milton, with Mr. Whittier's simple and true lines inscribed upon it, is unveiled to-day. Perhaps this gift in honour of Milton, of which I am asked to speak, is, even more than the gift in honour of Shakspeare, one to suggest edifying reflections to us.

Like Mr. Whittier, I treat the gift of Mr. Childs as a gift in honour of Milton, although the window given is in memory of his second wife, Catherine Woodcock, the 'late espoused saint' of the famous sonnet, who died in childbed at the end of the first year of her marriage with Milton, and who lies buried here with her infant. Milton is buried in Cripplegate, but he lived for a good while in this parish of St. Margaret's, Westminster, and here he composed part of *Paradise Lost,* and the whole of *Paradise Regained* and *Samson Agonistes.* When death deprived him of the Catherine whom the new window commemorates, Milton had still some eighteen years to live, and Cromwell, his 'chief of men,' was yet ruling England. But the Restoration, with its 'Sons of Belial,' was not far off; and in the meantime Milton's heavy affliction had laid fast hold upon him, his eyesight had failed totally, and he was blind. In what remained to him of life he had the consolation of producing the *Paradise Lost* and the *Samson Agonistes,* and such a consolation we may indeed count as no slight one. But the daily life of happiness in common things and in domestic affections—a life of which, to Milton as to Dante, too small a share was given—he seems to have known most, if not only, in his one married year with the wife who is here buried. Her form 'vested all in white,' as in his sonnet he relates that after her death she appeared to him, her face veiled, but with 'love, sweetness, and goodness' shining in her person,—this fair and gentle daughter of the rigid sectarist of Hackney, this lovable companion with whom Milton had rest and happiness one year, is a part of Milton indeed, and in calling up her memory, we call up his.

And in calling up Milton's memory we call up, let me say, a memory upon which, in prospect of the Anglo-Saxon contagion and of its dangers supposed and real, it may be well to lay stress even more than upon Shakspeare's. If to our English race an inadequate sense for perfection of work is a real danger, if the discipline of respect for a high and flawless excellence is peculiarly needed by us, Milton is of all our gifted men the best lesson, the most salutary influence. In the sure and flawless perfection of his rhythm and diction he is as admirable as Virgil or Dante, and in this respect he is unique amongst us. No one else in English literature and art possesses the like distinction.

Thomson, Cowper, Wordsworth, all of them good poets who have studied Milton, followed Milton, adopted his form, fail in their diction and rhythm if we try them by that high standard of excellence maintained by Milton constantly. From style really high and pure Milton never departs; their departures from it are frequent.

Shakspeare is divinely strong, rich, and attractive. But sureness of perfect style Shakspeare himself does not possess. I have heard a politician express wonder at the treasures of political wisdom in a certain celebrated scene of *Troilus and Cressida;* for my part I am at least equally moved to wonder at the fantastic and false diction in which Shakspeare has in that scene clothed them. Milton, from one end of *Paradise Lost* to the other, is in his diction and rhythm constantly a great artist in the great style. Whatever may be said as to the subject of his poem, as to the conditions under which he received his subject and treated it, that praise, at any rate, is assured to him.

For the rest, justice is not at present done, in my opinion, to Milton's management of the inevitable matter of a Puritan epic, a matter full of difficulties, for a poet. Justice is not done to the *architectonics,* as Goethe would have called them, of *Paradise Lost;* in these, too, the power of Milton's art is remarkable. But this may be a proposition which requires discussion and development for establishing it, and they are impossible on an occasion like the present.

That Milton, of all our English race, is by his diction and rhythm the one artist of the highest rank in the great style whom we have; this I take as requiring no discussion, this I take as certain.

The mighty power of poetry and art is generally admitted. But where the soul of this power, of this power at its best, chiefly resides, very many of us fail to see. It resides chiefly in the refining and elevation wrought in us by the high and rare excellence of the great style. We may feel the effect without being able to give ourselves clear account of its cause, but the thing is so. Now, no race needs the influences mentioned, the influences of refining and elevation, more than ours; and in poetry and art our grand source for them is Milton.

To what does he owe this supreme distinction? To nature first and foremost, to that bent of nature for inequality which to the worshippers of the average man is so unacceptable; to a gift, a divine favour. 'The older one grows,' says Goethe, 'the more one prizes natural gifts, because by no possibility can they be procured and stuck on.' Nature formed Milton to be a great poet. But what other poet has shown so sincere a sense of the grandeur of his vocation, and a moral effort so constant and sublime to make and keep himself worthy of it? The Milton of religious and political controversy, and perhaps of domestic life also, is not seldom disfigured by want of amenity, by acerbity. The Milton of poetry, on the other hand, is one of those great men 'who are modest'—to quote a fine remark of Leopardi, that gifted and stricken young Italian, who in his sense for poetic style is worthy to be named with Dante and Milton—'who are modest, because they continually compare themselves, not with other men, but with that idea of the perfect which they have before their mind.' The Milton of poetry is the man, in his own magnificent phrase, of 'devout prayer to that Eternal Spirit that can enrich with all utterance and knowledge, and sends out his Seraphim with the hallowed fire of his altar, to touch and purify the lips of whom he pleases.' And finally, the Milton of poetry is, in his own words again, the man of 'industrious and select reading.' Continually he lived in companionship with high and rare excellence, with the great Hebrew poets and prophets, with the great poets of Greece and Rome. The Hebrew compositions were not in verse, and can be not inadequately represented by the grand, measured prose of our English Bible. The verse of the poets of Greece and Rome no translation can adequately reproduce. Prose cannot have the power of verse; verse-translation may give whatever of charm is in the soul and talent of the translator himself, but never the specific charm of the verse and poet translated. In our race are thousands of readers, presently there will be millions, who know not a word of Greek and Latin, and will never learn those languages. If this host of readers are ever to gain any sense of the power and charm of the great poets of antiquity, their way to gain it is not through translations of the ancients, but through the original poetry of Milton, who has the like power and charm, because he has the like great style.

Through Milton they may gain it, for, in conclusion, Milton is English; this master in the great style of the ancients is English. Virgil, whom Milton loved and honoured, has at the end of the *Aeneid* a noble passage, where Juno, seeing the defeat of Turnus and the Italians imminent, the victory of the Trojan invaders assured, entreats Jupiter that Italy may nevertheless survive and be herself still, may retain her own mind, manners, and language, and not adopt those of the conqueror.

Sit Latium, sint Albani per secula reges! Jupiter grants the prayer; he promises perpetuity and the future to Italy—Italy reinforced by whatever virtue the Trojan race has, but Italy, not Troy. This we may take as a sort of parable suiting ourselves. All the Anglo-Saxon contagion, all the flood of

Anglo-Saxon commonness, beats vainly against the great style but cannot shake it, and has to accept its triumph. But it triumphs in Milton, in one of our own race, tongue, faith, and morals. Milton has made the great style no longer an exotic here; he has made it an inmate amongst us, a leaven, and a power. Nevertheless he, and his hearers on both sides of the Atlantic, are English, and will remain English—

Sermonem Ausonii patrium moresque tenebunt. The English race over-spreads the world, and at the same time the ideal of an excellence the most high and the most rare abides a possession with it for ever.

—Matthew Arnold, "Milton,"
Essays in Criticism, Second Series, 1888

FREDERICK POLLOCK "JOHN MILTON" (1890)

If we were to discuss the influence of Milton in the English poetry of the nineteenth century, we should have to analyse large portions of the works of recent and living English poets. Wordsworth's blank verse, when it is truly verse, is at times almost an echo of Milton; and Lord Tennyson, far too exquisite an artist to be ever a mere imitator, has in his perfection of form been a true follower of Milton's spirit. Neither has Milton's prose been fruit-less in the latter days; for something of its majestic reverberations may be heard in Landor, a master of English prose if ever there was one, from whom Milton received most loyal and yet unconstrained homage. rooted loyalty to letters had constrained him, too, to do homage; the last paragraph of his life of Milton redeems all the rest, effacing mistakes and prejudices in the fellow-feeling of a true scholar. He must be an exceedingly bold or an exceedingly fastidious Englishman who does not worship where Johnson and Landor have alike bowed the knee.

—Frederick Pollock, "John Milton,"
Fortnightly Review, 1890, p. 519

DONALD G. MITCHELL (1890)

Our amiable Dr. Channing, with excellent data before him, demonstrated his good Unitarian faith; but though Milton might have approved his nice reasonings, I doubt if he would have gone to church with him. He loved liberty; he could not travel well in double harness, not even in his household or with the elders. His exalted range of vision made light of the little aids and lorgnettes which the conventional teachers held out to him. Creeds and dogmas and vestments and canons, and all humanly consecrated helps, were but Jack-o'-lanterns to him, who was swathed all about with the glowing clouds of glory that rolled in upon his soul from the infinite depths.

—Donald G. Mitchell, *English Lands, Letters, and Kings: From Elizabeth to Anne*, 1890, p. 179

JAMES RUSSELL LOWELL "FRAGMENTS" (1891)

American poet, editor, essayist, and literary critic James Russell Lowell (1819–91) graduated from Harvard University in 1838 and earned his law degree in 1840 before turning to writing as his profession. After marrying poet Maria White in 1884, he began publishing poetry as well as abolitionist essays. He served as editor of the *Atlantic Monthly* from 1857 to 1861 and as coeditor of *The North American Review* from 1864 to 1872, where he wrote literary critical essays that were later published in two book-length collections. He was considered to be, along with Edgar Allan Poe, the foremost American critic of his time; the Modern Language Association continues to name its award for the top annual work in literary criticism the James Russell Lowell Prize.

Lowell assessed all other writers in relation to his "Five Indispensable Authors," Homer, Dante, Cervantes, Goethe, and Shakespeare. The following excerpt of his Milton criticism shows that, while Lowell lauds Milton's musicality, he does not see him as ranking with his favorites.

Where Milton's style is fine it is *very* fine, but it is always liable to the danger of degenerating into mannerism. Nay, where the imagination is absent and the artifice remains, as in some of the theological discussions in *Paradise Lost*, it becomes mannerism of the most wearisome kind. Accordingly, he is easily parodied and easily imitated. Philips, in his "Splendid Shilling," has caught the trick exactly. Philips has caught, I say, Milton's trick; his real secret he could never divine, for where Milton is best, he is incomparable. But all authors in whom imagination is a secondary quality, and whose merit lies less in what they say than in the way they say it, are apt to become mannerists, and to have imitators, because manner can be easily imitated. Milton has more or less colored all blank verse since his time, and, as those who imitate never fail to exaggerate, his influence has in some respects been mischievous. Thomson was well-nigh ruined by him. In him a leaf cannot fall without a Latinism, and there is circumlocution in the crow of a cock. Cowper was only saved by mixing equal proportions of Dryden in his verse, thus hitting upon a kind of cross between prose and poetry. In judging Milton, however, we should not forget that in verse the music makes a part of the meaning, and that no one before or since has been able to give to simple pentameters the majesty and compass of the organ. He was as much composer as poet.

—James Russell Lowell, "Fragments,"
The Century, 1891, pp. 24–25

JOHN AMPHLETT EVANS
"DRYDEN AND BEN JONSON" (1892)

The truth is, that in our literary history both Shakespeare and Milton stand apart by themselves, too inimitable and too spontaneous either to found a critical school or to carry with them any long train of followers. And as regards Milton, he may be viewed as a gigantic survival of the Elizabethan period, more Italianised than Spenser, more of the Puritan Englishman than was Shakespeare. "His soul was like a star, and dwelt apart."

—John Amphlett Evans, "Dryden and Ben
Jonson," *Temple Bar,* 1892, p. 109

WILLIAM WATSON "THE MYSTERY OF STYLE" (1893)

Admittedly and indisputably our highest summit in Style. He best proves the truth that in poetry Style is the paramount and invincible force. What else is the secret of his supremacy among our poets—a supremacy which no poet can doubt, and no true critic of poetry? For pure poetic endowment he sits unapproached on England's Helicon; yet, in comparison with Shakespeare, it cannot be said that his is a very rich or large nature uttering itself through literature. He has no geniality, he has no humour; he is often pedantic, sometimes pedagogic. Although his Invention was stupendous, in the quite distinct and finer quality of Imagination, or contagious spiritual vision, he has superiors; his human sympathies were neither warm nor broad; Shakespeare's contempt for the mass of mankind may be hesitatingly inferred from casual evidences, but Milton's is everywhere manifest.

—William Watson, "The Mystery of Style,"
Excursions in Criticism, 1893, pp. 105–10

GEORGE SAINTSBURY (1895)

In one respect Milton stands alone in his management of a great poetic medium. Shakespeare, because of the vast license of the English stage and its mixture of verse and prose, here stands out of the comparison, and we know nothing of Homer's predecessors. But no one, not Sophocles with the iambic trimeter, not even Virgil with the Latin hexameter, hardly even Dante with the Italian hendecasyllabic, has achieved such marvellous variety of harmony independent of meaning as Milton has with the English blank verse. All three, perhaps, had a better lexicon—it is permissible to think Milton's choice of words anything but infallible. But no one with his lexicon did such astonishing feats.

—George Saintsbury, *Social England*, 1895,
volume 4, edited by Traill, p. 425

FRANCIS TURNER PALGRAVE (1896)

British poet, critic, and editor Francis Turner Palgrave (1824–97) attended Balliol College at Oxford University, where he was part of Decade, a secret society that included Matthew Arnold. After he left Oxford, he visited Paris and then met Alfred, Lord Tennyson, whom Palgrave admired greatly and pursued as a friend. Palgrave wrote two novels and a poetry collection, then, in 1861, published a compendium for which he is most famous, *The Golden Treasury of the Best Songs and Lyrical Poems in the English Language*. He turned to art criticism, commissioned to compile the *Official Catalogue of the Fine Art Department of the International Exhibition of 1862*, which was attacked and withdrawn for the bias shown toward his friend Thomas Woolner. He served as art critic for the *Saturday Review* from 1863–66, publishing his compiled essays from that time in the 1866 volume *Essays on Art*. After continuing to write poetry and literary criticism, he served as chairman of poetry at Oxford from 1885 to 1895.

The following passage is excerpted from *Landscape in Poetry from Homer to Tennyson* (1897), a compilation of his Oxford lectures and his last book. Palgrave combines his knowledge of art and literature with his sensibilities as a poet in order to praise Milton's paired poems.

"L'Allegro" and "Il Penseroso," the earliest great lyrics of the landscape in our language, despite all later competition still remain supreme for range, variety, lucidity, and melodious charm within their style. And this style is essentially that of the Greek and the earlier English poets, but enlarged to the conception of whole scenes from Nature; occasionally even panoramic. What we gain from Milton, as these specimens in his very purest vein—his essence of landscape—illustrate, is the immense enlargement, the finer proportions, the greater scope, of his scenes from Nature. And with this we have that exquisite style, always noble, always music itself—Mozart without notes—in which

Milton is one of the few very greatest masters in all literature: in company—at least it pleases me to fancy—with Homer and Sophocles, with Vergil, with Dante, with Tennyson.

—Francis Turner Palgrave,
Landscape in Poetry, 1896, pp. 158–59

AUGUSTUS HOPKINS STRONG (1897)

It is certain that Milton deals with the invisible more than any other poet that ever lived. . . . Milton has not the spontaneity of imagination that distinguishes Shakespeare, nor has he so large a nature, but his sense of form is more unfailing, and in loftiness of character he towers far above the bard of Avon. Puritan as he is, he is more of an aristocrat, and more of a man, than is Shakespeare. His nobility of poetic form is but the expression of a lofty soul, thrilled to the center of its being with the greatest of possible themes—the struggle of good and evil, of God and Satan, and the triumph of the Almighty in the redemption of man. When this theme grows old, then will *Paradise Lost* and *Paradise Regained* grow old. But so long as man recognizes and values his own immortality, so long will the poetry of Milton vindicate its claim to be immortal.

—Augustus Hopkins Strong, *The Great Poets and
Their Theology,* 1897, pp. 246–56

FREDERIC IVES CARPENTER (1897)

Milton's lyric style is not so purely lyrical and personal; it is rather idyllic and objective. In this he is in a measure the poetic son of Spenser; and he, too, last of the Elizabethans, has a certain turn of lyric rhythm and phrase never afterwards recaptured. "L'Allegro" and "Il Penseroso" are the objective and idyllic presentations of the two fundamental subjective states of the human soul. In these poems all the rhythmical witchery and the subtle beauty of symbolism developed or suggested in the lyrics of Spenser, Shakespeare, Campion, Fletcher, Drummond, and Browne, is taken up and carried into the last perfection of English idyllic metre and fancy. And the "Lycidas" carries on the vein of earlier Ode and Elegy to a like perfection. Through all the concrete symbolism of these poems, however, we read the suggestion of the new ethical and subjective mood of the time, saturated with and subdued to the genius of the man Milton.

—Frederic Ives Carpenter, introduction to *English
Lyric Poetry 1500–1700,* 1897, p. liv

WALTER RALEIGH (1897)

Sir Walter Alexander Raleigh (1861–1922), professor of English and literary critic, received an M.A. degree from University College, London, and became professor of English literature at the Mohammedan Anglo-Oriental College, India. He returned in two years because of ill health, teaching at the universities of Liverpool and Glasgow before being appointed the first professor of English literature at Oxford University in 1904. He wrote books on Robert Lewis Stevenson, William Shakespeare, William Wordsworth, and John Milton, as well as his work titled *Style*, from which the following is excerpted.

Every page of the works of that great exemplar of diction, Milton, is crowded with examples of felicitous and exquisite meaning given to the infallible word. Sometimes he accepts the secondary and more usual meaning of a word only to enrich it by the interweaving of the primary and etymological meaning.

—Walter Raleigh, *Style*, 1897, p. 35

HENRY A. BEERS (1898)

American writer, critic, and Yale University professor Henry A. Beers (1847–1926) published books on American literature, composed poetry, and wrote two volumes on English romanticism, a movement he primarily defined as a return to medieval thought. The latter works were his most famous; an excerpt of the first volume, *A History of English Romanticism in the Eighteenth Century*, follows. In it, Beers notes the importance of Milton to the British romantic poets.

That the influence of Milton, in the romantic revival of the eighteenth century, should have been hardly second in importance to Spenser's is a confirmation of our remark that Augustan literature was "classical" in a way of its own. Milton is the most truly classical of English poets; and yet, from the angle of observation at which the eighteenth century viewed him, he appeared a romantic. It was upon his romantic side, at all events, that the new school of poets apprehended and appropriated him.

—Henry A. Beers, *A History of English Romanticism*, 1898, p. 146

JOHN A. HINES (1898)

Milton is one of the world's great minds. It is elevating to have intercourse with him and to follow his thought. Even in his partisanship—if to such independent and positive convictions as his that term can be applied—he is great. In carefulness and self-consistency he can give lessons to every living writer. He appears to best advantage when compared with other men of admitted power. Alongside of Homer he seems a kindred spirit. Bacon's interpretation of the ancient myths is puerile in comparison with his. His insight into the Sacred Scriptures often shames trained theologians. That his celebrated epic, the *Paradise Lost*, is even now but poorly understood is evidence of his superiority.

—John A. Hines, preface to *Paradise Lost*, 1898, p. iii

WILLIAM P. TRENT (1899)

William Peterfield Trent (1862–1939), professor, historian, and literary historian, was born in Richmond, Virginia, to an aristocratic southern family. He received undergraduate and master's degrees at the University of Virginia, planning on a career in law. He changed direction and entered Johns Hopkins University for further graduate work in history and political science, leaving to accept a professorship at the University of the South, in Sewanee, Tennessee, in political economy, history, and English, though he had no formal training in the latter. Trent labored to raise the level of scholarship in southern history, positing a revisionist point of view in a book-length study that criticized the antiquated values of Charleston, South Carolina, writer William Gilmore Simms; Trent followed that volume with *Southern Statesmen of the Old Régime*, in 1897, and *Robert E. Lee* in 1899.

Turning to his interests in literature, he published *John Milton: A Short Study of His Life and Works* and reestablished the *Sewanee Review* as a literary, rather than historical, journal. In 1900, upon the recommendation of Theodore Roosevelt, Trent was hired as a professor of English literature at Columbia University, where he collaborated on the *The Cambridge History of American Literature* (1917–21) and was chief editor of the 18-volume set of the works of John Milton as published by Columbia University Press.

Milton is the great idealist of our Anglo-Saxon race. In him there was no shadow of turning from the lines of thought and action marked out for him by his presiding genius. His lines may not be our lines; but if we cannot admire to the full his ideal steadfastness of purpose and his masterful accomplishment, it is because our own capacity for the comprehension and pursuit of the ideal is in so far weak and vacillating. And it is this pure idealism of his that makes him by far the most important figure, from a moral point of view, among all Anglo-Saxons.

—William P. Trent, *John Milton: A Short Study of His Life and Works,* 1899, p. 53

WORKS

Though known internationally and historically for one work, *Paradise Lost*, John Milton nonetheless produced a rich canon of writings, which, though they represent a variety of genres, are unified by his poetic craftsmanship, attention to detail, extensive knowledge of classical literature, and overriding, uncompromising religious-political ideology. Three themes are common to all his works: the importance of poetry and the divine calling of the poet, the problem of temptation, and the idea of an ultimate divine grace that allows life to continue in the midst of a corrupt world.

In his poetry, Milton did nothing that was not deliberate, including his intensive, self-imposed plan of study and tackling of a variety of poetic genres. He adhered to a modified version of the Roman poet Virgil's program of poetic hierarchies, beginning with pastoral, in "On the Morning of Christ's Nativity" and "Lycidas," proceeding to the sonnet form, then to the masque, with *Comus*, to the longer lyrical stylings of "L'Allegro" and "Il Penseroso," then to the serious prolonged classical epic form in *Paradise Lost* and *Paradise Regained*, and finally to tragedy in *Samson Agonistes*. Throughout, he also wrote prose works that represented his often radical views on religion and politics but were still elegantly crafted with writing marked by characteristic balance and clarity.

COMUS

Milton's *Comus* (first performed in 1634, published in 1637) is a court masque, or brief play for a courtly audience. Focusing on a mythical theme and incorporating song and usually choreographed dance, it was written for a specific occasion—the installation of the earl of Bridgewater, John Egerton, as lord president of Wales in 1634, and presented at Ludlow Castle, the earl's home. It was commissioned either by the Egerton family or by Henry Lawes, the renowned court musician, whose dedication to Egerton opens this volume's subsection. Milton was certainly aware of the masque's function within the Caroline court, as Inigo Jones produced the most lavish masques known from 1630 to 1639. Whether Milton was the violent antiroyalist evident in his later years or not at this point in his life, his puritan ideologies must have been offended to some extent at the masque's conspicuous consumption, which was compounded in its decadence by being presented on Sundays. Milton, in *Defensio Prima*, condemns Charles for his luxurious livery. *Comus*'s didacticism comes under fire from critics, originating from Samuel Johnson who condemned its speeches as "declamations deliberately composed and formally repeated on a moral question." Yet Milton uses a court drama, a medium that seems antithetical to his Puritan avoidance of such pleasures, to demonstrate the danger that might confront the young Alice Egerton, daughter of the earl, showing how she can overcome that danger with moral steadfastness and the assistance of her loving and noncorruptive family environment. Further, he portrays the immoral court of a lascivious ruler (Comus) as an abomination, looking to the earl of Bridgewater to govern with temperance and justice and using the genre's political nature to critique what he perceived as the immortality of Charles I's court in the process.

Criticism that takes Milton to task for the ways in which *Comus* deviates from the norms of the court masque overlooks Milton's political and religious radicalism, which would cause him to appropriate and then rewrite this mode that traditionally celebrated absolutist monarchy. Milton turns the court entertainment into one more approach to his central concern with temptation and the ability of the Christian to overcome it, to see through false appearances that masquerade as the real. Many of the following selections, however, are positive in their assessments of *Comus*, some asserting this brief work written early in Milton's career to be his best.

Henry Lawes
"To Lord-Viscount Brackly" (1637)

The leading songwriter associated with the court of Charles I, English composer Henry Lawes (1596–1662) also set to music the verse of many renowned poets of the era, including Robert Herrick, Thomas Carew, Richard Lovelace, Edmund Waller, and John Donne. Lawes also performed in and perhaps wrote some of the music for the Caroline court masques.

Lawes also composed a musical score for *Comus*; in the introduction that follows, Lawes, the famed artist, introduces the work of John Milton, who was a relative unknown at the time.

My Lord: This poem, which received its first occasion of birth from your self and others of your noble family, and much honour from your own person in the performance, now returns again to make a finall dedication of itself to you. Although not openly acknowledged by the author, yet it is a legitimate offspring, so lovely, and so much desired, that the often copying of it hath tired my pen to give my severall friends satisfaction, and brought me to a necessity of producing it to the publike view, and now to offer it up in all rightful devotion to those fair hopes and rare endowments of your much-promising youth, which gave a full assurance, to all that knew you, of a future excellence.

—Henry Lawes,
"To Lord-Viscount Brackly," *Comus*, 1637

Henry Wotton (1638)

Since your going, you have charged me with new obligations, both for a very kinde letter from you, dated the sixth of this month, and for a charity piece of entertainment which came therewith,—wherein I should much commend the tragical part if the lyrical did not ravish me with a certain Dorique delicacy in your songs and odes; whereunto I must plainly confess to have seen nothing parallel in our language.

—Henry Wotton, letter to John Milton,
April 13, 1638

Thomas Warton (1785)

On the whole, whether *Comus* be or be not deficient as a drama, whether it is considered as an epic drama, a series of lines, a mask, or a poem, I am of opinion that Milton is here only inferior to his own *Paradise Lost*.

—Thomas Warton, Miltons
Poems on Several Occasions, 1785, p. 263

Walter Scott (1805)

Popular and prolific Scottish poet, novelist, and literary scholar Sir Walter Scott (1771–1832) is famed for his works based on the medieval and Renaissance eras, which showed his depth of study of British history and letters. Among his most enduring works are the novels *Waverly, The Heart of Midlothian, Rob Roy, Ivanhoe,* and *Kenilworth.* His poetry earned him the post of poet laureate, which he declined. Scott also contributed to the field of literary criticism, writing articles for the *Quarterly Review,* and started, with James Ballantyne, the *Edinburgh Annual Register,* submitting an anonymous essay "The Living Poets of Great Britain," which included himself along with Robert Southey, Thomas Campbell, and William Wordsworth. In 1808, he published a critical edition of the works of John Dryden, complete with a well-researched biography; the following passage is taken from that book.

Even Milton deigned to contribute one of his most fascinating poems to the service of the drama; and, notwithstanding the severity of his puritanic tenets, *Comus* could only have been composed by one who felt the full enchantment of the theatre.

—Walter Scott, *The Life of John Dryden,* 1805

Nathan Drake (1817)

Can there be a test of merit more indisputable than this?—for *Comus,* though by no means faultless as a Masque, has to boast of a poetry more rich and imaginative than is to be found in any other composition save *The Tempest* of Shakspeare.

—Nathan Drake, *Shakspeare and His Times,*
1817, volume 2, p. 579

Robert Southey
"Todd's Edition of Milton" (1827)

A young girl and her brothers are benighted and separated as they pass through a forest in Herefordshire. How meagre is this solitary fact! how barren a paragraph would it have made for the Herefordshire journal,—had such a journal been then in existence! Submit it to Milton, and beautiful is the form which it assumes. Then rings that wood with the jocund revelry of Comus and his company; and the maiden draws near, in the strength of unblemished chastity, and her courage waxes strong as she sees

A sable cloud Turn forth her silver lining on the night—

and she calls upon Echo to tell her of the flowery cave which hides her brothers, and Echo betrays her to the enchanter. Then comes the spirit from the "starry threshold of Jove's court," and in shepherd-weeds leads on the brothers to her rescue; and the necromancer is put to flight, but not till he has bound up the lady in fetters of stone; and Sabrina hastens from under her "translucent wave" to dissolve the spell—and again they all three bend their happy steps back to the roof of their fathers. This is not extravagant rhapsody—the tale is still actually preserved; but it is preserved like a fly in amber. The image is a mere thing of wood, but Milton enshrines it, and it becomes an object of worship.

—Robert Southey, "Todd's Edition of Milton,"
Quarterly Review, 1827, p. 45

EDGAR ALLAN POE (1844)

American writer and critic Edgar Allan Poe (1809–49) achieved lasting fame with his tales of horror, his mysteries, and his haunting and lyrical poetry, yet he was also a literary critic of great repute. He anticipated the "art for art's sake" movement in his criticism, focusing on stylistic considerations and eschewing didacticism. This selection shows Poe's careful attention to the aural qualities of Milton's verse, as demonstrated in *Comus.*

The great force derivable from repetition of particular vowel sounds in verse, is little understood, or quite overlooked, even by those versifiers who dwell most upon what is commonly called "alliteration." How richly melodious are these lines of Milton's *Comus*

> May thy *brim*med waves for *this*
> Their full *tri*bute never *miss—*
> May thy *billows roll ashore*
> The beryl and the *golden ore!*

—and yet it seems especially singular that, with the full and noble volume of the long 6 resounding in his ears, the poet should have written, in the last line, "beryl," when he might so well have written "onyx."

—Edgar Allan Poe, *Marginalia,* 1844, *Complete
Works,* volume 16, edited by Harrison, pp. 26–27

HENRY REED (1855)

One of the last and lovelist radiations of the dramatic spirit, which seemed almost to live its life out in about half a century of English literature, beginning in the times of Queen Elizabeth, and ending in those of Charles the

First. Of *Comus*, I think, it might be said, as truly as of any poem in the language, that it is admirably adapted to inspire a real feeling for poetry. It abounds with so much of true imagination, such attractiveness of fancy, such grace of language and of metre, and withal contains so much thought and wisdom wherewith to win a mind unused to the poetic processes, that were I asked what poem might best be chosen to awaken the imagination to a healthful activity, I would point to Milton's *Comus*, as better fitted than almost any other for the purpose.

—Henry Reed, *Lectures on English Literature,*
from Chaucer to Tennyson, 1855, pp. 189–90

DAVID MASSON (1858)

Prolific British historical and literary scholar David Masson (1822–1907) was born in Aberdeen, Scotland. After attending the universities of Aberdeen and Edinburgh while preparing for the ministry, he abandoned that goal in the midst of religious controversies and became editor of the *Aberdeen Banner*. After leaving the publication, moving to London, and writing numerous anonymous articles for other periodicals, Masson produced *The British Museum, Historical and Descriptive* (1848) and "The Story of Thomas Chatterton," serialized in the *Dublin University Magazine*. His literary reputation grew, and in 1852 he became professor of English language and literature at University College, London. Masson's seven-volume set *The Life of John Milton, Narrated in Connexion with the Political, Ecclesiastical, and Literary History of His Time*, published from 1859–80, was to remain his major and most acclaimed work of literary criticism, placing him among preeminent Milton scholars even to the present day. As professor of rhetoric and English literature at the University of Edinburgh, where he was hired in 1865, he worked for the admission of women to the university and for women's right to vote. He continued to write literary historical works on British authors, including William Drummond, romantic poets, Thomas Carlyle, and William Shakespeare and became one of the most important Victorian biographers and literary critics.

Masson's excerpt on Milton's *Comus*, which follows, includes a description of the original setting of the work, in the earl of Bridgewater's castle, the ruins of which still remain. *Comus* is praised as the quintessential work of Milton; albeit written early in his career, it fuses the beauty of English place with language into a perfect creation.

With these sounds left on the ear, and a final glow of angelic light on the eye, the performance ends, and the audience rises and disperses through the castle. The castle is now a crumbling ruin, along the ivy-clad walls and through the dark passages of which the visitor clambers or gropes his way, disturbing the crows and the martlets in their recesses; but one can stand yet in the doorway through which the parting guests of that night descended into the inner court; and one can see where the stage was, on which the sister was lost by her brothers, and Comus revelled with his crew, and the lady was fixed as marble by enchantment, and Sabrina arose with her water-nymphs, and the swains danced in welcome of the earl, and the Spirit gloriously ascended to its native heaven. More mystic it is to leave the ruins, and, descending one of the winding streets that lead from the castle into the valley of the Teme, to look upwards to castle and town seen as one picture, and, marking more expressly the three long pointed windows that gracefully slit the chief face of the wall towards the north to realize that it was from that ruin, and from those windows in the ruin, that the verse of *Comus* was first shook into the air of England. Much as Milton wrote afterwards, he never wrote anything more beautiful, more perfect than *Comus*.

—David Masson, *The Life of John Milton,*
1858, volume 1, chapter 7

Adolphus William Ward (1875)

The sublimity of Milton's genius—the quality which, in the literature of his own country at all events, so pre-eminently distinguishes him as a poet— shines forth with marvellous fulness in this glorious work of his youth. The execution falls but little short of the conception. The lyric portions, although perhaps Macaulay goes too far in describing them as completely overshadowing the dramatic, are among the poet's noblest verse; and the dialogue, though its versification is less stately and its diction less ample than that of *Paradise Lost,* which indeed almost precludes dramatic decla- mation, rises at the climax of the moral interest—in the argument between Comus and the Lady—to almost matchless beauty. Indeed there may be those who cannot suppress a wish that Milton had always adhered to this earlier and easier treatment of his favourite metre—easier I mean to hands under which language passed into combinations "musical, as is Apollo's lute."

—Adolphus William Ward, *A History of English
Dramatic Literature,* 1875–99, volume 3, p. 200

PETER BAYNE (1878)

Peter Bayne's effusive praise of *Comus* places it even above the works of Shakespeare, long considered the touchstone of English literature.

The tale is told beautifully, simply; without plot or any artifice; and with no regard to superficial probabilities. Frankly discarding everything of the drama, except its form, the poet does not stoop, as, within certain limits, the successful dramatist must, to be a literary mocking-bird. Aloft on his perch, like a nightingale, he fills the grove with his music, varying his note as the subject varies, but always with the same volume of sound and the same rich and mellow tone. None of the masters of English poetry, Milton's predecessors, not Chaucer, not Spenser, not Shakespeare even, had done much to detract from the originality, or to herald the perfection of *Comus*. Chaucer's blank verse is not to be mentioned with that of Milton.

—Peter Bayne, *The Chief Actors in the Puritan Revolution*, 1878, p. 309

STOPFORD A. BROOKE (1879)

It is moreover raised above an ethical poem by its imaginative form and power; and its literary worth enables us to consider it, if we choose, apart from its dramatic form. Its imagination, however, sinks at times, and one can scarcely explain this otherwise than by saying that the Elizabethan habit of fantastic metaphor clung to Milton at this time. When he does fall, the fall is made more remarkable by the soaring strength of his loftier flight and by the majesty of the verse. Nothing can be worse in conception than the comparison of night to a thief who shuts up, for the sake of his felony, the stars whose lamps burn everlasting oil in his dark lantern. The better it is carried out and the finer the verse, the worse it is. And yet it is instantly followed by the great passage about the fears of night, the fantasies and airy tongues that syllable men's names, and by the glorious appeal to conscience, faith, and God, followed in its turn by the fantastic conceit of the cloud that turns out its silver lining on the night. This is the Elizabethan weakness and strength, the mixture of gold and clay, the want of that art-sensitiveness which feels the absurd: and Milton, even in *Paradise Lost*, when he had got further from his originals, falls into it not unfrequently. It is a fault which runs through a good deal of his earlier work, it is more seen in *Comus* than elsewhere; but it was the fault of that poetic age.

—Stopford A. Brooke, *Milton*, 1879, p. 24

SAMUEL R. GARDINER (1883)

The beautiful soul makes beautiful the outward form; the base act debases the soul of him who commits it. This was Milton's highest message to the world. This was the witness of Puritanism at its best. This was "the sage and serious doctrine of virginity," of that singleness of heart and spirit which is the safeguard of purity in marriage or out of marriage. Between the ideal of womanhood formed by Milton in his youth and that of even such a man as Massinger there is a great gulf. To Milton the world is a place in which the lady can break the spells of Comus by the very force of innocence. To Massinger it is a place to be shunned and avoided as altogether evil. His Camiola can only find rest by its renunciation.

—Samuel R. Gardiner, *History of England,*
1883, volume 7, p. 337

GEORGE SAINTSBURY (1887)

His greatest work, if scale and merit are considered. . . . The versification, as even Johnson saw, is the versification of *Paradise Lost,* and to my fancy at any rate it has a spring, a variety, a sweep and rush of genius, which are but rarely present later. As for its beauty in parts, *quis vituperavit?* It is impossible to single out passages, for the whole is golden. The entering address of Comus, the song "Sweet Echo," the descriptive speech of the Spirit, and the magnificent eulogy of the "sun-clad power of chastity," would be the most beautiful things where all is beautiful, if the unapproachable "Sabrina fair" did not come later, and were not sustained before and after, for nearly two hundred lines of pure nectar. If poetry could be taught by the reading of it, then indeed the critic's advice to a poet might be limited to this: "Give your days and nights to the reading of Comus."

—George Saintsbury, *A History of
Elizabethan Literature,* 1887, pp. 318–21

J. HOWARD B. MASTERMAN (1897)

Judged simply as a masque, *Comus* is perhaps inferior to some of Ben Jonson's. It is overweighted with moral teaching and lacks the lightening influence of humour. But Milton's genius overflowed the limits of its appointed task, and *Comus* remains a splendid protest, at an hour when such a protest was needed the most, on behalf of a reasonable life. For if *Comus* is the expression of the distaste with which Milton regarded the growing licence of Cavalier society, its production is no less clearly a repudiation of the doctrines of Prynne and the moroser Puritans, to whom the drama was an unholy thing.

—J. Howard B. Masterman,
The Age of Milton, 1897, p. 16

"LYCIDAS"

Milton's pastoral elegy "Lycidas" (1638) combines personal, literary, and political concerns. The work was written for *Justa Edovardo King Naufrago* or *Obsequys for Edward King, Shipwrecked,* a volume of 36 poems collected from various Cambridge associates in memory of fellow Christ's College classmate Edward King. "Lycidas" ostensibly seems to lament the death of a young man, the same age as Milton, who was similarly preparing for the ministry and composing Latin poetry. King died on August 10, 1637, crossing the Irish Sea, thus spawning the myriad watery images that swim through "Lycidas." The city of Cambridge is threaded by the River Cam, another source for the multiple allusions to water in the work. Milton modeled the poem on classical pastoral elegies: the Greek Theocritus's first idyll and Virgil's fifth eclogue. Pastoral poetry is classical rustic poetry, focusing on poet-shepherds, shepherdesses, simple living, an age of innocence that parallels Eden before the Fall, and communion among mortals and immortals. Virgil is of particular interest for Milton throughout his writing career; Milton follows the Virgilian schedule of composition for a developing poet by beginning with the pastoral, then moving to works of increasing difficulty and gravity, including the epic. Milton himself terms the work a "monody," a subset of pastoral elegy that focuses on an interior monologic lament by one shepherd.

Critic Samuel Johnson questioned Milton's sincerity in appropriating the pastoral mode for this work mourning his classmate, but Cambridge was a sylvan setting that brought to mind the beauty summoned by pastorals. Milton also fuses seventeenth-century puritan views of Christ as the Great Shepherd and the reproach of corrupt courtly life, as contrasted with simple, honest rural people. It is unknown how close Milton personally was to King, and he chooses to make the poem more than a personal lament. It is a poem that engages several concerns Milton returns to throughout his career: the role of the poet and the austere life required by the true poet, immortality (here, through poetry), the idea of a utopia merging the human and the divine, and temptations that corrupt that relationship by presenting false substitutes for one's true calling.

The passage in the poem that has received the most censure is the introduction of the false shepherds as an opportunity to rail against Anglican bishops who Milton saw as leading astray the true flock. Within the work, Saint Peter authors the declamation against the English state church, speaking out against one of Milton's long-established targets. However, one could tie this section into an earlier passage that upholds the "homely slighted Shepherd trade," that is, the solitudinous composition of poetry, as a divine calling; both passages admonish Lycidas and the reader to stand steadfast against temptations that weaken faith and virtuous fame.

"Lycidas" is also faulted for a perceived lack of unity within the work, including the shift in voice from first to third person from the poem's opening to closing lines. "Lycidas'" commentators often criticize the depth of emotions within the poem as well, augmenting Samuel Johnson's vituperative remarks, but frequently appreciate its depth of thought and lyrical qualities. Despite any weaknesses marked by its detractors, the work inspired later elegies by Percy Bysshe Shelly and Matthew Arnold and has been placed alongside Tennyson's *In Memoriam A.H.H.* as a renowned treatment of grief for a young male friend.

THOMAS WARTON (1785)

In "Lycidas" there is perhaps more poetry than sorrow. But let us read it for its poetry. It is true that passion plucks no berries from the myrtle and ivy, nor calls upon Arethus and Mincius, nor tells of rough satyrs with cloven heel. But poetry does this; and in the hands of Milton does it with a peculiar and irresistible charm.

—Thomas Warton, *Milton's Poems
on Several Occasions*, 1785, p. 36

THOMAS GREEN (1810)

"Lycidas,"—though highly poetical,—I agree, with Johnson, breathes little sincere sorrow, and is therefore essentially defective as a Monody.

—Thomas Green, *Extracts from the
Diary of a Lover of Literature*, 1810

ROBERT SOUTHEY
"TODD'S EDITION OF MILTON" (1827)

It has been said that this is not the natural mode of expressing passion—that where it is real, its language is less figurative and that "where there is leisure for fiction there is little grief." In general this may be true; in the case of Milton its truth may be doubted. . . . The mind of Milton was perfect fairy-land; and every thought which entered it, whether grave or gay, magnificent or mean, quickly partook of a fairy form.

—Robert Southey, "Todd's Edition of Milton,"
Quarterly Review, 1827, p. 46

EDWIN GUEST (1838)

Historian and literary researcher Edwin Guest (1800–80) is noted for his thorough volume on English rhythms, excerpted here. Guest singles out the appearance of Saint Peter as an absurd element of the poem but allows that "Lycidas" is not without its aesthetic merits.

The common *metre* of six accents, which spread so widely during the sixteenth century, seldom tolerated a verse with a compound section. The reluctance to admit these verses was strengthened by the example of Drayton, who rigidly excluded them from the *Polyolbion*. There are, however, a few poems, in which they are admitted freely enough to give a peculiar character to the rhythm. One of these poems is the "Elegy" written by Brysket, (though generally ascribed to Spenser), on the death of Sir Philip Sidney. It has very little poetical merit, but deserves attention, as having undoubtedly been in Milton's eye, when he wrote his "Lycidas." From it Milton borrowed his irregular rhimes, and that strange mixture of Christianity and Heathenism, which shocked the feelings and roused the indignation of Johnson. It may be questioned, if the peculiarity in the meter can fairly be considered as a blemish. Like endings, recurring at uncertain distances, impart a wildness and an appearance of negligence to the verse, which suits well with the character of elegy. But to bring in St. Peter hand in hand with a pagan deity is merely ludicrous; it was the taste of the age, and that is all that can be urged in its excuse. Still, however, the beauties of this singular poem may well make us tolerant of even greater absurdity. No work of Milton has excited warmer admiration, or called forth more strongly the zeal of the partizan.

—Edwin Guest, *A History of English Rhythms*,
1838, volume I, p. 274

STOPFORD A. BROOKE (1879)

"Lycidas" appeals not only to the imagination, but to the educated imagination. There is no ebb and flow of poetical power as in *Comus*; it is an advance on all his previous work, and it fitly closes the poetic labour of his youth. It is needless to analyse it, and all criticism is weaker than the poem itself. Yet we may say that one of its strange charms is its solemn undertone rising like a religious chaunt through the elegiac musick; the sense of a stern national crisis in the midst of its pastoral mourning; the sense of Milton's grave force of character among the flowers and fancies of the poem; the sense of the Christian religion pervading the classical imagery. We might say that these things are ill-fitted to each other. So they would be, were not the art so fine and the poetry so over-mastering; were they not fused together by genius into a whole so that the unfitness itself becomes fascination.

—Stopford A. Brooke, *Milton*, 1879, p. 26

MARK PATTISON (1879)

In "Lycidas' (1637) we have reached the high-water mark of English poesy and of Milton's own production. A period of a century and a half was to elapse before poetry in England seemed, in Wordsworth's *Ode on Immortality* (1807), to be rising again toward the level of inspiration which it had once attained in "Lycidas." "Lycidas" opens up a deeper vein of feeling, a patriot passion so vehement and dangerous that, like that which stirred the Hebrew prophet, it is compelled to veil itself from power, or from sympathy, in utterance made purposely enigmatical.

—Mark Pattison, *Milton*, 1879, pp. 27–28

FRANCIS HASTINGS DOYLE (1886)

Mr. Arnold, like everyone else who speaks with authority on such matters, is horrified when Dr. Johnson bluntly condemns "Lycidas." Now I could read over the "Allegro" and "Penseroso" a thousand times without tiring of them. *Comus, Paradise Regained,* the other secondary poems, all of them, give me great pleasure, though in different degrees; but as for "Lycidas," well, I say ditto to old Sam. In the first place the kind of idyll is not to my taste. If a poet really sorrows over the death of a friend to that degree that he cannot, as a relief to the soul, refrain from pouring out his sorrow in song, I think his utterance should be natural and straightforward; he should not speak in a falsetto tone, or overlay his theme with classical affectations. On the other hand, if the grief is only a half grief, conjured up by the imagination to play with like a toy, then, in my opinion, the bard had better hold his tongue. In the second place, the jumbling together of Christian and heathen traditions jars upon me just as it jarred upon the tough old dictionary-maker. Nay, besides all this, "Lycidas" appears to me not so much a spontaneous outburst as a self-appointed task. One of Milton's editors tells us that Mr.

King's friends—Milton being one of those friends—agreed to write, and bind up together, a lot of verses on his death, but that when "Lycidas" made its appearance, it proved so much more important than all the other poems put together, that it was withdrawn from the book, to be afterwards separately published; and even now, I think, traces of the original business-like arrangement are to be found in the elegy as we have it.

> —Francis Hastings Doyle,
> *Reminiscences and Opinions*, 1886, p. 184

George Saintsbury (1887)

There are indeed blotches in it. The speech of Peter, magnificently as it is introduced, and strangely as it has captivated some critics, who seem to think that anything attacking the Church of England must be poetry, is out of place, and in itself is obscure, pedantic, and grotesque. There is some over-classicism, and the scale of the piece does not admit the display of quite such sustained and varied power as in *Comus*. But what there is, is so exquisite that hardly can we find fault with Mr. Pattison's hyperbole when he called "Lycidas" the "high-water mark of English poetry." High-water mark even in the physical world is a variable limit. Shakespere constantly, and some other poets here and there in short passages go beyond Milton. But in the same space we shall nowhere find anything that can outgo the passage beginning "Alas what boots it," down to "head of thine," and the whole conclusion from "Return Alpheus." For melody of versification, for richness of images, for curious felicity of expression, these cannot be surpassed.

> —George Saintsbury, *A History of Elizabethan*
> *Literature*, 1887, p. 322

Eugene Lee-Hamilton "Lycidas to Milton (1637)" (1888)

The flowers that we lay upon a tomb
Are withered by the morrow,—ere the crowd
Which for a moment ceased its hum, and bowed
Its head, as Death flew by and made a gloom,
Resumes its whirl. And scarcely longer bloom
The sculptured wreathes with which a tomb more proud,
In some pale minster, may have been endowed;
For marble petals share the common doom.

But thou canst twine the wreaths that never die;
And something tells me thou wilt stay behind
When I am gone; I know it, I know not why.
The sea-gull's scream, the wailing of the wind,
The ocean's roar, sound like Death's prophecy:
I fain would have a garland thou hadst twined.

—Eugene Lee-Hamilton, "Lycidas to Milton
(1637)," *Imaginary Sonnets*, 1888

J. Howard B. Masterman (1897)

"Lycidas" is the elegy of much more than Edward King; it is the last note of the inspiration of an age that was passing away. It is redolent of the "sweet mournfulness of the Spenserian time, upon whose joys Death is the only intruder." No such elegy was to adorn our English literature until "two hundred years after." Shelley and Matthew Arnold produced the two elegiac poems which alone in our language deserve to rank with Milton's—for the wider scope of *In Memoriam* removes it from this category. "Thyrsis" excels "Lycidas" in the expression of chastened sorrow and tender recollection, but Matthew Arnold loved Clough and Oxford as Milton never loved King of Cambridge. *Adonais* is charged with deeper thought and more harmonious passion; but both owe to "Lycidas" a debt which "Lycidas" owes to no other poem.

—J. Howard B. Masterman,
The Age of Milton, 1897, p. 24

William R. Trent (1899)

"Lycidas" has a beauty and passion unknown to its Alexandrian predecessors, and it has not a touch of their oriental effeminacy and licentiousness. The rhythm is varied, and flows now in leaping waves, now in long rolling billows that carry all before them, like the surging periods of *Paradise Lost*. There is probably no short poem in the language the rhythm of which has been more deservedly praised and studied, or more despaired of by other poets. Milton's mastery of rhythm, remarkable from the first, almost culminated in "Lycidas," in spite of the fact that he was there subjected (practically for the last time) to what he afterward called "the troublesome and modern boundage of riming."

—William R. Trent, *John Milton: A Short Study of
His Life and Works*, 1899, p. 140

PARADISE LOST

Nothing in any language quite compares to *Paradise Lost*, first published in 1667 in ten books, then reissued in 12 volumes in 1674. John Milton's foremost work is the apex of the English epic and of all works based on Christian myth. The scope of it alone is remarkable. The plot spans divine history from the Creation to the second coming of Christ, while focusing primarily on the characters of Satan, Adam, and Eve. Milton's also exceeds other literary works in presenting developed portrayals of God, the Son, and the angels. *Paradise Lost* has proved to be so enduring that it has shaped popular views of the temptation of Adam and Eve and the character of Satan; Milton filled in narrative gaps in the biblical texts concerning the war in Heaven and Satan's subsequent fall in ways that have augmented Christian Scripture itself in the perceptions of many.

The composition of *Paradise Lost* is noteworthy in itself, for this epic actually began as a drama; manuscripts from 1640–42 show four drafts of the work as a morality play and a five-act tragedy in its first conceptions. The character interplay and plotting still resonate with Milton's dramatic impulse, as he reshaped the raw materials into an epic. The resulting verse is unsurpassed in English. In its more than 10,000 lines of blank verse, the poem employs such technical skill that each line varies slightly metrically, using enjambment to break up end-stopped lines and employ careful phrasing. Milton wrote *Paradise Lost* at the peak of his poetic powers and while blind; all that he had read, studied, and written was preparing him for this ultimate outpouring of rhetorical prowess and lyrical beauty in the creation of a classically and biblically grounded work. The epic poem could not have been produced in any other age or circumstance. *Paradise Lost* is most literally an homage to the failed great Puritan parliamentary governmental experiment, the initial glimmer of democracy amid centuries of monarchy. It is a memorial to the loss of utopia, the failed dream of bringing the kingdom of God to Earth.

Paradise Lost has attracted critical attention since its initial publication; it has attracted equal measures of praise and controversy, as is fitting for a work written by an author marked by radicalism. Some critics have focused primarily on the formal qualities of the work, its versification, stylistics, and characterization most prominently discussed. Others have studied its classicism, including allusions to ancient works and adherence to or violation of the mechanics of classical epic. Many have interrogated its theology, juxtaposing it with its biblical sources and seventeenth-century religious beliefs to see where Milton's views of divine workings, scripture, and human agency fall. Biographical information has influenced another host of readers, Milton's blindness, marital problems, and personal foibles most affecting perceptions of the work. Finally, the most outspoken critics have brought Milton's political views into their readings of the poem, rejecting or celebrating the epic as it aligns with their beliefs.

The selections that follow showcase the panoply of critical opinion, as well as its stratification along historical lines. As in the section relating to Milton's biography, the commentators of each era read *Paradise Lost* through their own horizons of expectations. The eighteenth-century critics and Victorians show little patience for Milton's puritanism. The neoclassicists condemn Milton's slightest violation of classical decorum and Aristotelian unities, especially the blending of "pagan" and Christian sources, as well as irregularities of meter. The romantic poets frequently celebrate Milton's nonconformity they detect in his portrayals of God, Jesus Christ, and Satan; yet most admit Milton's genius, however they express that particular concept.

ANDREW MARVELL
"ON MR. *MILTON'S* PARADISE LOST" (1674)

The son of a Calvinist preacher, English seventeenth-century poet Andrew Marvell (1621–78) grew up in Hull and started attending Trinity College at Cambridge University in 1633. He completed a B.A. in 1639, after a mysterious period of absence rumored to be caused by either a conversion to Catholicism or service in the English civil war. He then began to pursue a master's degree, leaving after his father's death in 1641. While at Cambridge, he had written a Greek and a Latin poem for a student collection in honor of Charles I's fifth child. After Cambridge, Marvell travelled throughout continental Europe, learning four languages and gathering materials for later poetry. His earlier poems showed a royalist sympathy, such as "Richard Lovelace," commemorating the Cavalier poet, and "Upon the Death of Lord Hastings." These were followed by a poem that established Marvell's fame and showcased his balanced political views, "An Horatian Ode upon Cromwell's Return from Ireland," which presents both praise and blame of Oliver Cromwell in his military actions against the monarchical government. Marvell became a tutor to Thomas, Lord Fairfax's daughter from 1650–53 at Appleton House, the subject of his lengthy poem, then asked Cromwell for a government appointment, using a recommendation from John Milton. After serving first as a tutor to William Dutton, a suitor to Cromwell's daughter, Marvell was named

Latin secretary to the Puritan government in 1657, assisting John Milton, and then was elected to Parliament in 1659 as a representative of Hull.

Marvell's work is often viewed as combining metaphysical and Cavalier strains of seventeenth-century poetry; his carpe diem poem "To His Coy Mistress" is his best-known work and shows the perfect combination of Cavalier subject matter of sexual conquest rendered in a deeply intellectual and deconstructive metaphysical style. After producing numerous lyrical poems on political, philosophical, and amatory themes, Marvell turned to writing social-political satires in prose and poetry that conveyed his disillusionment with the Restoration government, despite being a member of Parliament. Marvell concluded his writing with the polemical work *An Account of the Growth of Popery, and Arbitrary Government in England* (1677).

There is widespread belief that Andrew Marvell, through his Parliamentary office, was instrumental in saving John Milton's life, when Milton was charged with treason by the restored monarch Charles II. Literary scholars currently debate the actual relationship of Marvell and Milton, questioning the closeness of the friendship and the amount of agreement between the two on political issues.

This debate affects the interpretation of the following poem, "On Mr. Milton's Paradise Lost," by Marvell. It combines his personal knowledge of Milton with his poet's sensibility to produce the most famous encomium of *Paradise Lost*. It is possible, however, to note ironies in Marvell's praise poem, as the fact that he applauds Milton's use of unrhymed verse as superior while using rhyme himself. The poem was used as frontmatter to editions of *Paradise Lost* from 1674 onward. The poem, in acknowledging the politically radical aspects of Milton's art, notes that the poet's blindness has not thwarted his enterprise; Milton becomes a type of Tiresias, the blind seer of classical myth. Marvell's poem references as well the subject of Samson Agonistes, Sampson the blind prophet and judge of Israel who would pull down the columns of the Philistines' temple in revenge for his blinding at their hands. The poem also marvels at the enormity of the subject matter of *Paradise Lost*, as well as the previously unmatched brilliance and rhetorical skill in dealing with divine material. Finally, Marvell continues to defend Milton's use of blank verse, castigating rhyme as an empty adornment.

⟨⟨⟨⟩⟩⟩   ⟨⟨⟨⟩⟩⟩   ⟨⟨⟨⟩⟩⟩

When I beheld the Poet blind, yet bold,
In slender Book his vast Design unfold,

Messiah Crown'd, *Gods* Reconcil'd Decree,
Rebelling *Angels,* the Forbidden Tree,
Heav'n, Hell, Earth, Chaos, All; the Argument
Held me a while misdoubting his Intent,
That he would ruine (for I saw him strong)
The sacred Truths to Fable and old Song,
(So *Sampson* groap'd the Temples Posts in spight)
The World o'rewhelming to revenge his Sight.

    Yet as I read, soon growing less severe,
I lik'd his Project, the success did fear;
Through that wide Field how he his way should find
O're which lame Faith leads Understanding blind;
Lest he perplext the things he would explain,
And what was easie he should render vain.

    Or if a Work so infinite he spann'd,
Jealous I was that some less skilful hand
(Such as disquiet alwayes what is well,
And by ill imitating would excell)
Might hence presume the whole Creations day
To change in Scenes, and show it in a Play.

    Pardon me, *mighty Poet,* nor despise
My causeless, yet not impious, surmise.
But I am now convinc'd, and none will dare
Within thy Labours to pretend a Share.
Thou hast not miss'd one thought that could be fit,
And all that was improper dost omit:
So that no room is here for Writers left,
But to detect their Ignorance or Theft.

    That Majesty which through thy Work doth Reign
Draws the Devout, deterring the Profane.
And things divine thou treatst of in such state
As them preserves, and Thee inviolate.
At once delight and horrour on us seize,
Thou singst with so much gravity and ease;
And above humane flight dost soar aloft,
With Plume so strong, so equal, and so soft.
The *Bird* nam'd from that *Paradise* you sing
So never Flags, but alwaies keeps on Wing.

    Where couldst thou Words of such a compass find?
Whence furnish such a vast expense of Mind?

Just Heav'n Thee, like *Tiresias,* to requite,
Rewards with *Prophesie* thy loss of Sight.
     Well mightst thou scorn thy Readers to allure
With tinkling Rhime, of thy own Sense secure;
While the Town-Bays writes all the while and spells,
And like a Pack-Horse tires without his Bells.
Their Fancies like our bushy Points appear,
The Poets tag them; we for fashion wear.
I too transported by the *Mode* offend,
And while I meant to *Praise* thee, must Commend.
Thy verse created like thy *Theme* sublime,
In Number, Weight, and Measure, needs not *Rhime.*

> —Andrew Marvell, "On Mr. *Milton's* Paradise
> lost," 1674

Thomas Rymer (1678)

That *Paradise lost* of *Miltons,* which some are pleas'd to call a Poem.

> —Thomas Rymer, *The Tragedies of the Last Age,*
> 1678

John Oldham "A Pastoral on the Death of the Earl of Rochester" (1680)

Milton, whose Muse with such a daring Flight,
Led out the warring Saraphims to fight.

> —John Oldham, "A Pastoral on the Death of the
> Earl of Rochester," 1680

John Dryden (1685)

Imitation is a nice point, and there are few Poets who deserve to be Models in all they write. *Miltons Paradice Lost* is admirable; but am I therefore bound to maintain, that there are no flats amongst his Elevations, when 'tis evident he creeps along sometimes, for above an Hundred lines together? cannot I admire the height of his Invention, and the strength of his expression, without defending his antiquated words, and the perpetual harshness of their sound? 'Tis as much commendation as a Man can bear, to own him excellent; all beyond it is Idolatry.

> —John Dryden, preface to *Sylvae,* 1685

JOHN DRYDEN (1692)

As for Mr. *Milton,* whom we all admire with so much Justice, his Subject is not that of an Heroique Poem; properly so call'd: His Design is the Losing of our Happiness; his Event is not prosperous, like that of all other Epique Works: His Heavenly Machines are many, and his Humane Persons are but two. But I will not take Mr. *Rymer's* Work out of his Hands. He has promis'd the World a Critique on that Author; wherein, tho' he will not allow his Poem for Heroick, I hope he will grant us, that his Thoughts are elevated, his Words Sounding, and that no Man has so happily Copy'd the Manner of *Homer;* or so copiously translated his *Grecisms,* and the *Latin* Elegancies of *Virgil.* 'Tis true, he runs into a flat of Thought, sometimes for a Hundred Lines together, but 'tis when he is got into a Track of Scripture: His Antiquated words were his Choice, not his Necessity; for therein he imitated *Spencer,* as *Spencer* did *Chawcer.* And tho', perhaps, the love of their Masters, may have transported both too far, in the frequent use of them; yet in my Opinion, Obsolete Words may then be laudably reviv'd, when either they are more Sounding, or more Signifcant than those in practice: And when their Obscurity is taken away, by joining other Words to them which clear the Sense; according to the Rule *of Horace,* for the admission of new Words. But in both cases, a Moderation is to be observ'd, in the use of them: For unnecessary Coynage, as well as unnecessary Revival, runs into Affectation; a fault to be avoided on either hand. Neither will I Justifie *Milton* for his Blank Verse, tho' I may excuse him, by the Example of *Hannibal Cam,* and other *Italians,* who have us'd it: For whatever Causes he alledges for the abolishing of Rhyme (which I have not now the leisure to examine) his own particular Reason is plainly this, that Rhyme was not his Talent; he had neither the Ease of doing it, nor the Graces of it; which is manifest in his *Juvenilia,* or Verses written in his Youth: Where his Rhyme is always constraint and forc'd, and comes hardly from him at an Age when the Soul is most pliant; and the Passion of Love, makes almost every Man a Rhymer, tho' not a Poet.

—John Dryden, *Discourse Concerning the Original and Progress of Satire,* 1692

JOSEPH ADDISON (1712)

An enormously influential eighteenth-century Milton critic, Joseph Addison wrote a series of essays on Milton in *The Spectator,* a newspaper he had co-founded with Richard Steele. The writings were reprinted numerous times as a collection and even appeared in some editions of

Milton's works. The following essay assesses *Paradise Lost* as a classical epic by comparing Milton to Homer and Virgil on specific points of Aristotle's *Poetics*. In some parts, Milton is found wanting: Addison sees Homer's characters as exceeding those in any other epic and dislikes Milton's use of the allegorical figures of Sin and Death. In other ways, however, *Paradise Lost* compares favorably: in its greatness of subject matter, action, structure, and elevated style of language. Most of all, Addison praises Milton for his philosophical depth, proclaiming: "Milton's chief Talent, and indeed his distinguishing Excellence, lies in the Sublimity of his Thoughts."

No. 267, January 5, 1712

Cedite Romani Scriptores, cedite Graii. (Propert.)

There is nothing in Nature more irksom than general Discourses, especially when they turn chiefly upon Words. For this Reason I shall wave the Discussion of that Point which was started some Years since, Whether Milton's *Paradise Lost* may be called an *Heroick Poem?* Those who will not give it that Title, may call it (if they please) a *Divine Poem.* It will be sufficient to its Perfection, if it has in it all the Beauties of the highest kind of Poetry; and as for those who alledge it is not an Heroick Poem, they advance no more to the Diminution of it, than if they should say *Adam* is not *Aeneas,* nor *Eve Helen.*

I shall therefore examine it by the Rules of Epic Poetry, and see whether it falls short of the *Iliad* or *Aeneid* in the Beauties which are essential to that kind of Writing. The first thing to be considered in an Epic Poem, is the Fable, which is perfect or imperfect, according as the Action which it relates is more or less so. This Action should have three Qualifications in it. First, It should be but one Action. Secondly, It should be an entire Action; and Thirdly, It should be a great Action. To consider the Action of the *Iliad, Aeneid,* and *Paradise Lost* in these three several Lights. *Homer* to preserve the Unity of his Action hastens into the midst of things, as *Horace* has observed: Had he gone up to *Leda's* Egg, or begun much later, even at the Rape of *Helen,* or the Investing of *Troy,* it is manifest that the Story of the Poem would have been a Series of several Actions. He therefore opens his Poem with the Discord of his Princes, and artfully interweaves in the several succeeding parts of it, an account of every thing material which relates to them, and had passed before this fatal Dissension. After the same manner *Aeneas* makes his first appearance in the *Tyrrhene* Seas, and within sight of *Italy,* because the Action proposed to be celebrated was that of his Settling himself in *Latium.* But because it was necessary for the Reader to know what had happened to him in the taking of *Troy,* and in the preceding parts of his Voyage, *Virgil* makes his Hero relate it by way of Episode in the second and third Books of the *Aeneid*. The Contents of both which Books come before those of the first Book in the Thread of the Story, tho' for preserving of this Unity of Action, they follow it in the Disposition of the Poem. *Milton*, in Imitation of these two great Poets, opens his *Paradise Lost* with an Infernal Council plotting the Fall of Man, which is the Action he proposed to celebrate; and as for those great Actions, the Battel of the Angels, and the Creation of the World, (which preceded in point of time, and which, in my Opinion, would have entirely destroyed the Unity of his Principal Action, had he related them in the same Order that they happened) he cast them into the fifth, sixth and seventh Books, by way of Episode to this noble Poem.

Aristotle himself allows, that *Homer* has nothing to boast of as to the Unity of his Fable, tho' at the same time that great Critick and Philosopher endeavours to palliate this Imperfection in the *Greek* Poet, by imputing it in some Measure to the very Nature of an Epic Poem. Some have been of Opinion, that the *Aeneid* also labours in this particular, and his Episodes which may be looked upon as Excrescencies rather than as Parts of the Action. On the contrary, the Poem which we have now under our Consideration, hath no other Episodes than such as naturally arise from the Subject, and yet is filled with such a multitude of astonishing Incidents, that it gives us at the same time a Pleasure of the greatest Variety, and of the greatest Simplicity; uniform in its Nature, tho' diversified in the Execution.

I must observe also, that as *Virgil* in the Poem which was designed to celebrate the Original of the Roman Empire, has described the Birth of its great Rival, the *Carthaginian* Commonwealth: *Milton* with the like Art in his Poem on the Fall of Man, has related the Fall of those Angels who are his professed Enemies. Besides the many other Beauties in such an Episode, it's running Parallel with the great Action of the Poem, hinders it from breaking the Unity so much as another Episode would have done, that had not so great an Affinity with the principal Subject. In short, this is the same kind of Beauty which the Criticks admire in the *Spanish Fryar,* or the *Double Discovery,* where the two different Plots look like Counterparts and Copies of one another.

The second Qualification required in the Action of an Epic Poem is, that it should be an *entire* Action: An Action is entire when it is compleat in all its Parts; or as *Aristotle* describes it, when it consists of a Beginning, a Middle, and an End. Nothing should go before it, be intermix'd with it, or follow after it, that is not related to it. As on the contrary, no single Step should be omitted in that just and regular Progress which it must be supposed to take from its Original to its Consummation. Thus we see the Anger *of Achilles* in its Birth, its Continuance and Effects; and *Aeneas's* Settlement in *Italy,* carried on through all the Oppositions in his way to it both by Sea and Land. The Action in *Milton* excels (I think) both the former in this particular; we see it contrived in Hell, executed upon Earth, and punished by Heaven. The parts of it are told in the most distinct manner, and grow out of one another in the most natural Order.

The third Qualification of an Epic Poem is its *Greatness.* The Anger of *Achilles* was of such Consequence, that it embroiled the Kings of *Greece,* destroy'd the Heroes of Asia, and engaged all the Gods in Factions. *Aeneas's* Settlement in *Italy* produced the *Caesars,* and gave Birth to the Roman Empire. *Milton's* Subject was still greater than either of the former; it does not determine the Fate of single Persons or Nations, but of a whole Species. The united Powers of Hell are joyned together for the Destruction of Mankind, which they effected in part, and would have completed, had not Omnipotence it self interposed. The principal Actors are Man in his greatest Perfection, and Woman in her highest Beauty. Their Enemies are the fallen Angels: The Messiah their Friend, and the Almighty their Protecior. In short, every thing that is great in the whole Circle of Being, whether within the Verge of Nature, or out of it, has a proper Part assigned it in this admirable Poem.

In Poetry, as in Architecture, not only the whole, but the principal Members, and every part of them, should be Great. I will not presume to say, that the Book of Games in the *Aeneid,* or that in the *Iliad,* are not of this nature, nor to reprehend *Virgil's* Simile of the Top, and many other of the same Kind in the *Iliad,* as liable to any Censure in this Particular; but I think we may say, without derogating from those wonderful Performances, that there is an Indisputable and Unquestioned Magnificence in every Part of *Paradise Lost,* and indeed a much greater than could have been formed upon any Pagan System.

But *Aristotle,* by the Greatness of the Action, does not only mean that it should be great in its Nature, but also in its Duration, or in other Words, that it should have a due length in it, as well as what we properly call Greatness. The just Measure of this kind of Magnitude, he explains by the following Similitude. An Animal, no bigger than a Mite, cannot appear perfect to the Eye, because the Sight takes it in at once, and has only a confused Idea of the whole, and not a distinct Idea of all its Parts; If on the contrary you should suppose an Animal of ten thousand Furlongs in length, the Eye would be so filled with a single Part of it, that it could not give the Mind an Idea of the whole. What these Animals are to the Eye, a very short or a very long Action would be to the Memory. The first would be, as it were, lost and swallowed up by it, and the other difficult to be contained in it. *Homer* and *Virgil* have shewn their principal Art in this Particular; the Action of the *Iliad,* and that of the *Aeneid,* were in themselves exceeding short, but are so beautifully extended and diversified by the Invention of *Episodes,* and the Machinery of Gods, with the like Poetical Ornaments, that they make up an agreeable Story sufficient to employ the Memory without overcharging it. Milton's Action is enriched with such a variety of Circumstances, that I have taken as much Pleasure in reading the Contents of his Books, as in the best invented Story I ever met with. It is possible, that the Traditions on which the *Iliad* and *Aeneid* were built, had more Circumstances in them than the History of *the Fall of Man,* as it is related in Scripture. Besides it was easier for *Homer* and *Virgil* to dash the Truth with Fiction, as they were in no danger of offending the Religion of their Country by it. But as for *Milton,* he had not only a very few Circumstances upon which to raise his Poem, but was also obliged to proceed with the greatest Caution in every thing that he added out of his own Invention. And, indeed, notwithstanding all the Restraints he was under, he has filled his Story with so many surprising Incidents, which bear so close Analogy with what is delivered in Holy Writ, that it is capable of pleasing the most delicate Reader, without giving Offence to the most scrupulous.

The Modern Criticks have collected from several Hints in the *Iliad* and *Aeneid* the Space of Time, which is taken up by the Action of each of those Poems; but as a great part of *Milton's* Story was transacted in Regions that lie out of the reach of the Sun and the Sphere of Day, it is impossible to gratifie the Reader with such a Calculation, which indeed would be more curious than instructive; none of the Criticks, either Ancient or Modern, having laid down Rules to circumscribe the Action of an Epic Poem with any determined number of Years, Days or Hours.

But of this more particularly hereafter.

No. 273. *January 12, 1712*

. . . *Notandi sunt tibi* Mores. (Hor.)

Having examined the Action *of Paradise Lost,* let us in the next place consider the Actors. This is *Aristotle's* Method of considering; first the Fable, and secondly the Manners, or, as we generally call them in *English,* the Fable and the Characters.

Homer has excelled all the Heroic Poets that ever wrote, in the multitude and variety of his Characters. Every God that is admitted into his poem, acts a Part which would have been suitable to no other Deity. His Princes are as much distinguished by their Manners as by their Dominions; and even those among them, whose Characters seem wholly made up of Courage, differ from one another as to the particular kinds of Courage in which they excell.

In short, there is scarce a Speech or Action in the *Iliad,* which the Reader may not ascribe to the Person that speaks or acts, without seeing his Name at the Head of it.

Homer does not only out-shine all other Poets in the Variety, but also in the Novelty of his Characters. He has introduced among his *Graecian* Princes a Person, who had lived in three Ages of Men, and conversed with *Theseus, Hercules, Polyphemus,* and the first Race of Heroes. His principal Actor is the Son of a Goddess, not to mention the Off-spring of other Deities, who have likewise a Place in his Poem, and the venerable *Trojan* Prince, who was the Father of so many Kings and Heroes. There is in these several Characters of *Homer,* a certain Dignity as well as Novelty, which adapts them in a more peculiar manner to the Nature of an Heroic Poem. Tho', at the same time, to give them the greater variety, he has described a *Vulcan,* that is, a Buffoon among his Gods, and a *Thersites* among his Mortals.

Virgil falls infinitely short of *Homer* in the Characters of his Poem, both as to their Variety and Novelty. *Aeneas* is indeed a perfect Character, but as for *Achates,* tho' he is stiled the Hero's Friend, he does nothing in the whole Poem which may deserve that Title. *Gyas, Mnestheus, Sergestus,* and *Cloanthus,* are all of them Men of the same Stamp and Character,

> . . . *Fortemque Gyan, fortemque Cloanthum:* Virg.

There are indeed several very natural Incidents in the Part of *Ascanius;* as that of *Dido* cannot be sufficiently admired. I do not see any thing new or particular in *Turnus. Pallas* and *Evander* are remote Copies of *Hector* and *Priam,* as *Lausus* and *Mezentius* are almost Parallels to *Pallas* and *Evander.* The Characters of *Nisus* and *Eurialus* are beautiful, but common. We must not forget the Parts of *Sinon, Camilla,* and some few others, which are fine Improvements on the *Greek* Poet. In short, there is neither that Variety nor Novelty in the Persons of the *Aeneid,* which we meet with in those of the *Iliad.*

If we look into the Characters of *Milton,* we shall find that he has introduced all the Variety his Fable was capable of receiving. The whole Species of Mankind was in two Persons at the time to which the Subject of his Poem is confined. We have, however, four distinct Characters in these two Persons. We see Man and Woman in the highest Innocence and Perfection, and in the most abject State of Guilt and Infirmity. The two last Characters are, indeed, very common and obvious, but the two first are not only more magnificent, but more new than any Characters either in *Virgil,* or *Homer,* or indeed in the whole Circle of Nature.

Milton was so sensible of this Defect in the Subject of his Poem, and of the few Characters it would afford him, that he has brought into it two Actors of a Shadowy and Fictitious Nature, in the Persons of Sin and Death, by which means he has wrought into the Body of his Fable a very beautiful and well invented Allegory. But not withstanding the Fineness of this Allegory may attone for it in some measure; I cannot think that Persons of such a Chymerical Existence are proper Actors in an Epic Poem; because there is not that measure of Probability annexed to them, which is requisite in Writings of this kind, as I shall shew more at large hereafter.

Virgil has, indeed, admitted *Fame* as an Actress in the *Aeneid,* but the Part she acts is very short, and none of the most admired Circumstances in that Divine Work. We find in Mock-Heroic Poems, particularly in the *Dispensary* and the *Lutrin,* several Allegorical Persons of this Nature, which are very beautiful in those Compositions, and may, perhaps, be used as an Argument, that the Authors of them were of Opinion, such Characters might have a Place in an Epic Work. For my own part, I should be glad the Reader would think so, for the sake of the Poem I am now examining, and must further add, that if such empty unsubstantial Beings may be ever made use of on this occasion, never were any more nicely imagined, and employed in more proper Actions, than those of which I am now speaking. Another Principal Actor in this Poem is the great Enemy of Mankind. The part of *Ulysses* in *Homer's Odissey* is very much admired by *Aristotle,* as perplexing that Fable with very agreeable Plots and Intricacies, not only by the many Adventures in his Voyage, and the Subtilty of his Behaviour, but by the various Concealments and Discoveries of his Person in several parts of that Poem. But the Crafty Being I have now mentioned, makes a much longer Voyage than *Ulysses,* puts in practice many more Wiles and Stratagems, and hides himself under a greater variety of Shapes and Appearances, all of which are severally detected, to the great Delight and Surprize of the Reader.

We may likewise observe with how much Art the Poet has varied several Characters of the Persons that speak in his infernal Assembly. On the contrary, how has he represented the whole Godhead exerting it self towards Man in its full Benevolence under the Three-fold Distinction of a Creator, a Redeemer and a Comforter!

Nor must we omit the Person *of Raphael,* who amidst his Tenderness and Friendship for Man, shews such a Dignity and Condescention in all his Speech and Behaviour, as are suitable to a Superior Nature. The Angels are indeed as much diversified in *Milton,* and distinguished by their proper Parts, as the Gods are in *Homer* or *Virgil.* The Reader will find nothing ascribed to *Uriel, Gabriel, Michael,* or *Raphael,* which is not in a particular manner suitable to their respective Characters.

There is another Circumstance in the principal Actors of the *Iliad* and *Aeneid,* which gives a peculiar Beauty to those two Poems, and was therefore contrived with very great Judgment. I mean the Authors having chosen for their Heroes Persons who were so nearly related to the People for whom they wrote. *Achilles* was a *Greek,* and *Aeneas* the remote Founder of *Rome.* By this means their Countrymen (whom they principally proposed to themselves for their Readers) were particularly attentive to all the parts of their Story, and sympathized with their Heroes in all their Adventures. A *Roman* could not but rejoice in the Escapes, Successes and Victories of *Aeneas,* and be grieved at any Defeats, Misfortunes or Disappointments that befel him; as a *Greek* must have had the same regard for *Achilles.* And it is plain, that each of those Poems have lost this great Advantage, among those Readers to whom their Heroes are as Strangers, or indifferent Persons.

Milton's Poem is admirable in this respect, since it is impossible for any of its Readers, whatever Nation, Country or People he may belong to, not to be related to the persons who are the principal Actors in it; but what is still infinitely more to its Advantage, the principal Actors in this Poem are not only our Progenitors, but our Representatives. We have an actual Interest in every thing they do, and no less than our utmost Happiness is concerned, and lies at Stake in all their Behaviour.

I shall subjoyn as a Corollary to the foregoing Remark, an admirable Observation out of *Aristotle,* which hath been very much misrepresented in the Quotations of some Modern Criticks. 'If a Man of perfect and consummate Virtue falls into a Misfortune, it raises our Pity, but not our Terror, because we do not fear that it may be our own Case, who do not resemble the Suffering Person. But as that great Philosopher adds, 'If we see a Man of Virtue mixt with Infirmities, fall into any Misfortune, it does not only raise our Pity but our Terror; because we are afraid that the like Misfortunes may happen to our selves, who resemble the Character of the Suffering Person.'

I shall only remark in this Place, that the foregoing Observation of *Aristotle,* tho' it may be true in other Occasions, does not hold in this; because in the present Case, though the Persons who fall into Misfortune are of the most perfect and consummate Virtue, it is not to be considered as what may possibly be, but what actually is our own Case; since we are embark'd with them on the same Bottom, and must be partakers of their Happiness or Misery.

In this, and some other very few Instances, *Aristotle's* Rules for Epic Poetry (which he had drawn from his Reflections upon *Homer)* cannot be supposed to square exactly with the Heroic Poems which have been made since his Time; since it is evident to every impartial Judge his Rules would still have been more perfect, cou'd he have perused the *Aeneid* which was made some hundred Years after his Death.

In my next I shall go through other parts of *Milton's* Poem; and hope that what I shall there advance, as well as what I have already written, will not only serve as a Comment upon *Milton,* but upon *Aristotle.*

No. 279. January 19, 1712

Reddere personal scit convenientia cuique. (Hor.)

We have already taken a general Survey of the Fable and Characters in *Milton's Paradise Lost:* The Parts which remain to be consider'd, according to *Aristotle's* Method, are the Sentiments and the Language. Before I enter upon the first of these, I must advertise my Reader, that it is my Design as soon as I have finished my general Reflections on these four several Heads, to give particular Instances out of the poem now before us of Beauties and Imperfections which may be observed under each of them, as also of such other Particulars as may not properly fall under any of them. This I thought fit to premise, that the Reader may not judge too hastily of this Piece of Criticism, or look upon it as Imperfect, before he has seen the whole Extent of it.

The Sentiments in an Epic Poem are the Thoughts and Behaviour which the Author ascribes to the Persons whom he introduces, and are *just* when they are comformable to the Characters of the several Persons. The Sentiments have likewise a relation to *Things* as well as *Persons,* and are then perfect when they are such as are adapted to the Subject. If in either of these Cases the Poet endeavours to argue or explain, to magnifie or diminish, to raise Love or Hatred, Pity or Terror, or any other Passion, we ought to consider whether the Sentiments he makes use of are proper for those Ends. *Homer* is censured by the Criticks for his Defect as to this Particular in several parts of the *Iliad* and *Odyssey,* tho' at the same time those who have treated this great Poet with Candour, have attributed this Defect to the Times in which he lived. It was the fault of the Age, and not of *Homer,* if there wants that Delicacy in some of his Sentiments, which now appears in the Works of Men of a much inferior Genius. Besides, if there are Blemishes in any particular Thoughts, there is an infinite Beauty in the greatest part of them. In short, if there are many Poets who wou'd not have fallen into the meanness of some of his Sentiments, there are none who cou'd have risen up to the Greatness of others. *Virgil* has excelled all others in the Propriety of his Sentiments. *Milton* shines likewise very much in this Particular: Nor must we omit one Consideration which adds to his Honour and Reputation. *Homer* and *Virgil* introduced Persons whose Characters are commonly known among Men, and such as are to be met with either in History, or in ordinary Conversation. *Milton's* Characters, most of them, lie out of Nature, and were to be formed purely by his own Invention. It shews a greater Genius in *Shakespear* to have drawn his *Calyban*, than his *Hotspur* or *Julius Cassar*. The one was to be supplied out of his own Imagination, whereas the other might have been formed upon Tradition, History and Observation. It was much easier therefore for *Homer* to find proper Sentiments for an Assembly of *Grecian* Generals, than for *Milton* to diversifie his Infernal Council with proper Characters, and inspire them with a variety of Sentiments. The Loves of *Dido* and *Aeneas* are only Copies of what has passed between other Persons. *Adam* and *Eve*, before the Fall, are a different Species from that of Mankind, who are descended from them; and none but a Poet of the most unbounded Invention, and the most exquisite Judgment, cou'd have filled their Conversation and Behaviour with so many apt Circumstances during their State of Innocence.

Nor is it sufficient for an Epic Poem to be filled with such Thoughts as are *Natural*, unless it abound also with such as are *Sublime*. *Virgil* in this Particular falls short of *Homer*. He has not indeed so many Thoughts that are Low and Vulgar; but at the same time has not so many Thoughts that are Sublime and Noble. The truth of it is, *Virgil* seldom rises into very astonishing Sentiments, where he is not fired by the *Iliad*. He every where charms and pleases us by the force of his own Genius; but seldom elevates and transports us where he does not fetch his Hints from *Homer*.

Milton's chief Talent, and indeed his distinguishing Excellence, lies in the Sublimity of his Thoughts. There are others of the Moderns who rival him in every other part of Poetry; but in the greatness of his Sentiments he triumphs over all the Poets both Modern and Ancient, *Homer* only excepted. It is impossible for the Imagination of Man to distend it self with greater Ideas, than those which he has laid together in his first, second and sixth Books. The Seventh, which describes the Creation of the World, is likewise wonderfully Sublime, tho' not so apt to stir up Emotion in the Mind of the Reader, nor consequently so perfect in the Epic way of Writing, because it is filled with less Action. Let the judicious Reader compare what *Longinus* has observed on several Passages in *Homer*, and he will find Parallels for most of them in the *Paradise Lost*.

From what has been said we may infer, that as there are two kinds of Sentiments, the Natural and the Sublime, which are always to be pursued in an Heroic Poem, there are also two kinds of Thoughts which are carefully to be avoided. The first are such as are affected and unnatural; the second such as are mean and vulgar. As for the first kind of Thoughts we meet with little or nothing that is like them in *Virgil*: He has none of those trifling Points and Puerilities that are so often to be met with in *Ovid*, none of the Epigrammatick Turns of *Lucan*, none of those swelling Sentiments which are so frequent in *Statius* and *Claudian*, none of those mixed Embellishments of *Tasso*. Every thing is just and natural. His Sentiments shew that he had a perfect Insight into Human Nature, and that he knew every thing which was the most proper to affect it.

Mr. *Dryden* has in some Places, which I may hereafter take notice of, misrepresented *Virgil's* way of thinking as to this Particular, in the Translation he has given us of the *Aeneid*. I do not remember that *Homer* any where falls into the Faults above mentioned, which were indeed the false Refinements of later Ages. *Milton*, it must be confest, has sometimes erred in this Respect, as I shall shew more at large in another Paper; tho' considering all the Poets of the Age in which he writ, were infected with this wrong way of thinking, he is rather to be admired that he did not give more into it, than that he did sometimes comply with the vicious Taste which prevails so much among Modern Writers.

But since several Thoughts may be natural which are low and groveling, an Epic Poet should not only avoid such Sentiments as are unnatural or affected, but also such as are mean and vulgar. *Homer* has opened a great Field of Raillery to Men of more Delicacy than Greatness of Genius, by the Homeliness of some of his Sentiments. But, as I have before said, these are rather to be imputed to the Simplicity of the Age in which he lived, to which I may also add, of that which he described, than to any Imperfection in that Divine Poet. *Zoilus*, among the Ancients, and Monsieur *Perrault*, among the Moderns, pushed their Ridicule very far upon him, on account of some such Sentiments. There is no Blemish to be observed in *Virgil* under this Head, and but a very few in *Milton*.

I shall give but one Instance of this Impropriety of Thought in *Homer*, and at the same time compare it with an Instance of the same nature, both in *Virgil* and *Milton*. Sentiments which raise Laughter, can very seldom be admitted with any decency into an Heroic Poem, whose Business is to excite Passions of a much nobler Nature. *Homer*, however, in his Characters of *Vulcan* and *Thersites*, in his Story of *Mars* and *Venus*, in his Behaviour of *Irus*, and in other Passages, has been observed to have lapsed into the Burlesque Character, and to have departed from that serious Air which seems essential to the Magnificence of an Epic Poem. I remember but one Laugh in the whole *Aeneid*, which rises in the Fifth Book upon *Monoetes*, where he is represented as thrown overboard, and drying himself upon a Rock. But this Piece of Mirth is so well timed, that the severest Critick can have nothing to say against it, for it is in the Book of Games and Diversions, where the Reader's Mind may be supposed to be sufficiently relaxed for such an Entertainment. The only Piece of Pleasantry in *Paradise Lost,* is where the Evil Spirits are described as rallying the Angels upon the Success of their new invented Artillery. This Passage I look upon to be the most exceptionable in the whole Poem, as being nothing else but a String of Punns, and those too very indifferent.

> . . . Satan beheld their Plight,
> And to his Mates thus in derision call'd.
>> O Friends, why come not on these Victors
>> proud!
> E'er while they fierce were coming, and when we,
> To entertain them fair with *open Front,*
> And Breast, (what could we more) propounded terms
> *Of Composition,* strait they chang'd their Minds,
> *Flew off,* and into strange Vagaries fell,
> As they would dance, yet for a Dance they seem'd
> Somewhat extravagant, and wild, perhaps
> For Joy of offer'd Peace: but I suppose
> If our Proposals once again were *heard,*
> We should compel them to a quick *Result.*
>> To whom thus *Belial* in like gamesome mood.
> Leader, the Terms we sent, were Terms *of weight,*
> Of *hard Contents,* and full of force urg'd home,
> Such as we might perceive amus'd them all,
> And *stumbled* many; who receives them right,
> Had need, from Head to Foot, well *understand;*
> Not *understood,* this Gift they have besides,
> They shew us when our Foes *walk not upright.*
>> Thus they among themselves in pleasant vein
> Stood scoffing. . . .

No. 285. January 26, 1712

Ne quicunque Deus, quicunque adhibebitur heros,

Regali conspectus in auro nuper & ostro,

Migret in Obscuras humili sermone tabernas:

Aut dum vitat humum, nubes & inania captet. (Hor.)

Having already treated of the Fable, the Characters, and Sentiments in the *Paradise Lost,* we are in the last place to consider the *Language;* and as the learned World is very much divided upon *Milton* as to this Point, I hope they will excuse me if I appear particular in any of my Opinions, and encline to those who judge the most advantagiously of the Author.

It is requisite that the Language of an Heroic Poem should be both Perspicuous and Sublime. In proportion as either of these two Qualities are wanting, the Language is imperfect. Perspicuity is the first and most necessary Qualification; insomuch, that a good-natured Reader sometimes overlooks a little Slip even in the Grammar or Syntax, where it is impossible for him to mistake the Poet's Sense. Of this kind is that Passage in *Milton*, wherein he speaks of *Satan*.

. . . God and his Son except,
Created thing nought valu'd be nor shunn'd.

And that in which he describes *Adam* and Eve.

Adam the goodliest Man of Men since born
His Sons, the fairest of her Daughters *Eve*.

It is plain, that in the former of these Passages, according to the natural Syntax, the Divine Persons mentioned in the first Line are represented as created Beings; and that in the other, *Adam* and *Eve* are confounded with their Sons and Daughters. Such little Blemishes as these, when the Thought is great and natural, we should, with *Horace,* impute to a pardonable Inadvertency, or to the Weakness of Human Nature, which cannot attend to each minute Particular, and give the last finishing to every Circumstance in so long a Work. The Ancient Criticks therefore, who were acted by a Spirit of Candour, rather than that of Cavilling, invented certain figures of Speech, on purpose to palliate little Errors of this nature in the Writings of those Authors, who had so many greater Beauties to attone for them.

If Clearness and Perspicuity were only to be consulted, the Poet would have nothing else to do but to cloath his Thoughts in the most plain and natural Expressions. But, since it often happens, that the most obvious Phrases, and those which are used in ordinary Conversation, become too familiar to the Ear, and contract a kind of Meanness by passing through the Mouths of the Vulgar, a Poet should take particular care to guard himself against Idiomatick ways of speaking. Ovicf and *Lucan* have many Poornesses of Expression upon this account, as taking up with the first Phrases that offered, without putting themselves to the trouble of looking after such as would not only be natural, but also elevated and sublime. *Milton* has but a few

Failings in this kind, of which, however, you may meet with some Instances, as in the following Passages.

> Embrio's and Idiots, Eremites and Fryars
> *White, Black and Grey,* with all their *Trumpery,*
> Here Pilgrims roam . . .
> . . . A while Discourse they hold,
> *No fear lest Dinner cool;* when thus began
> Our Author . . .
> Who of all Ages to succeed, but feeling
> The Evil on him brought by me, will curse
> My Head, ill fare our Ancestor impure,
> *For this we may thank* Adam . . .

The great Masters in Composition know very well that many an elegant Phrase becomes improper for a Poet or an Orator, when it has been debased by common use. For this reason the Works of Ancient Authors, which are written in dead Languages, have a great Advantage over those which are written in Languages that are now spoken. Were there any mean Phrases or Idioms in *Virgil* and *Homer,* they would not shock the Ear of the most delicate Modern Reader, so much as they would have done that of an old *Greek* or *Roman,* because we never hear them pronounced in our Streets, or in ordinary Conversation.

It is not therefore sufficient, that the Language of an Epic Poem be Perspicuous, unless it be also Sublime. To this end it ought to deviate from the common Forms and ordinary Phrases of Speech. The Judgment of a Poet very much discovers it self in shunning the common Roads of Expression, without falling into such ways of Speech as may seem stiff and unnatural; he must not swell into a false Sublime, by endeavouring to avoid the other Extream. Among the *Greeks, Æschylus,* and sometimes *Sophocles,* were guilty of this Fault; among the *Latins, Claudian* and *Statius;* and among our own Countrymen, *Shakespear* and *Lee.* In these Authors the Affectation of Greatness often hurts the Perspicuity of the Stile, as in many others the Endeavour after Perspicuity prejudices its Greatness.

Aristotle has observed, that the Idiomatick Stile may be avoided, and the Sublime formed, by the following Methods. First, by the use of Metaphors: such are those in *Milton.*

> *Imparadis'd* in one anothers Arms,
> . . . And in his Hand a Reed

Stood waving *tipt* with Fire; . . .
The grassie Clods now *calv'd.* . . .
Spangled with Eyes . . .

In these and innumerable other Instances, the Metaphors are very bold but just; I must however observe, that the Metaphors are not thick sown in *Milton,* which always savours too much of Wit; that they never clash with one another, which as *Aristotle* observes, turns a Sentence into a kind of an Enigma or Riddle; and that he seldom has Recourse to them where the proper and natural Words will do as well.

Another way of raising the Language, and giving it a Poetical Turn, is to make use of the Idioms of other Tongues. *Virgil* is full of the *Greek* Forms of Speech, which the Criticks call *Hellenisms,* as *Horace* in his Odes abounds with them much more than *Virgil.* I need not mention the several Dialects which *Homer* has made use of for this end. *Milton,* in conformity with the Practice of the Ancient Poets, and with *Aristotle's* Rule has infused a great many *Latinisms,* as well as *Graicisms,* and sometimes *Hebraisms,* into the Language of his Poem, as towards the Beginning of it.

Nor did they *not* perceive the evil plight
In which they were, *or* the fierce Pains *not* feel.
Yet *to* their Gen'ral's Voice they soon obey'd.
. . . Who shall tempt with wandring Feet
The dark unbottom'd Infinite *Abyss,*
And through the *palpable Obscure* find out
His uncouth way, or spread his airy Flight
Upborn with indefatigable Wings
Over the *vast Abrupt!*
. . . So both ascend
In the Visions of God . . .

(B.II.)

Under this Head may be reckoned the placing the Adjective after the Substantive, the transposition of Words, the turning the Adjective into a Substantive, with several other Foreign Modes of Speech, which this Poet has naturalized to give his Verse the greater Sound, and throw it out of Prose.

The third Method mentioned by *Aristotle,* is what agrees with the Genius of the *Greek* Language more than with that of any other Tongue, and is therefore more used by *Homer* than by any other Poet. I mean the lengthning of a

Phrase by the Addition of Words, which may either be inserted or omitted, as also by the extending or contracting of particular Words by the Insertion or Omission of certain Syllables. *Milton* has put in practice this Method of raising his Language, as far as the nature of our Tongue will permit, as in the Passage above-mentioned, *Eremite*, for what is Hermit, in common Discourse. If you observe the Measure of his Verse, he has with great Judgment suppressed a Syllable in several Words, and shortned those of two Syllables into one, by which Method, besides the above-mentioned Advantage, he has given a greater Variety to his Numbers. But this Practice is more particularly remarkable in the Names of Persons and of Countries, as *Beelzebub*, *Hessebon*, and in many other Particulars, wherein he has either changed the Name, or made use of that which is not the most commonly known, that he might the better depart from the Language of the Vulgar.

The same Reason recommended to him several old Words, which also makes his Poem appear the more venerable, and gives it a greater Air of Antiquity.

I must likewise take notice, that there are in *Milton* several Words of his own Coining, as *Cerberean, miscreated, Hell-doom'd, Embryon* Atoms, and many others. If the Reader is offended at this Liberty in our *English* Poet, I would recommend him to a Discourse in *Plutarch,* which shews us how frequently *Homer* has made use of the same Liberty.

Milton, by the above-mentioned Helps, and by the choice of the noblest Words and Phrases which our Tongue wou'd afford him, has carried our Language to a greater height than any of the *English* Poets have ever done before or after him, and made the Sublimity of his Stile equal to that of his Sentiments.

I have been the more particular in these Observations on Milton's Stile, because it is that part of him in which he appears the most singular. The Remarks I have here made upon the Practice of other Poets, with my Observations out of *Aristotle,* will perhaps alleviate the Prejudice which some have taken to his Poem upon this Account; tho' after all, I must confess, that I think his Stile, tho' admirable in general, is in some places too much stiffened and obscured by the frequent use of those Methods, which *Aristotle* has prescribed for the raising of it.

This Redundancy of those several ways of Speech which *Aristotle* calls *foreign Language,* and with which *Milton* has so very much enriched, and in some places darkned the Language of his Poem, was the more proper for his use, because his Poem is written in Blank Verse. Rhyme, without any other Assistance, throws the Language off from Prose, and very often makes an indifferent Phrase pass unregarded; but where the Verse is not built upon Rhymes, there Pomp of Sound, and Energy of Expression, are indispensably necessary to support the Stile, and keep it from falling into the Flatness of Prose.

Those who have not a Taste for this Elevation of Stile, and are apt to ridicule a Poet when he goes out of the common Forms of Expression, would do well to see how *Aristotle* has treated an Ancient Author, called *Euclid,* for his insipid Mirth upon this Occasion. Mr. *Dryden* used to call this sort of Men his Prose-Criticks.

I should, under this Head of the Language, consider *Milton's* Numbers, in which he has made use of several Elisions, that are not customary among other *English* Poets, as may be particularly observed in his cutting off the Letter Y. when it precedes a Vowel. This, and some other Innovations in the Measure of his Verse, has varied his Numbers in such a manner, as makes them incapable of satiating the Ear and cloying the Reader, which the same uniform Measure would certainly have done, and which the perpetual Returns of Rhime never fail to do in long Narrative Poems. I shall close these Reflections upon the Language of *Paradise Lost,* with observing that *Milton* has copied after *Homer,* rather than *Virgil,* in the length of his Periods, the Copiousness of his Phrases, and the running of his Verses into one another.

—Joseph Addison,
from *The Spectator,* January 1712

RICHARD BLACKMORE (1716)

It must be acknowledged that till about forty years ago Great Britain was barren of critical learning, though fertile in excellent writers; and in particular had so little taste for epic poetry, and was so unacquainted with the essential properties and peculiar beauties of it, that *Paradise Lost,* an admirable work of that kind, published by Mr. Milton, the great ornament of his age and country, lay many years unspoken of and entirely disregarded, till at length it happened that some persons of great delicacy and judgment found out the merit of that excellent poem, and, by communicating their sentiments to their friends, propagated the esteem of the author, who soon acquired universal applause.

—Richard Blackmore,
Essays on Several Subjects, 1716

FRANÇOIS MARIE AROUET DE VOLTAIRE (1727)

A major philosopher, critic, historian, and writer of eighteenth-century France, Voltaire (1694–1778) was born François Marie Arouet in Paris, to a solicitor father who wanted his son to follow his career in law. Instead, Voltaire wrote inflammatory articles about the regent Phillipe d'Orleans, earning himself exile at the chateau of the duc de Sully and, later, imprisonment in the Bastille. His epic on Henri IV, which protested religious intolerance, again stirred up trouble, and Voltaire was exiled to England in 1726, where he became acquainted with the leading satirists Alexander Pope and Jonathan Swift. His 1734 *Letters Concerning the English Nation* was ordered burned for its alleged criticism of French institutions. Voltaire returned to writing plays, which he had begun with the 1719 *Oedipe*, had an affair with the marquise du Chatelet, living with her for a while in Cirey before moving to Potsdam from 1750–53 at the request of Frederick II, king of Prussia, when the affair ended. Upon Voltaire's return trip to France, he was arrested, accused of stealing a manuscript of Frederick's poems.

Paris was no longer receptive to Voltaire, so he purchased a property in Geneva. His relationship there with the progressive Jean Le Rond d'Alembert, who had written an article in the *Encyclopédie* advocating tolerance for the theater, which had been suppressed by the Calvinists, spurred a religious argument with Jean-Jacques Rousseau. Incited by the Lisbon earthquake of 1755, Voltaire wrote his best-known work, *Candide* (published 1759), as a response to Rousseau's optimism over providential workings and an attempt to dispute the idea that everything happens for the best reasons. He moved back to France, settling in Ferney, where he increased his campaign against religious intolerance, following the burning of the *Encyclopédie* and Voltaire's poem *La religion naturelle*, as well as the horrific torture and execution of a Protestant man accused (falsely, in Voltaire's mind) of murdering his son. Voltaire wrote *A Treatise on Religious Toleration* in 1764, in protest to these and other events that he saw as evidence of the extreme narrowmindedness of his era. He also produced a pocket dictionary of philosophy, written using the scientific method, including a dissection of Scriptures that was viewed as scandalous by some but popular with many. Altogether, Voltaire wrote numerous dramas, novels, short stories, and philosophical works that invited controversy at nearly every turn.

Here, Voltaire's critique of *Paradise Lost* shows his respect for British writing. His banishment to England had instilled in him a sense that the British enjoyed more liberties in the realm of religion and philosophy than the French, whom he castigated for intolerance. Thus, while Milton's puritanical views could have earned Voltaire's ire, he is instead celebrated for following his conscience against the state religion. Voltaire's sensibilities are shaped as well by his neoclassical aesthetics, emphasizing the use of classical epic and the form of the poem.

⸻ ❧ ⸻ ❧ ⸻ ❧ ⸻

Milton is the last in *Europe* who wrote an *Epick* Poem, for I wave all those whose Attempts have been unsuccessful, my Intention being not to descant on the many who have contended for the Prize, but to speak only of the very few who have gain'd it in their respective Countries.

Milton, as he was travelling through *Italy* in his Youth, saw at *Florence* a Comedy call'd *Adamo,* writ by one *Andreino* a Player, and dedicated to *Mary de Medicis* Queen of *France.* The Subject of the Play was the *Fall of Man;* the Actors, God, the Devils, the Angels, *Adam, Eve,* the Serpent, Death, and the Seven Mortal Sins. That Topick so improper for a Drama, but so suitable to the absurd Genius of the *Italian* Stage, (as it was at that Time) was handled in a Manner intirely conformable to the Extravagance of the Design. The Scene opens with a Chorus of Angels, and a Cherubim thus speaks for the Rest: "Let the Rainbow be the Fiddlestick of the Fiddle of the Heavens, let the Planets be the Notes of our Musick, let Time beat carefully the Measure, and the Winds make the Sharps, &c." Thus the Play begins, and every Scene rises above the last in Profusion of Impertinence.

Milton pierc'd through the Absurdity of that Performance to the hidden Majesty of the Subject, which being altogether unfit for the Stage, yet might be (for the Genius of *Milton,* and for his only) the Foundation of an *Epick* Poem.

He took from that ridiculous Trifle the first Hint of the noblest Work, which human Imagination hath ever attempted, and which he executed more than twenty Years after.

In the like Manner, *Pythagoras* ow'd the Invention of Musick to the Noise of the Hammer of a Blacksmith. And thus in our Days Sir *Isaak Newton* walking in his Gardens had the first Thought of his System of Gravitation, upon seeing an Apple falling from a Tree.

If the Difference of Genius between Nation and Nation, ever appear'd in its full Light, 'tis in *Milton's* Paradise lost.

The *French* answer with a scornful Smile, when they are told there is in *England* an *Epick* Poem, the Subject whereof is the Devil fighting against God, and *Adam* and *Eve* eating an Apple at the Persuasion of a Snake. As that Topick hath afforded nothing among them, but some lively Lampoons, for which that Nation is so famous; they cannot imagine it possible to build an *Epick* Poem upon the subject of their Ballads. And indeed such an Error ought to be excused; for if we consider with what Freedom the politest Part of Mankind throughout all *Europe,* both Catholicks and Protestants, are wont to ridicule in Conversation those consecrated Histories; nay, if those who have the highest Respect for the Mysteries of the Christian Religion, and who are struck with Awe at some Parts of it, yet cannot forbear now and then making free with the *Devil,* the *Serpent,* the Frailty of our first Parents, the Rib which *Adam* was robb'd of, and the like; it seems a very hard Task for a profane Poet to endeavour to remove those Shadows of Ridicule, to reconcile together what is Divine and what looks absurd, and to command a Respect that the sacred Writers could hardly obtain from our frivolous Minds.

What *Milton* so boldly undertook, he perform'd with a superior Strength of Judgement, and with an Imagination productive of Beauties not dream'd of before him. The *Meaness* (if there is any) of some Parts of the Subject is lost in the Immensity of the Poetical Invention. There is something above the reach of human Forces to have attempted the Creation without Bombast, to have describ'd the Gluttony and Curiosity of a Woman without Flatness, to have brought Probability and Reason amidst the Hurry of imaginary Things belonging to another World, and as far remote from the Limits of our Notions as they are from our Earth; in short to force the Reader to say, "If God, if the Angels, if Satan would speak, I believe they would speak as they do in *Milton.*"

I have often admir'd how barren the Subject appears, and how fruitful it grows under his Hands.

The *Paradise Lost* is the only Poem wherein are to be found in a perfect Degree that Uniformity which satisfies the Mind and that Variety which pleases the Imagination. All its Episodes being necessary Lines which aim at the Centre of a perfect Circle. Where is the Nation who would not be pleas'd with the Interview *of Adam* and the *Angel?* With the Mountain of Vision, with the bold Strokes which make up the Relentless, undaunted, and sly Character of Satan? But above all with that sublime Wisdom which *Milton* exerts, whenever he dares to describe God, and to make him speak? He seems indeed to draw the Picture of the Almighty, as like as human Nature can reach to, through the mortal Dust in which we are clouded.

The *Heathens* always, the *Jews* often, and our Christian Priests sometimes, represent God as a Tyrant infinitely powerful. But the God *of Milton* is always a Creator, a Father, and a Judge, nor is his Vengeance jarring with his Mercy, nor his Predeterminations repugnant to the Liberty of Man. These are the Pictures which lift up indeed the Soul of the Reader. *Milton* in that Point as well as in many others is as far above the ancient Poets as the Christian Religion is above the *Heathen* Fables.

But he hath especially an indisputable Claim to the unanimous Admiration of Mankind, when he descends from those high Flights to the natural Description of human Things. It is observable that in all other Poems Love is represented as a Vice, in *Milton* only 'tis a Virtue. The Pictures he draws of it, are naked as the Persons he speaks of, and as venerable. He removes with a chaste Hand the Veil which covers everywhere else the enjoyments of that Passion. There is Softness, Tenderness and Warmth without Lasciviousness; the Poet transports himself and us, into that State of innocent Happiness in which *Adam* and *Eve* continued for a short Time: He soars not above human, but above corrupt Nature, and as there is no Instance of such Love, there is none of such Poetry.

How then it came to pass that the *Paradise Lost* had been so long neglected, (nay almost unknown) in *England*, (till the Lord *Sommers* in some Measure *taught Mankind to admire it,)* is a Thing which I cannot reconcile, *neither* with the Temper, *nor* with the Genius of the *English* Nation.

The Duke of *Buckingham* in his Art of Poetry gives the Preference to *Spencer.* It is reported in the Life of the Lord *Rochester,* that he had no Notion of a better Poet than *Cowley.*

Mr. *Dryden's* Judgement on *Milton* is still more unaccountable. He hath bestow'd some Verses upon him, in which he puts him upon a Level with, nay above *Virgil* and *Homer;*

The Force of Nature could not further go,
To make a third she join'd the former two.

The same Mr. *Dryden* in his Preface upon his Translation of the *Æneid,* ranks *Milton* with *Chapellain* and *Lemoine* the most impertinent Poets who ever scribbled. How he could extol him so much in his Verses, and debase him so low in his Prose, is a Riddle which, being a Foreigner, I cannot understand. In short one would be apt to think that Milton has not obtained his true Reputation till Mr. *Adisson,* the best Critick as well as the best Writer of his Age, pointed out the most hidden Beauties of the *Paradise Lost,* and settled forever its Reputation.

It is an easy and a pleasant Task to take Notice of the many Beauties of *Milton* which I call universal: But 'tis a ticklish Undertaking to point out what would be reputed a Fault in any other Country.

I am very far from thinking that one Nation ought to judge of its Productions by the Standard of another, nor do I presume that the *French* (for Example) who have no *Epick* Poets, have any Right to give Laws on *Epick* Poetry.

But I fancy many *English* Readers, who are acquainted with the *French* language, will not be displeas'd to have some Notion of the Taste of that Country: And I hope they are too just either to submit to it, or despise it barely upon the Score of its being foreign to them.

Would each Nation attend a little more than they do, to the Taste and the Manners of their respective Neighbours, perhaps a general good Taste might diffuse itself through all *Europe* from such an intercourse of Learning, and from that useful Exchange of Observations. The *English* Stage, for Example, might be clear'd of mangled Carcasses, and the Style of their tragick Authors, come down from their forced Metaphorical Bombast to a nearer Imitation of Nature. The *French* would learn from the *English* to animate their Tragedies with more Action, and would contract now and then their long Speeches into shorter and warmer Sentiments.

The *Spaniards* would introduce in their Plays more Pictures of human Life, more Characters and Manners, and not puzzle themselves always in the Entanglements of confus'd Adventures, more romantick than natural. The *Italian* in Point of Tragedy would catch the Flame from the English, and all the Rest from the *French*. In Point of Comedy, they would learn from Mr. *Congreve* and some other Authors, to prefer Wit and Humour to Buffoonery.

To proceed in that View, I'll venture to say that none of the *French* Criticks could like the Excursions which *Milton* makes sometimes beyond the strict Limits of his Subject. They lay down for a Rule that an Author himself ought never to appear in his Poem; and his own Thoughts, his own Sentiments must be spoken by the Actors he introduces. Many judicious Men in *England* comply with that Opinion, and Mr. *Adisson* favours it. I beg Leave in this place to hazard a Reflection of my own, which I submit to the Reader's Judgement.

Milton breaks the Thread of his Narration in two Manners. The first consists of two or three kinds of prologues, which he premises at the Beginning of some Books. In one Place he expatiates upon his own Blindness; in another he compares his Subject and prefers it to that of the *Iliad,* and to the common Topicks of War, which were thought before him the only Subject fit for *Epick* Poetry; and he adds that he hopes to soar as high as all his Predecessors, unless the cold Climate of *England damps his Wings.*

His other Way of interrupting his Narration, is by some Observations which he intersperses now and then upon some great Incident, or some interesting Circumstance. Of that Kind is his Digression on Love in the fourth Book;

Whatever *Hippocrites* austerely talk
Defaming as impure, what God declares
Pure, and commands to some, leaves free to all.

Our Maker bids increase, who bids abstain
But our Destroyer foe to God and Men?
Hail wedded Love, &c.

As to the first of these two Heads, I cannot but own that an Author is generally guilty of an impardonable Self-love, when he lays aside his Subject to descant on his own Person; but that human Frailty is to be forgiven in *Milton*; nay, I am pleas'd with it. He gratifies the Curiosity, it raises in me about his Person, when I admire the Author, I desire to know something of the Man, and he whom all Readers would be glad to know, is allow'd to speak of himself. But this however is a very dangerous Example for a Genius of an inferior Order, and is only to be justified by Success.

As to the second Point I am so far from looking on that Liberty as a Fault, that I think it to be a great Beauty. For if Morality is the aim of Poetry, I do not apprehend why the Poet should be forbidden to intersperse his Descriptions with moral Sentences and useful Reflexions, provided he scatters them with a sparing Hand, and in proper Places either when he wants Personages to utter those Thoughts, or when their Character does not permit them to speak in the Behalf of Virtue.

'Tis strange that *Homer* is commended by the Criticks for his comparing *Ajax* to an Ass pelted away with Stones by some Children, *Ulysses* to a Pudding, the Council-board of *Priam* to Grashoppers. 'Tis strange, I say, that they defend so clamorously those Similes tho' never so foreign to the Purpose, and will not allow the natural Reflexions, the noble Digressions of *Milton* tho' never so closely link'd to the Subject.

I will not dwell upon some small Errors of *Milton*, which are obvious to every Reader, I mean some few Contradictions and those frequent Glances at the *Heathen* Mythology, which Fault by the by is so much the more unexcusable in him, by his having premis'd in his first Book that those Divinities were but Devils worshipp'd under different Names, which ought to have been a sufficient Caution to him not to speak of the Rape of *Proserpine*, of the Wedding *of Juno* and *Jupiter*, &c. as Matters of Fact.

I lay aside likewise his preposterous and aukward Jests, his Puns, his too familiar Expressions so inconsistent with the Elevation of his Genius, and of his Subject.

To come to more essential Points and more *liable* to be debated. I dare affirm that the Contrivance of the *Pandaemonium* would have been entirely disapprov'd of by Criticks like *Boyleau, Racine*, &c.

That Seat built for the Parliament of the Devils, seems very preposterous: Since Satan hath summon'd them altogether, and harangu'd them just before in an ample Field. The Council was necessary; but where it was to be held, 'twas very indifferent. The Poet seems to delight in building his *Pandaemonium* in *Doric* Order with Freeze and Cornice, and a Roof of Gold. Such a Contrivance savours more of the wild Fancy of our Father *le Moine,* then of the serious spirit of *Milton.* But when afterwards the Devils turn dwarfs to fill their Places in the House, as if it was impracticable to build a Room large enough to contain them in their natural Size; it is an idle Story which would match the most extravagant Tales. And to crown all, Satan and the chief Lords preserving their own monstrous Forms, while the rabble of the Devils shrink into Pigmees, heightens the Ridicule of the whole Contrivance to an unexpressible Degree. Methinks the true Criterion for discerning what is really ridiculous in an *Epick* Poem, is to examine if the same Thing would not fit exactly the Mock heroick. Then I dare say that no-thing is so adapted to that ludicrous way of Writing as the Metamorphosis of the Devils into Dwarfs.

The Fiction of *Death* and *Sin* seems to have in it some great Beauties and many gross Defects. In order to canvass this Matter with Order. We must first lay down that such shadowy Beings, as *Death, Sin, Chaos,* are intolerable when they are not allegorical. For Fiction is nothing but Truth in Disguise. It must be granted too, that an Allegory must be short, decent and noble. For an Allegory carried too far or too low, is like a beautiful Woman who wears always a Mask. An Allegory is a long Metaphor; and to speak too long in metaphor's must be tiresom, because unnatural. This being premis'd, I must say that in general those Fictions, those imaginary beings, are more agreeable to the Nature of *Milton's* Poem, than to any other; because he hath but two natural Persons for his Actors, I mean *Adam* and *Eve.* A great Part of the Action lies in imaginary Worlds, and must *of course* admit of imaginary Beings.

Then Sin springing out of the Head of Satan, seems a beautiful Allegory of Pride, which is look'd upon as the first Offence committed against God. But I question if *Satan,* getting his Daughter with Child, is an Invention to be approv'd off. I am afraid that Fiction is but a meer Quibble; for if Sin was of a masculine Gender in *English, as it is in all the other Languages,* that whole Affair Drops, and the Fiction vanishes away. But suppose we are not so nice, and we allow Satan to be in Love with Sin, *because this Word is made feminine in* English (as Death passes also for masculine) what a horrid and loathsome Idea does *Milton* present to the Mind, in this Fiction? *Sin* brings forth Death, this Monster inflam'd with Lust and Rage, lies with his Mother, as she had done with her Father. From that new Commerce, springs a Swarm of Serpents, which creep in and out of their Mother's Womb, and gnaw and tear the Bowels they are born from.

Let such a Picture be never so beautifully drawn, let the Allegory be never so obvious, and so clear, still it will be intolerable, on the Account of its Foulness. That Complication of Horrors, that Mixture of Incest, that Heap of Monsters, that Loathsomeness so far fetch'd, cannot but shock a Reader of delicate Taste.

But what is more intolerable, there are Parts in that Fiction, which bearing no Allegory at all, have no Manner of Excuse. There is no Meaning in the Communication between Death and Sin, 'tis distasteful without any Purpose; or if any Allegory lies under it, the filthy Abomination of the Thing is certainly more obvious than the Allegory.

I see with Admiration, *Sin*, the *Portress* of Hell, opening the Gates of the Abiss, but unable to shut them again; that is really beautiful, because 'tis true. But what signifies Satan and Death quarrelling together, grinning at one another, and ready to fight?

The Fiction of *Chaos, Night,* and *Discord,* is rather a Picture, than an Allegory; and for ought I know, deserves to be approv'd, because it strikes the Reader with Awe, not with Horror.

I know the Bridge built by Death and Sin, would be dislik'd in *France.* The nice Criticks of that Country would urge against that Fiction, that it seems too common, and that it is useless; for Men's Souls want no paved Way, to be thrown into Hell, after their Separation from the Body.

They would laugh justly at the Paradise of Fools, at the Hermits, Fryars, Cowles, Beads, Indulgences, Bulls, Reliques, toss'd by the Winds, at *St. Peter's* waiting with his Keys at the Wicket of Heaven. And surely the most passionate Admirers of *Milton,* could not vindicate those low comical Imaginations, which belong by Right to *Ariosto.*

Now the sublimest of all the Fictions calls me to examine it. I mean the War in Heaven. The Earl of *Roscommon,* and Mr. *Addison* (whose Judgement seems either to guide, or to justify the Opinion of his Countrymen) admire chiefly that Part of the Poem. They bestow all the Skill of their Criticism and the Strength of their Eloquence, to set off that favourite Part. I may affirm, that the very Things they admire, would not be tolerated by the *French* Criticks. The Reader will perhaps see with Pleasure, *in what consists so strange a Difference,* and what may be the Ground of it.

First, they would assert, that a War in Heaven being an imaginary Thing, which lies out of the Reach of our Nature, should be contracted in two or three Pages, rather than lengthen'd out into two Books; because we are naturally impatient of removing from us the Objects which are not adapted to our Senses.

According to that Rule, they would maintain that 'tis an idle Task to give the Reader the full Character of the Leaders of that War, and to describe *Raphael, Michael, Abdiel, Moloch,* and *Nisroth,* as *Homer* paints *Ajax, Diomede,* and *Hector.*

For what avails it to draw at length the Picture of these Beings, so utterly Strangers to the Reader, that he cannot be affected any Way towards them; by the same Reason, the long Speeches of these imaginary Warriors, either before the Battle or in the Middle of the Action, their mutual Insults, seem an injudicious Imitation of *Homer.*

The aforesaid Criticks would not bear with the Angels plucking up the Mountains, with their Woods, their Waters, and their Rocks, and flinging them on the Heads of their Enemies. Such a Contrivance (they would say) is the more puerile, the more it aims at Greatness. Angels arm'd with Mountains in Heaven, resemble too much the Dipsodes in *Rabelais,* who wore an Armour of *Portland* Stone six Foot thick.

The Artillery seems of the same Kind, yet more trifling, because more useless.

To what Purpose are these Engines brought in? Since they cannot wound the Enemies, but only remove them from their Places, and make them tumble down: Indeed (if the Expression may be forgiven) 'tis to play at Nine-Pins. And the very Thing which is so dreadfully great on Earth, becomes very low and ridiculous in Heaven.

I cannot omit here, the visible Contradiction which reigns in that Episode. God sends his faithful Angels to fight, to conquer and to punish the Rebels. *Go* (says He, to *Michael* and *Gabriel)*

> . . . And to the Brow of Heaven
> Pursuing, drive them out from God and Bliss,
> Into their Place of Punishment, the Gulph
> Of *Tartarus,* which ready opens wide
> His fiery Chaos to receive their Fall.

How does it come to pass, after such a positive Order, that the Battle hangs doubtful? And why did God the Father command *Gabriel* and *Raphael,* to do what He executes afterwards by his Son only.

I leave it to the Readers, to pronounce, if these Observations are right, or ill-grounded, and if they are carried to far. But in case these Exceptions are just, the severest Critick must however confess there are Perfections enough in *Milton,* to attone for all his Defects.

I must beg leave to conclude this Article on Milton with two Observations.

His Hero (I mean *Adam,* his first Personage) is unhappy. That demonstrates against all the Criticks, that a very good Poem may end unfortunately, in Spight of all their pretended Rules. Secondly, the *Paradise Lost* ends compleatly. The Thread of the Fable is spun out to the last. *Milton* and *Tasso* have been careful of not stopping short and abruptly. The one does not abandon *Adam* and Eve, till they are driven out of *Eden.* The other does not conclude, before *Jerusalem* is taken. *Homer* and *Virgil* took a contrary Way, the *Iliad* ends with the Death of *Hector,* the *Æneid,* with that of *Turnus:* The Tribe of Commentators have upon that enacted a Law, that a House ought never to be finish'd, because *Homer* and *Virgil* did not compleat their own; but if *Homer* had taken *Troy,* and *Virgil* married *Lavinia* to *Æneas,* the Criticks would have laid down a Rule just the contrary.

—François Marie Arouet de Voltaire, from *An Essay upon Epick Poetry,* 1727

Jonathan Swift (1732)

When Milton first published his famous poem, the first edition was very long going off; few either read, liked, or understood it; and it gained ground merely by its merit.

—Jonathan Swift, letter to Charles Wogan, Aug. 2, 1732

Alexander Pope (1736)

Milton's style, in his *Paradise Lost,* is not natural; 'tis an exotic style.—As his subject lies a good deal out of our world, it has a particular propriety in those parts of the poem: and, when he is on earth, wherever he is describing our parents in Paradise, you see he uses a more easy and natural way of writing.— Though his formal style may fit the higher parts of his own poem, it does very ill for others who write on natural and pastoral subjects.

—Alexander Pope, *Spence's Anecdotes,* 1734–36, p. 131

Theophilus Cibber (1753)

The British nation, which has produced the greatest men in every profession, before the appearance of Milton could not enter into any competition with antiquity, with regard to the sublime excellencies of poetry. Greece could boast an Euripides, Eschylus, Sophocles and Sappho; England was proud of her Shakespeare, Spenser, Johnson and Fletcher; but their then ancients had still a poet in reserve superior to the rest, who stood unrivalled by all succeeding times, and in epic poetry, which is justly esteemed the highest effort of genius, Homer had no rival. When Milton appeared, the pride of Greece was humbled, the competition became more equal, and since *Paradise Lost* is ours; it would, perhaps, be an injury to our national fame to yield the palm to any state, whether ancient or modern.

—Theophilus Cibber, *Lives of the Poets*,
1753, volume 2, p. 108

THOMAS GRAY (1757)

Nor second He, that rode sublime
Upon the seraph-wings of Extasy,
The secrets of th' Abyss to spy.
    He pass'd the flaming bounds of Place and Time:
The living Throne, the sapphire-blaze,
Where Angels tremble, while they gaze,
He saw; but blasted with excess of light,
Closed his eyes in endless night.

—Thomas Gray, *The Progress of Poesy*, 1757

FRANÇOIS MARIE AROUET DE VOLTAIRE (1759)

"What? the barbarian who constructed a long commentary on the first chapter of Genesis in ten books of harsh verse? The clumsy imitator of the Greeks who caricatures creation and who, while Moses represents the Eternal Being as creating the world by his word, makes the Messiah take a big compass out of a cupboard in heaven to trace out the work? What? I admire the man who has spoilt Tasso's hell and Tasso's devil; who makes Lucifer masquerade, now as a toad, now as a pigmy; who puts the same speech in his mouth a hundred times over; who represents him as arguing on divinity; who, in attempting a serious imitation of Ariosto's comic invention of fire-arms, makes the devils fire cannon in heaven? Neither I, nor anybody in Italy, has ever been able to take pleasure in all these dismal extravagances. His marriage of Sin and Death, and the snakes of which Sin is delivered, make any man of tolerably delicate taste sick, and his long description of a hospital is only good for a grave-digger. This obscure, eccentric, and disgusting poem was despised at its birth: and I treat it to-day as it was treated in its own country by its own contemporaries. Anyhow, I say what I think, and I really care very little whether others agree with me or not."

—François Marie Arouet de Voltaire,
Candide, 1759, chapter 25

JOHN WESLEY (1763)

Founder of the Methodist movement, an evangelical revival within the Anglican Church, John Wesley (1703–91) was one of seven surviving children born to the rector of Epworth, Samuel Wesley, and Susannah Wesley, who also held large Bible meetings in their kitchen. Wesley graduated from Christ's Church, Oxford, in 1724 and was ordained an Anglican priest in 1728. While at Oxford, he and his brother, Charles, became involved with a group of students who were mockingly called Methodists because of their methodical study of Scripture and austere habits, such as fasting two days a week. The group was also known for its work in helping those at the margins of society. In 1735, John Wesley left for a missionary trip to Georgia, in the American colonies, returning two years later after a lack of success in reaching the native tribes of the region and an ill-fated romantic attachment. After Wesley returned to London, he underwent a mystical experience, feeling a divine touch while in a worship service led by Moravians, and thereafter devoted his life to reaching people both within and without the church through itinerant preaching and organizing small groups called Methodist societies, as well as continuing to promote social justice for the poor.

Although Charles Wesley, who was also a preacher and a co-founder of the Methodist movement, is best known for writing poetry and composing thousands of hymns, John Wesley also wrote hymns and poetry. The Wesley brothers found inspiration in seventeenth-century poets, especially George Herbert and John Milton. John Wesley appreciated Milton's work to such an extent that he published an edition of *Paradise Lost*, an abridged version with annotations aimed at a nonscholarly audience. What follows is Wesley's preface to his edition, lauding Milton's preeminence as poet, while admitting the difficulty of reading *Paradise Lost*.

To the Reader.

Of all the poems which have hitherto appeared in the World, in whatever Age or Nation, the Preference has generally been given by impartial judges, to *Milton's Paradise Lost*. But this inimitable Work amidst all its Beauties, is unintelligible to abundance of Readers: The immense Learning which he has every where crowded together, making it quite obscure to persons of a common Education.

This Difficulty, almost insuperable as it appears, I have endeavored to remove in the following Extract: First, By omitting those Lines, which I despaired of explaining to the unlearned, without using abundance of Words: And, Secondly, by adding short and easy Notes, such as I trust will make the Main of this excellent Poem, clear and intelligible to any uneducated Person, of a tolerable good understanding.

To those Passages which I apprehend to be peculiarly Excellent, either with regard to Sentiment or Expression, I have prefixed a Star: And these, I believe, it would be worth while to read over and over, and even to commit to Memory.

London, January 2, 1763

—John Wesley, *An Extract from*
Milton's Paradise Lost, 1763

JAMES BEATTIE (1776)

Adam and Eve, in the state of innocence, are well imagined, and admirably supported; and the different sentiments arising from difference of sex, are traced out with inimitable delicacy, and philosophical propriety. After the fall, he makes them retain the same characters, without any other change than what the transition from innocence to guilt might be supposed to produce: Adam has still that preeminence in dignity, and Eve in loveliness, which we should naturally look for in the father and mother of mankind.—Of the blessed spirits, Raphael and Michael are well distinguished; the one for affability, and peculiar good-will to the human race; the other for majesty, but such as commands veneration, rather than fear.—We are sorry to add, that Milton's attempt to soar still higher, only shows, that he had already soared as high, as, without being "blasted with excess of light," it is possible for the human imagination to rise.

—James Beattie, *An Essay on Poetry and Music*, 1776

WILLIAM COWPER (1779)

Was there ever any thing so delightfull as the Music of the *Paradise Lost*? It is like that of a fine Organ; has the fullest & the deepest Tones of Majesty, with all the Softness & Elegance of the Dorian Flute. Variety without End! & never equal'd unless perhaps by Virgil. Yet the Doctor has little or nothing to say upon this copious Theme, but talks something about the unfitness of the English Language for Blank Verse, & how apt it is, in the Mouth of some Readers to degenerate into Declamation. Oh! I could thresh his old Jacket 'till I made his Pension Jingle in his Pocket.

—William Cowper, letter to
William Unwin, October 31, 1779

WILLIAM GODWIN "OF CHOICE IN READING" (1797)

Milton has written a sublime poem upon a ridiculous story of eating an apple, and of the eternal vengeance decreed by the Almighty against the whole human race, because their progenitor was guilty of this black and detestable offence.

—William Godwin, "Of Choice in Reading,"
The Enquirer, 1797, p. 135

FRIEDRICH VON SCHLEGEL (1815)

German writer, philosopher, and critic Friederich von Schlegel (1772–1819) studied and published on classical works, trying to connect ancient Greece with modern culture and asserting that poetry should combine mysticism with classicism. Together with his brother August Wilhelm, he edited and contributed essays to the journal *Athenäum*, developing a literary theory that would lead to German romanticism. He delivered two lecture series in Vienna, on modern history and on literature, that were important in developing the idea of a new incarnation of the Middle Ages; the following passage was taken from his lectures on literature. Here, Schlegel is intrigued by Milton's subject matter, "the holy mysteries of religion," but finds his narrow Protestant view has limited the deeper symbolism Schlegel finds in the Italian epics. He also prefers what he sees as the Germanic language of Edmund Spenser, as opposed to Milton's Latinate diction.

His epic is, at the very outset, exposed to the difficulties which beset all Christian poems that celebrate the holy mysteries of religion. It is strange that he failed to discover the incompleteness of *Paradise Lost* as a unique whole, and that it could only appear, as it really is, the first act of a great Christian drama, of which the Creation, the Fall, and Redemption, are so many successive acts, closely linked together. He eventually perceived the defect, it is true, and appended *Paradise Regained:* but the proportions of this latter to the first performance were not in keeping, and much too slight to admit of its constituting an efficient key-stone. When compared with Dante and Tasso, who were his models, Milton, as a Protestant, laboured under considerable disadvantages, since he was deprived of a vast storehouse of emblematical representation, tales, and traditions, which considerably enriched their verse. Accordingly, he sought to supply the deficiency by means of fables and allegories selected from the Koran and the Talmud, a remedy not at all in harmonious unison with the general complexion of a serious Christian poem. The merits of his epic do not, accordingly, consist in regularity of plan so much as in scattered passages of independent beauty, and in the perfection of his poetic diction. The universal admiration of Milton in the eighteenth century is based on his isolated descriptions of paradisaic innocence and beauty, his awful picture of Hell, with the character of its inhabitants, whom he sketched, after the antique, as giants of the Abyss. It is questionable if any real benefit accrued to the language of English poetry from its increased leaning to the Latinism of Milton rather than to the Germanism of Spenser: but this tendency being a fact, Milton must be regarded as the greatest master of style, and in many respects the standard of dignified poetic expression. It is not, however, easy to propose any fixed normal standard for a language composed, as the English is, of mixed ingredients: suspended between two extremes, it cannot but be subject to occasional oscillation to and fro. Shakspere alone exhibits the varied elements of copiousness, power, and brilliancy inherent in it.

—Friedrich von Schlegel,
Lectures on the History of Literature, 1815

John Keats
"Notes on Milton's *Paradise Lost*" (1818)

The Genius of Milton, more particularly in respect to its span in immensity, calculated him, by a sort of birth-right, for such an "argument" as the *Paradise Lost:* he had an exquisite passion for what is properly, in the sense of ease and pleasure, poetical Luxury; and with that, it appears to me, he would fain have been content, if he could, so doing, have preserved his self-respect and feel[ing] of duty performed; but there was working in him, as it were, that same sort of thing as operates in the great world to the end of a Prophecy's being accomplish'd: therefore he devoted himself rather to the ardours than the pleasures of song, solacing himself at intervals with cups of old wine; and those are, with some exceptions the finest parts of the poem.

—John Keats, "Notes on Milton's *Paradise Lost,*"
1818

Samuel Taylor Coleridge "Milton" (1818)

Samuel Taylor Coleridge's comments on Milton have appeared several times in this volume. In his more developed essay that follows, Coleridge gives some background to Milton's era and then discusses *Paradise Lost* as it relates to the Aristotelian rules of classical epic. In most cases, Milton's epic lines up favorably, though his language when it comes to God is limited in some cases by the biblical texts. Coleridge, nonetheless, praises Milton's interconnection of diction and poetic style, asserting, "The language and versification of the *Paradise Lost* are peculiar in being so much more necessarily correspondent to each than those in any other poem or poet." Finally, Coleridge moves past classical studies to show his preference for romantic criteria and declare, "Sublimity is the pre-eminent characteristic of the *Paradise Lost.*"

If we divide the period from the accession of Elizabeth to the Protectorate of Cromwell into two unequal portions, the first ending with the death of James I. the other comprehending the reign of Charles and the brief glories of the Republic, we are forcibly struck with a difference in the character of the illustrious actors, by whom each period is rendered severally memorable. Or rather, the difference in the characters of the great men in each period, leads us to make this division. Eminent as the intellectual powers were that were displayed in both; yet in the number of great men, in the various sorts of excellence, and not merely in the variety but almost diversity of talents united in the same individual, the age of Charles falls short of its predecessor; and the stars of the Parliament, keen as their radiance was, in fulness and richness of lustre, yield to the constellation at the court of Elizabeth;—which can only be paralleled by Greece in her brightest moment, when the titles of the poet, the philosopher, the historian, the statesman and the general not seldom formed a garland round the same head, as in the instances of our Sidneys and Raleighs. But then, on the other hand, there was a vehemence of will, an enthusiasm of principle, a depth and an earnestness of spirit, which the charms of individual fame and personal aggrandisement could not pacify,—an aspiration after reality, permanence, and general good,—in short, a moral grandeur in the latter period, with which the low intrigues, Machiavellic maxims, and selfish and servile ambition of the former, stand in painful contrast.

The causes of this it belongs not to the present occasion to detail at length; but a mere allusion to the quick succession of revolutions in religion, breeding a political indifference in the mass of men to religion itself, the enormous increase of the royal power in consequence of the humiliation of the nobility and the clergy—the transference of the papal authority to the crown,—the unfixed state of Elizabeth's own opinions, whose inclinations were as popish as her interests were protestant—the controversial extravagance and practical imbecility of her successor—will help to explain the former period; and the persecutions that had given a life and soul-interest to the disputes so imprudently fostered by James,—the ardour of a conscious increase of power in the commons, and the greater austerity of manners and maxims, the natural product and most formidable weapon of religious disputation, not merely in conjunction, but in closest combination, with newly awakened political and republican zeal, these perhaps account for the character of the latter sra.

In the close of the former period, and during the bloom of the latter, the poet Milton was educated and formed; and he survived the latter, and all the fond hopes and aspirations which had been its life; and so in evil days, standing as the representative of the combined excellence of both periods, he produced the *Paradise Lost* as by an after-throe of nature. "There are some persons (observes a divine, a contemporary of Milton's) of whom the grace of God takes early hold, and the good spirit inhabiting them, carries them on in an even constancy through innocence into virtue, their Christianity bearing equal date with their manhood, and reason and religion, like warp and woof, running together, make up one web of a wise and exemplary life. This (he adds) is a most happy case, wherever it happens; for, besides that there is no sweeter or more lovely thing on earth than the early buds of piety, which drew from our Saviour signal affection to the beloved disciple, it is better to have no wound than to experience the most sovereign balsam, which, if it work a cure, yet usually leaves a scar behind." Although it was and is my intention to defer the consideration of Milton's own character to the conclusion of this Lecture, yet I could not prevail on myself to approach the *Paradise Lost* without impressing on your minds the conditions under which such a work was in fact producible at all, the original genius having been assumed as the immediate agent and efficient cause; and these conditions I find in the character of the times and in his own character. The age in which the foundations of his mind were laid, was congenial to it as one golden era of profound erudition and individual genius;—that in which the superstructure was carried up, was no less favourable to it by a sternness of discipline and a show of self-control, highly flattering to the imaginative dignity of an heir of fame, and which won Milton over from the dear-loved delights of academic groves and cathedral aisles to the anti-prelatic party. It acted on him, too, no doubt, and modified his studies by a characteristic controversial spirit, (his presentation of God is tinted with it)—a spirit not less busy indeed in political than in theological and ecclesiastical dispute, but carrying on the former almost always, more or less, in the guise of the latter. And so far as Pope's censure of our poet,—that he makes God the Father a school divine—is just, we must attribute it to the character of his age, from which the men of genius, who escaped, escaped by a worse disease, the licentious indifference of a Frenchified court.

Such was the *nidus* or soil, which constituted, in the strict sense of the word, the circumstances of Milton's mind. In his mind itself there were purity and piety absolute; an imagination to which neither the past nor the present were interesting, except as far as they called forth and enlivened the great ideal, in which and for which he lived; a keen love of truth, which, after many weary pursuits, found a harbour in a sublime listening to the still voice in his own spirit, and as keen a love of his country, which, after a disappointment still more depressive, expanded and soared into a love of man as a probationer of immortality. These were, these alone could be, the conditions under which such a work as the *Paradise Lost* could be conceived and accomplished. By a life-long study Milton had known—

> What was of use to know,
> What best to say could say, to do had done.
> His actions to his words agreed, his words
> To his large heart gave utterance due, his heart
> Contain'd of good, wise, fair, the perfect shape;

and he left the imperishable total, as a bequest to the ages coming, in the PARADISE LOST.

Difficult as I shall find it to turn over these leaves without catching some passage, which would tempt me to stop, I propose to consider, 1st, the general plan and arrangement of the work;—2ndly, the subject with its difficulties and advantages;—3rdly, the poet's object, the spirit in the letter, the *enthymion en mytho*, the true school-divinity; and lastly, the characteristic excellencies of the poem, in what they consist, and by what means they were produced.

1. As to the plan and ordonnance of the Poem. Compare it with the *Iliad*, many of the books of which might change places without any injury to the thread of the story. Indeed, I doubt the original existence of the *Iliad* as one poem; it seems more probable that it was put together about the time of the Pisistratidae. The *Iliad*—and, more or less, all epic poems, the subjects of which are taken from history—have no rounded conclusion; they remain, after all, but single chapters from the volume of history, although they are ornamental chapters. Consider the exquisite simplicity of the *Paradise Lost*. It and it alone really possesses a beginning, a middle, and an end; it has the totality of the poem as distinguished from the *ab ovo* birth and parentage, or straight line, of history.

2. As to the subject.

In Homer, the supposed importance of the subject, as the first effort of confederated Greece, is an after-thought of the critics; and the interest, such as it is, derived from the events themselves, as distinguished from the manner of representing them, is very languid to all but Greeks. It is a Greek poem. The superiority of the *Paradise Lost* is obvious in this respect, that the interest transcends the limits of a nation. But we do not generally dwell on this excellence of the *Paradise Lost,* because it seems attributable to Christianity itself;—yet in fact the interest is wider than Christendom, and comprehends the Jewish and Mohammedan worlds;—nay, still further, inasmuch as it represents the origin of evil, and the combat of evil and good, it contains matter of deep interest to all mankind, as forming the basis of all religion, and the true occasion of all philosophy whatsoever.

The Fall of Man is the subject; Satan is the cause; man's blissful state the immediate object of his enmity and attack; man is warned by an angel who gives him an account of all that was requisite to be known, to make the warning at once intelligible and awful; then the temptation ensues, and the Fall; then the immediate sensible consequence; then the consolation, wherein an angel presents a vision of the history of men with the ultimate triumph of the Redeemer. Nothing is touched in this vision but what is of general interest in religion; any thing else would have been improper.

The inferiority of Klopstock's *Messiah* is inexpressible. I admit the prerogative of poetic feeling, and poetic faith; but I cannot suspend the judgment even for a moment. A poem may in one sense be a dream, but it must be a waking dream. In Milton you have a religious faith combined with the moral nature; it is an efflux; you go along with it. In Klopstock there is a wilfulness; he makes things so and so. The feigned speeches and events in the *Messiah* shock us like falsehoods; but nothing of that sort is felt in the *Paradise Lost,* in which no particulars, at least very few indeed, are touched which can come into collision or juxta-position with recorded matter.

But notwithstanding the advantages in Milton's subject, there were concomitant insuperable difficulties, and Milton has exhibited marvellous skill in keeping most of them out of sight. High poetry is the translation of reality into the ideal under the predicament of succession of time only. The poet is an historian, upon condition of moral power being the only force in the universe. The very grandeur of his subject ministered a difficulty to Milton. The statement of a being of high intellect, warring against the supreme Being, seems to contradict the idea of a supreme Being. Milton precludes our feeling this, as much as possible, by keeping the peculiar attributes of divinity less in sight, making them to a certain extent allegorical only. Again, poetry implies the language of excitement; yet how to reconcile such language with God? Hence Milton confines the poetic passion in God's speeches to the language of scripture; and once only allows the *passio vera,* or *quasi- humana* to appear, in the passage, where the Father contemplates his own likeness in the Son before the battle:—

Go then, thou Mightiest, in thy Father's might,
Ascend my chariot, guide the rapid wheels
That shake Heaven's basis, bring forth all my war,
My bow and thunder; my almighty arms
Gird on, and sword upon thy puissant thigh;
Pursue these sons of darkness, drive them out
From all Heaven's bounds into the utter deep:
There let them learn, as likes them, to despise
God and Messiah his anointed king.

                                                            (B. VI. v. 710.)

3. As to Milton's object:—

It was to justify the ways of God to man! The controversial spirit observable in many parts of the poem, especially in God's speeches, is immediately attributable to the great controversy of that age, the origination of evil. The Arminians considered it a mere calamity. The Calvinists took away all human will. Milton asserted the will, but declared for the enslavement of the will out of an act of the will itself. There are three powers in us, which distinguish us from the beasts that perish;—1, reason; 2, the power of viewing universal truth; and 3, the power of contracting universal truth into particulars. Religion is the will in the reason, and love in the will.

The character of Satan is pride and sensual indulgence, finding in self the sole motive of action. It is the character so often seen *in little* on the political stage. It exhibits all the restlessness, temerity, and cunning which have marked the mighty hunters of mankind from Nimrod to Napoleon. The common fascination of men is, that these great men, as they are called, must act from some great motive. Milton has carefully marked in his Satan the intense selfishness, the alcohol of egotism, which would rather reign in hell than serve in heaven. To place this lust of self in opposition to denial of self or duty, and to show what exertions it would make, and what pains endure to accomplish its end, is Milton's particular object in the character of Satan. But around this character he has thrown a singularity of daring, a grandeur of sufferance, and a ruined splendour, which constitute the very height of poetic sublimity.

Lastly, as to the execution:—

The language and versification of the *Paradise Lost* are peculiar in being so much more necessarily correspondent to each than those in any other poem or poet. The connexion of the sentences and the position of the words are exquisitely artificial; but the position is rather according to the logic of passion or universal logic, than to the logic of grammar. Milton attempted to make the English language obey the logic of passion as perfectly as the Greek and Latin. Hence the occasional harshness in the construction.

Sublimity is the pre-eminent characteristic of the *Paradise Lost*. It is not an arithmetical sublime like Klopstock's, whose rule always is to treat what we might think large as contemptibly small. Klopstock mistakes bigness for greatness. There is a greatness arising from images of effort and daring, and also from those of moral endurance; in Milton both are united. The fallen angels are human passions, invested with a dramatic reality.

The apostrophe to light at the commencement of the third book is particularly beautiful as an intermediate link between Hell and Heaven; and observe, how the second and third book support the subjective character of the poem. In all modern poetry in Christendom there is an under consciousness of a sinful nature, a fleeting away of external things, the mind or subject greater than the object, the reflective character predominant. In the *Paradise Lost*, the sublimest parts are the revelations of Milton's own mind, producing itself and evolving its own greatness; and this is so truly so, that when that which is merely entertaining for its objective beauty is introduced, it at first seems a discord.

In the description of Paradise itself you have Milton's sunny side as a man; here his descriptive powers are exercised to the utmost, and he draws deep upon his Italian resources. In the description of Eve, and throughout this part of the poem, the poet is predominant over the theologian. Dress is the symbol of the Fall, but the mark of intellect; and the metaphysics of dress are, the hiding what is not symbolic and displaying by discrimination what is. The love of Adam and Eve in Paradise is of the highest merit—not phantomatic, and yet removed from every thing degrading. It is the sentiment of one rational being towards another made tender by a specific difference in that which is essentially the same in both; it is a union of opposites, a giving and receiving mutually of the permanent in either, a completion of each in the other.

Milton is not a picturesque, but a musical, poet; although he has this merit that the object chosen by him for any particular foreground always remains prominent to the end, enriched, but not incumbered, by the opulence of descriptive details furnished by an exhaustless imagination. I wish the *Paradise Lost* were more carefully read and studied than I can see any ground for believing it is, especially those parts which, from the habit of always looking for a story in poetry, are scarcely read at all,—as for example, Adam's vision of future events in the 11th and 12th books. No one can rise from the perusal of this immortal poem without a deep sense of the grandeur and the purity of Milton's soul, or without feeling how susceptible of domestic enjoyments he really was, notwithstanding the discomforts which actually resulted from an apparently unhappy choice in marriage. He was, as every truly great poet has ever been, a good man; but finding it impossible to realize his own aspirations, either in religion, or politics, or society, he gave up his heart to the living spirit and light within him, and avenged himself on the world by enriching it with this record of his own transcendant ideal.

—Samuel Taylor Coleridge, "Milton,"
1818, *Literary Remains*, ed. Coleridge,
volume 1, 1836, pp. 166–78

WILLIAM HAZLITT "ON SHAKSPEARE AND MILTON" (1818)

One of the great romantic critics, essayists, and reformers, William Hazlitt (1778–1830) was the son of a Presbyterian minister and dissenter who moved his family from Kent to Ireland and to the American colonies while working for religious and social issues. Reverend Hazlitt helped establish the first Unitarian church in Boston. The family returned to England, where Hazlitt attended New Unitarian College at Hackney intending to enter the ministry as well, but, influenced by William Godwin, he decided against not only a career in religion but also religion itself. After dabbling in painting, Hazlitt turned to writing his radical views, with his first publication *An Essay on the Principles of Human Action: being an Argument in favour of the National Disinterestedness of the Human Mind* (1805), one that he worked on for years, meeting Coleridge and Wordsworth in the process, who in turn introduced him to Charles and Mary Lamb, major influences on Hazlitt's later literary writing and journalism career. In addition to a number of other political-philosophical works, Hazlitt published a grammar book, gave a philosophical lecture series in London, and turned to journalism to support himself. Serving as reporter for the *Morning Chronicle*, Hazlitt also wrote articles for other periodicals including the *Times*. Revealing his controversial nature, some of Hazlitt's articles attacked writers for giving up their idealism, including Robert Southey for accepting the position of poet laureate and William Wordsworth for his sinecure as distributor of stamps in Westmorland.

Hazlitt produced a number of occasional essays and lectures on literature that were later compiled in book form. The following passage is
from his first lecture series on the English poets; Shakespeare was the
long-standing favorite of Hazlitt, the subject of a number of his works.
Yet, in the prolonged discussion of Milton, Hazlitt finds much to admire,
particularly his genius and imagination that were central to Hazlitt's
metaphysical philosophy, nonconformity, and romantic sensibilities.

Milton has borrowed more than any other writer, and exhausted every
source of imitation, sacred or profane; yet he is perfectly distinct from every
other writer. He is a writer of centos, and yet in originality scarcely inferior
to Homer. The power of his mind is stamped on every line. The fervour
of his imagination melts down and renders malleable, as in a furnace, the
most contradictory materials. In reading his works, we feel ourselves under
the influence of a mighty intellect, that the nearer it approaches to others,
becomes more distinct from them. The quantity of art in him shews the
strength of his genius: the weight of his intellectual obligations would have
oppressed any other writer. Milton's learning has the effect of intuition. He
describes objects, of which he could only have read in books, with the vividness of actual observation. His imagination has the force of nature. He makes
words tell as pictures.

> Him followed Rimmon, whose delightful seat
> Was fair Damascus, on the fertile banks
> Of Abbana and Pharphar, lucid streams.

The word *lucid* here gives to the idea all the sparkling effect of the most
perfect landscape. And again:

> As when a vulture on Imaus bred,
> Whose snowy ridge the roving Tartar bounds,
> Dislodging from a region scarce of prey,
> To gorge the flesh of lambs and yeanling kids
> On hills where flocks are fed, flies towards the springs
> Of Ganges or Hydaspes, Indian streams;
> But in his way lights on the barren plains
> Of Sericana, where Chineses drive
> With sails and wind their cany waggons light.

If Milton had taken a journey for the express purpose, he could not have
described this scenery and mode of life better. Such passages are like

demonstrations of natural history. Instances might be multiplied without end.

We might be tempted to suppose that the vividness with which he describes visible objects, was owing to their having acquired an unusual degree of strength in his mind, after the privation of his sight; but we find the same palpableness and truth in the descriptions which occur in his early poems. In 'Lycidas' he speaks of 'the great vision of the guarded mount,' with that preternatural weight of impression with which it would present itself suddenly to 'the pilot of some small night-foundered skiff: and the lines in the 'Penseroso,' describing 'the wandering moon,'

Riding near her highest noon,
Like one that had been led astray
Through the heaven's wide pathless way,

are as if he had gazed himself blind in looking at her. There is also the same depth of impression in his descriptions of the objects of all the different senses, whether colours, or sounds, or smells—the same absorption of his mind in whatever engaged his attention at the time. It has been indeed objected to Milton, by a common perversity of criticism, that his ideas were musical rather than picturesque, as if because they were in the highest degree musical, they must be (to keep the sage critical balance even, and to allow no one man to possess two qualities at the same time) proportionably deficient in other respects. But Milton's poetry is not cast in any such narrow, common-place mould; it is not so barren of resources. His worship of the Muse was not so simple or confined. A sound arises 'like a stream of rich distilled perfumes'; we hear the pealing organ, but the incense on the altars is also there, and the statues of the gods are ranged around! The ear indeed predominates over the eye, because it is more immediately affected, and because the language of music blends more immediately with, and forms a more natural accompaniment to, the variable and indefinite associations of ideas conveyed by words. But where the associations of the imagination are not the principal thing, the individual object is given by Milton with equal force and beauty. The strongest and best proof of this, as a characteristic power of his mind, is, that the persons of Adam and Eve, of Satan, &c. are always accompanied, in our imagination, with the grandeur of the naked figure; they convey to us the ideas of sculpture. As an instance, take the following

He soon
Saw within ken a glorious Angel stand,

The same whom John saw also in the sun:
His back was turned, but not his brightness hid;
Of beaming sunny rays a golden tiar
Circled his head, nor less his locks behind
Illustrious on his shoulders fledge with wings
Lay waving round; on some great charge employ'd
He seem'd, or fix'd in cogitation deep.
Glad was the spirit impure, as now in hope
To find who might direct his wand'ring flight
To Paradise, the happy seat of man,
His journey's end, and our beginning woe.
But first he casts to change his proper shape,
Which else might work him danger or delay
And now a stripling cherub he appears,
Not of the prime, yet such as in his face
Youth smiled celestial, and to every limb
Suitable grace diffus'd, so well he feign'd:
Under a coronet his flowing hair
In curls on either cheek play'd; wings he wore
Of many a colour'd plume sprinkled with gold,
His habit fit for speed succinct, and held
Before his decent steps a silver wand.

The figures introduced here have all the elegance and precision of a Greek statue; glossy and impurpled, tinged with golden light, and musical as the strings of Memnon's harp! Again, nothing can be more magnificent than the portrait of Beelzebub:

With Atlantean shoulders fit to bear
The weight of mightiest monarchies:

Or the comparison of Satan, as he lay floating many a rood,' to 'that sea beast,'

Leviathan, which God of all his works
Created hugest that swim the ocean-stream!

What a force of imagination is there in this last expression! What an idea it conveys of the size of that hugest of created beings, as if it shrunk up the ocean to a stream, and took up the sea in its nostrils as a very little thing?

Force of style is one of Milton's greatest excellences. Hence, perhaps, he stimulates us more in the reading, and less afterwards. The way to defend Milton against all impugners, is to take down the book and read it.

Milton's blank verse is the only blank verse in the language (except Shakspeare's) that deserves the name of verse. Dr. Johnson, who had modelled his ideas of versification on the regular sing-song of Pope, condemns the *Paradise Lost* as harsh and unequal. I shall not pretend to say that this is not sometimes the case; for where a degree of excellence beyond the mechanical rules of art is attempted, the poet must sometimes fail. But I imagine that there are more perfect examples in Milton of musical expression, or of an adaptation of the sound and movement of the verse to the meaning of the passage, than in all our other writers, whether of rhyme or blank verse, put together, (with the exception already mentioned). Spenser is the most harmonious of our stanza writers, as Dryden is the most sounding and varied of our rhymists. But in neither is there any thing like the same ear for music, the same power of approximating the varieties of poetical to those of musical rhythm, as there is in our great epic poet. The sound of his lines is moulded into the expression of the sentiment, almost of the very image. They rise or fall, pause or hurry rapidly on, with exquisite art, but without the least trick or affectation, as the occasion seems to require . . .

Dr. Johnson and Pope would have converted his vaulting Pegasus into a rocking-horse. Read any other blank verse but Milton's,—Thomson's, Young's, Cowper's, Wordsworth's,—and it will be found, from the want of the same insight into 'the hidden soul of harmony,' to be mere lumbering prose.

To proceed to a consideration of the merits of *Paradise Lost,* in the most essential point of view, I mean as to the poetry of character and passion. I shall say nothing of the fable, or of other technical objections or excellences; but I shall try to explain at once the foundation of the interest belonging to the poem. I am ready to give up the dialogues in Heaven, where, as Pope justly observes, 'God the Father turns a school-divine'; nor do I consider the battle of the angels as the climax of sublimity, or the most successful effort of Milton's pen. In a word, the interest of the poem arises from the daring ambition and fierce passions of Satan, and from the account of the paradisaical happiness, and the loss of it by our first parents. Three-fourths of the work are taken up with these characters, and nearly all that relates to them is unmixed sublimity and beauty. The two first books alone are like two massy pillars of solid gold.

Satan is the most heroic subject that ever was chosen for a poem; and the execution is as perfect as the design is lofty. He was the first of created beings, who, for endeavouring to be equal with the highest, and to divide the empire of heaven with the Almighty, was hurled down to hell. His aim was no less than the throne of the universe; his means, myriads of angelic armies bright, the third part of the heavens, whom he lured after him with his countenance, and who durst defy the Omnipotent in arms. His ambition was the greatest, and his punishment was the greatest; but not so his despair, for his fortitude was as great as his sufferings. His strength of mind was matchless as his strength of body; the vastness of his designs did not surpass the firm, inflexible determination with which he submitted to his irreversible doom, and final loss of all good. His power of action and of suffering was equal. He was the greatest power that was ever overthrown, with the strongest will left to resist or to endure. He was baffled, not confounded. He stood like a tower; or

> As when Heaven's fire
> Hath scathed the forest oaks or mountain pines.

He was still surrounded with hosts of rebel angels, armed warriors, who own him as their sovereign leader, and with whose fate he sympathises as he views them round, far as the eye can reach; though he keeps aloof from them in his own mind, and holds supreme counsel only with his own breast. An outcast from Heaven, Hell trembles beneath his feet, Sin and Death are at his heels, and mankind are his easy prey.

> All is not lost; th' unconquerable will,
> And study of revenge, immortal hate,
> And courage never to submit or yield,
> And what else is not to be overcome,

are still his. The sense of his punishment seems lost in the magnitude of it; the fierceness of tormenting flames is qualified and made innoxious by the greater fierceness of his pride; the loss of infinite happiness to himself is compensated in thought, by the power of inflicting infinite misery on others. Yet Satan is not the principle of malignity, or of the abstract love of evil—but of the abstract love of power, of pride, of self-will personified, to which last principle all other good and evil, and even his own, are subordinate. From this principle he never once flinches. His love of power and contempt for suffering are never once relaxed from the highest pitch of intensity. His thoughts burn like a hell within him; but the power of thought holds dominion in his mind over every other consideration. The consciousness of a determined purpose, of 'that intellectual being, those thoughts that wander through eternity,' though accompanied with endless pain, he prefers to nonentity, to 'being swallowed up and lost in the wide womb of uncreated night.' He expresses the sum and substance of all ambition in one line. 'Fallen cherub, to be weak is miserable, doing or suffering!' After such a conflict as his, and such a defeat, to retreat in order, to rally, to make terms, to exist at all, is something; but he does more than this—he founds a new empire in hell, and from it conquers this new world, whither he bends his undaunted flight, forcing his way through nether and surrounding fires. The poet has not in all this given us a mere shadowy outline; the strength is equal to the magnitude of the conception. The Achilles of Homer is not more distinct; the Titans were not more vast; Prometheus chained to his rock was not a more terrific example of suffering and of crime. Wherever the figure of Satan is introduced, whether he walks or flies, 'rising aloft incumbent on the dusky air,' it is illustrated with the most striking and appropriate images: so that we see it always before us, gigantic, irregular, portentous, uneasy, and disturbed—but dazzling in its faded splendour, the clouded ruins of a god. The deformity of Satan is only in the depravity of his will; he has no bodily deformity to excite our loathing or disgust. The horns and tail are not there, poor emblems of the unbending, unconquered spirit, of the writhing agonies within. Milton was too magnanimous and open an antagonist to support his argument by the bye-tricks of a hump and cloven foot; to bring into the fair field of controversy the good old catholic prejudices of which Tasso and Dante have availed themselves, and which the mystic German critics would restore. He relied on the justice of his cause, and did not scruple to give the devil his due. Some persons may think that he has carried his liberality too far, and injured the cause he professed to espouse by making him the chief person in his poem. Considering the nature of his subject, he would be equally in danger of running into this fault, from his faith in religion, and his love of rebellion; and perhaps each of these motives had its full share in determining the choice of his subject.

Not only the figure of Satan, but his speeches in council, his soliloquies, his address to Eve, his share in the war in heaven, or in the fall of man, shew the same decided superiority of character. To give only one instance, almost the first speech he makes:

> Is this the region, this the soil, the clime,
> Said then the lost archangel, this the seat
> That we must change for Heaven; this mournful
>   gloom
> For that celestial light? Be it so, since he
> Who now is sov'rain can dispose and bid
> What shall be right: farthest from him is best,

Whom reason hath equal'd, force hath made
   supreme
Above his equals. Farewel happy fields,
Where joy for ever dwells: Hail horrors, hail
Infernal world, and thou profoundest Hell,
Receive thy new possessor: one who brings
A mind not to be chang'd by place or time.
The mind is its own place, and in itself
Can make a Heav'n of Hell, a Hell of Heav'n.
What matter where, if I be still the same,
And what I should be, all but less than he
Whom thunder hath made greater? Here at least
We shall be free; th' Almighty hath not built
Here for his envy, will not drive us hence:
Here we may reign secure, and in my choice
To reign is worth ambition, though in Hell:
Better to reign in Hell, than serve in Heaven.

The whole of the speeches and debates in Pandemonium are well worthy of the place and the occasion—with Gods for speakers, and angels and archangels for hearers. There is a decided manly tone in the arguments and sentiments, an eloquent dogmatism, as if each person spoke from thorough conviction; an excellence which Milton probably borrowed from his spirit of partisanship, or else his spirit of partisanship from the natural firmness and vigour of his mind. In this respect Milton resembles Dante, (the only modern writer with whom he has any thing in common) and it is remarkable that Dante, as well as Milton, was a political partisan. That approximation to the severity of impassioned prose which has been made an objection to Milton's poetry, and which is chiefly to be met with in these bitter invectives, is one of its great excellences. The author might here turn his philippics against Salmasius to good account. The rout in Heaven is like the fall of some mighty structure, nodding to its base, 'with hideous ruin and combustion down.' But, perhaps, of all the passages in *Paradise Lost,* the description of the employments of the angels during the absence of Satan, some of whom 'retreated in a silent valley, sing with notes angelical to many a harp their own heroic deeds and hapless fall by doom of battle,' is the most perfect example of mingled pathos and sublimity.—What proves the truth of this noble picture in every part, and that the frequent complaint of want of interest in it is the fault of the reader, not of the poet, is that when any interest of a practical kind takes a shape that can be at all turned into this, (and there is little doubt that Milton had some such in his eye in writing it) each party converts it to its own purposes, feels the absolute identity of these abstracted and high speculations; and that, in fact, a noted political writer of the present day has exhausted nearly the whole account of Satan in the *Paradise Lost,* by applying it to a character whom he considered as after the devil, (though I do not know whether he would make even that exception) the greatest enemy of the human race. This may serve to shew that Milton's Satan is not a very insipid personage.

Of Adam and Eve it has been said, that the ordinary reader can feel little interest in them, because they have none of the passions, pursuits, or even relations of human life, except that of man and wife, the least interesting of all others, if not to the parties concerned, at least to the by-standers. The preference has on this account been given to Homer, who, it is said, has left very vivid and infinitely diversified pictures of all the passions and affections, public and private, incident to human nature—the relations of son, of brother, parent, friend, citizen, and many others. Longinus preferred the *Iliad* to the *Odyssey,* on account of the greater number of battles it contains; but I can neither agree to his criticism, nor assent to the present objection. It is true, there is little action in this part of Milton's poem; but there is much repose, and more enjoyment. There are none of the every-day occurrences, contentions, disputes, wars, fightings, feuds, jealousies, trades, professions, liveries, and common handicrafts of life; 'no kind of traffic; letters are not known; no use of service, of riches, poverty, contract, succession, bourne, bound of land, tilth, vineyard none; no occupation, no treason, felony, sword, pike, knife, gun, nor need of any engine.' So much the better; thank Heaven, all these were yet to come. But still the die was cast, and in them our doom was sealed. In them

The generations were prepared; the pangs,
The internal pangs, were ready, the dread strife
Of poor humanity's afflicted will,
Struggling in vain with ruthless destiny.

In their first false step we trace all our future woe, with loss of Eden. But there was a short and precious interval between, like the first blush of morning before the day is overcast with tempest, the dawn of the world, the birth of nature from 'the unapparent deep,' with its first dews and freshness on its cheek, breathing odours. Theirs was the first delicious taste of life, and on them depended all that was to come of it. In them hung trembling all our hopes and fears. They were as yet alone in the world, in the eye of nature, wondering at their new being, full of enjoyment and enraptured with one another, with the voice of their Maker walking in the garden, and ministering angels attendant on their steps, winged messengers from heaven like rosy clouds descending in their sight. Nature played around them her virgin fancies wild; and spread for them a repast where no crude surfeit reigned. Was there nothing in this scene, which God and nature alone witnessed, to interest a modern critic? What need was there of action, where the heart was full of bliss and innocence without it! They had nothing to do but feel their own happiness, and 'know to know no more.' "They toiled not, neither did they spin; yet Solomon in all his glory was not arrayed like one of these.' All things seem to acquire fresh sweetness, and to be clothed with fresh beauty in their sight. They tasted as it were for themselves and us, of all that there ever was pure in human bliss. 'In them the burthen of the mystery, the heavy and the weary weight of all this unintelligible world, is lightened.' They stood awhile perfect, but they afterwards fell, and were driven out of Paradise, tasting the first fruits of bitterness as they had done of bliss. But their pangs were such as a pure spirit might feel at the sight—their tears 'such as angels weep.' The pathos is of that mild contemplative kind which arises from regret for the loss of unspeakable happiness, and resignation to inevitable fate. There is none of the fierceness of intemperate passion, none of the agony of mind and turbulence of action, which is the result of the habitual struggles of the will with circumstances, irritated by repeated disappointment, and constantly setting its desires most eagerly on that which there is an impossibility of attaining. This would have destroyed the beauty of the whole picture. They had received their unlooked-for happiness as a free gift from their Creator's hands, and they submitted to its loss, not without sorrow, but without impious and stubborn repining.

> In either hand the hast'ning angel caught
> Our ling'ring parents, and to th' eastern gate
> Led them direct, and down the cliff as fast
> To the subjected plain; then disappear'd.
> They looking back, all th' eastern side beheld
> Of Paradise, so late their happy seat,
> Wav'd over by that flaming brand, the gate
> With dreadful faces throng'd, and fiery arms:
> Some natural tears they dropt, but wip'd them soon;

The world was all before them, where to choose
Their place of rest, and Providence their guide.
—William Hazlitt, from "On Shakspeare and
Milton," *Lectures on the English Poets,* 1818

MARY SHELLEY (1818)

British novelist Mary Wollstonecraft Shelley (1797–1851) was the daughter of political radicals William Godwin and Mary Wollstonecraft, who died soon after giving birth to her. Her father sent her to Scotland at age 14 to live with another family; on one of her visits home, Mary Godwin met the romantic poet Percy Bysshe Shelley, fell in love, became pregnant at 16, and eloped, with Shelley leaving his first wife Harriet Westbrook. They lived in a common-law marriage until they married formally in 1816 after Harriet's suicide. Percy Bysshe Shelley encouraged his wife's literary ambitions; Mary Shelley first published travel writing based on their excursions throughout Europe and then began, in 1816, the project that was to be her most important: *Frankenstein; Or, The Modern Prometheus*, published as a three-volume set in 1819 and revised into a single volume in 1831. The Shelleys' marriage was plagued with tragedies; Mary had three children who died and a miscarriage that nearly claimed her life; her husband, who had been unfaithful to her, died by drowning in Italy in 1822. At the age of 24, Mary Shelley returned to London with her surviving son, Percy Florence, and continued her writing career, but none of her later works matched the reputation of *Frankenstein*.

From the title page onward, *Frankenstein* announces its indebtedness to Milton's *Paradise Lost*. Mary Shelley uses the following quotation of Adam in book 10 as an epigraph to her novel: "Did I request thee, Maker, from my clay / To mould me man? Did I solicit thee / From darkness to promote me?" Frankenstein's creation becomes a second Adam, unwittingly identified with Satan, as Shelley probes religious, philosophical, social, and scientific concerns of her era. Frankenstein's personal Prometheus did not ask to be created and is at the mercy of the Creator, as Adam is in relation to God. In volume 2, chapter 2, the monster confronts Frankenstein with "Remember, that I am thy creature: I ought to be thy Adam; but I am rather the fallen angel, whom thou drivest for joy for no misdeed." Branded demonic, the creature is a social outcast who begins a program of reading that raises his awareness of his self, both internally and in relation to others. In the following passage, the creature turns to *Paradise Lost* for meaning, finding in Milton's work the words to describe his destitute state.

But *Paradise Lost* excited different and far deeper emotions. I read it, as I had read the other volumes which had fallen into my hands, as a true history. It moved every feeling of wonder and awe, that the picture of an omnipotent God warring with his creatures was capable of exciting. I often referred the several situations, as their similarity struck me, to my own. Like Adam, I was created apparently united by no link to any other being in existence; but his state was far different from mine in every other respect. He had come forth from the hands of God a perfect creature, happy and prosperous, guarded by the especial care of his Creator; he was allowed to converse with, and acquire knowledge from beings of a superior nature: but I was wretched, helpless, and alone. Many times I considered Satan as the fitter emblem of my condition; for often, like him, when I viewed the bliss of my protectors, the bitter gall of envy rose within me.

Another circumstance strengthened and confirmed these feelings. Soon after my arrival in the hovel, I discovered some papers in the pocket of the dress which I had taken from your laboratory. At first I had neglected them; but now that I was able to decipher the characters in which they were written, I began to study them with diligence. It was your journal of the four months that preceded my creation. You minutely described in these papers every step you took in the progress of your work; this history was mingled with accounts of domestic occurrences. You, doubtless, recollect these papers. Here they are. Every thing is related in them which bears reference to my accursed origin; the whole detail of that series of disgusting circumstances which produced it is set in view; the minutest description of my odious and loathsome person is given, in language which painted your own horrors, and rendered mine ineffaceable. I sickened as I read. 'Hateful day when I received life!' I exclaimed in agony. 'Cursed creator! Why did you form a monster so hideous that even you turned from me in disgust? God in pity made man beautiful and alluring, after his own image; but my form is a filthy type of your's, more horrid from its very resemblance. Satan had his companions, fellow-devils, to admire and encourage him; but I am solitary and detested.'

—Mary Shelley, excerpt from *Frankenstein;
Or, The Modern Prometheus*, 1818

GEORGE GORDON, LORD BYRON (1820)

I am not persuaded that the *Paradise Lost* would not have been more nobly conveyed to posterity, not perhaps in heroic couplets, although even *they* could sustain the subject if well balanced, but in the stanza of Spenser or of Tasso, or in the terza rima of Dante, which the powers of Milton could easily have grafted on our language.

—George Gordon, Lord Byron,
"Some Observations upon an Article in
Blackwood's Magazine," 1820

Percy Bysshe Shelley (1821)

This section from English poet Percy Bysshe Shelley's *A Defence of Poetry* is the most famous work of criticism addressing Milton's Satan; like other romantics, Shelley regarded Satan as the hero of *Paradise Lost*, but his statement "Miltons' Devil as a moral being is as far superior to his God" exceeds other elevations of Satan's character. According to Shelley, Milton's quality of creative genius violated his own religious views to create the fully realized character of Satan who was heroic in his rebellion and revenge. Shelley originally intended this passage to be part of an 1819 essay, "On the Devil, and Devils," redefining satanism as a positive force for affecting societal reform by overcoming the tyranny of God as seen in organized religion.

The poetry of Dante may be considered as the bridge thrown over the stream of time, which unites the modern and antient World. The distorted notions of invisible things which Dante and his rival Milton have idealised, are merely the mask and the mantle in which these great poets walk through eternity enveloped and disguised. It is a difficult question to determine how far they were conscious of the distinction which must have subsisted in their minds between their own creeds and that of the people. Dante at least appears to wish to mark the full extent of it by placing Riphaeus, whom Virgil calls *justissimus units,* in Paradise, and observing a most heretical caprice in his distribution of rewards and punishments. And Milton's poem contains within itself a philosophical refutation of that system, of which, by a strange and natural antithesis, it has been a chief popular support. Nothing can exceed the energy and magnificence of the character of Satan as expressed in *Paradise Lost*. It is a mistake to suppose that he could ever have been intended for the popular personification of evil. Implacable hate, patient cunning and a sleepless refinement of device to inflict the extremest anguish on an enemy, these things are evil; and, although venial in a slave, are not to be forgiven in a tyrant; although redeemed by much that ennobles his defeat in one subdued, are marked by all that dishonours his conquest in the victor. Miltons' Devil as a moral being is as far superior to his God, as One who perseveres in some purpose which he has conceived to be excellent in spite of adversity and torture, is to One who in the cold security of undoubted triumph inflicts the most horrible revenge upon his enemy, not from any mistaken notion of inducing him to repent of a perseverance in enmity, but with the alleged design of exasperating him to deserve new torments. Milton has so far violated the popular creed (if this shall be judged to be a violation) as to have alleged no superiority of moral virtue to his God over his Devil. And this bold neglect of a direct moral purpose is the most decisive proof of the supremacy of Milton's genius. He mingled as it were the elements of human nature as colours upon a single pallet, and arranged them in the composition of his great picture according to the laws of epic truth; that is, according to the laws of that principle by which a series of actions of the external universe and of intelligent and ethical beings is calculated to excite the sympathy of succeeding generations of mankind. The *Divina Commedia* and *Paradise Lost* have conferred upon modern mythology a systematic form; and when change and time shall have added one more superstition to the mass of those which have arisen and decayed upon the earth, commentators will be learnedly employed in elucidating the religion of ancestral Europe, only not utterly forgotten because it will have been stamped with the eternity of genius.

—Percy Bysshe Shelley, *A Defence of Poetry,* 1821

Henry Neele (1829)

The Second great name in the annals of English poetry is Milton: which is the First, of course, I need not say. Many other Poets have excelled him in variety and versatility; but none ever approached him in intensity of style and thought, in unity of purpose and in the power and grandeur with which he piles up the single monument of Genius, to which his mind is for the time devoted. His Harp may have but one string, but that is such an one, as none but his own finger knows how to touch. *Paradise Lost* has few inequalities; few feeblenesses. It seems not like a work taken up and continued at intervals; but one continuing effort; lasting, perhaps, for years, yet never remitted: elaborated with the highest polish, yet all the marks of ease and simplicity in it's composition.

—Henry Neele, *Lectures on English Poetry,*
1827–29, lecture 2

SAMUEL TAYLOR COLERIDGE (1833)

In this famous quotation, Samuel Taylor Coleridge uses the term *egotism* in a positive sense; to Coleridge, Milton's unequivocal commitment to presenting his own self, no matter what others thought, is what made him a great creative genius.

In the *Paradise Lost*—indeed in every one of his poems—it is Milton himself whom you see; his Satan, his Adam, his Raphael, almost his Eve—are all John Milton; and it is a sense of this intense egotism that gives me the greatest pleasure in reading Milton's works. The egotism of such a man is a revelation of spirit.

—Samuel Taylor Coleridge,
Table Talk, August 18, 1833

FRANÇOIS RENÉ
"MILTON IN *PARADISE LOST*" (1837)

François René, vicomte de Chateaubriand, aligns Milton's political thought with French republicanism, here praising *Paradise Lost* for its spiritual and ideological genius.

The republican is conspicuous in every verse of *Paradise Lost:* the speeches of Satan breathe a hatred of subjection. Milton, however, who, although an enthusiast of liberty, had nevertheless served Cromwell, reveals the kind of republic which accorded with his ideas: it is not a republic of equality, a plebeian republic; he desired an aristocratic republic, in which gradations of rank are admitted. Satan says:—

> if not equal all, yet free,
> Equally free; for orders and degrees
> Jar not with liberty, but well consist.
> Who can in reason then, or right, assume
> Monarchy over such as live by right
> His equals, if in power or splendour less,
> In freedom equal? or can introduce
> Law and edict on us, who without law
> Err not? much less for this to be our Lord,
> And look for adoration, to the abuse

Of those imperial titles, which assert
Our being ordained to govern, not to serve.

(Paradise Lost, Book V)

If there could remain any doubt on this subject, Milton, in his tract entitled *The Ready and Easy Way to Establish a Free Commonwealth,* speaks a language calculated to dispel all uncertainty; he therein avows that the republic should be governed *by a grand or general perpetual council;* he rejects the *popular remedy* adopted to check the ambition of this permanent council, as the people would plunge headlong into a *licentious and unbridled democracy.* Milton, the proud republican, had a coat of arms: he bore on a field sable, an eagle argent, double-headed gules, beak and legs sable. An eagle was, for the poet at least, a speaking escutcheon. The Americans have escutcheons of a more feudal character than those of the knights of the fourteenth century; such fancies are altogether harmless.

The speeches which constitute the greater part of *Paradise Lost,* have acquired new interest since we have had a representative government. The poet has introduced into his work the political forms of the government of his native land. Satan convokes in hell a real parliament; he divides it into two chambers; Tartarus rejoices in a chamber of peers. Eloquence is one of the essential qualities of the author's talent; the speeches delivered by his personages are frequently models of skill and energy. Abdiel, when parting from the rebel angels, addresses Satan in these words:—

O alienate from God, O spirit accurs'd,
Forsaken of all good! I see thy fall
Determined, and thy hapless crew involv'd
In this perfidious fraud, contagion spread
Both of thy crime and punishment: henceforth
No more be troubled how to quit the yoke
Of God's Messiah; those indulgent laws
Will not be now vouchsaf'd; other decrees
Against thee are gone forth without recall;
That golden sceptre, which thou didst reject,
Is now an iron rod to bruise and break
Thy disobedience. Well thou didst advise;
Yet not for thy advice and threats I fly
These wicked tents devoted, lest the wrath
Impendent, raging into sudden flame,

Distinguish not: for soon expect to feel
His thunder on thy head, devouring fire.
Then who created thee lamenting learn,
When who can uncreate thee thou shalt know.

There is, in the poem, something which at first sight appears unaccountable: the infernal republic attempts to overthrow the celestial monarchy;
Milton, though his sentiments are wholly republican, invariably ascribes
justice and victory to the Almighty! The reason of this is that the poet was
swayed by his religious opinions. In accordance with the Independents,
he desired a theocratic republic, a hierarchical liberty, subject only to the
dominion of Heaven; he had represented Cromwell as the lieutenant-general
of God and the protector of the republic:—

Cromwell, our chief of men, who, through a
      cloud
Not of war only, but detractions rude,
Guided by faith and matchless fortitude,
To peace and truth thy glorious way hast
      plough'd,
And on the neck of crowned fortune proud
Hast rear'd God's trophies, and his works
      pursued,
While Darwen stream, with blood of Scots
      imbrued,
And Dunbar field resounds thy praises loud,
And Worcester's laureat wreath. Yet much remains
To conquer still; peace hath her victories
No less renown'd than war: new foes arise
Threat'ning to bind our souls with secular chains:
Help us to save free conscience from the paw
Of hireling wolves, whose gospel is their maw.

Satan and his angels were pictured to Milton's imagination by the proud
Presbyterians, who refused to submit to the *Saints,* Milton's own faction, of
which he hailed the inspired Cromwell as the godly leader.

We discern in Milton a man of troubled spirit; still under the influence
of revolutionary scenes and passions, he stood erect after the downfall of the
revolution which had fled to him for shelter, and palpitated in his bosom. But
the earnestness of that revolution overpowers him; religious gravity forms the
counterpoise to his political agitations. Stunned, however, at the overthrow of

his fondest illusions, at the dissipation of his dreams of liberty, he knows not which way to turn, but remains in a state of perplexity, even respecting religious truth.

An attentive perusal *of Paradise Lost* fixes on the mind the impression that Milton fluctuated between a variety of systems. In the very opening of his poem, he avows himself a Socinian by the celebrated expression "one greater man;" he is silent respecting the Holy Ghost, never names the Trinity, nowhere states the Son to be equal to the Father. The Son is not begotten of all eternity; the poet even places his creation after that of the angels. Milton is, if anything, an Arian; he does not admit what is properly called the *creation*, but supposes a pre-existing matter, co-eternal with the spirit. The particular creation of the universe is no more, in his opinion, than the arrangement of a little corner of chaos, which is ever threatening to return to its previous state of confusion. All the known philosophical theories of the poet have more or less taken root amongst his beliefs; at one time, Plato with the exemplars of ideas, or Pythagoras with the harmony of the spheres; at another, Epicurus, or Lucretius, with his materialism, as when he exhibits to view the half-formed animals issuing from the earth. He is a fatalist when making the rebel angel say of himself and his companions:—

We know no time when we were not as now;
Know none before us, self-begot, self-rais'd
By our own quick'ning power, when fatal course
Had circled his full orb.

Milton is, moreover, a pantheist or Spinozist, but his pantheism is of an extraordinary kind.

The poet first appears to admit of the known pantheism, a medley of matter and mind; but, if man had not sinned, Adam would have gradually extricated himself from matter, and acquired the nature of angels. Adam falls into sin. With a view to redeem the spiritual part of man, the Son of God, who is all spirit, assumes a material substance, descends upon earth, dies, and re-ascends into heaven, after passing through matter. Christ thus becomes the vehicle by means of which matter, brought into contact with intelligence, becomes spiritualised. At length, the due time having elapsed, matter or the material world is at an end, and merges into the other principle. "The Son," says Milton, "shall be absorbed in the bosom of the Father, with the rest of the creatures; God shall be all in all." This is a spiritual pantheism, succeeding the pantheism of the two principles.

Thus our soul will be absorbed in the source of spirituality. What is that sea of intelligence, a single drop of which, contained within matter, is sufficiently powerful to comprehend the motion of the spheres and to investigate the nature of God? What is the Infinite? What! still worlds after worlds! Imagination is bewildered in its endeavours to penetrate those abysses, and Milton is wrecked in the attempt. Nevertheless, amidst this chaos of principles, the poet remains biblical and a Christian; he rehearses the fall and the redemption. A Puritan at first, then an Independent and an Anabaptist, he becomes a *saint,* a quietist, and an enthusiast; it is at length but a voice that sings the praises of the Almighty. Milton had forsaken the house of God; he no longer gave any external signs of religion; in *Paradise Lost* he declares that prayer is the only worship acceptable to God.

This poem, which opens in hell, and, passing over the earth, terminates in heaven, exhibits only two human beings in the vast wilderness of the new creation; the rest are the supernatural inhabitants of the abyss of endless felicity, or of the gulf of everlasting misery. Well, then, the poet has dared to penetrate this solitude, where he presents himself as the child of Adam, a deputy of the human race, fallen through disobedience. He there appears as the hierophant, the prophet, commissioned to learn the history of man's fall, and to sing it on the harp devoted to the penances of David. He is so full of genius, holiness, and grandeur, that his noble head is not misplaced near that of our first parent, in the presence of God and of his angels. Issuing forth from the abyss of darkness, he hails that holy light which is denied to his eyes.

> Hail, holy light, offspring of heaven first-born,
> Or of the Eternal co-eternal beam,
> May I express thee unblam'd? since God is light,
> And never but in unapproached light
> Dwelt from eternity, dwelt there in thee,
> Bright effluence of bright essence increate!
> Or hear'st thou rather, pure ethereal stream,
> Whose fountain who shall tell? Before the sun,
> Before the heavens, thou wert, and, at the voice
> Of God, as with a mantle, didst invest
> The rising world of waters, dark and deep,
> Won from the void and formless infinite.
> Thee I revisit now with bolder wing,
> Escap'd the Stygian pool. . . .

And feel thy sovran, vital lamp; but thou
Revisit'st not these eyes, that roll in vain
To find thy piercing ray, and find no dawn;
So thick a drop serene hath quench'd their orbs,
Or dim suffusion veil'd. Yet not the more
Cease I to wander where the muses haunt
Clear spring or shady grove. . . .
       . . . nor sometimes forget
Those other two equall'd with me in fate.
So were I equall'd with them in renown,
Blind Thamyris, and blind Maeonides,
And Tiresias and Phineus, prophets old;
There feed on thoughts, that voluntary move
Harmonious numbers; as the wakeful bird
Sings darkling, and in shadiest covert hid
Tunes her nocturnal note. Thus with the year
Seasons return; but not to me returns
Day, or the sweet approach of even or morn,
Or sight of vernal bloom, or summer's rose,
Or flocks, or herds, or human face divine;
But clouds instead, and ever-during dark
Surrounds me, from the cheerful ways of men
Cut off, and for the book of knowledge fair
Presented with a universal blank
Of Nature's works, to me expung'd and ras'd,
And wisdom at one entrance quite shut out.
So much the rather thou, celestial light,
Shine inward, and the mind through all her powers
Irradiate; there plant eyes, all mist from thence
Purge and disperse; that I may see and tell
Of things invisible to mortal sight.

Elsewhere he exclaims in not less pathetic strains:

If answerable style I can obtain
Of my celestial patroness, who deigns
Her nightly visitation unimplor'd,
       . . . higher argument
Remains; sufficient of itself to raise
That name, unless an age too late, or cold

Climate, or years, damp my intended wing
Depress'd.

How lofty must have been the intelligence of Milton, which could sustain this intercourse face to face with God, and the wonderful beings he has created! No man ever displayed a more sober and at the same time a more delicate genius. "It was," says Hume, "during a state of poverty, blindness, disgrace, danger, and old age, that Milton composed his wonderful poem, which not only surpassed all the performances of his contemporaries, but all the compositions which had flowed from his pen during the vigour of his age and the height of his prosperity." We actually distinguish in this poem, through the ardour of youthful years, the maturity of age and the gravity of misfortune; this imparts to *Paradise Lost* an extraordinary fascination of old age and youth, of restlessness and peace, of sadness and joy, of reason and love.

—François René, vicomte de Chateaubriand,
"Milton in *Paradise Lost*," *Sketches of English
Literature*, volume 2, 1837, pp. 145–54

Henry Hallam (1839)

The slowness of Milton's advance to glory is now generally owned to have been much exaggerated: we might say that the reverse was nearer the truth. It would hardly, however, be said, even in this age, of a poem 3,000 copies of which had been sold in eleven years, that its success had been small; and some, perhaps, might doubt whether *Paradise Lost,* published eleven years since, would have met with a greater demand. There is sometimes a want of congeniality in public taste which no power of genius will overcome. For Milton it must be said by every one conversant with the literature of the age that preceded Addison's famous criticism, from which some have dated the reputation of *Paradise Lost,* that he took his place among great poets from the beginning.

—Henry Hallam, *Introduction to the Literature of
Europe,* 1837–39, part 4, chapter 5, paragraph 34

Thomas Carlyle (1838)

Adam and Eve are beautiful, graceful objects, but no one has breathed the Pygmalion life into them; they remain cold statues. Milton's sympathies were with things rather than with men, the scenery and phenomena of nature, the trim gardens, the burning lake; but as for the phenomena of the mind, he was not able to see them. He has no delineations of mind except Satan, of which we may say that Satan was his own character, the black side of it. I wish however, to be understood not to speak at all in disparagement of Milton; far from that.

—Thomas Carlyle, *Lectures on the History of Literature,* 1838, p. 166

Thomas De Quincey "On Milton" (1839)

In the following discussion, Thomas De Quincey develops a defense of Milton's *Paradise Lost* against eighteenth-century criticism, notably by Samuel Johnson, that denigrates Milton's works for violating neoclassical literary principles. De Quincey argues against the charges of Milton's overly pedantic diction and the lack of decorum in blending classical and Christian materials. De Quincey asserts that the use of particular vocabulary, images, and allusions is necessary to produce the work of art that is *Paradise Lost.* Most forcefully, De Quincey proclaims Milton a master of the sublime, the foremost quality informing eighteenth-century aesthetic theory. De Quincey had been much influenced by the works of Emmanuel Kant, who, in 1764, had written *Observations on the Feeling of the Beautiful and Sublime.* Kant connects the sublime with the faculty of reason, saying that it surpasses the sensory and imaginative functions of the mind and is the highest human experience.

Who and what *is* Milton? Dr. Johnson was furiously incensed with a certain man, by trade an author and manufacturer of books, wholesale and retail, for introducing Milton's name into a certain index under the letter M thus—"Milton, Mr. John." That Mister, undoubtedly, was hard to digest. Yet very often it happens to the best of us—to men who are far enough from "thinking small beer of themselves"—that about ten o'clock A.M. an official big-wig, sitting at Bow Street, calls upon the man to account for his *sprees* of the last night, for his feats in knocking down lamp-posts, and extinguishing watchmen, by this ugly demand of—"Who and what are you, sir?" And perhaps the poor man, sick and penitential for want of soda-water, really finds a considerable difficulty in replying satisfactorily to the worthy *beak's* apostrophe, although, at five o'clock in the evening, should the culprit be returning into the country in the same coach as his awful interrogator, he might be very apt to look fierce and retort this amiable inquiry, and with equal thirst for knowledge to demand, "Now, sir, if you come to *that,* who and what are *you?*" And the *beak* in *his* turn, though so apt to indulge his own curiosity at the expense of the public, might find it very difficult to satisfy that of others.

The same thing happens to authors; and to great authors beyond all others. So accustomed are we to survey a great man through the cloud of years that has gathered round him—so impossible is it to detach him from the pomp and equipage of all who have quoted him, copied him, echoed him, lectured about him, disputed about him, quarrelled about him, that in the case of any Anacharsis the Scythian coming amongst us—any savage, that is to say, uninstructed in our literature, but speaking our language, and feeling an intelligent interest in our great men—a man could hardly believe at first how perplexed he would feel, how utterly at a loss for any *adequate* answer to this question, suddenly proposed—*"Who and what was Milton?"* That is to say, what is the place which he fills in his own vernacular literature? what station does he hold in universal literature?

I, if abruptly called upon in that summary fashion to convey a *commensurate* idea of Milton, one which might at once correspond to his pretensions, and yet be readily intelligible to the savage, should answer perhaps thus:—Milton is not an author amongst authors, not a poet amongst poets, but a power amongst powers; and the *Paradise Lost* is not a book amongst books, not a poem amongst poems, but a central force amongst forces. Let me explain:—There is this great distinction amongst books: some, though possibly the best in their class, are still no more than books—not indispensable, not incapable of supplementary representation by other books. If they had never been, if their place had continued for ages unfilled, not the less, upon a sufficient excitement arising, there would always have been found the ability either directly to fill up the vacancy, or at least to meet the same passion virtually, though by a work differing in form. Thus, supposing Butler to have died in youth, and the *Hudibras* to have been intercepted by his premature death, still the ludicrous aspects of the Parliamentary War and its fighting saints were too striking to have perished. If not in a narrative form, the case would have come forward in the drama. puritanical sanctity, in collision with the ordinary interests of life and with its militant propensities, offered too striking a field for the Satiric Muse, in any case, to have passed in total neglect. The impulse was too strong for repression—it was a volcanic agency, that, by some opening or other, must have worked a way for itself to the upper air. Yet Butler was a most original poet, and a creator within his own province. But, like many another original mind, there is little doubt that he quelled and repressed, by his own excellence, other minds of the same cast. Mere despair of excelling him, so far as not, after all, to seem imitators, drove back others who would have pressed into that arena, if not already brilliantly filled. Butler failing, there would have been another Butler, either in the same, or in some analogous form.

But with regard to Milton and the Miltonic power the case is far otherwise. If the man had failed, the power would have failed. In that mode of power which he wielded the function was exhausted in the man, the species was identified with the individual, the poetry was incarnated in the poet.

Let it be remembered that, of all powers which act upon man through his intellectual nature, the very rarest is that which we moderns call the *sublime*. The Grecians had apparently no word for it, unless it were that which they mean by *to semnon*: for *hypsos* was a comprehensive expression for all qualities which gave a character of life or animation to the composition,—such even as were philosophically opposed to the sublime. In the Roman poetry, and especially in Lucan, at times also in Juvenal, there is an exhibition of a moral sublime, perfectly distinct from anything known to the Greek poetry. The delineations of republican grandeur, as expressing itself through the principal leaders in the Roman camps, or the trampling under foot of ordinary superstitions, as given in the reasons assigned to Labienus for passing the oracle of the Libyan Jupiter unconsulted, are in a style to which there is nothing corresponding in the whole Grecian literature; nor would they have been comprehensible to an Athenian. The famous line "Jupiter est quodcunque vides, quocunque moveris," and the brief review of such questions as might be worthy of an oracular god, with the summary declaration that every one of those points we know already by the light of nature, and could not know them better though Jupiter Ammon himself were to impress them on our attention—

Scimus, et haec nobis non altius inseret
Ammon:
We know it, and no Ammon will ever sink it deeper
into our hearts:

all this is truly Roman in its sublimity, and so exclusively Roman that there, and not in poets like the Augustan, expressly modelling their poems on Grecian types, ought the Roman mind to be studied.

On the other hand, for that species of the sublime which does not rest purely and merely on moral energies, but on a synthesis between man and nature—for what may properly be called the ethico-physical sublime—there is but one great model surviving in the Greek poetry: viz. the gigantic drama of the Prometheus crucified on Mount Elborus. And this drama differs so much from everything else even in the poetry of Æschylus,—as the mythus itself differs so much from all the rest of the Grecian mythology (belonging apparently to an age and a people more gloomy, austere, and nearer to the *incunabula mundi* than those which bred the gay and sunny superstitions of Greece),—that much curiosity and speculation have naturally gathered round the subject of late years. Laying this one insulted case apart, and considering that the Hebrew poetry of Isaiah and Ezekiel, as having the benefit of inspiration, does not lie within the just limits of competition, we may affirm that there is no human composition which can be challenged as constitutionally sublime,—sublime equally by its conception and by its execution, or as uniformly sublime from first to last,—excepting the *Paradise Lost.* In Milton only, first and last, is the power of the sublime revealed. In Milton only does this great agency blaze and glow as a furnace kept up to a white heat, without suspicion of collapse.

If, therefore, Milton occupies this unique position—and let the reader question himself closely whether he can cite any other book than the Paradise Lost as continuously sublime, or sublime even by its prevailing character—in that case there is a peculiarity of importance investing that one book which belongs to no other; and it must be important to dissipate any erroneous notions which affect the integrity of that book's estimation. Now, there are two notions, countenanced by Addison and by Dr. Johnson, which tend greatly to disparage the character of its composition. If the two critics, one friendly, the other very malignant, but both endeavouring to be just, have in reality built upon sound principles, or at least upon a sound appreciation of Milton's principles, in that case there is a mortal taint diffused over the whole of the Paradise Lost: for not a single book is clear of one or other of the two errors which they charge upon him. We will briefly state the objections, and then as briefly reply to them, by exposing the true philosophy of Milton's practice. For we are very sure that, in doing as he did, this mighty poet was governed by no carelessness or oversight (as is imagined), far less by affectation or ostentation, but by a most refined theory of poetic effects.

1. The first of these two charges respects a supposed pedantry, or too ambitious a display of erudition. It is surprising to us that such an objection should have occurred to any man: both because, after all, the quantity of learning cannot be great for which any poem can find an opening; and because, in any poem burning with concentrated fire, like the Miltonic, the passion becomes a law to itself, and will not receive into connexion with itself any parts so deficient in harmony as a cold ostentation of learned illustrations must always have been found. Still, it is alleged that such words as *frieze, architrave, cornice, zenith, &c,* are words of art, out of place amongst

the primitive simplicities of Paradise, and at war with Milton's purpose of exhibiting the paradisaical state.

Now, here is displayed broadly the very perfection of ignorance, as measured against the very perfection of what may be called poetic science. We will lay open the true purpose of Milton by a single illustration. In describing impressive scenery as occurring in a hilly or a woody country, everybody must have noticed the habit which young ladies have of using the word *amphitheatre:* "amphitheatre of woods," "amphitheatre of hills"—these are their constant expression. Why? Is it because the word *amphitheatre* is a Grecian word? We question if one young lady in twenty knows that it is; and very certain we are that no word would recommend itself to her use by that origin, if she happened to be aware of it. The reason lurks here:—In the word *theatre* is contained an evanescent image of a great audience, of a populous multitude. Now, this image—half-withdrawn, half-flashed upon the eye, and combined with the word *hills* or *forests*—is thrown into powerful collision with the silence of hills, with the solitude of forests; each image, from reciprocal contradiction, brightens and vivifies the other. The two images act, and react, by strong repulsion and antagonism.

This principle I might exemplify and explain at great length; but I impose a law of severe brevity upon myself. And I have said enough. Out of this one principle of subtle and lurking antagonism may be explained everything which has been denounced under the idea of pedantry in Milton. It is the key to all that lavish pomp of art and knowledge which is sometimes put forward by Milton in situations of intense solitude, and in the bosom of primitive nature—as, for example, in the Eden of his great poem, and in the Wilderness of his *Paradise Regained*. The shadowy exhibition of a regal banquet in the desert draws out and stimulates the sense of its utter solitude and remotion from men or cities. The images of architectural splendour suddenly raised in the very centre of Paradise, as vanishing shows by the wand of a magician, bring into powerful relief the depth of silence and the unpopulous solitude which possess this sanctuary of man whilst yet happy and innocent Paradise could not in any other way, or by any artifice less profound, have been made to give up its essential and differential characteristics in a form palpable to the imagination. As a place of rest, it was necessary that it should be placed in close collision with the unresting strife of cities; as a place of solitude, with the image of tumultuous crowds; as the centre of mere natural beauty in its gorgeous prime, with the images of elaborate architecture and of human workmanship; as a place of perfect innocence in seclusion, that it should be exhibited as the antagonist pole to the sin and misery of social man.

Such is the covert philosophy which governs Milton's practice, and which might be illustrated by many scores of passages from both the *Paradise Lost* and the *Paradise Regained*.[1] In fact, a volume might be composed on this one chapter. And yet, from the blindness or inconsiderate examination of his critics, this latent wisdom, this cryptical science of poetic effects, in the mighty poet has been misinterpreted, and set down to the effect of defective skill, or even of puerile ostentation.

2. The second great charge against Milton is, *prima facie*, even more difficult to meet. It is the charge of having blended the Pagan and Christian forms. The great realities of Angels and Archangels are continually combined into the same groups with the fabulous impersonations of the Greek Mythology. Eve is interlinked in comparisons with Pandora, with Aurora, with Proserpine. Those impersonations, however, may be thought to have something of allegoric meaning in their conceptions which in a measure corrects this paganism of the idea. But Eve is also compared with Ceres, with Hebe, and other fixed forms of pagan superstition. Other allusions to the Greek mythologic forms, or direct combination of them with the real existences of the Christian heavens, might be produced by scores, were it not that we decline to swell our paper beyond the necessity of the case. Now, surely this at least is an error. Can there be any answer to this?

At one time we were ourselves inclined to fear that Milton had been here caught tripping. In this instance, at least, he seems to be in error. But there is no trusting to appearances. In meditating upon the question, we happened to remember that the most colossal and Miltonic of painters had fallen into the very same fault, if fault it were. In his *Last Judgment* Michael Angelo has introduced the pagan deities in connexion with the hierarchy of the Christian Heavens. Now, it is very true that one great man cannot palliate the error of another great man by repeating the same error himself. But, though it cannot avail as an excuse, such a conformity of ideas serves as a summons to a much more vigilant examination of the case than might else be instituted. One man might err from inadvertency; but that two, and both men trained to habits of constant meditation, should fall into the same error, makes the marvel tenfold greater.

Now we confess that, as to Michael Angelo, we do not pretend to assign the precise key to the practice which he adopted. And to our feelings, after all that might be said in apology, there still remains an impression of incongruity in the visual exhibition and direct juxtaposition of the two orders of supernatural existence so potently repelling each other. But, as regards Milton, the justification is complete. It rests upon the following principle:—

In all other parts of Christianity the two orders of superior beings, the Christian Heaven and the Pagan Pantheon, are felt to be incongruous—not as the pure opposed to the impure (for, if that were the reason, then the Christian fiends should be incongruous with the angels, which they are not), but as the unreal opposed to the real. In all the hands of other poets we feel that Jupiter, Mercury, Apollo, Diana, are not merely impure conceptions, but that they are baseless conceptions, phantoms of air, nonentities; there is much the same objection, in point of just taste, to the combination of such fabulous beings in the same groups with glorified saints and angels as there is to the combination by a painter or a sculptor of real flesh-and-blood creatures with allegoric abstractions.

This is the objection to such combination in all other poets. But this objection does not apply to Milton; it glances past him, and for the following reason:—Milton has himself laid an early foundation for his introduction of the Pagan Pantheon into Christian groups: *the false gods of the heathen world were, according to Milton, the fallen Angels.* See his inimitable account of the fallen angels—who and what they subsequently became. In itself, and even if detached from the rest of the *Paradise Lost,* this catalogue is an *ultra-* magnificent poem. They are not false, therefore, in the sense of being unreal, baseless, and having a merely fantastical existence, like our European Fairies, but as having drawn aside mankind from a pure worship. As ruined angels under other names, they are no less real than the faithful and loyal angels of the Christian heavens. And in that one difference of the Miltonic creed, which the poet has brought pointedly and elaborately under his reader's notice by his matchless roll-call of the rebellious angels, and of *their pagan transformations,* in the very first book of the *Paradise Lost,* is laid beforehand[2] the amplest foundation for his subsequent practice, and at the same time, therefore, the amplest answer to the charge preferred against him by Dr. Johnson, and by so many other critics, who had not sufficiently penetrated the latent theory on which he acted.

Notes

1. For instance, this is the key to that image in the *Paradise Regained* where Satan, on first emerging into sight, is compared to an old man gathering sticks, "to warm him on a winter's day." This image, at first sight, seems little in harmony with the wild and awful character of the supreme fiend. No; it is *not in* harmony, nor is it meant to be in harmony. On the contrary, it is meant to be in antagonism and intense repulsion. The household image of old age, of human infirmity, and of domestic hearths, are all meant as a machinery for provoking and

soliciting the fearful idea to which they are placed in collision, and as so many repelling poles.

2. Other celebrated poets have laid no such preparatory foundations for their intermixture of heathen gods with the heavenly host of the Christian revelation; for example, amongst thousands of others, Tasso, and still more flagrantly Camoens, who is not content with allusions or references that suppose the Pagan Mythology still substantially existing, but absolutely introduces them as potent agencies amongst superstitious and bigoted worshippers of papal saints. Consequently, they, beyond all apology, are open to the censure which for Milton is subtly evaded.

—Thomas De Quincey, from "On Milton," 1839,
Collected Writings, edited by Masson,
volume 10, 1890, pp. 398–406

DAVID MASSON "THE THREE DEVILS: LUTHER'S, MILTON'S, AND GOETHE'S" (1844)

David Masson's essay consists of a prolonged discussion of Milton's Satan in *Paradise Lost,* from his conception to his relation to other angelic beings and to God. Masson does this to uncover Satan's motivation for his actions. In creating the character of Satan, Masson sees Milton as working in the manner of Homer, "[d]evoting the whole strength of his genius to the object, not of being discursive and original, not of making profound remarks on everything as he goes along, but of carrying on a sublime and stately narrative."

The difficulties which Milton had to overcome in writing his *Paradise Lost* were immense. The gist of those difficulties may be defined as consisting in this, that the poet had at once to represent a supernatural condition of being and to construct a story. He had to describe the ongoings of Angels, and at the same time to make one event follow another. It is comparatively easy for Milton to sustain his conception of those superhuman beings as mere objects or phenomena—to represent them flying singly through space like huge black shadows, or standing opposite to each other in hostile battalions; but to construct a story in which these beings should be the agents, to exhibit these beings thinking, scheming, blundering, in such a way as to produce a likely succession of events, was enormously difficult. The difficulty was to make the course of events correspond with the reputation of the objects. To do this perfectly was literally impossible. It is possible for the human mind to conceive twenty-four great supernatural beings existing together at any given moment in space; but it is utterly impossible to conceive what would occur among those twenty-four beings during twenty-four hours. The value of time, the amount of history that can be transacted in a given period, depends on the nature and prowess of the beings whose volitions make the chain of events; and so a lower order of beings can have no idea at what rate things happen in a higher. The mode of causation will be different from that with which they are acquainted.

This is the difficulty with which Milton had to struggle; or, rather, this is the difficulty with which he did not struggle. He had to construct a narrative; and so, while he represents to us the full stature of his superhuman beings as mere objects or phenomena, he does not attempt to make events follow each other at a higher rate among those beings than they do amongst ourselves, except in the single respect of their being infinitely more powerful physical agents than we are. Whatever feeling of inconsistency is experienced in reading the *Paradise Lost* may be traced, perhaps, to the fact that the necessities of the story obliged the poet not to attempt to make the rate of causation among those beings as extraordinary as his description of them as phenomena. Such a feeling of inconsistency there is; and yet Milton sustains his flight as nobly as mortal could have done. Throughout the whole poem we see him recollecting his original conception of Satan as an object:

> Thus Satan, talking to his nearest mate,
> With head uplift above the waves, and eyes
> That sparkling blazed; his other parts besides,
> Prone on the flood, extended long and large,
> Lay floating many a rood.

And this is a great thing to have done. If the poet ever flags in his conception of those superhuman beings as objects, it is when he finds it necessary to describe a multitude of them assembled together in some *place*; and his usual device then is to reduce the bulk of the greatest number. This, too, is for the behoof of the story. If it is necessary, for instance, to assemble the Angels to deliberate, this must be done in an audience-hall, and the human mind refuses to go beyond certain limits in its conception of what an audience-hall is. Again the gate of Hell is described, although the Hell of Milton is a mere vague extent of fiery element, which, in strict keeping, could not be described as having a gate. The narrative, however, requires the conception. And so in other cases. Still, consistency of description is well sustained.

Nor is it merely as objects or phenomena that Milton sustains throughout his whole poem a consistent conception of the Angels. He is likewise consistent in his description of them as physical agents. Lofty stature and appearance carry with them a promise of so much physical power; and hence, in Milton's case, the necessity of finding words and figures capable of expressing modes and powers of mechanical action, on the part of the Angels, as superhuman as the stature and appearance he has given to them. This complicated his difficulties very much. It is quite conceivable that a man should be able to describe the mere appearance of a gigantic being standing up, as it were, with his back to a wall, and yet utterly break down, and not be able to find words, when he tried to describe this gigantic being stepping forth into colossal activity and doing some characteristic thing. Milton has overcome the difficulty. His conception of the Angels as physical agents does not fall beneath his conception of them as mere objects. In his description, for instance, in the sixth book, of the Angels tearing up mountains by the roots and flinging them upon each other, we have strength suggested corresponding to the reputed stature of the beings. In extension of the same remark, we may observe how skilfully Milton has aggrandized and eked out his conception of the superhuman beings he is describing by endowing them with the power of infinitely swift motion through space. On this point we offer our readers an observation which they may verify for themselves:—Milton, we are persuaded, had it vaguely in his mind, throughout *Paradise Lost,* that the bounding peculiarity between the human condition of being and the angelic one he is describing is the law of gravitation. We, and all that is cognisable by us, are subject to this law; but Creation may be peopled with beings who are not subject to it, and to us these beings are as if they were not. But, whenever one of those beings becomes cognisable by us, he instantly becomes subject to gravitation; and he must resume his own mode of being ere he can be free from its consequences. The Angels were not subject to gravitation; that is to say, they had the means of moving in any direction at will. When they rebelled, and were punished by expulsion from Heaven, they did not *fall* out; for, in fact, so far as the description intimates, there existed no planet, no distinct material element, towards which they could gravitate. They were *driven* out by a pursuing fire. Then, after their fall, they had the power of rising upward, of navigating space, of quitting Hell, directing their flight to one glittering planet, alighting on its rotund surface, and then bounding off again, and away to another. A corollary of this fundamental difference between the human condition of being and the angelic would be that angels are capable of direct vertical action, whereas men are capable mainly of horizontal. An army of men can exist only as a square, or other plane figure, whereas an army of angels can exist as a cube or parallelopiped.

Now, in everything relating to the physical action of the Angels, even in carrying out this notion of their mode of being, Milton is most consistent. But it was impossible to follow out the superiority of these beings to its whole length. The attempt to do so would have made a narrative impossible. Exalting our conception of these beings as mere objects, or as mere physical agents, as much as he could, it would have been suicidal in the poet to attempt to realize history as it must be among such beings. No human mind could do it. He had, therefore, except where the notion of physical superiority assisted him, to make events follow each other just as they would in a human narrative. The motives, the reasonings, the misconceptions of those beings, all that determined the succession of events, he had to make substantially human. The whole narrative, for instance, proceeds on the supposition that those supernatural beings had no higher degree of knowledge than human beings, with equal physical advantages, would have had under similar circumstances. Credit the spirits with a greater degree of insight—credit them even with such a strong conviction of the Divine omnipotence as, in their reputed condition of being, we can hardly conceive them not attaining—and the whole of Milton's story is rendered impossible. The crushing conviction of the Divine omnipotence would have prevented them from rebelling with the alleged motive; or, after they had rebelled, it would have prevented them from struggling with the alleged hope. In *Paradise Lost* the working notion which the devils have about God is exactly that which human beings have when they hope to succeed in a bad enterprise. Otherwise the poem could not have been written. Suppose the fallen Angels to have had a working notion of the Deity as superhuman as their reputed appearance and physical greatness: then the events of the *Paradise Lost* might have happened nevertheless, but the chain of volitions would not have been the same, and it would have been impossible for any human poet to realize the narrative.

These remarks are necessary to prepare us for conceiving the Satan of Milton. Except, as we have said, for an occasional feeling during a perusal of the poem that the style of thinking and speculating about the issue of their enterprise is too meagre and human for a race of beings physically so superhuman, one's astonishment at the consistency of the poet's conceptions is unmitigated throughout. Such keeping is there between one conception and another, such a distinct material grasp had the poet of his whole subject, so little is there of the mystic or the hazy in his descriptions from beginning to end, that it would be quite possible to prefix to the *Paradise Lost* an illustrative diagram exhibiting the universal space in which Milton conceived his beings moving to and fro, divided, as he conceived it, at first into two or three, and afterwards into four tropics or regions. Then his narrative is so clear that a brief prose version of it would be a history of Satan in the interval between his own fall and the fall of Man.

It is to be noted that Milton as a poet proceeds on the Homeric method, and not on the Shakespearian, devoting the whole strength of his genius to the object, not of being discursive and original, not of making profound remarks on everything as he goes along, but of carrying on a sublime and stately narrative. We should hardly be led to assert, however, that the difference between the epic and the drama lies in this, that the latter may be discursive and reflective while the former cannot. We can conceive an epic written after the Shakespearian method; that is, one which, while strictly sustaining a narrative, should be profoundly expository in its spirit. Certain it is, however, that Milton wrote after the Homeric method, and did not exert himself chiefly in strewing his text with luminous propositions. One consequence of this is that the way to obtain an idea of Milton's Satan is not to lay hold of specific sayings that fall from his mouth, but to go through his history. Goethe's Mephistopheles, we shall find, on the other hand, reveals himself in the characteristic propositions which he utters. Satan is to be studied by following his progress; Mephistopheles by attending to his remarks.

In the history of Milton's Satan it is important to begin at the time of his being an Archangel. Before the creation of our World, there existed, according to Milton, a grand race of beings altogether different from what we are. Those beings were Spirits. They did not lead a planetary existence; they tenanted space in some strange, and, to us, inconceivable way. Or, rather, they did not tenant all space, but only that upper and illuminated part of infinity called Heaven. For Heaven, in Milton, is not to be considered as a locality, but as a region stretching infinitely out on all sides—an immense extent of continent and kingdom. The infinite darkness, howling and blustering underneath Heaven, was Chaos or Night. What was the exact mode of being of the Spirits who lived in dispersion through Heaven is unknown to us; but it was social. Moreover, there subsisted between the multitudinous far-extending population of Spirits and the Almighty Creator a relation closer, or at least more sensible and immediate, than that which exists between human beings and Him. The best way of expressing this relation in human language is by the idea of physical nearness. They were God's Angels. Pursuing, each individual among them, a life of his own, agreeable to his wishes and his character, yet they all recognised themselves as the Almighty's ministering spirits. At times they were summoned, from following their different occupations in all the ends of Heaven, to assemble near the Divine presence. Among these Angels there were degrees and differences. Some were, in their very essence and constitution, grander and more sublime intelligences than the rest; others, in the course of their long existence, had become noted for their zeal and assiduity. Thus, although really a race of beings living on their own account as men do, they constituted a hierarchy, and were called Angels.

Among all the vast angelic population three or four individuals stood pre-eminent and unapproachable. These were the Archangels. Satan was one of these: if not the highest Archangel in Heaven, he was one of the four highest. After God, he could feel conscious of being the greatest being in the Universe. But, although the relation between the Deity and the angelic population was so close that we can only express it by having recourse to the conception of physical nearness, yet even to the Angels the Deity was so shrouded in clouds and mystery that the highest Archangel might proceed on a wrong notion of his character, and, just as human beings do, might believe the Divine omnipotence as a theological proposition, and yet, in going about his enterprises, might not carry a working consciousness of it along with him. There is something in the exercise of power, in the mere feeling of existence, in the stretching out of a limb, in the resisting of an obstacle, in being active in any way, which generates a conviction that our powers are self-contained, hostile to the recollection of inferiority or accountability. A messenger, employed in his master's business, becomes, in the very act of serving him, forgetful of him. As the feeling of enjoyment in action grows strong, the feeling of a dependent state of being, the feeling of being a messenger, grows weak. Repose and physical weakness are favourable to the recognition of a derived existence: hence the beauty of the feebleness of old age preceding the approach of death. The feebleness of the body weakens the self-sufficient feeling, and disposes to piety. The young man, rejoicing in his strength, cannot believe that his breath is in his nostrils. In some such way the Archangel fell. Rejoicing in his strength, walking colossal through Heaven, gigantic in his conceptions, incessant in his working, ever scheming, ever imagining new enterprises, Satan was in his very nature the most active of God's Archangels. He was ever doing some great thing, and ever thirsting for some greater thing to do. And, alas! his very wisdom became his folly. His notion of the Deity was higher and grander than that of any other Angel: but, then, he was not a contemplative spirit; and his feeling of derived existence grew weak in the glow and excitement of constant occupation. As the feeling of enjoyment in action grew strong, the feeling of being an Angel grew weak. Thus the mere duration of his existence had undermined his strength and prepared him for sin. Although the greatest Angel in Heaven—nay, just because he was such—he was the readiest to fall.

At last an occasion came. When the intimation was made by the Almighty in the Congregation of the Angels that he had anointed his only-begotten Son King on the holy hill of Zion, the Archangel frowned and became a rebel: not because he had weighed the enterprise to which he was committing himself, but because he was hurried on by the impetus of an overwrought nature. Even had he weighed the enterprise, and found it wanting, he would have been a rebel nevertheless; he would have rushed into ruin on the wheels of his old impulses. He could not have said to himself "It is useless to rebel, and I will not;" and, if he could, what a hypocrite to have remained in Heaven! His revolt was the natural issue of the thoughts to which he had accustomed himself; and his crime lay in having acquired a rebellious constitution, in having pursued action too much, and spurned worship and contemplation. Herein lay the difference between him and the other Archangels, Raphael, Gabriel, and Michael.

Satan in his revolt carried a third part of the Angels with him. He had accustomed many of the Angels to his mode of thinking. One of the ways in which he gratified his desire for activity had been that of exerting a moral and intellectual influence over the inferior Angels. A few of these he had liked to associate with, discoursing with them, and observing how they imbibed his ideas. His chief associate, almost his bosom-companion, had been Beelzebub, a princely Angel. Moloch, Belial, and Mammon, had likewise been admitted to his confidence. These five had constituted a kind of clique in Heaven, giving the word to a whole multitude of inferior Angels, all of them resembling their leader in being fonder of action than of contemplation. Thus, in addition to the mere hankering after action, there had grown up in Satan's mind a love of power. This feeling that it was a glorious thing to be a leader seems to have had much to do with his voluntary sacrifice of happiness. We may conceive it to have been voluntary. Foreseeing never so much misery would not have prevented such a spirit from rebelling. Having a third of the Angels away with him in some dark, howling region, where he might rule over them alone, would have seemed, even if he had foreseen it, infinitely preferable to the puny sovereignty of an Archangel in that world of gold and emerald: "better to reign in Hell than serve in Heaven." Thus we conceive him to have faced the anticipation of the future. It required little persuasion to gain over the kindred spirit of Beelzebub. These two appear to have conceived the enterprise from the beginning in a different light from that in which they represented it to their followers. Happiness with the inferior Spirits was a more important consideration than with such Spirits as Satan and Beelzebub; and to have hinted the possibility of losing happiness in the enterprise would have been to terrify them away. Satan and Beelzebub were losing happiness to gain something which they thought better; to the inferior Angels nothing could be mentioned that would appear better. Again, the inferior Angels, judging from narrower premises, might indulge in enthusiastic expectations which the greater knowledge of the leaders would prevent them from entertaining. At all events, the effect of the intercourse with the Angels was that a third of their number joined the standard of Satan. Then began the wars in Heaven, related in the poem.

It may be remarked that the carrying on those wars by Satan with the hope of victory is not inconsistent with what has been said as to the possibility of his not having proceeded on a false calculation. We are apt to imagine those wars as wars between the rebel Angels and the armies of God. Now this is true; but it is scarcely the proper idea in the circumstances. How could Satan have hoped for victory in that case? You can only suppose that he did so by lessening his intellect, by making him a mere blundering Fury, and not a keen, far-seeing Intelligence. But in warring with Michael and his followers he was, until the contrary should be proved, warring merely against his fellow-beings of the same Heaven, whose strength he knew and feared not. The idea of physical nearness between the Almighty and the Angels confuses us here. Satan had heard the threat which had accompanied the proclamation of the Messiah's sovereignty; but it may have been problematical in his mind whether the way in which God would fulfil the threat would be to make Michael conquer him. So he made war against Michael and his Angels. At last, when all Heaven was in confusion, the Divine omnipotence interfered. On the third day the Messiah rode forth in his strength, to end the wars and expel the rebel host from Heaven. They fled, driven before his thunder. The crystal wall of Heaven opened wide, and the two lips, rolling inward, disclosed a spacious gap yawning into the wasteful Deep. The reeling Angels saw down, and hung back affrighted; but the terror of the Lord was behind them: headlong they threw themselves from the verge of Heaven into the fathomless abyss, eternal wrath burning after them down through the blackness like a hissing fiery funnel.

And now the Almighty determined to create a new kind of World, and to people it with a race of beings different from that already existing, inferior in the meantime to the Angels, but with the power of working themselves up into the Angelic mode of being. The Messiah, girt with omnipotence, rode out on this creating errand. Heaven opened her everlasting gates, moving on their golden hinges, and the King of Glory, uplifted on the wings of Cherubim, rode on and on into Chaos. At last he stayed his fervid wheels and took the golden compasses in his hand. Centering one point where he stood, he turned the other silently and slowly round through the profound obscurity. Thus were the limits of *our* Universe marked out—that azure region in which the stars were to shine, and the planets were to wheel. On the huge fragment of Chaos thus marked out the Creating Spirit brooded, and the light gushed down. In six days the work of creation was completed. In the centre of the new Universe hung a silvery star. That was the Earth. Thereon, in a paradise of trees and flowers, walked Adam and Eve, the last and the fairest of all God's creatures.

Meanwhile the rebel host lay rolling in the fiery gulf underneath Chaos. The bottom of Chaos was Hell. Above it was Chaos proper, a thick, black, sweltering confusion. Above it again was the new experimental World, cut out of it like a mine, and brilliant with stars and galaxies. And high over all, behind the stars and galaxies, was Heaven itself. Satan and his crew lay rolling in Hell, the fiery element underneath Chaos. Chaos lay between them and the new World. Satan was the first to awake out of stupor and realize the whole state of the case—what had occurred, what was to be their future condition of being, and what remained to be attempted. In the first dialogue between him and Beelzebub we see that, even thus early, he had ascertained what his function was to be for the future, and decided in what precise mode of being he could make his existence most pungent and perceptible.

> Of this be sure,
> To do aught good never will be our task,
> But ever to do evil our sole delight,
> As being the contrary to His high will
> Whom we resist.

Here the ruined Archangel first strikes out the idea of existing for ever after as the Devil. It is important to observe that his becoming a Devil was not the mere inevitable consequence of his being a ruined Archangel. Beelzebub, for instance, could see in the future nothing but a prospect of continued suffering, until Satan communicated to him his conception of a way of enjoying action in the midst of suffering. Again, some of the Angels appear to have been ruminating the possibility of retrieving their former condition by patient enduring. The gigantic scheme of becoming a Devil was Satan's. At first it existed in his mind only as a vague perception that the way in which he would be most likely to get the full worth of his existence was to employ himself thenceforward in doing evil. The idea afterwards became more definite. After glancing round their new domain, Beelzebub and he aroused their abject followers. In the speech which Satan addresses to them after they had

all mustered in order we find him hint an opening into a new career, as if the
idea had just occurred to him:—

    Space may produce new worlds; whereof so rife
    There went a fame in Heaven that He ere long
    Intended to create, and therein plant
    A generation whom His choice regard
    Should favour equal to the sons of Heaven:
    Thither, if but to pry, shall be perhaps
    Our first eruption.

Here is an advance in definiteness upon the first proposal—that, namely,
of determining to spend the rest of existence in doing evil. Casting about
in his mind for some specific opening, Satan had recollected the talk they
used to have in Heaven about the new World that was to be cut out of
Chaos, and the new race of beings that was to be created to inhabit it; and
it instantly struck his scheming fancy that *this* would be the weak point of
the Universe. If he could but insert the wedge here! He did not, however,
announce the scheme fully at the moment, but went on thinking. In the
council of gods which was summoned some advised one thing, some
another. Moloch was for open war; Belial had great faith in the force of
circumstances; and Mammon was for organizing their new kingdom so as
to make it as comfortable as possible. No one, however, could say the exact
thing that was wanted. At last Beelzebub, prompted by Satan, rose and
detailed the project of their great leader:—

                 There is a place
    (If ancient and prophetic fame in Heaven
    Err not), another world, the happy seat
    Of some new race called Man, about this time
    To be created, like to us, though less
    In power and excellence, but favoured more
    Of Him who rules above. So was His will
    Pronounced among the gods, and by an oath
    That shook Heaven's whole circumference
        confirmed.
    Thither let us bend all our thoughts, and learn
    What creatures there inhabit, of what mould
    Or substance, how endued, and what their power
    And where their weakness: how attempted best;
    By force or subtlety.

This was Satan's scheme. The more he had thought on it the more did it recommend itself to him. It was more feasible than any other. It held out an indefinite prospect of action. Success in it would be the addition of another fragment of the Universe to Satan's kingdom, mingling and confounding the new World with Hell, and dragging down the new race of beings to share the perdition of the old. The scheme was universally applauded by the Angels; who seem to have differed from their leaders in this, that they were sanguine of being able to better their condition, whereas their leaders sought only the gratification of their desire of action.

The question next was, Who would venture out of Hell to explore the way to the new World? Satan volunteered the perilous excursion. Immediately, putting on his swiftest wings, he directs his solitary flight towards Hell-gate, where sat Sin and Death. When, at length, the gate was opened to give him exit, it was like a huge furnace-mouth, vomiting forth smoke and flames into the womb of Chaos. Issuing thence, Satan spread his sail-broad wings for flight, and began his toilsome way upward, half on foot, half on wing, swimming, sinking, wading, climbing, flying, through the thick and turbid element. At last he emerged out of Chaos into the glimmer surrounding the new Universe. Winging at leisure now through the balmier ether, and still ascending, he could discern at last the whole empyrean Heaven, his former home, with its opal towers and sapphire battlements, and, depending thence by a golden chain, our little World or Universe, like a star of smallest magnitude on the full moon's edge. At the point of suspension of this World from Heaven was an opening, and by that opening Satan entered.

When Satan thus arrived in the new Creation the whole phenomenon was strange to him, and he had no idea what kind of a being Man was. He asked Uriel, whom he found on the sun fulfilling some Divine errand, in which of all the shining orbs round him Man had fixed his seat, or whether he had a fixed seat at all, and was not at liberty to shift his residence, and dwell now in one star, now in another. Uriel, deceived by the appearance which Satan had assumed, pointed out the way to Paradise.

Alighting on the surface of the Earth, Satan walks about immersed in thought. Heaven's gate was in view. Overhead and round him were the quiet hills and the green fields. Oh, what an errand he had come upon! His thoughts were sad and noble. Fallen as he was, all the Archangel stirred within him. Oh, had he not been made so high, should he ever have fallen so low? Is there no hope even now, no room for repentance? Such were his first thoughts. But he roused himself and shook them off. "The past is gone and away; it is to the future that I must look. Perish the days of my Archangelship! perish the name of Archangel! Such is my name no longer. My future, if less happy, shall be more glorious. Ah, and this is the World I have singled out for my experiment! Formerly, in the days of my Archangelship, I ranged at will through infinity, doing one thing here and another there. Now I must contract the sphere of my activity, and labour nowhere but here. But it is better to apply myself to the task of thoroughly impregnating one point of space with my presence than henceforth to beat my wings vaguely all through infinitude. Ah, but may not my nature suffer by the change? In thus selecting a specific aim, in thus concerning myself exclusively with one point of space, and forswearing all interest in the innumerable glorious things that may be happening out of it, shall I not run the risk of degenerating into a smaller and meaner being? In the course of ages of dealing with the puny offspring of these new beings, may I not dwindle into a mere pungent, pettifogging Spirit? What would Raphael, Gabriel, and Michael say, were they to see their old co-mate changed into such a being? But be it so. If I cannot cope with the Almighty on the grand scale of infinitude, I shall at least make my existence felt by opposing His plans respecting this new race of beings. Besides, by beginning with this, may I not worm my way to a more effective position even in infinitude? At all events, I shall have a scheme on hand, and be incessantly occupied. And, as time makes the occupation more congenial, if I do become less magnanimous, I shall, at the same time, become happier. And, whether my fears on this point are visionary or not, it will, at least, be a noble thing to be able to say that I have caused a whirlpool that shall suck down generation after generation of these new beings, before their Maker's eyes, into the same wretched condition of being to which He has doomed us. It will be something so to vitiate the Universe that, let Him create, create on, as He chooses, it will be like pouring water into a broken vessel."

In the very course of this train of thinking Satan begins to degenerate into a meaner being. He is on the very threshold of that career in which he will cease for ever to be the Archangel and become irrevocably the Devil. The very manner in which he tempts the first pair is devil-like. It is in the shape of a cormorant on a tree that he sits watching his victims. He sat at the ear of Eve "squat like a toad." It was in the shape of a serpent that he tempted her. And, when the evil was done, he slunk away through the brush wood. In the very act of ruining Man he committed himself to a life of ignominious activity: he was to go on his belly and eat dust all his days.

—David Masson, from "The Three Devils:
Luther's, Milton's, and Goethe's," 1844, <i>The Three</i>
Devils, 1874, pp. 9–32

WILLIAM H. PRESCOTT "CHATEAUBRIAND'S ENGLISH LITERATURE" (1845)

Its sale was no evidence that its merits were comprehended, and may be referred to the general reputation of its author; for we find so accomplished a critic as Sir William Temple, some years later, omitting the name of Milton in his roll of writers who have done honour to modern literature, a circumstance which may, perhaps, be imputed to that reverence for the ancients which blinded Sir William to the merits of their successors. How could Milton be understood in his own generation, in the grovelling, sensual court of Charles the Second? How could the dull eyes, so long fastened on the earth, endure the blaze of his inspired genius? It was not till time had removed him to a distance that he could be calmly gazed on and his merits fairly contemplated. Addison, as is well known, was the first to bring them into popular view, by a beautiful specimen of criticism that has permanently connected his name with that of his illustrious subject. More than half a century later, another great name in English criticism, perhaps the greatest in general reputation, Johnson, passed sentence of a very different kind on the pretensions of the poet. A production more discreditable to the author is not to be found in the whole of his voluminous works; equally discreditable, whether regarded in an historical light or as a sample of literary criticism.

—William H. Prescott, "Chateaubriand's
English Literature," 1839, *Biographical
and Critical Miscellanies,* 1845

EDWARD EVERETT (1850)

In *Paradise Lost* we feel as if we were admitted to the outer courts of the Infinite. In that all-glorious temple of genius inspired by truth, we catch the full diapason of the heavenly organ. With its first choral swell the soul is lifted from the earth. In the *Divina Commedia* the man, the Florentine, the exiled Ghibelline, stands out, from first to last, breathing defiance and revenge. Milton, in some of his prose works, betrays the partisan also; but in his poetry we see him in the white robes of the minstrel, with upturned though sightless eyes, rapt in meditation at the feet of the heavenly muse. Dante, in his dark vision, descends to the depths of the world of perdition, and, homeless fugitive as he is, drags his proud and prosperous enemies down with him, and buries them, doubly destroyed, in the flaming sepulchres of the lowest hell. Milton, on the other hand, seems almost to have purged off the dross of humanity. Blind, poor, friendless, in solitude and sorrow, with quite as much reason as his Italian rival to repine at his fortune and war against mankind, how calm and unimpassioned is he in all that concerns his own personality! He deemed too highly of his divine gift, to make it the instrument of immortalizing his hatreds. One cry, alone, of sorrow at his blindness, one pathetic lamentation over the evil days on which he had fallen, bursts from his full heart. There is not a flash of human wrath in all his pictures of woe. Hating nothing but evil spirits, in the childlike simplicity of his heart, his pure hands undefiled with the pitch of the political intrigues in which he had lived, he breathes forth his inexpressibly majestic strains,—the poetry not so much of earth as of heaven.

—Edward Everett, *Orations and Speeches*, 1850,
volume 2, p. 222

ALPHONSE DE LAMARTINE (1854)

Milton is one of the three great Christian poets who were to the theogony of the Middle Ages what Homer was to the Olympus of paganism. The triumvirate consists of Dante, Tasso, and Milton. The *Divine Comedy* of Dante, the *Jerusalem Delivered* of Tasso, the *Paradise Lost* of Milton, are the *Iliads* and *Odysseys* of our theological system. Milton is the least original of the three great Christian poets. At first he imitates Homer, then Virgil, and lastly Dante and Tasso; but his real model is Dante. He impresses the same supernatural subject on the Christian theogony; he sings to England what Italy has already heard—the strife of created angels in revolt against their Maker—the blissful loves of Eden—the seduction of woman—the fall of man—the intercession of the Son of God with the Father—the mercy obtained by his own sacrifice, and the redemption partially gleaming through the distance, as the *denouement* of this sublime tragedy. Finally, he embraces the entire series of mysteries which the philosopher penetrates with his conjectures, the theologian explains, and the poet describes, without demanding of them other components than miracles, images, and emotions. Why, then, did Milton select this overpowering theological subject, and transplant it to England, so rich in Saxon and Celtic traditions, already popular, and admirably adapted for the text of a grand national and original northern epic? The answer is to be found in his character and his life. By nature he was theological, and the youngest half of his existence had been passed in Italy. The first voyage of a youth is a second birth; from it he imbibes new sensations and ideas, which produce a species of personal transformation. The phenomenon of petrification is not confined to the effect of water upon a plant; it operates upon man through the air that he breathes.

—Alphonse de Lamartine,
Memoirs of Celebrated Characters, 1854

Walter Bagehot "John Milton" (1859)

English essayist, literary critic, editor, and economist Walter Bagehot (1826–77) received B.A. and M.A. degrees from University College, London. Although called to the Bar for a law career, he left that field to enter banking. Writing, however, drew his attention most; after graduating from the university, he wrote articles for the *Prospective Review*, including one on Shakespeare (1853). In 1855, he co-founded the London *National Review* with Richard Hutton, essentially functioning as co-editor, despite his friend's title of editor. Bagehot wrote long essays on literary topics and figures for each issue of the quarterly journal, then turned to political writing with a well-received piece on former prime minister Robert Peel. A collection of Bagehot's essays from the *Prospective Review* and *National Review* was published in 1858. Continuing to garner attention for his literary analysis, Bagehot wrote on Walter Scott, Charles Dickens, and, in the following selection, John Milton, then began also writing for the *Economist*, taking over the publication after the death of his father-in-law, James Wilson, editor of the magazine and financial secretary of the national treasury. Bagehot resigned his banking post and became a full-time editor and writer. His current fame rests primarily on *The English Constitution*, a volume collected from his serialized installments in the *Fortnightly Review* from 1865–67. The work shows Bagehot's moderate political views in advocating for a limited democracy in which the working class would have to be educated before being allowed to vote. He finished his career with two other books, *Physics and Politics* (1872), which reasserted many of his previously published views from a more theoretical perspective, and an economic work focusing on the London banking system, *Lombard Street* (1873).

Bagehot's essay on Milton was originally written for the *National Review*. It is impressionistic in its reading of *Paradise Lost*, commenting on everything from the work's classicism to its theology to the purpose of poetry. Two comments stand out in the selection: The first is Bagehot's declamation of "the great error which pervades *Paradise Lost*. Satan is made *interesting*." Bagehot supports his argument at length, seeing Milton as undermining his own theology and his theodicy, as the positive portrayal of Satan removes any possibility of justifying God's ways to humans. The second is his appraisal of Eve as a more successfully created character than Adam, asserting, "Eve's character, indeed, is one of the most wonderful efforts of the human imagination." As she is more interesting than Adam, according to Bagehot, she left Adam to take a nap, as she "must have found him tiresome."

If from the man we turn to his works, we are struck at once with two singular contrasts. The first of them is this. The distinction between ancient and modern art is sometimes said, and perhaps truly, to consist in the simple bareness of the imaginative conceptions which we find in ancient art, and the comparatively complex clothing in which all modern creations are embodied. If we adopt this distinction, Milton seems in some sort ancient, and in some sort modern. Nothing is so simple as the subject-matter of his works. The two greatest of his creations—the character of Satan and the character of Eve—are two of the simplest—the latter probably the very simplest—in the whole field of literature. On this side Milton's art is classical. On the other hand, in no writer is the imagery more profuse, the illustrations more various, the dress altogether more splendid. And in this respect the style of his art seems romantic and modern. In real truth, however, it is only ancient art in a modern disguise. The dress is a mere dress, and can be stripped off when we will. We all of us do perhaps in memory strip it off for ourselves. Notwithstanding the lavish adornments with which her image is presented, the character of Eve is still the simplest sort of feminine essence,—the pure embodiment of that inner nature which we believe and hope that women have. The character of Satan, though it is not so easily described, has nearly as few elements in it. The most purely modern conceptions will not bear to be unclothed in this manner. Their romantic garment clings inseparably to them. Hamlet or Lear are not to be thought of except as complex characters, with very involved and complicated embodiments. They are as difficult to draw out in words as the common characters of life are; that of Hamlet, perhaps, is more so. If we make it, as perhaps we should, the characteristic of modern and romantic art that it presents us with creations which we cannot think of or delineate except as very varied, and, so to say, circumstantial, we must not rank Milton among the masters of romantic art. And without involving the subject in the troubled sea of an old controversy, we may say that the most striking of the poetical peculiarities of Milton is the bare simplicity of his ideas, and the rich abundance of his illustrations. Another of his peculiarities is equally striking. There seems to be such a thing as second-hand poetry. Some poets, musing on the poetry of other men, have unconsciously shaped it into something of their own: the new conception is like the original, it would never probably have existed had not the original existed previously; still it is sufficiently different from the original to be a new thing, not a copy or a plagiarism; it is a creation, though, so to say, a suggested creation. Gray is as good an example as can be found of a poet whose works abound in this species of semi-original conceptions. Industrious critics track his best lines back, and find others like them which doubtless lingered near his fancy while he was writing them. The same critics have been equally busy with the works of Milton, and equally successful. They find traces of his reading in half his works; not, which any reader could do, in overt similes and distinct illustrations, but also in the very texture of the thought and the expression. In many cases, doubtless, they discover more than he himself knew. A mind like his, which has an immense store of imaginative recollections, can never know which of his own imaginations is exactly suggested by which recollection. Men awake with their best ideas; it is seldom worth while to investigate very curiously whence they came. Our proper business is to adapt, and mould, and act upon them. Of poets perhaps this is true even more remarkably than of other men; their ideas are suggested in modes, and according to laws, even more impossible to specify than the ideas of the rest of the world. Second-hand poetry, so to say, often seems quite original to the poet himself; he frequently does not know that he derived it from an old memory; years afterwards it may strike him as it does others. Still, in general, such inferior species of creation is not so likely to be found in minds of singular originality as in those of less. A brooding, placid, cultivated mind, like that of Gray, is the place where we should expect to meet with it. Great originality disturbs the adaptive process, removes the mind of the poet from the thoughts of other men, and occupies it with its own heated and flashing thoughts. Poetry of the second degree is like the secondary rocks of modern geology,—a still, gentle, alluvial formation; the igneous glow of primary genius brings forth ideas like the primeval granite, simple, astounding, and alone. Milton's case is an exception to this rule. His mind has marked originality, probably as much of it as any in literature; but it has as much of moulded recollection as any mind too. His poetry in consequence is like an artificial park, green, and soft, and beautiful, yet with outlines bold, distinct, and firm, and the eternal rock ever jutting out; or, better still, it is like our own lake scenery, where nature has herself the same combination—where we have Rydal Water side by side with the everlasting upheaved mountain. Milton has the same union of softened beauty with unimpaired grandeur; and it is his peculiarity.

These are the two contrasts which puzzle us at first in Milton, and which distinguish him from other poets in our remembrance afterwards. We have a superficial complexity in illustration, and imagery, and metaphor; and in contrast with it we observe a latent simplicity of idea, an almost rude strength of conception. The underlying thoughts are few, though the flowers on the surface are so many. We have likewise the perpetual contrast of the soft poetry of the memory, and the firm, as it were fused, and glowing poetry of the imagination. His words, we may half fancifully say, are like his character. There is the same austerity in the real essence, the same exquisiteness of sense, the same delicacy of form which we know that he had, the same music which we imagine there was in his voice. In both his character and his poetry there was an ascetic nature in a sheath of beauty.

No book, perhaps, which has ever been written is more difficult to criticise than *Paradise Lost*. The only way to criticise a work of the imagination, is to describe its effect upon the mind of the reader,—at any rate, of the critic; and this can only be adequately delineated by strong illustrations, apt similies, and perhaps a little exaggeration. The task is in its very nature not an easy one; the poet paints a picture on the fancy of the critic, and the critic has in some sort to copy it on the paper. He must say what it is before he can make remarks upon it. But in the case of *Paradise Lost* we hardly like to use illustrations. The subject is one which the imagination rather shrinks from. At any rate, it requires courage, and an effort to compel the mind to view such a subject as distinctly and vividly as it views other subjects. Another peculiarity of *Paradise Lost* makes the difficulty even greater. It does not profess to be a mere work of art; or rather, it claims to be by no means that, and that only. It starts with a dogmatic aim; it avowedly intends to

> assert eternal Providence,
> And justify the ways of God to men.

In this point of view we have always had a sympathy with the Cambridge mathematician who has been so much abused. He said, 'After all, *Paradise Lost proves* nothing;' and various persons of poetical tastes and temperament have been very severe on the prosaic observation. Yet, 'after all,' he was right. Milton professed to prove something. He was too profound a critic,—rather, he had too profound an instinct of those eternal principles of art which criticism tries to state,—not to know that on such a subject he must prove something. He professed to deal with the great problem of human destiny; to show why man was created, in what kind of universe he lives, whence he came, and whither he goes. He dealt of necessity with the greatest of subjects. He had to sketch the greatest of objects. He was concerned with infinity and eternity even more than with time and sense; he undertook to delineate the ways, and consequently the character, of Providence, as well as the conduct and the tendencies of man. The essence of success in such an attempt is to satisfy the religious sense of man; to bring home to our hearts what we know to be true; to teach us what we have not seen; to awaken us to what we have forgotten;

to remove the 'covering' from all people, and 'the veil' that is spread over all nations; to give us, in a word, such a conception of things, divine and human, as we can accept, believe, and trust. The true doctrine of criticism demands what Milton invites—an examination of the degree in which the great epic attains this aim. And if, in examining it, we find it necessary to use unusual illustrations, and plainer words than are customary, it must be our excuse that we do not think the subject can be made clear without them.

The defect of *Paradise Lost* is that, after all, it is founded on a *political* transaction. The scene is in heaven very early in the history of the universe, before the creation of man or the fall of Satan. We have a description of a court. The angels,

> By imperial summons called,
> appear
> Under their hierarchs in orders bright.
> Ten thousand thousand ensigns high advanced,
> Standards and gonfalons, 'twixt van and rear,
> Stream in the air, and for distinction serve
> Of hierarchies, of orders, and degrees.

To this assemblage 'th' Omnipotent' speaks:

> Hear, all ye Angels, progeny of light,
> Thrones, Dominations, Princedoms, Virtues,
>   Powers,
> Hear my decree, which unrevoked shall stand!
> This day I have begot whom I declare
> My only Son, and on this holy hill
> Him have anointed, whom ye now behold
> At my right hand. Your head I him appoint;
> And by myself have sworn to him shall bow
> All knees in Heaven, and shall confess him Lord.
> Under his great vicegerent reign abide,
> United as one individual soul,
> For ever happy. Him who disobeys
> Me disobeys, breaks union, and, that day,
> Cast out from God and blessed vision, falls
> Into utter darkness deep engulfed, his place
> Ordained without redemption, without end.

This act of patronage was not popular at court; and why should it have been? The religious sense is against it. The worship which sinful men owe to God is not transferable to lieutenants and vicegerents. The whole scene of the court jars upon a true feeling. We seem to be reading about some emperor of history, who admits his son to a share in the empire, who confers on him a considerable jurisdiction, and requires officials, with 'standards and gonfalons,' to bow before him. The orthodoxy of Milton is quite as questionable as his accuracy. The old Athanasian creed was not made by persons who would allow such a picture as that of Milton to stand before their imaginations. The generation of the Son was to them a fact 'before all time,' an eternal fact. There was no question in their minds of patronage or promotion. The Son was the Son before all time, just as the Father was the Father before all time. Milton had in such matters a bold but not very sensitive imagination. He accepted the inevitable materialism of biblical, and, to some extent, of all religious language as distinct revelation. He certainly believed, in contradiction to the old creed, that God had both 'parts and passions.' He imagined that earth

> Is but the shadow of Heaven, and, things therein
> Each to other like, more than on Earth is thought!

From some passages it would seem that he actually thought of God as having 'the members and form' of a man. Naturally, therefore, he would have no toleration for the mysterious notions of time and eternity which are involved in the traditional doctrine. We are not, however, now concerned with Milton's belief, but with his representation of his creed—his picture, so to say, of it in *Paradise Lost*; still, as we cannot but think, that picture is almost irreligious, and certainly different from that which has been generally accepted in Christendom. Such phrases as 'before all time,' 'eternal generation,' are doubtless very vaguely interpreted by the mass of men; nevertheless, no sensitively orthodox man *could* have drawn the picture of a generation, not to say an exaltation, *in* time.

We shall see this more clearly by reading what follows in the poem:

> All seemed well pleased; all seemed, but were not all.

One of the archangels, whose name can be guessed, decidedly disapproved, and calls a meeting, at which he explains that

> orders and degrees
> Jar not with liberty, but well consist;

but still, that the promotion of a new person, on grounds of relationship merely, above, even infinitely above, the old angels with imperial titles, was 'a new law,' and rather tyrannical. Abdiel,

> than whom none with more zeal adored
> The Deity, and divine commands obeyed,

attempts a defence:

> Grant it thee unjust
> That equal over equals monarch reign—
> Thyself, though great and glorious, dost thou count,
> Or all angelic nature join'd in one,
> Equal to him, begotten Son, by whom?
> As by his Word, the mighty Father made
> All things, even thee, and all the Spirits of Heaven
> By him created in their bright degrees,
> Crowned them with glory, and to their glory named
> Thrones, Dominations, Princedoms, Virtues,
>   Powers?—
> Essential Powers; nor by his reign obscured,
> But more illustrious made; since he, the head,
> One of our number thus reduced becomes;
> His laws our laws; all honour to him done
> Returns our own. Cease then this impious rage,
> And tempt not these; but hasten to appease
> The incensed Father and the incensed Son,
> While pardon may be found, in time besought.

Yet though Abdiel's intentions were undeniably good, his argument is rather specious. Acting as an instrument in the process of creation would scarcely give a valid claim to the obedience of the created being. Power may be shown in the act, no doubt; but mere power gives no true claim to the obedience of moral beings. It is a kind of principle of all manner of idolatries and false religions to believe that it does so. Satan, besides, takes issue on the fact:

> That we were formed then, say'st thou? and the work
> Of secondary hands, by task transferred
> From Father to his Son? Strange point and new!
> Doctrine which we would know whence learned!

And we must say that the speech in which the new ruler is introduced to the 'thrones, dominations, princedoms, virtues, powers,' is hard to reconcile with Abdiel's exposition. '*This day* he seems to have come into existence, and could hardly have assisted at the creation of the angels, who are not young, and who converse with one another like old acquaintances.

We have gone into this part of the subject at length, because it is the source of the great error which pervades *Paradise Lost*. Satan is made *interesting*. This has been the charge of a thousand orthodox and even heterodox writers against Milton. Shelley, on the other hand, has gloried in it; and fancied, if we remember rightly, that Milton intentionally ranged himself on the Satanic side of the universe, just as Shelley himself would have done, and that he wished to show the falsity of the ordinary theology. But Milton was born an age too early for such aims, and was far too sincere to have advocated any doctrine in a form so indirect. He believed every word he said. He was not conscious of the effect his teaching would produce in an age like this, when scepticism is in the air, and when it is not possible to help looking coolly on his delineations. Probably in our boyhood we can recollect a period when any solemn description of celestial events would have commanded our respect; we should not have dared to read it intelligently, to canvass its details and see what it meant: it was a religious book; it sounded reverential, and that would have sufficed. Something like this was the state of mind of the seventeenth century. Even Milton probably shared in a vague reverence for religious language. He hardly felt the moral effect of the pictures he was drawing. His artistic instinct, too, often hurries him away. His Satan was to him, as to us, the hero of his poem. Having commenced by making him resist on an occasion which in an earthly kingdom would have been excusable and proper, he probably a little sympathised with him, just as his readers do.

The interest of Satan's character is at its height in the first two books. Coleridge justly compared it to that of Napoleon. There is the same pride, the same satanic ability, the same will, the same egotism. His character seems to grow with his position. He is far finer after his fall, in misery and suffering, with scarcely any resource except in himself, than he was originally in heaven; at least if Raphael's description of him can be trusted. No portrait which imagination or history has drawn of a revolutionary anarch is nearly so perfect; there is all the grandeur of the greatest human mind, and a certain infinitude in his circumstances which humanity must ever want. Few Englishmen feel a profound reverence for Napoleon I. There was no French alliance in *his* time; we have most of us some tradition of antipathy to him. Yet hardly any Englishman can read the account of the campaign of 1814 without feeling his interest for the Emperor to be strong, and without perhaps being conscious of a latent wish that he may succeed. Our opinion is against him, our serious wish is of course for England; but the imagination has a sympathy of its own, and will not give place. We read about the great general—never greater than in that last emergency—showing resources of genius that seem almost infinite, and that assuredly have never been surpassed, yet vanquished, yielding to the power of circumstances, to the combined force of adversaries, each of whom singly he outmatches in strength, and all of whom together he surpasses in majesty and in mind. Something of the same sort of interest belongs to the Satan of the first two books *of Paradise Lost*. We know that he will be vanquished; his name is not a recommendation. Still we do not imagine distinctly the minds by which he is to be vanquished; we do not take the same interest in them that we do in him; our sympathies, our fancy, are on his side.

Perhaps much of this was inevitable; yet what a defect it is! Especially what a defect in Milton's own view, and looked at with the stern realism with which he regarded it! Suppose that the author of evil in the universe were the most attractive being in it; suppose that the source of all sin were the origin of all interest to us! We need not dwell upon this.

As we have said, much of this was difficult to avoid, if indeed it could be avoided, in dealing with such a theme. Even Milton shrank, in some measure, from delineating the divine character. His imagination evidently halts when it is required to perform that task. The more delicate imagination of our modern world would shrink still more. Any person who will consider what such an attempt must end in will find his nerves quiver. But by a curiously fatal error, Milton has selected for delineation exactly that part of the divine nature which is most beyond the reach of the human faculties, and which is also, when we try to describe our fancy of it, the least effective to our minds. He has made God *argue*. Now, the procedure of the divine mind from truth to truth must ever be incomprehensible to us; the notion, indeed, of his proceeding at all, is a contradiction: to some extent, at least, it is inevitable that we should use such language, but we know it is in reality inapplicable. A long train of reasoning in such a connection is so out of place as to be painful; and yet Milton has many. He relates a series of family prayers in heaven, with sermons afterwards, which are very tedious. Even Pope was shocked at the notion of Providence talking like 'a school-divine.' And there is the still worse error, that if you once attribute reasoning to Him, subsequent logicians may discover that He does not reason very well.

Another way in which Milton has contrived to strengthen our interest in Satan is the number and insipidity of his good angels. There are old rules as to the necessity of a supernatural machinery for an epic poem, worth some fraction of the paper on which they are written, and derived from the practice of Homer, who believed his gods and goddesses to be real beings, and would have been rather harsh with a critic who called them machinery. These rules had probably an influence with Milton, and induced him to manipulate these serious angels more than he would have done otherwise. They appear to be excellent administrators with very little to do; a kind of grand chamberlains with wings, who fly down to earth and communicate information to Adam and Eve. They have no character; they are essentially messengers, merely conductors, so to say, of the providential will: no one fancies that they have an independent power of action; they seem scarcely to have minds of their own. No effect can be more unfortunate. If the struggle of Satan had been with Deity directly, the natural instincts of religion would have been awakened; but when an angel with mind is only contrasted to angels with wings, we sympathise with the former.

In the first two books, therefore, our sympathy with Milton's Satan is great; we had almost said unqualified. The speeches he delivers are of well-known excellence. Lord Brougham, no contemptible 'judge of emphatic oratory, has laid down that if a person had not an opportunity of access to the great Attic masterpieces, he had better choose these for a model. What is to be regretted about the orator is that he scarcely acts up to his sentiments. 'Better to reign in hell than serve in heaven' is, at any rate, an audacious declaration. But he has no room for exhibiting similar audacity in action. His offensive career is limited. In the nature of the subject there was scarcely the possibility for the fallen archangel to display in the detail of his operations the surpassing intellect with which Milton has endowed him. He goes across chaos, gets into a few physical difficulties; but these are not much. His grand aim is the conquest of our first parents; and we are at once struck with the enormous inequality of the conflict. Two beings just created, without experience, without guile, without knowledge of good and evil, are expected to contend with a being on the delineation of whose powers every resource of art and imagination, every subtle suggestion, every emphatic simile, has been lavished. The idea in every reader's mind is, and must be, not surprise that our first parents should yield, but wonder that Satan should not think it beneath him to attack them. It is as if an army should invest a cottage.

We have spoken more of theology than we intended; and we need not say how much the monstrous inequalities attributed to the combatants affect our estimate of the results of the conflict. The state of man is what it is, because the defenceless Adam and Eve of Milton's imagination yielded to the nearly all-powerful Satan whom he has delineated. Milton has in some sense invented this difficulty; for in the book of Genesis there is no such inequality. The serpent may be subtler than any beast of the field; but he is not necessarily subtler or cleverer than man. So far from Milton having justified the ways of God to man, he has loaded the common theology with a new encumbrance.

We may need refreshment after this discussion; and we cannot find it better than in reading a few remarks of Eve.

That day I oft remember, when from sleep,
I first awaked, and found myself reposed,
Under a shade, on flow'rs, much wond'ring where
And what I was, whence thither brought, and how.
Not distant far from thence a murm'ring sound
Of waters issued from a cave, and spread
Into a liquid plain; then stood unmoved,
Pure as the expanse of Heav'n. I thither went
With unexperienced thought, and laid me down
On the green bank, to look into the clear
Smooth lake, that to me seem'd another sky.
As I bent down to look, just opposite
A shape within the watery gleam appear'd,
Bending to look on me. I started back;
It started back: but pleased I soon returned;
Pleased it returned as soon with answering looks
Of sympathy and love. There I had fix'd
Mine eyes till now, and pined with vain desire,
Had not a voice thus warned me: 'What thou seest,
What there thou seest, fair creature, is thyself;
With thee it came and goes: but follow me,
And I will bring thee where no shadow stays
Thy coming, and thy soft embraces—he
Whose image thou art; him thou shalt enjoy
Inseparably thine; to him shalt bear
Multitudes like thyself, and thence be call'd
Mother of Human Race.' What could I do
But follow straight, invisibly thus led?
Till I espied thee, fair, indeed, and tall,
Under a platan; yet methought less fair,
Less winning soft, less amiably mild,
Than that smooth watery image. Back I turn'd:
Thou, following, cry'dst aloud, 'Return, fair Eve;
Whom fly'st thou?'

Eve's character, indeed, is one of the most wonderful efforts of the human imagination. She is a kind of abstract woman; essentially a typical being; an official 'mother of all living.' Yet she is a real interesting woman, not only full of delicacy and sweetness, but with all the undefinable fascination, the charm of personality, which such typical characters hardly ever have. By what consummate miracle of wit this charm of individuality is preserved, without impairing the general idea which is ever present to us, we cannot explain, for we do not know.

Adam is far less successful. He has good hair,—'hya-cinthine locks' that 'from his parted forelock manly hung;' a 'fair large front' and 'eye sublime;' but he has little else that we care for. There is, in truth, no opportunity of displaying manly virtues, even if he possessed them. He has only to yield to his wife's solicitations, which he does. Nor are we sure that he does it well. He is very tedious; he indulges in sermons which are good; but most men cannot but fear that so delightful a being as Eve must have found him tiresome Eve's character, indeed, is one of the most wonderful efforts of the human imagination. . . . She steps away, however, and goes to sleep at some of the worst points.

Dr. Johnson remarked, that, after all, *Paradise Lost* was one of the books which no one wished longer: we fear, in this irreverent generation, some wish it shorter. Hardly any reader would be sorry if some portions of the later books had been spared him. Coleridge, indeed, discovered profound mysteries in the last; but in what could not Coleridge find a mystery if he wished? Dryden more wisely remarked, that Milton became tedious when he entered upon a 'tract of Scripture.' Nor is it surprising that such is the case. They style of many parts of Scripture is such that it will not bear addition or subtraction. A word less, or an idea more, and the effect upon the mind is the same no longer. Nothing can be more tiresome than a sermonic amplification of such passages. It is almost too much when, as from the pulpit, a paraphrastic commentary is prepared for our spiritual improvement. In deference to the intention we bear it, but we bear it unwillingly; and we cannot endure it at all when, as in poems, the object is to awaken our fancy rather than to improve our conduct. The account of the creation in the book of Genesis is one of the compositions from which no sensitive imagination would subtract an iota, to which it could not bear to add a word. Milton's paraphrase is alike copious and ineffective. The universe is, in railway phrase, 'opened,' but not created; no green earth springs in a moment from the indefinite void. Instead, too, of the simple loneliness of the Old Testament, several angelic officials are in attendance, who help in nothing, but indicate that heaven must be plentifully supplied with tame creatures.

There is no difficulty in writing such criticisms, and, indeed, other unfavourable criticisms, on *Paradise Lost*. There is scarcely any book in the world which is open to a greater number, or which a reader who allows plain words to produce a due effect will be less satisfied with. Yet what book is really greater? In the best parts the words have a magic in them; even in the inferior passages you are hardly sensible of their inferiority till you translate them into your own language. Perhaps no style ever written by man expressed so adequately the conceptions of a mind so strong and so peculiar; a manly strength, a haunting atmosphere of enhancing suggestions, a firm continuous music, are only some of its excellencies. To comprehend the whole of the others, you must take the volume down and read it,—the best defence of Milton, as has been said most truly, against all objections.

Probably no book shows the transition which our theology has made, since the middle of the seventeenth century, at once so plainly and so fully. We do not now compose long narratives to 'justify the ways of God to men.' The more orthodox we are, the more we shrink from it; the more we hesitate at such a task, the more we allege that we have no powers for it. Our most celebrated defences of established tenets are in the style of Butler, not in that of Milton. They do not profess to show a satisfactory explanation of human destiny; on the contrary, they hint that probably we could not understand such an explanation if it were given us; at any rate, they allow that it is not given us. Their course is palliative. They suggest an 'analogy of difficulties.' If our minds were greater, so they reason, we should comprehend these doctrines: now we cannot explain analogous facts which we see and know. No style can be more opposite to the bold argument, the boastful exposition of Milton. The teaching of the eighteenth century is in the very atmosphere we breathe. We read it in the teachings of Oxford; we hear it from the missionaries of the Vatican. The air of the theology is clarified. We know our difficulties, at least; we are rather prone to exaggerate the weight of some than to deny the reality of any.

We cannot continue a line of thought which would draw us on too far for the patience of our readers. We must, however, make one more remark, and we shall have finished our criticism on *Paradise Lost*. It is analogous to that which we have just made. The scheme of the poem is based on an offence against positive morality. The offence of Adam was not against nature or conscience, not against anything of which we can see the reason, or conceive the obligation, but against an unexplained injunction of the Supreme Will. The rebellion in heaven, as Milton describes it, was a rebellion, not against known ethics, or immutable spiritual laws, but against an arbitrary selection and an unexplained edict. We do not say that there is no such thing as positive morality; we do not think so; even if we did, we should not insert a proposition so startling at the conclusion of a literary criticism. But we are sure that wherever a positive moral edict is promulgated, it is no subject, except perhaps under a very peculiar treatment, for literary art. By the very nature of it, it cannot satisfy the heart and conscience. It is a difficulty; we need not attempt to explain it away. There are mysteries enough which will never be explained away. But it is contrary to every principle of criticism to state the difficulty as if it were not one; to bring forward the puzzle, yet leave it to yourself; to publish so strange a problem, and give only an untrue solution of it: and yet such, in its bare statement, is all which Milton has done.

Of Milton's other writings we have left ourselves no room to speak; and though every one of them, or almost every one of them, would well repay a careful criticism, yet few of them seem to throw much additional light on his character, or add much to our essential notion of his genius, though they may exemplify and enhance it. *Comus* is the poem which does so the most. Literature has become so much lighter than it used to be, that we can scarcely realise the position it occupied in the light literature of our forefathers. We have now in our own language many poems that are pleasanter in their subject, more graceful in their execution, more flowing in their outline, more easy to read. Dr. Johnson, though perhaps no very excellent authority on the more intangible graces of literature, was disposed to deny to Milton the capacity of creating the lighter literature: 'Milton, madam, was a genius that could cut a colossus from a rock, but could not carve heads upon cherrystones.' And it would not be surprising if this generation, which has access to the almost indefinite quantity of lighter compositions which have been produced since Johnson's time, were to echo his sentence. In some degree, perhaps, the popular taste does so. *Comus* has no longer the peculiar exceptional popularity which it used to have. We can talk without general odium of its defects. Its characters are nothing, its sentiments are tedious, its story is not interesting. But it is only when we have realised the magnitude of its deficiences that we comprehend the peculiarity of its greatness. Its power is in its style. A grave and firm music pervades it: it is soft, without a thought of weakness; harmonious and yet strong; impressive, as few such poems are, yet covered with a bloom of beauty and a complexity of charm that few poems have either. We have, perhaps, light literature in itself better, that we read oftener and more easily, that lingers more in our memories; but we have not any, we question if there ever will be any, which gives so true a conception of the capacity and the dignity of the mind by which it was produced. The breath of solemnity which hovers round the music attaches us to the writer. Every line, here as elsewhere in Milton, excites the idea of indefinite power.

And so we must draw to a close. The subject is an infinite one, and if we pursued it, we should lose ourselves in miscellaneous commentary, and run on far beyond the patience of our readers. What we have said has at least a defined intention. We have wished to state the impression which the character of Milton and the greatest of Milton's works are likely to produce on readers of the present generation,—a generation, almost more than any other, different from his own.

> —Walter Bagehot, from "John Milton," 1859,
> *Collected Works,* edited by St. John-Stevas,
> volume 2, 1965, pp. 134–48

MATTHEW ARNOLD (1861)

How noble this metre is in Milton's hands, how completely it shows itself capable of the grand, nay of the grandest, style, I need not say. To this metre, as used in the *Paradise Lost,* our country owes the glory of having produced one of the only two poetical works in the grand style which are to be found in the modern languages; the *Divine Comedy* of Dante is the other. England and Italy here stand alone; Spain, France and Germany have produced great poets, but neither Calderon, nor Corneille, nor Schiller, nor even Goethe, has produced a body of poetry in the true grand style, in the sense in which the style of the body of Homer's poetry, or Pindar's, or Sophocles's, is grand. But Dante has, and so has Milton; and in this respect Milton possesses a distinction which even Shakespeare, undoubtedly the supreme poetical power in our literature, does not share with him. Not a tragedy of Shakespeare but contains passages in the worst of all styles, the affected style; and the grand style, although it may be harsh, or obscure, or cumbrous, or over-laboured, is never affected. In spite, therefore, of objections which may justly be urged against the plan and treatment of the *Paradise Lost,* in spite of its possessing, certainly, a far less enthralling force of interest to attract and to carry forward the reader than the *Iliad* or the *Divine Comedy,* it fully deserves, it can never lose, its immense reputation; for, like the *Iliad* and the *Divine Comedy,* nay in some respects to a higher degree than either of them, it is in the grand style.

> —Matthew Arnold, *On Translating Homer,* 1861

EDMOND SCHERER
"MILTON AND *PARADISE LOST*" (1868)

French theologian, politician, and literary critic Edmond Henri Adolphe Scherer (1815–89) studied law, then received his doctorate in theology from Strasbourg University and was ordained. Appointed professor at the École Evangelique in Geneva, his growing religious liberalism prompted his resignation six years later, and he eventually moved away from Protestantism altogether. After serving in politics, he devoted himself primarily to writing literary-historical criticism. Here, we see Scherer's theological analysis of Milton's religious views. Castigating seventeenth-century Puritan views, he asserts that *Paradise Lost* becomes didactic because of Milton's belief system.

VI

Paradise Lost is a work of the Renaissance, full of imitation of the ancients. The plan is modelled upon the consecrated patterns, especially on that of the *Aeneid*. There is an exposition, there is an invocation; after which the author plunges *in medias res*. Satan and his accomplices are discovered stranded on the floor of hell, like Æneas on the coast of Carthage. At this point the action begins. It is and will be very simple throughout. As /Eneas triumphs over Turnus, so Satan will ruin humanity in the person of our first parents. This unity of action is demanded by the rules; but it is necessary, on the other hand, that the poet should tell us what has gone before, and what will come after, otherwise there would not be material enough. So resource is had to narratives. Æneas tells Dido of the Fall of Troy: Raphael narrates to Adam the revolt of the angels and the creation of the world. Thus we are posted up as to the past: but the future remains. The poet cannot leave us with the death of Turnus or the Fall of the first human beings, because the true interest of the two poems lies in the relations of Æneas with the destinies of the Roman people and in the relations of Adam's sin with the lot of all mankind. Patience! a new device will get us out of the difficulty. Æneas descends to Hades, and there finds Anchises, who shows him the procession of his posterity. The archangel Michael leads Adam to a hill and delivers a complete course of lectures to him on sacred history, from the death of Abel to the coming of Christ, and even to the Last Judgment.

Such is the plan of *Paradise Lost*: there is nothing more regular or more classical. We recognize the superstitions of the Renaissance in this faithfulness to models. But the result is that Milton's poem presents a sort of tertiary formation, the copy of a copy. It is to the Latin epics what these are to Homer. We shall see presently what Milton has succeeded in throwing into the traditional mould; but as for the form of his poem he did not create it for himself, he received it. It is a legacy of antiquity.

VII

If the form of *Paradise Lost* was supplied by the Renaissance the substance was furnished by Puritanism. *Paradise Lost* is an epic, but it is a theological epic, and the theology of the poem is made up of the favorite dogmas of the Puritans—the Fall, Justification, the sovereign laws of God. Moreover, Milton makes no secret of the fact that he is defending a thesis: his end, he says in the first lines, is to "assert eternal providence And justify the ways of God to man."

There are, therefore, in *Paradise Lost* two things which must be kept distinct: an epic poem and a theodicy. Unluckily, these two elements—answering to the two men of which Milton was himself made up, and to the two tendencies which his age obeyed—these two elements, I say, were incapable of thorough fusion. Nay, they are at complete variance, and from their juxtaposition there results an undertone of contradiction which runs through the whole work, affects its solidity, and endangers its value. It would be vain to plead the example of the classical epic. The Gods no doubt hold a great place both in the *Iliad* and the *Aeneid;* but Christianity is in this respect very differently situated from Paganism. Christianity is a religion which has been formally "redacted" and settled; and it is impossible, without doing it violence, to add anything to it or subtract anything from it. Moreover, Christianity is a religion serious in itself and insisting upon being taken seriously, devoted to ideas the gravest, not to say the saddest, that imagination can form: those of sin, redemption, self-denial, good works—all of them things which, as Boileau says, are not fitted for being smartened up by ornament.

L'evangile a l'esprit n'offre de tous cotes
Que penitence a faire et tourments merites,
Et de vos fictions le melange coupable
Meme a ses vérités donne l'air de la fable.[1]

But this is not all. Christianity is a religion of dogma: in place of the fantastic and intangible myths of which the Aryan religions were made up, it has abstruse distinctions, paradoxical mysteries, subtle teachings. In short, it amounts to a meta-physic, or, to return to the expression I used at first, a theology. And theology has never had the reputation of being favorable to poetry. Lastly, and as a climax, this theology is still alive. It is for thousands an object of faith and hope: it is not "to let," if I may so speak, there is no vacancy in it; and the poet who carries into it the creations of his fantasy has all the appearance of committing sacrilege.

This, as it is, looks ill for Milton's poem; but we have not yet said all. *Paradise Lost* is not only a theological poem—two words which cry out at finding themselves united—but it is at the same time a commentary on texts of Scripture. The author has chosen for his subject the first chapters of Genesis, that is to say a story, which the stoutest or the simplest faith hesitates to take quite literally, a story in which serpents are heard speaking, and the ruin of the human race is seen to be bound up with a fault merely childish in appearance. In fixing on such a subject, Milton was obliged to treat the whole story as a literal and authentic history; and, worse still, to take a side on the questions which it starts. Now, these questions are the very thorniest in theology: and so it comes about that Milton, who intended to instruct us, merely launches us on a sea of difficulties. What are we to understand by the Son of the Most High, who, one fine day, is begotten and raised to the rank of viceroy of creation? How are we to comprehend an angel who enters on a conflict with God, that is to say, with a being whom he knows to be omnipotent? What kind of innocence is it which does not prevent a man from eating forbidden fruit? How, again, can this fault extend its effects to ourselves? By what effort of imagination or of faith can we regard the history of Adam as part of our own history, and acknowledge solidarity with his crime in ourselves? And if Milton does not succeed in arousing this feeling in us, what becomes of his poem? What is its value, what its interest? It becomes equally impossible to take it seriously as a profession of faith (since this faith escapes us) and even to regard it as the poetical expression of a theodicy which is out of date, because that theodicy could only become poetic on the terms of being intelligible.

Paradise Lost has shared the fate of its hero, that is to say, of the devil. The idea of Satan is a contradictory idea: for it is contradictory to know God and yet attempt rivalry with Him. Accordingly, the flourishing time of belief in the devil was a time of logical impotence. The devil at this time of day has been riddled through and through, he has become a comic character, he supplies us with our little jokes.[2] As for *Paradise Lost* it lives still, but it is none the less true that its fundamental conceptions have become strange to us, and that if the work survives, it is in spite of the subject which it celebrates.

VIII

Nor is this the only trick which Milton's theology has played upon his poetry. The marvellous is an essential part of classical poetry, and this is intelligible enough. In a certain sense Paganism is more religious than Christianity, and associates the Deity with every act of human life more naturally and more of necessity. From the very fact that it has Gods for everything—for the domestic hearth, for love, for marriage, for fighting—there is not a circumstance in which these Gods have not a *locus standi*. Much more is this so when the subject is a hero whose valor is inconceivable without divine protection, or a great historical event, whereof the decrees of Zeus supply the sovereign explanation. It is by no means the same with the moderns, in whom the much more exalted, but much vaguer idea of divine Providence, has replaced the crowd of special deities. If there is in this a metaphysical progress, there is at the same time a poetical impoverishment. It is not that Christianity also has not produced its own mythology: we have a whole Catholic Olympus, pretty well populated. But the attributes are uncertain, the parts ill distributed: and, in spite of everything, there clings to these creations a sort of inborn spiritualism, which is proof against the materialism of popular beliefs. Christianity, I have said, is a religion wanting in ductility. Since it damns those who do not believe it, it perceives the necessity of offering them clearly defined doctrines. Everything in it is more or less settled and agreed upon. Imagination, therefore, can only assign very narrow limits, or, so to say, a circle drawn beforehand, to the utterances of God or the actions of angels. Hence the awkwardness of poets who have tried to draw from the Christian theology the marvels of which they had need. They satisfy the demands neither of piety nor of poetry. They are hampered by the fear of going too far; and, however timid they show themselves, they still have an air of temerity. The *Gerusalemme Liberata*, the *Henriade*, the *Messiade, Les Martyrs,* show the faults of the kind palpably. Dante alone escapes, because with admirable tact or, if anyone pleases, art, he has brought into play only the sinners and the saved.

Yet Milton has been more fortunate than most of the epic poets of the Christian period. Indeed, there was no necessity for him to make a shift to supply his epic with the element of the marvellous, since the whole was already placed straight off in the region of the supernatural. God and his Son, the devils and the angels, were not kept in the background and reserved for the denouement. They themselves filled the principal parts. Even our first parents, placed as they were in the garden of Eden and in a state of innocence, shared in a kind of superior existence. Thus there was from the first no need to introduce the divinity arbitrarily. The author of *Paradise Lost* had but to remain within the conditions of his subject and to extend a little the outlines of the sacred history.

But if Milton avoided factitious marvels it was at the cost of inconvenience elsewhere, of baldness in story, of poverty in ethical quality. Not only is the reader lifted into the sphere of religious abstractions, where the eye of man cannot see or his breast draw breath; but the whole action and actors alike are too destitute of complexity. In strictness there is but one personage in possession of the stage—God the Father; since God cannot show Himself without eclipsing all the rest, nor speak without His will being done. The Son is but a double of the Father. The angels and archangels are but his messengers; nay, they are even less—personifications of his decrees, supers in a drama which would have gone on equally well without them.

Milton did not yield without a struggle to the conditions of his chosen subject. He tried to evade them, and only made the defect more sensible. The long discourses with which he fills the gaps between the action are only sermons, and do but make evident the absence of dramatic matter. Then, since after all some sort of action, some sort of contest was necessary, the poet had recourse to the revolt of the angels. But, unluckily, the fundamental defects of the subject were such that this expedient turned in a fashion against him. What the drama gains in movement, it loses in verisimilitude. We see a battle, but we cannot take either the fight or the fighters seriously. A God who can be resisted is not a God. A struggle with Omnipotence is not only rash, but silly. Belial saw that very well when, in the Infernal Council, he rejected the idea of a contest, either open or concealed, with Him who is all-seeing and all-powerful. Nor can one, indeed, comprehend how his colleagues did not at once give way to so self-evident a consideration. But, I repeat, the poem only became possible at the cost of this impossibility; and so Milton bravely made up his mind to it. He urged to the last, he accepted, even in its uttermost consequences, the most inadmissible of fictions. He presents to us Jehovah anxious for His omnipotence, afraid of seeing His position turned, His palace surprised, His throne usurped.[3] He sketches for us angels throwing mountains, and firing cannon, at each other's heads. He shows us victory evenly balanced till the Son arrives armed with thunder and mounted on a car with four cherubs harnessed to it.

We have still to inquire whether Milton had an epic imagination, or whether his subject did not do him good service by dispensing him from drawing more largely on his own resources. As a matter of fact, he scarcely ever strays from this subject without falling into burlesque. His prince of the rebel angels, who changes himself into a toad and a cormorant; his demons, who become dwarfs in order to be less crowded in their Parliament house; the punishment inflicted on them, which consists of being changed once a year into serpents; the Paradise of Fools; the famous, but extravagant allegory of Sin and Death—all these fictions give us but a feeble notion of Milton's inventive genius, and make it permissible to think that he would not have succeeded in a subject where he had to create his heroes and imagine his situations.

IX

Let me not be misunderstood. I do not reproach Milton, because, with his sixteenth century Calvinism, he is found out of harmony with nineteenth century thought. I care very little about his believing in witches and in astrology. Where would Homer be, where Dante, if, refusing to place ourselves at their point of view, we judged them from the level of our modern criticism? Not a single work of art could support such a trial. But the position of Milton is not exactly this. Milton wants to prove something, he is sustaining a thesis, he means to do the work of a theologian as well as of a poet. In a word, whether intentionally or merely as a fact, *Paradise Lost* is a didactic work, and, as a consequence, its form cannot be separated from its matter. Now, it so happens that the idea of the poem does not bear examination; that its explanation of the problem of evil verges on the burlesque; that the characters of its heroes, Jehovah and Satan, are incoherent; that the fate of Adam touches us little; and finally, that the action passes in regions where the interests and the passions of our common humanity have nothing to do. I have already pointed out this contradiction in Milton's epic. The story on which it rests has neither meaning nor value unless it retains its dogmatic import, and at the same time it cannot retain this import without falling into theology, that is to say, into a domain foreign to art. The subject of the poem is nothing unless it is real, unless it touches us as the secret of our destinies; and the more the poet tries to grasp this reality the more it escapes him.

So intangible in character are these conceptions, that Milton knew not even where to pitch the scene of his drama. He is obliged to forge a system of the world on purpose, a system in which he himself only half believes. He is hampered by the science of his time. Men are no longer in the fourteenth century, when Dante could image hell as a great hole burrowing beneath the surface of our globe. Copernicus and Galileo have intervened. So the cosmology of the Scriptures must be modified and accommodated to the enlightenment of the day. There is nothing more curious than to read *Paradise Lost* from this point of view, and to note the modifications imposed by science on tradition. Milton regards space as infinite, but divided into two regions, that of light or creation, and that of darkness or of chaos. On earth, in the country of Eden, is the Earthly Paradise, communicating by a staircase with the abode of the Most High. Chaos surrounds the whole of this created world, but on the edge of chaos, in the twilight, is the Limbo of vanity, and beyond chaos, in the depths of uncreated space, is found Hell, with a gate and a bridge constructed by Sin and Death, over which is the road from earth to the abyss.[4]

A vague conception, half literal, half symbolic, whereof the author had need as a scene for his personages, but in which he himself has no entire confidence—a striking example of the kind of antinomy with which I charge the whole poem, of the combined necessity, and impossibility of taking things at the foot of the letter.

X

Let us sum up. *Paradise Lost* is an unreal poem, a grotesque poem, a tiresome poem. There is not one reader in a hundred who can read Books Nine and Ten without a smile, or Books Eleven and Twelve without a yawn. The thing does not hold together: it is a pyramid balanced on its apex, the most terrible of problems solved by the most childish of means. And yet *Paradise Lost* is immortal. It lives by virtue of some episodes which will be for ever famous. In contrast with Dante, who must be read as a whole if we wish really to grasp his beauties, Milton ought not to be read except in fragments; but these fragments form a part of the poetic patrimony of the human race. The invocation to Light, the character of Eve, the description of the earthly Paradise, of the morning of the world, of its first love, are all masterpieces. The discourses of the Prince of Hell are incomparably eloquent. Lord Brougham used to cite them as worthy to be set side by side with the greatest models of antiquity, and another orator of our time, Mr. Bright, is said to be a constant reader of Milton. *Paradise Lost* is, moreover, strewn with incomparable lines. The poetry of Milton is the very essence of poetry. The author seems to think but in images, and these images are grand and proud as his own soul—a marvellous mingling of the sublime and the picturesque. Every word of his vocabulary of expression is a discovery and unique. "Darkness visible" is well known. If he would paint night he shows us the fairies dancing by the woodside:

> while overhead the moon
> Sits arbitress, and nearer to the earth
> Wheels her pale course.

The sun shines on the expanse of the deluge waters and begins to evaporate them:

> And the clear sun on his wide watery glass
> Gaz'd hot, and of the fresh wave largely drew,
> As after thirst.

Peace follows fighting:

The brazen throat of war had ceased to roar.

The chaste happiness of the wedded pair is drawn in a word:

Imparadised in one another's arms.

Verses of this kind, always as exact as they are beautiful, are innumerable in Milton, and one is almost ashamed to cite them, so capricious does choice seem in the midst of such riches.

Besides, all is not said when some verses of Milton have been quoted. He has not only imagery and vocabulary, but the period, the great musical phrase, a little long, a little loaded with ornament and convolved with inversions, but swaying all with it in its superb undulation. After all, and above all, he has an indefinable serenity and victoriousness, a sustained equality, an indomitable power; one might almost say that he wraps us in the skirt of his robe and wafts us with him to the eternal regions where he himself dwells.[5]

Notes

1. [In Gospel truth nought's by the mind discerned
   But penance due and punishments well-earned;
   And when your art a blameful blend supplies
   You give its very truths the air of lies.—*Trans.*]
2. [There is, however, a proverb in M. Scherer's language, *Rira bien qui rira le dernier;* and one may also think of Sandy Mackaye's very pregnant and luminous protest against the premature interment of this personage.—*Trans.*]
3. *Paradise Lost,* v. 719, *et seq.* In fact and in fine Satan *has* won something, and *has* succeeded. His own lot is made no worse, and, on the other hand, a great many men will be damned, x. 375. It is useless, therefore, to represent Evil as merely passing, or even as a means to good, x. 629.
4. Milton introduced not merely his cosmology but also his politics into his poem. See his republicanism and tyranny, xii. 64–101.
5. Milton himself has given the rule of poetry. According to him, it must be "simple, sensuous, and impassioned," which comes to the three conditions of simplicity, fulness of imagery, and movement.

—Edmond Scherer, from "Milton and *Paradise Lost,*" 1868, *Essays on English Literature,* translated by Saintsbury, 1891, pp. 134–49

Hippolyte Taine (1871)

In *Samson* he finds a cold and lofty tragedy, in *Paradise Regained* a cold and noble epic; he composes an imperfect and sublime poem in *Paradise Lost.* . Adam and Eve, the first pair! I approach, and it seems as though I discovered the Adam and Eve of Raphael Sanzio, imitated by Milton, so his biographers tell us, glorious, strong, voluptuous children, naked in the light of heaven, motionless and absorbed before grand landscapes, with bright vacant eyes, with no more thought than the bull or the horse on the grass beside them. I listen, and I hear an English household, two reasoners of the period— Colonel Hutchinson and his wife. Heavens! dress them at once. Folk so culti- vated should have invented before all a pair of trousers and modesty. What dialogues! Dissertations capped by politeness, mutual sermons concluded by bows. This Adam entered Paradise *via* England. There he learned respect- ability, and there he studied moral speechifying.

—Hippolyte Taine, *History of English Literature*,
1871, volume 1, translated by
Van Laun, book 2, chapter 6

David Masson (1871)

Let *Paradise Lost*, then, be called a *Vorstellung*. But what a *Vorstellung* it is! That World of Man, the world of all our stars and starry transparencies, hung but drop-like after all from an Empyrean; the great Empyrean itself, "unde- termined square or round," so that, though we do diagram it for form's sake, it is beyond all power of diagram; A Hell, far beneath, but still measurably far, with its outcast infernal Powers tending disastrously upwards or tugging all downwards; finally, between the Empyrean and Hell, a blustering blackness of unimaginable Chaos, roaring around the Mundane Sphere and assaulting everlastingly its outermost bosses, but unable to break through, or to disturb the serenity of the golden poise that steadies it from the zenith—what phan- tasmagory more truly all-significant than this has the imagination of poet ever conceived? What expense of space comparable to this for vastness has any other poet presumed to fill with visual symbolisms, or to occupy with a coherent story? The physical universe of Dante's great poem would go into a nutshell as compared with that to which the imagination must stretch itself out in *Paradise Lost*. In this respect—in respect of the extent of physical immensity through which the poem ranges, and which it orbs forth with soul-dilating clearness and maps out with never-to-be-obliterated accuracy before the eye—no possible poem can ever overpass it. And then the story itself! What story mightier or more full of meaning can there ever be than that of the Archangel rebelling in Heaven, degraded from Heaven into Hell, reascending from Hell to the Human Universe, winging through the starry spaces of that Universe, and at last possessing himself of our central Earth, and impregnating its incipient history with the spirit of Evil? Vastness of scene and power of story together, little wonder that the poem should have so impressed the world. Little wonder that it should now be Milton's Satan, and Milton's narrative of the Creation in its various transcendental connexions, that are in possession of the British imagination, rather than the strict Biblical accounts from which Milton so scrupulously derived the hints to which he gave such marvellous expansion.

—David Masson, *The Poetical Works of John Milton*, 1874, volume 1, p. 101

EDWARD FITZGERALD (1876)

I don't think I've read him these forty years; the whole Scheme of the Poem, and certain Parts of it, looming as grand as anything in my Memory; but I never could read ten lines together without stumbling at some Pedantry that tipped me at once out of Paradise, or even Hell, into the Schoolroom, worse than either.

—Edward FitzGerald, letter to C. E. Norton, February 7, 1876, *Letters*, volume 3, edited by Terhune and Terhune, p. 655

E. S. NADEL "THE COSMOGONY OF *PARADISE LOST*" (1877)

The cosmogony of the universe as conceived by Milton in *Paradise Lost*, though very simple, is very little understood. Nobody confesses to not reading the poem. Many do read it; many more to their own loss, begin and do not finish it; all attempt it. And yet how few know the simple plan of creation which it presupposes, and without a just conception of which it is totally impossible to understand the poem. Indeed, it is no doubt in large part the want of this conception which induces many readers to forego the further perusal of the work after having reached the third book. They are wearied by the very peculiar and incomprehensible movements of Satan on his journey earthward. In what kind of a world is it that Satan, Raphael, Michael, Uriel, and the rest move about? How does it happen that Satan, in going from Hell to Earth, flies downward? and how is it that in the journey he is compelled to pass by the gate of Heaven? Where is the Paradise of Fools through which the poet, in one of the most scornful and extraordinary passages in the book, makes him wander? Where is the throne of Chaos and old Night? There is little use in attempting to read the poem without understanding these things. They are very simple. A diagram or two will be sufficient to explain them.

—E. S. Nadel, "The Cosmogony of *Paradise Lost*," *Harper's*, December 1877, p. 137

Peter Bayne (1878)

The triumph of the Puritan poet was as signal as the triumph of the Puritan king. No Anglican minstrel is nearly equal to Milton; neither the Temple nor the Christian Year will compare with *Paradise Lost*. We naturally place it side by side with the poem in which Dante enshrined Catholicism. Dante excels Milton in tenderness; in intimate knowledge of the human heart; in the delineation of all passions, except revenge and ambition, pride and hatred. Dante has the infallible Shakespearian touch whenever his theme is love; Milton in the like case paints with great literary dexterity and with a frank audacity of sensuous colour which would fain be passionate and tender; but he never gets beyond painted love. For Eve's face he has not a word; not one syllable for the crimson of the lip, for the ravishment of the smile. Conventional golden tresses, slender waist, and ringlets "wanton," which surely they had no call to be in Eden;—this is what we find in Milton's first woman, whom Charlotte Bronte says he never saw. Against Dante, on the other hand, and in favour of Milton, we have to put the traces of Middle-age childishness, the nursery goblinism, grotesquerie, and allegorical wire-drawing, which are present in the *Divine Comedy*. The sustained grandeur which has made "Miltonic" a convertible term with "sublime" is far above all that.

—Peter Bayne, *The Chief Actors in the Puritan Revolution*, 1878, pp. 335–36

Stopford A. Brooke (1879)

The style is always great. On the whole it is the greatest in the whole range of English poetry, so great that when once we have come to know and honour and love it, it so subdues the judgment that the judgment can with difficulty do its work with temperance. It lifts the low, gives life to the commonplace, dignifies even the vulgar, and makes us endure that which is heavy and dull. We catch ourselves admiring things not altogether worthy of admiration, because the robe they wear is so royal. No style, when one has lived in it, is so spacious and so majestic a place to walk in. . . . Fulness of sound, weight of march, compactness of finish, fitness of words to things, fitness of pauses to thought, a strong grasp of the main idea while other ideas play round it, power of digression without loss of the power to return, equality of power over vast spaces of imagination, sustained splendour when he soars

With plume so strong, so equal and so soft,

a majesty in the conduct of thought, and a music in the majesty which fills it with solemn beauty, belong one and all to the style; and it gains its highest influence on us, and fulfils the ultimate need of a grand style in being the easy and necessary expression of the very character and nature of the man. It reveals Milton, as much, sometimes even more than his thought.

—Stopford A. Brooke, *Milton*, 1879, p. 83

MARK PATTISON (1879)

Whatever conclusion may be the true one from the amount of the public demand, we cannot be wrong in asserting that from the first, and now as then, *Paradise Lost* has been more admired than read. The poet's wish and expectation that he should find "fit audience, though few," has been fulfilled. Partly this has been due to his limitation, his unsympathetic disposition, the deficiency of the human element in his imagination, and his presentation of mythical instead of real beings. But it is also in part a tribute to his excellence, and is to be ascribed to the lofty strain, which requires more effort to accompany than an average reader is able to make, a majestic demeanour which no parodist has been able to degrade, and a wealth of allusion demanding more literature than is possessed by any but the few whose life is lived with the poets. An appreciation of Milton is the last reward of consummated scholarship; and we may apply to him what Quintilian has said of Cicero, "Ille se profecisse sciat, cui Cicero valde place-bit."

—Mark Pattison, *Milton*, 1879, p. 210

FREDERIC HARRISON
"THE CHOICE OF BOOKS" (1879)

Who now reads the ancient writers? Who systematically reads the great writers, be they ancient or modern, whom the consent of ages has marked out as classics: typical, immortal, peculiar teachers of our race? Alas! the *Paradise Lost* is lost again to us beneath an inundation of graceful academic verse, sugary stanzas of ladylike prettiness, and ceaseless explanations in more or less readable prose of what John Milton meant or did not mean, or what he saw or did not see, who married his great aunt, and why Adam or Satan is like that, or unlike the other. We read a perfect library about the *Paradise Lost,* but the *Paradise Lost* itself we do not read.

> —Frederic Harrison, "The Choice of Books,"
> 1879, *The Choice of Books and Other Literary*
> *Pieces,* 1886, p. 13

WILLIAM SCHERER (1886)

Klopstock made up his mind to fulfil the prophecy in himself. When he left school in 1745, he had already conceived the plan of the *Messias,* and in his farewell speech on the nature and office of the epic poet, he distinctly alludes to the great work which he contemplated. It was the most popular subject that he could choose, and as yet no poet had exhausted it or brought it once and for all into definite shape, as Milton had the history of the Fall, to the exclusion of all possible rivals on the same ground. It was the vision of Milton that floated before the poet's eyes, and indeed he could not have had a better model, for Milton had achieved the highest that could be done for the Biblical tradition. Milton's *Paradise Lost* stood unrivalled in grandeur of conception and effective development of the theme. Amid Klopstock's many debts to Milton, the following may be mentioned: the detailed description of hell, the council of the devils, the differences of opinion amongst them, their punishment by metamorphosis, the paths through the universe along which devils and angels wander and fly, and the vision of the Last Judgment at the close of the poem. But Klopstock did not profit half enough by Milton's example. While Milton leads us from hell into paradise, and thus relieves a gloomy scene by a bright one, Klopstock, on the contrary, begins with the glories of heaven, and then keeps us in his irksome limbo of disembodied spirits till we long for a change out of very weariness. Milton exerts himself to the utmost not to let the interest flag, and pays particular attention to unity of composition, steady unfolding of the plot, and graphic narration; Klopstock, on the other hand, lets the thread of his narrative decidedly drag, and accompanies each step of the gradual *denouement* with the sentiments of all the spectators. His poetry is full of the very faults which Milton condemned, and, however much Milton may have been his model, yet his *Messias* is more closely related to the religious oratorios than to *Paradise Lost.*

> —Wilhelm Scherer, *A History of German Literature,*
> 1883–86, translated by Conybeare, volume 2, pp. 31–33

Aubrey De Vere (1887)

The dust of the conflict had fallen; and the mountain heights shone out once more from the serene distance: once more he confronted the mighty works of ancient genius. They pleased him still, from their severity and their simplicity; but they did not satisfy him—because they wanted elevation. In his *Paradise Lost* he raised and endeavoured to spiritualise the antique epic. There are many who will always regard St. Peter's temple in the air as the first of architectural monuments. The admirers of the classic will, however, feel that the amplitude and height of the wondrous dome are no sufficient substitute for that massive simplicity and breadth of effect which belong to the Parthenon; while those who revere our cathedrals will maintain that it lacks the variety, the mystery, the aspiration, and the infinitude which characterise the Christian architecture of the North. On analogous grounds the more devoted admirers of Homer and of Shakespeare will ever be dissatisfied with Milton's work, however they may venerate his genius. It is obviously composite in its character—the necessary result of its uniting a Hebraic spirit with a classic form. Dante, like Milton, uses the Greek mythology freely; considering it, no doubt, as part of that "inheritance of the Heathen," into possession of which Christendom had a right to enter; but he uses it as a subordinate ornament, and in matters of mere detail. His poem is a Vision, not an Epic, that vision of supernatural truth, of Hell, Purgatory, and Paradise, which passed before the eyes of the mediaeval Church as she looked up in nocturnal vigil; not the mundane circle of life and experience, of action and of passion, exhibited in its completeness, and contemplated with calm satisfaction by a Muse that looks down from heaven.

—Aubrey De Vere, *Essays,*
Chiefly on Poetry, 1887, vol. 2, p. 112

Donald G. Mitchell (1890)

I cannot stay to characterize his great poem; nor is there need; immortal in more senses than one; humanity counts for little in it; one pair of human creatures only, and these looked at, as it were, through the big end of the telescope; with gigantic, Godlike figures around one, or colossal demons prone on fiery floods. It is not a child's book; to place it in schools as a parsing-book is an atrocity that I hope is ended. Not, I think, till we have had some fifty years to view the everlasting fight between good and evil in this world, can we see in proper perspective the vaster battle which, under Milton's imagination, was pictured in Paradise between the same foes. Years only can so widen one's horizon as to give room for the reverberations, of that mighty combat of the powers of light and darkness.

—Donald G. Mitchell, *English Lands, Letters, and Kings: From Elizabeth to Anne,* 1890, p. 171

EDMUND CLARENCE STEDMAN (1892)

I have said that the grandest of English supernatural creations is Milton's Satan. No other personage has at once such magnitude and definiteness of outline as that sublime, defiant archangel, whether in action or in repose. Milton, like Dante, has to do with the unknown world. The Florentine bard soars at last within the effulgence of "the eternal, coeternal beam." Milton's imagination broods "in the wide womb of uncreated night." We enter that "palpable obscure," where there is "no light, but rather darkness visible," and where lurk many a "grisly terror and execrable shape."

—Edmund Clarence Stedman, *The Nature and Elements of Poetry,* 1892, p. 245

WILLIAM DEAN HOWELLS (1895)

Long after I had thought never to read it—in fact when I was *nel mezzo del cammin di nostra vita*—I read Milton's *Paradise Lost,* and found in it a splendor and majestic beauty that justified to me the fame it wears, and eclipsed the worth of those lesser poems which I had stupidly and ignorantly accounted his worthiest.

—William Dean Howells, *My Literary Passions,* 1895, p. 239

VIDA M. SCUDDER (1895)

What a magnificent opportunity for describing the gradual dawn of living beauty was in the hands of the man who did not hesitate to write poetry about the creation! Does he avail himself of it? Does he give us any suggestion of the tender grace of the young, wondering world, the slow awakening and unfolding of all fair things till they reach the perfection of their loveliness? Oh no! There is chaos, void, abyss, emptiness. We wait and watch. Suddenly—hey! presto! The world is made. There it whirls,—round, smooth, neatly finished. There are the oceans with the fishes, the mountains, the trees, yes, and the flowers and beasts.

—Vida M. Scudder, *The Life of the Spirit in the Modern English Poets,* 1895, p. 19

J. Howard B. Masterman (1897)

Paradise Lost is the product of two great movements—Puritanism and the Renaissance. Or, to put the same thought in another way, the conception of the poem is Hebraic, its form and imagery are classical. Within the limits of the sacred narrative, from which Milton would not allow himself to deviate, his luxuriant imagination found ample scope for all its stored wealth of learning; and the issue is something far different from the Hebrew original. Few of us, probably, realize how often we unconsciously read into the Scriptural narrative of the Creation and the Fall ideas instilled by Milton's splendid poem.

—J. Howard B. Masterman,
The Age of Milton, 1897, p. 54

Virginia Woolf (1918)

Novelist, essayist, and critic Virginia Woolf (1882–1941) was born Adeline Virginia Stephen to famous biographer Leslie Stephen and his wife, Julia, in London. Virginia read extensively in her father's library to develop her literary knowledge and lived in Bloomsbury after his death, becoming part of England's intellectually elite group of artists and writers. In 1912, she married fellow Bloomsburian Leonard Woolf, and together they founded Hogarth Press. Virginia Woolf produced numerous novels, including *Jacob's Room* (1922), *Mrs. Dalloway* (1925), *To the Lighthouse* (1927), *The Waves* (1931), and *Orlando* (1928), a work in which the protagonist morphs back and forth between male and female, demonstrating Woolf's belief that humans are essentially androgynous. She developed a style that focused on the inner workings of her characters, framed by a modified stream of consciousness. Famed as well for her essays that helped strengthen the first-wave feminist movement, Woolf is particularly noted for *A Room of One's Own* (1929), taken from a lecture series given at Girton and Newham colleges, in which she argues for the rights of women to write, recognizing their need for autonomy and income in the creative process. In her diaries, Woolf records her extensive readings, setting down her insights on *Paradise Lost* in the following selection. Woolf faults Milton for dealing with externals rather than internal feelings, although she praises his poetic style. Most famously, from the perspective of later feminist readings of *Paradise Lost*, she terms Milton "the first of the masculinists," declaiming his negative portrayal of Eve and marriage.

Though I am not the only person in Sussex who reads Milton, I mean to write down my impressions of Paradise Lost while I am about it. Impressions fairly well describes the sort of thing left in my mind. I have left many riddle unread. I have slipped on too easily to taste the full flavour. However I see, & agree to some extent in believing, that this extreme difference between this poem & any other. It lies, I think, in the sublime aloofness & impersonality of the emotions. I have never read Cowper on the Sofa, but I can imagine that the sofa is a degraded substitute for Paradise Lost. The substance of Milton is all made of wonderful, beautiful, & masterly descriptions of angels bodies, battles, flights, dwelling places. He deals in horror & immensity & squalor & sublimity, but never in the passions of the human heart. Has any great poem ever let in so little light upon ones own joys & sorrows? I get no help in judging life; I scarcely feel that Milton lived or knew men & women; except for the peevish personalities about marriage & the woman's duties. He was the first of the masculinists; but his disparagement rises from his own ill luck, & seems even a spiteful last word in his domestic quarrels. But how smooth, strong & elaborate it all is! What poetry! I can conceive that even Shakespeare after this would seem a little troubled, personal, hot & imperfect. I can conceive that this is the essence, of which almost all other poetry is the dilution. The inexpressible fineness of the style, in which shade after shade is perceptible, would alone keep one gazing in to, long after the surface business in progress has been despatched. Deep down one catches still further combinations, rejections, felicities, & materies. Moreover, though there is nothing like Lady Macbeth's terror or Hamlet's cry, no pity or sympathy or intuition, the figures are majestic; in them is summed up much of what men though of our place in the universe, of our duty to God, our religion.

—Virginia Woolf, entry from *Diary*, September 3, 1918

PARADISE REGAINED

Paradise Regained (1671) is often overlooked by readers; it is the opposite of *Paradise Lost*. Whereas *Paradise Lost* is richly verbose, thickly allusional, and hyperambitious in its project, *Paradise Regained* is controlled—in its tone, its use of other literature, and its rhetorical style. This restraint stems from its focused subject matter: the temptation of Christ by Satan, following Christ's 40-day fast in the wilderness at the start of his ministry. In overcoming Satan, Christ has already triumphed, assuring redemption through the cross and the restoration of relations between the human and the divine. Christ, the quiet hero, has silenced the glossy-tongued antagonist of both this brief epic and its forerunner, *Paradise Lost*.

Thomas Ellwood (1714)

Thomas Ellwood here claims his conversation with Milton, about a follow-up to *Paradise Lost*, to be the primary impetus for the creation of *Paradise Regained*. Literary historians question the accuracy of Ellwood's account, as many think Milton had already begun *Paradise Regained* 10 to 20 years before this encounter in 1665.

Some little time before I went to Aylesbury prison I was desired by my quondam master, Milton, to take a house for him in the neighbourhood where I dwelt, that he might go out of the city, for the safety of himself and his family, the pestilence then growing hot in London. I took a pretty box for him in Giles Chalfont, a mile from me, of which I gave him notice, and intended to have waited on him, and seen him sell settled in it, but was prevented by that imprisonment.

But now being released and returned home, I soon made a visit to him, to welcome him into the country.

After some common discourses had passed between us, he called for a manuscript of his; which being brought he delivered to me, bidding me take it home with me, and read it at my leisure; and when I had so done, return it to him with my judgment thereupon.

When I came home, and had set myself to read it, I found it was that excellent poem which he entituled *Paradise Lost*. After I had, with the best attention, read it through, I made him another visit, and returned him his book, with due acknowledgment of the favour he had done me in communicating it to me. He asked me how I liked it and what I thought of it, which I modestly but freely told him, and after some further discourse about it, I pleasantly said to him, "Thou hast said much here of *Paradise Lost,* but what hast thou to say of *Paradise Found?*" He made me no answer, but sat some time in a muse; then brake off that discourse, and fell upon another subject.

After the sickness was over, and the city well cleansed and become safely habitable again, he returned thither.

And when afterwards I went to wait on him there, which I seldom failed of doing whenever my occasions drew me to London, he showed me his second poem, called *Paradise Regained,* and in a pleasant tone said to me, "This is owing to you, for you put it into my head by the question you put to me at Chalfont, which before I had not thought of."

—Thomas Ellwood, *The History of the Life of Thomas Ellwood,* 1714, edited by Crump, pp. 144–45

SAMUEL TAYLOR COLERIDGE
"NOTES ON MILTON" (1807)

Readers would not be disappointed in this latter poem, if they proceeded to a perusal of it with a proper preconception of the kind of interest intended to be excited in that admirable work. In its kind it is the most perfect poem extant, though its kind may be inferior in interest—being in its essence didactic—to that other sort, in which instruction is conveyed more effectively, because less directly, in connection with stronger and more pleasurable emotions, and thereby in a closer affinity with action. But might we not as rationally object to an accomplished woman's conversing, however agreeably, because it has happened that we have received a keener pleasure from her singing to the harp?

—Samuel Taylor Coleridge, "Notes on Milton,"
1807, *Literary Remains,* volume 1,
edited by Coleridge, p. 179

JOHN WILSON "WORDSWORTH" (CA. 1826)

Milton has no idealism,—not even in the *Paradise Regained,* where there was most scope for it. His poetry is for the most part quite literal; and the objects he describes have all a certain definiteness and individuality which separates them from the infinite. He has often endeavoured to present images where every thing should have been lost in sentiment.

—John Wilson, "Wordsworth," ca. 1826, *Essays*
Critical and Imaginary, 1856

HENRY HALLAM (1839)

The neglect which *Paradise Lost* never experienced seems to have been long the lot *of Paradise Regained.* It was not popular with the world: it was long believed to manifest a decay of the poet's genius; and, in spite of all that the critics have written, it is still but the favorite of some whose predilections for the Miltonic sytle are very strong. The subject is so much less capable of calling forth the vast powers of his mind, that we should be unfair in comparing it throughout with the greater poem: it has been called a model of the shorter epic, an action comprehending few characters and a brief space of time. The love of Milton for dramatic dialogue, imbibed from Greece, is still more apparent than in *Paradise Lost:* the whole poem, in fact, may almost be accounted a drama of primal simplicity; the narrative and descriptive part serving rather to diversify and relieve the speeches of the actors, than their speeches, as in the legitimate epic, to enliven the narration. *Paradise Regained* abounds with passages equal to any of the same nature in *Paradise Lost*; but the argumentative tone is kept up till it produces some tediousness; and perhaps, on the whole, less pains have been exerted to adorn and elevate that which appeals to the imagination.

—Henry Hallam, *Introduction to the Literature of Europe*, 1837–39, part 4, chapter 5, paragraph 35

MARK PATTISON (1879)

In this poem he has not only curbed his imagination, but has almost suppressed it. He has amplified, but has hardly introduced any circumstance which is not in the original. *Paradise Regained* is little more than a paraphrase of the Temptation as found in the synoptical gospels. It is a marvel of ingenuity that more than two thousand lines of blank verse can have been constructed out of some twenty lines of prose, without the addition of any invented incident, or the insertion of any irrelevant digression. In the first three books of *Paradise Regained* there is not a single simile. Nor yet can it be said that the version of the gospel narrative has the fault of most paraphrases, viz., that of weakening the effect, and obliterating the chiselled features of the original.

—Mark Pattison, *Milton*, 1879, p. 187

EDMUND GOSSE (1897)

As he grew older the taste of Milton grew more austere. The change in the character of his ornament is deeply marked when we ascend from the alpine meadows of *Paradise Lost* to the peaks of *Paradise Regained*, where the imaginative air is so highly rarefied that many readers find it difficult to breathe.

—Edmund Gosse, *Short History of Modern English Literature*, 1897, p. 167

AUGUSTUS HOPKINS STRONG (1897)

The latter epic indubitably shows some falling off in the poet's powers; the supernatural vein has already yielded the best of its ore; earth must now be the main scene of the drama; the piercing splendors of the poet's earlier verse give place to something more like grand and sonorous prose. Yet now and then the old inspiration seems to seize him.

—Augustus Hopkins Strong, *The Great Poets and Their Theology*, 1897, p. 252

WILLIAM MOODY "LIFE OF MILTON" (1899)

In this poem there is noticeable a distinct change from Milton's earlier manner,—a sudden purging away of ornament, a falling back on the naked concept, a preference for language as slightly as possible tinctured with metaphoric suggestion. A portion of this change may be due to failing vividness of imagination; certainly the abandonment of rapid narrative for tedious argumentation marks the increasing garrulity of age. Christ and Satan in the wilderness dispute with studied casuistry, until the sense of the spiritual drama in which they are protagonists is almost lost. As this same weakness is apparent also in the later books *of Paradise Lost,* we must lay it largely to the score of flagging creative energy. But in still greater measure the change seems to be a deliberate experiment in style, or perhaps more truly a conscious reproduction, in language, of that rarefied mental atmosphere to which the author had climbed from the rich valley mists of his youth.

—William Moody, "Life of Milton," *Poetical
Works of Milton,* 1899, Cambridge edition, p. xxxi

SAMSON AGONISTES

Modeled on Greek tragedy, Milton's *Samson Agonistes,* published in 1671, was a closet drama; that is, it was not intended for the stage but for reading. The work is thought by many, though not all, critics to be the last of Milton's canon; following the Aristotelian literary hierarchy, which places tragedy above all other genres, it would seem that Milton chooses this mode for his ultimate piece. Structurally, *Samson Agonistes* follows most closely Aeschylus's classic tragedy *Prometheus Bound.* Both works feature a protagonist who is physically static, anchored in place by chains, as the plays' episodes are primarily dialogues between the protagonist and the visitors/antagonists who come to argue their points of view. In its opening, Milton's tragedy also mirrors Sophocles' *Oedipus at Colonus,* which portrays the self-blinded Oedipus being brought onto the stage. Selecting as his subject Samson, an Old Testament judge from Judges chapters 13–16, Milton deals once more with his favorite themes of temptation and service to God.

The work's autobiographical elements, as related to Milton's physical attributes, religion, and politics, are frequently noted. Samson, like Milton, is blind; the circumstances, however, are far from parallel. Milton has lost his eyesight from overuse through reading and probable eye disease; Samson has been the victim of female temptation. He has exposed the secret of his superhuman strength to Dalila (Delilah from Judges), his Philistine wife, after her repeated probing; his hair, which has never been cut, by order of God, has been the source of his strength. Dalila has cut off his hair while he slept and enabled the Philistines to bind and blind the weakened hero. This action has occurred before the opening of the tragedy, as explained in the exposition. While Milton had a disastrous first marriage, in which his first wife, Mary Powell, left him one month after the wedding and stayed away for three years, she returned, had two children, died, and he proceeded to remarry two more times, his second wife dying in childbirth. It is difficult, therefore, to see a direct causal connection between the temptress portrayed by Dalila and Milton's blindness. However, Dalila's character brings to mind another of Milton's female creations, *Paradise Lost*'s Eve, and Samson's situation parallels Adam's overfondness for his beautiful wife.

More generally, both Milton's and Samson's blindness represent a threatened ineffectuality to perform their divinely appointed tasks. Both feel called by God to bring to its knees what they perceive as a corrupt and heretical government. Both puzzle over how that action can take place with their physical inadequacy. Milton's sonnet "When I Consider How My Light Is Spent" dealt with this issue previously, concluding that, "They also serve who only stand and wait"; it is not necessary to fight using physical prowess, as God can use other talents of those who make themselves available. Now, Samson must stand and wait for the return of his strength and divine guidance to allow him to complete the task for which he has been set aside. The play's conclusion shows that he is indeed capable of destroying the enemy, as he pulls down tremendous pillars on the mass of assembled Philistines. Likewise, Milton's blindness has not thwarted his calling as a poet inspired by God to weaken the British monarchy and state religion, as he continued to dictate his works to scribes, and they continued to be published.

The issue of temptation both encompasses and supersedes the biographical concerns, as the action plays off the interchange of human agency and divine will. What has been ordained as the goal of human giftedness still requires free will to coincide; that is, the hero Samson must not submit to despair but remain faithfully committed to his cause. Temptation comes not only through the beguilements of his wife (who, in the scriptural text is actually a prostitute, without mention of being married to Samson), but also through the well-meaning words of Samson's father who wants to intercede for Samson through pity, an action that would counter Samson's ability to bring down the Philistines.

The play's end recalls Aristotle's *Poetics* once again, which stated that tragedy's purpose was to cause in the viewers a catharsis, raising and then purging their emotions of pity and fear. The poet's line "All passion spent" seems appropriate to both Samson's death and the last work of Milton, who channeled his passions for religion and politics into poetry. Though the biographical approach to reading *Samson Agonistes* is not accepted by all contemporary critics, it informs several of the following selections.

Johann Wolfgang von Goethe (1830)

The greatest German writer, Johann Wolfgang von Goethe (1749–1832) wrote dramas, poetry, novels, essays, and memoirs. Best-known for the chief work of the German romantic movement, *Faust*, Goethe here characterizes Samson's blindness as a projection of Milton's and praises Milton's poetic genius, as is typical of the romantics.

I have lately read his *Samson*, which has more of the antique spirit than any production of any other modern poet. He is very great, and his own blindness enabled him to describe with so much truth the situation of Samson. Milton was really a poet; one to whom we owe all possible respect.

> —Johann Wolfgang von Goethe, *Conversations*
> *with Eckermann,* 1830, volume 2, translated by
> Oxenford, p. 220

François René (1837)

The tragedy of *Samson* breathes all the energy and simplicity of the antique. The poet himself is depicted in the person of the Israelite, blind, a prisoner, and unfortunate. A noble way of revenging himself on his age.

> —François René, vicomte de Chateaubriand,
> *Sketches of English Literature,* 1837, volume 2, p. 106

Edwin Guest (1838)

Johnson considered the versification of these choruses "so harsh and dissonant, as scarce to preserve (whether the lines end with or without rhyme) any appearance of metrical regularity;" and it must be confessed there are lines which almost seem to merit a censure thus severe. But modern pronunciation is *not* the pronunciation of Milton. Many verses, as they are now read by some of Milton's admirers, would disgust the poet, full as much as his critic.

> —Edwin Guest, *A History of English Rhythms,*
> 1838, volume 2, p. 259

James Russell Lowell
"Swinburne's Tragedies" (1871)

The most successful attempt at reproducing the Greek tragedy, both in theme and treatment, is the *Samson Agonistes,* as it is also the most masterly piece of English versification. Goethe admits that it alone, among modern works, has caught life from the breath of the antique spirit.

—James Russell Lowell, "Swinburne's Tragedies,"
My Study Windows, 1871, p. 220

Adolphus William Ward (1875)

From a purely literary point of view the tragedy of *Samson Agonistes,* which, as the Preface needlessly states, was "never intended to the stage," cannot be said to possess merits commensurate with its historical and biographical value. That it has escaped representation under conditions wholly uncongenial to it, may be due not only to the sacred character of the source of the subject, but also to the circumstance that by composing music to it as an oratorio Handel has removed it for ever from possible contact with the play-house.

—Adolphus William Ward, *A History of English
Dramatic Literature,* 1875–99, volume 3, p. 204

George Edmundson (1885)

We have now shown that the two most noticeable characteristics of the *Samson Agonistes,* the personal element which runs through it and its dramatic form, modelled upon that of the ancient Greek tragedy; are even more markedly the special features of the *Samson* of Vondel. We know, further, that the Dutch play preceded the English one by at least five years. It only remains for us to show from internal evidence that Milton was acquainted with the language of Vondel's play in order to complete the chain of evidence, and make it more than probable that the one is the direct descendant of the other.

—George Edmundson,
Milton and Vondel, 1885, p. 170

Frederick William Farrar
"Three Portraits of Milton" (1891)

The *Samson Agonistes,* the most Greek-like drama ever written since the death of Euripides, gives us some insight into the passion-seething abysses of his soul, whose swelling turbulence was only kept down by a sovereign faith. Professor Seeley finely calls it "the thundering reverberation of a mighty spirit struck by the plectrum of disappointment;" but though that plectrum struck the reverberant chords into thunder, it was the last sob of the retiring storm beyond which we already see the gleam of blue.

—Frederick William Farrar, "Three Portraits of Milton," *The English Illustrated Magazine*, 1891, p. 120

ROBERT BRIDGES (1893)

The opinions which critics have ventured on the versification of the choruses in *Samson Agonistes* would be sufficient proof that they had met with something not well understood, even if they had never misinterpreted the rhythm. It is not less than an absurdity to suppose that Milton's carefully-made verse could be unmusical: on the other hand it is easy to see how the farsought effects of the greatest master in any art may lie beyond the general taste.

—Robert Bridges, *Milton's Prosody*, 1893, p. 32

SONNETS

Published chronologically in two editions of Milton's collected verse in 1645 and 1673, Milton's 23 sonnets include six Italian sonnets and *canzone* closely modeled on works of Italian poets Francesco Petrarch, Giovanni della Casa, Pietro Bembo, and Torquato Tasso. Milton's sonnets were written to his friend and former classmate Charles Diodati and his family before the poet visited them in Italy at the time of Charles's death in 1638. Milton had learned the Italian language and read Italian poetry only from books at the time of writing. The Italian sonnets and early English sonnets, numbers one through ten, appeared in the 1645 *Poems*, printed by Humphrey Moseley. The later English sonnets appeared in *Poems, &c. Upon Several Occasions*, printed by Thomas During in 1673. Milton's English sonnets often focused on public figures, acquaintances, or events, such as Henry Lawes, Milton's pupil Cyriack Skinner, and the Piedmont Massacre; other unpublished sonnets found in the Trinity College manuscript include poems on General Fairfax and Oliver Cromwell. Milton's most popular sonnets today are more personal in nature, notably Sonnet 19, "When I Consider How My Light Is Spent," written on his blindness, and Sonnet 23, "Methought I Saw," on the death of one of his wives (probably Mary Powell Milton) in childbirth.

NATHAN DRAKE (1820)

The sonnets of Milton, like those of Dante, are frequently deficient in sweetness of diction and harmony of versification, yet they possess, what seldom is discernible in compositions of this kind, energy and sublimity of sentiment. The sonnets to Cyriac Skinner, to Fairfax, Cromwell, and Vane, are remarkable for these qualities, and for vigour of expression, whilst those addressed to the Nightingale and to Mr. Laurence, can boast, I may venture to assert, both of melody in language and elegance in thought. It should also be observed, that Milton has altogether avoided the quaint and metaphysic concetti of Petrarch.

—Nathan Drake, *Literary Hours,*
1798–1820, volume 1, p. 80

WILLIAM HAZLITT
"ON MILTON'S SONNETS" (1821–22)

The great object of the Sonnet seems to be, to express in musical numbers, and as it were with undivided breath, some occasional thought or personal feeling, 'some fee-grief due to the poet's breast.' It is a sigh uttered from the fulness of the heart, an involuntary aspiration born and dying in the same moment. I have always been fond of Milton's *Sonnets* for this reason, that they have more of this personal and internal character than any others; and they acquire a double value when we consider that they come from the pen of the loftiest of our poets. Compared with *Paradise Lost,* they are like tender flowers that adorn the base of some proud column or stately temple. The author in the one could work himself up with unabated fortitude 'to the height of his great argument;' but in the other he has shewn that he could condescend to men of low estate, and after the lightning and the thunder-bolt of his pen, lets fall some drops of 'natural pity' over hapless infirmity, mingling strains with the nightingale's, 'most musical, most melancholy.' The immortal poet pours his mortal sorrows into our breasts, and a tear falls from his sightless orbs on the friendly hand he presses. The *Sonnets* are a kind of pensive record of past achievements, loves, and friendships, and a noble exhortation to himself to bear up with cheerful hope and confidence to the last. Some of them are of a more quaint and humorous character; but I speak of those only, which are intended to be serious and pathetical.—I do not know indeed but they may be said to be almost the first effusions of this sort of natural and personal sentiment in the language. Drummond's ought perhaps to be excepted, were they formed less closely on the model of Petrarch's, so as to be often little more than translations of the Italian poet. But Milton's *Sonnets* are truly his own in allusion, thought, and versification. Those of Sir Philip Sidney, who was a great transgressor in this way, turn sufficiently on himself and his own adventures; but they are elaborately quaint and intricate, and more like riddles than sonnets. They are 'very tolerable and not to be endured.' Shakespear's, which some persons better-informed in such matters than I can pretend to be, profess to cry up as 'the divine, the matchless, what you will,'—to say nothing of the want of point or a leading, prominent idea in most of them, are I think overcharged and monotonous, and as to their ultimate drift, as for myself, I can make neither head nor tail of it. Yet some of them, I own, are sweet even to a sense of faintness, luscious as the woodbine, and graceful and luxuriant like it. Here is one.

> From you have I been absent in the spring,
> When proud-pied April, dress'd in all his trim,
> Hath put a spirit of youth in every thing;
> That heavy Saturn laugh'd and leap'd with him.
> Yet nor the lays of birds, nor the sweet smell
> Of different flowers in odour and in hue,
> Could make me any summer's story tell,
> Or from their proud lap pluck them where they grew:
> Nor did I wonder at the lilies white,
> Nor praise the deep vermilion in the rose;
> They were but sweet, but figures of delight,
> Drawn after you, you pattern of all those.
> Yet seem'd it winter still; and you away,
> As with your shadow, I with these did play.

I am not aware of any writer of Sonnets worth mentioning here till long after Milton, that is, till the time of Warton and the revival of a taste for Italian and for our own early literature. During the rage for French models, the Sonnet had not been much studied. It is a mode of composition that depends entirely on *expression;* and this the French and artificial style gladly dispenses with, as it lays no particular stress on any thing—except vague, general common-places. Warton's Sonnets are undoubtedly exquisite, both in style and matter: they are poetical and philosophical effusions of very delightful sentiment; but the thoughts, though fine and deeply felt, are not, like Milton's subjects, iden-tified completely with the writer, and so far want a more individual interest. Mr. Wordsworth's are also finely conceived and high-sounding Sonnets. They mouth it well, and are said to be sacred to Liberty. Brutus's exclamation, 'Oh Virtue, I thought thee a substance, but I find thee a shadow,' was not considered as a compliment, but as a bitter sarcasm. The beauty of Milton's *Sonnets* is their sincerity, the spirit of poetical patriotism which they breathe. Either Milton's or the living bard's are defective in this respect. There is no Sonnet of Milton's on the Restoration of Charles II. There is no Sonnet of Mr. Wordsworth's corresponding to that of 'the poet blind and bold,' 'On the late Massacre in Piedmont.' It would be no niggard praise to Mr. Wordsworth to grant that he was either half the man or half the poet that Milton was. He has not his high and various imagination, nor his deep and fixed principle. Milton did not worship the rising sun, nor turn his back on a losing and fallen cause.

Such recantation had no charms for him!

Mr. Southey has thought proper to put the author of *Paradise Lost* into his late Heaven, on the understood condition that he is 'no longer to kings and to hierarchs hostile.' In his life-time, he gave no sign of such an alteration; and it is rather presumptuous in the poet-laureate to pursue the deceased antagonist of Salmasius into the other world to compliment him with his own infirmity of purpose. It is a wonder he did not add in a note that Milton called him aside to whisper in his ear that he preferred the new English hexameters to his own blank verse!

Our first of poets was one of our first of men. He was an eminent instance to prove that a poet is not another name for the slave of power and fashion; as is the case with painters and musicians—things without an opinion—and who merely aspire to make up the pageant and shew of the day. There are persons in common life who have that eager curiosity and restless admiration of bustle and splendour, that sooner than not be admitted on great occasions of feasting and luxurious display, they will go in the character of livery-servants to stand behind the chairs of the great. There are others who can so little bear to be left for any length of time out of the grand carnival and masquerade of pride and folly, that they will gain admittance to it at the expense of their characters as well as of a change of dress. Milton was not one of these. He had too much of the *ideal* faculty in his composition, a lofty contemplative principle, and consciousness of inward power and worth, to be tempted by such idle baits. We have plenty of chaunting and chiming in among some modern writers with the triumphs over their own views and principles; but none of a patient resignation to defeat, sustaining and nourishing itself with the thought of the justice of their cause, and with firm-fixed rectitude. I do not pretend to defend the tone of Milton's political writings (which was borrowed from the style of controversial divinity) or to say that he was right in the part he took:—I say that he was consistent in it, and did not convict himself of error: he was consistent in it in spite of danger and obloquy, 'on evil days though fallen, and evil tongues,' and therefore his character has the salt of honesty about it. It does not offend in the nostrils of posterity. He had taken his part boldly and stood to it manfully, and submitted to the change of times with pious fortitude, building his consolations on the resources of his own mind and the recollection of the past, instead of endeavouring to make himself a retreat for the time to come. As an instance of this, we may take one of the best and most admired of these Sonnets, that addressed to Cyriac Skinner, on his own blindness.

> Cyriac, this three years' day, these eyes, though clear,
> To outward view, of blemish or of spot,
> Bereft of light their seeing have forgot,
> Nor to their idle orbs doth sight appear
> Of sun or moon or star throughout the year,
> Or man or woman. Yet I argue not
> Against Heav'n's hand or will, nor bate a jot
> Of heart or hope; but still bear up and steer
> Right onward. What supports me, dost thou ask?
> The conscience, Friend, to have lost them overply'd
> In liberty's defence, my noble task,
> Of which all Europe talks from side to side.
> This thought might lead me through the world's vain mask,
> Content though blind, had I no better guide.

Nothing can exceed the mild, subdued tone of this Sonnet, nor the striking grandeur of the concluding thought. It is curious to remark what seems to be a trait of character in the two first lines. From Milton's care to inform the reader that 'his eyes were still clear to outward view of spot or blemish,' it would be thought that he had not yet given up all regard to personal appearance; a feeling to which his singular beauty at an earlier age might be supposed naturally enough to lead.—Of the political or (what may be called) his *State-Sonnets,* those to Cromwell, to Fairfax, and to the younger Vane, are full of exalted praise and dignified advice. They are neither familiar nor servile. The writer knows what is due to power and to fame. He feels the true, unassumed equality of greatness. He pays the full tribute of admiration for great acts achieved, and suggests becoming occasion to deserve higher praise. That to Cromwell is a proof how completely our poet maintained the erectness of his understanding and spirit in his intercourse with men in power. It is such a compliment as a poet might pay to a conqueror and head of the state, without the possibility of self-degradation. . . .

There could not have been a greater mistake or a more unjust piece of criticism than to suppose that Milton only shone on great subjects; and that on ordinary occasions and in familiar life, his mind was unwieldy, averse to the cultivation of grace and elegance, and unsusceptible of harmless pleasures. The whole tenour of his smaller compositions contradicts this opinion, which however they have been cited to confirm. The notion first got abroad from the bitterness (or vehemence) of his controversial writings, and has been kept up since with little meaning and with less truth. His *Letters to Donatus* and others are not more remarkable for the display of a scholastic enthusiasm, than for that of the most amiable dispositions. They are 'severe in youthful virtue unreproved.' There is a passage in his prose-works (the *Treatise on Education*) which shews, I think, his extreme openness and proneness to pleasing outward impressions in a striking point of view. 'But to return to our own institute,' he says, 'besides these constant exercises at home, there is another opportunity of gaining experience to be won from pleasure itself abroad. *In those vernal seasons of the year, when the air is calm and pleasant, it were an injury and sullen-ness against nature, not to go out and see her riches, and partake in her rejoicing with Heaven and earth.* I should not therefore be a persuader to them of studying much then, but to ride out in companies with prudent and well staid guides, to all quarters of the land,' &c. Many other passages might be quoted, in which the poet breaks through the groundwork of prose, as it were, by natural fecundity and a genial, unrestrained sense of delight. To suppose that a poet is not easily accessible to pleasure, or that he does not take an interest in individual objects and feelings, is to suppose that he is no poet; and proceeds on the false theory, which has been so often applied to poetry and the Fine Arts, that the whole is not made up of the particulars. If our author, according to Dr. Johnson's account of him, could only have treated epic, high-sounding subjects, he would not have been what he was, but another Sir Richard Blackmore.—I may conclude with observing, that I have often wished that Milton had lived to see the Revolution of 1688. This would have been a triumph worthy of him, and which he would have earned by faith and hope. He would then have been old, but would not have lived in vain to see it, and might have celebrated the event in one more undying strain!

—William Hazlitt, from "On Milton's Sonnets,"
Table-Talk, 1821–22

William Wordsworth "Sonnet" (1827)

Scorn not the Sonnet; . . .

   . . . when a damp
Fell round the path of Milton, in his hand
The thing became a trumpet; whence he blew
Soul-animating strains—alas, too few!

                              —William Wordsworth, "Sonnet," 1827

Walter Savage Landor "To the President
of the French Republic" (1848)

'Twas not unseemly in the bravest bard
From Paradise and angels to descend,
And crown his country's saviour with a wreath
Above the regal: Few his words, but strong,
And sounding through all ages and all climes.
He caught the sonnet from the dainty hand
Of Love, who cried to lose it; and he gave
The notes to Glory.

                      —Walter Savage Landor, "To the President of the
                                      French Republic," 1848

James Ashcroft Noble
"The Sonnet in England" (1880)

Even when Milton's matter repels or fails to interest, there is always something in his manner which compels an attentive and fascinated hearing. The
personal quality, which was of pure and high self-containedness all compact,
informs the language and gives it a magical power. He on his mountain-top
had learned from the silent stars and voiceful winds a speech which was not
the dialect of the crowd, and, whatever be the burden of the saying, there is a
spell in the mere intonation. We feel the spell sometimes almost humorously,
as in the rough-hewn sonnet with its harsh, unpoetic, bald, monosyllabic
rhymes—"clogs," "dogs," "frogs," "hogs,"—which leaves almost the same sense
of weight and mass that we derive from his nobler and more delightful utterances. Among these, it is needless to say, one stands apart in unapproached
and unapproachable majesty. The great sonnet "On the late Massacres in
Piedmont" is one of those achievements in which matter of the noblest order
moulds for itself a form of the highest excellence, matter and form being, as

in music and in all supreme art, so bound up and interfused that, though we know both of them to be there, we cannot know them or think of them apart. Much has been said in eulogy of this sonnet, and said worthily and well; but there is a perfection which mocks praise, and it is this perfection that is here attained; not the perfection which consists in this quality or in that, but which comes when all qualities which may be displayed, all potentialities which can be exerted, meet in triumphant, satisfying, utter accomplishment.

—James Ashcroft Noble, "The Sonnet in England,"
1880, *The Sonnet in England and Other Essays*,
1893, p. 33

RICHARD HENRY STODDARD
"THE SONNET IN ENGLISH POETRY" (1881)

They differ from all the sonnets of the time, in that they are simple in thought and unstudied in expression, and that they convince us of the entire sincerity of the singer. We feel that they were not written because other poets had made a reputation by such compositions, but because their writer had something to say, and knew that the best way for him to say it was in this form. If he had read Shakspere and Drummond, or Drayton and Daniel, he forgot them in his remembrance of Petrarch, whose form he mastered, at the age of twenty-three, as no English poet since Sidney had done. They do not read like the productions of a young man, for they are mature in conception and severe in execution—demanding our deepest respect as well as our highest admiration. The credentials of a strong intellect, which knows itself and the work it has to do, their gravity is Shaksperean. They bear a weight of thought which had never before laid upon the English sonnet, and they bear it lightly as a flower.

—Richard Henry Stoddard, "The Sonnet in
English Poetry," *Scribner's Monthly*, 1881, p. 915

HALL CAINE (1882)

Hallam and certain other writers have declared themselves unable to reconcile their judgment to the frequent violation of the legitimate structure in Milton's sonnets. It is true that the pause between the major and minor portions of the sonnet (so uniformly observed in the best Italian examples) is not to be found in Milton, but the rhyme-scheme is always faultlessly in conformity with the most rigid rule, and the sonnets, even where they link themselves together—as in the cases of the two divorce sonnets and the two sonnets on his blindness—stand alone in self-centered unity, and never become sonnet stanzas. The serious divergence favoured by Milton in his practice of running octave into sestet was clearly the result of a deliberate conviction that the sonnet in his hands was too short a poem to be broken into halves, and hence his sonnets, each done in a breath as to metrical flow, possess the intellectual unity of oneness of conception, at the same time that they are devoid of the twofold metrical and intellectual unity which comes of the rounded perfectness of linked and contrasted parts. Much may be said for the beauty of the sonnet structure adopted by Milton, and indeed the model has been so much in requisition in recent years, that it appears to merit the distinct nomenclature which, in the index of metrical groups, I have ventured to give it.

—Hall Caine, *Sonnets of Three Centuries*,
1882, p. 280

Thomas R. Lounsbury (1892)

Some of Milton's most famous sonnets were never published in his lifetime. They were not even printed until 1694, and then from copies which had been circulating from hand to hand in manuscript. It was not until 1753 that the text was published from the originals. These at once made it plain that the variations which had crept in were, with one possible exception, variations for the worse, and, in some instances, grossly for the worse.

—Thomas R. Lounsbury, *Studies in Chaucer*, 1892,
volume 1, p. 232

A. T. Quiller-Couch (1897)

His sonnets were no chamber exercises: each owed its inspiration to a real occasion, and that inspiration of reality lifted it high above mere simulation of the Horatian mode.

—A. T. Quiller-Couch, introduction to *English
Sonnets*, 1897, p. xvi

"ON THE MORNING
OF CHRIST'S NATIVITY"

"On the Morning of Christ's Nativity" is also known as Milton's nativity ode. This early work, written in 1619 and sent to his friend Charles Diodati when Milton was 21, is Milton's declaration of intention to become a great

Christian poet, as he recounts the routing of classical deities by the birth of Christ. Milton often includes classical allusions, only to overturn them, in much of his great works, culminating in *Paradise Lost*, in which he appropriates and then subverts the model of the classical epic hero in his creation of Satan. Here, Milton first cites the heavenly muse as his source of inspiration, both a poetic stance and a religious belief that comes full circle with *Paradise Lost*. He employs his musical skills gained as the son of a composer to produce a rhyming poem with crescendos and decrescendos, moving from a quiet opening to an exuberant angelic hymn of praise to the newborn Christ back to a quiet conclusion that anticipates the quiet conclusion of *Paradise Regained*. Both the nativity ode and *Paradise Regained* anticipate the necessary heroic action of Christ in the crucifixion and resurrection before the ultimate celebration can be engaged. "On the Morning of Christ's Nativity" looks forward to the defeat of Satan who is now "in straiter limits bound," while *Paradise Regained* celebrates the defeat of Satan through Christ's fortitude against temptation in his ministry's initiation.

Henry Hallam (1839)

The "Ode on the Nativity," far less popular than most of the poetry of Milton, is perhaps the finest in the English language. A grandeur, a simplicity, a breadth of manner, an imagination at once elevated and restrained by the subject, reign throughout it. If Pindar is a model of lyric poetry, it would be hard to name any other ode so truly Pindaric; but more has naturally been derived from the Scriptures. Of the other short poems, that on the death of the Marchioness of Westminister deserves particular mention.

—Henry Hallam, Introduction to the Literature of
Europe, 1837–39, part 3, chapter 5, paragraph 63

Henry Reed (1855)

The most distinct foreshadowing of Milton's great epic poem, and of his own independent genius, is an earlier poem—"The Hymn of the Nativity"—which gives the poet the fame of having composed almost in his youth the earliest of the great English odes, the like of which had not, I believe, been heard, since Pindar, two thousand years before, had struck the lyre for assembled Greece. It is a lyric that might have burst from that religious bard of paganism, could he have had prophetic vision of the Advent. It is a poem that revealed a new mastery of English versification, disciplined afterward to such power in the blank verse of *Paradise Lost*. Nothing in the way of meter can be grander than some of the transitions from the gentle music of the quiet passages to the passionate parts, and their deep reverberating lines that seem to go echoing on, spiritually sounding, long after they are heard no more.

—Henry Reed, *Lectures on English Literature,*
from Chaucer to Tennyson, 1855, p. 193

GEORGE MACDONALD (1868)

Show me one who delights in the "Hymn on the Nativity," and I will show you one who may never indeed be a singer in this world, but who is already a listener to the best.

—George Macdonald, *England's Antiphon,* 1868,
p. 200

EDMUND GOSSE (1897)

When, at the close of 1629, Milton began his "Ode on the Morning of Christ's Nativity," he was still closely imitating the form of these favourites of his, the Fletchers, until the fifth stanza was reached, and then he burst away in a magnificent measure of his own, pouring forth that hymn which carried elaborate lyrical writing higher than it had ever been taken before in England.

—Edmund Gosse, *Short History of*
Modem English Literature, 1897, p. 143

ALBERT PERRY WALKER (1900)

The "Hymn'" may be reckoned the first fully opened flower of Milton's poetic springtime. . . . It would be difficult to find a poem that would better exemplify certain of the characteristics of a lyric poem than does the "Hymn on the Nativity." The religious fervor of the young poet informs every stanza of the poem; the pictures are painted for their dynamic emotional value only; the language is adorned with "rich and various gems" of expression; the sentiment is elevated; the metrical form is graceful and harmonious with the thought.

—Albert Perry Walker, *Selections from the Poetical*
Works of John Milton, 1900, p. 257

"L'ALLEGRO" AND "IL PENSEROSO"

Milton's companion poems "L'Allegro" and "Il Penseroso," first published in 1645, are enjoyed by readers at all levels, from undergraduates through specialists. The works focus on contrasting personalities, the happy person and the pensive or thoughtful person, but the poems are not exact opposites, as each personality contains aspects of the other within it. One interpretation of the pair is that the two works combined comprise the qualities of a well-rounded individual. However, the second poem can also be viewed as the final word in the dichotomy, as introspection trumps surface happiness, pointing once again to Milton's emphasis on the importance of the poet as one set apart from the pleasures of the world. Similar to "On the Morning of Christ's Nativity," these poems are most enthusiastically praised for their musical and lyrical qualities.

OLIVER GOLDSMITH
"INTRODUCTORY CRITICISM" (1767)

Irish dramatist, novelist, poet, and essayist Oliver Goldsmith (1730–74) was known for his eccentric personal demeanor and wit and for his works, the 1766 novel, *The Vicar of Wakefield,* and the 1773 comedy, *She Stoops to Conquer.* Here, in his introduction to his essay *The Beauties of English Poetry,* Goldsmith criticizes Milton's poetry for its lack of English metrical style.

———

I have heard a very judicious critic say, that he had an higher idea of Milton's style in poetry from the two following poems, than from his *Paradise Lost.* It is certain the imagination shewn in them is correct and strong. The introduction to both in irregular measure is borrowed from the Italians, and hurts an English ear.

—Oliver Goldsmith, "Introductory Criticism,"
The Beauties of English Poetry, 1767

HUGH BLAIR (1783)

Of all the English poems in the descriptive style, the richest and most remarkable are, Milton's "Allegro" and "Penseroso." The collection of gay images on the one hand, and of melancholy ones on the other, exhibited in these to small, but inimitably fine poems, are as exquisite as can be conceived. They are, indeed, the storehouse whence many succeeding poets have enriched their descriptions of similar subjects; and they alone are sufficient for illustrating the observations which I made, concerning the proper selection of circumstances in descriptive writing.

—Hugh Blair, *Lectures on Rhetoric and Belles-Lettres,* 1783, edited by Mills, lecture 40

WILLIAM ELLERY CHANNING (1826)

We find nowhere in his writings that whining sensibility and exaggeration of morbid feeling, which makes so much of modern poetry effeminating. If he is not gay, he is not spirit-broken. His "L'Allegro" proves, that he understood thoroughly the bright and joyous aspects of nature; and in his "Penseroso," where he was tempted to accumulate images of gloom, we learn, that the saddest views which he took of creation, are such as inspire only pensive musing or lofty contemplation.

—William Ellery Channing, *Remarks on the*
Character and Writings of John Milton, 1826

JOHN W. HALES (1872)

There can be little doubt as to which of the two characters he portrays was after Milton's own heart. He portrays "L'Allegro" with much skill and excellence; but he cannot feign with him the sympathy he genuinely feels with the other; into his portrait of "Il Penseroso" he throws himself, so as to speak, with all his soul.

—John W. Hales,
Longer English Poems, 1872, p. 231

GEORGE SAINTSBURY (1887)

As for "L'Allegro" and "Il Penseroso," who shall praise them fitly? They are among the few things about which there is no difference of opinion, which are as delightful to childhood as to criticism, to youth as to age. To dwell on their technical excellences (the chief of which is the unerring precision with which the catalectic and acatalectic lines are arranged and interchanged) has a certain air of impertinence about it. Even a critical King Alfonso El Sabio could hardly think it possible that Milton might have taken a hint here, although some persons have, it seems, been disturbed because skylarks do not come to the window, just as others are troubled because the flowers in "Lycidas" do not grow at the same time, and because they think they could see stars through the "star-proof" trees of the "Arcades."

—George Saintsbury, *A History of Elizabethan*
Literature, 1887, p. 320

A. C. BENSON "ANDREW MARVELL" (1896)

Of course Milton's "Il Penseroso" and "L'Allegro" have far more value even as country poems than hundreds of more literal transcripts. From a literary point of view indeed the juxtapositions of half a dozen epithets alone would prove the genius of the writer. But there are no sharp outlines; the scholar pauses in his walk to peer across the watered flat, or raises his eyes from his book to see the quiver of leaves upon the sunlit wall; he notes an effect it may be; but his images do not come like treasures lavished from a secret storehouse of memory.

> —A. C. Benson, "Andrew Marvell,"
> *Essays*, 1896, p. 71

WILLIAM VAUGHN MOODY (1899)

The language of these two little masterpieces has been the despair of poets. It is not that it is so beautiful, for others have equaled or excelled it in the mere conjuring power of suggestion; but that it is, as a French critic has finely said, so *just* in its beauty. The means are exquisitely proportioned to the end. The speech incarnates the thought as easily, as satisfyingly, as the muscles of a Phidian youth incarnate the motor-impulse of his brain. Always fruition is just gently touched. To the connoisseur in language there is a sensation of almost physical soothing in its perfect poise and play.

> —William Vaughn Moody, *Poetical Works of*
> *Milton*, 1899, Cambridge edition, p. 26

Chronology

1608	Born in London on December 9.
1617	Enters St. Paul's School in London.
1625	Enters Christ's College, Cambridge University.
1629	Earns a bachelor's of arts degree from Cambridge.
1632	Receives a master's degree from Cambridge.
1632–38	Studies at home in London and at Horton in Buckinghamshire.
1634	Performance of the masque *Comus* at Ludlow Castle.
1638–39	Travels in Italy.
1641	*Of Reformation in England* is published.
1642	*The Reason of Church-Government* is published. Marries Mary Powell, who subsequently returns to her parents.
1643	*The Doctrine and Discipline of Divorce* is published.
1644	*Areopagitica* is published.
1645	Mary Powell Milton returns to her husband in London. *Poems of Mr. John Milton, Both English and Latin* is released.
1649	*The Tenure of Kings and Magistrates* is published. Milton becomes secretary of foreign tongues to Cromwell's Council of State.
1651	*Defense of the English People* is published.
1652	Goes blind. The death of wife and son.
1656	Marries Katherine Woodcock.
1657	Death of Katherine Woodcock Milton.
1660	*The Ready and Easy Way to Establish a Free Commonwealth* is published.
1663	Marries Elizabeth Minshull.
1667	*Paradise Lost* is published in 10 volumes.
1671	*Paradise Regained* and *Samson Agonistes* are published.
1674	A 12-volume edition of *Paradise Lost* is released. Milton dies on November 8.

Index